BASIC TEACHINGS OF
THE GREAT PSYCHOLOGISTS

S. Stansfeld Sargent is a graduate of Haverford College and took his doctorate in Psychology at Columbia University. In his years of teaching at Adelphi College, Central YMCA College (now Roosevelt University), Barnard College, and Columbia University, he was primarily involved with General, Experimental, and Social Psychology. Since 1956 he has been a clinical psychologist at the VA Hospital in Phoenix, Arizona, and does part-time private practice there. He is a former president of the Society for Psychological Study of Social Issues, a division of the American Psychological Association. Besides *Basic Teachings of the Great Psychologists* (1944), Dr. Sargent has written a textbook in Social Psychology (revised with R. C. Williamson) and edited a volume entitled *Culture and Personality* (with Marian W. Smith).

Kenneth R. Stafford was educated at the University of Oklahoma and received his Ph.D. there. He has taught Educational Psychology, General Psychology, Measurement, and Learning Theory at the University of Arkansas, East Texas State College, and Arizona State University, where he is presently located. He was also a counseling psychologist with the Phoenix Veterans Administration, has done private practice in child psychology, and was a staff member in one of the teacher training projects of the Fund for Advancement of Education. Dr. Stafford's research and writing interests are in the area of cognition, specifically language and problem solving.

BASIC TEACHINGS OF
THE GREAT PSYCHOLOGISTS

S. STANSFELD SARGENT, Ph.D.
Clinical Psychologist, VA Hospital
Phoenix, Arizona

REVISED EDITION

in Collaboration with
KENNETH R. STAFFORD, Ph.D.
Associate Professor of Educational Psychology
Arizona State University

DOLPHIN BOOKS
DOUBLEDAY & COMPANY, INC.
GARDEN CITY, NEW YORK

Grateful acknowledgment is made for permission to reprint material from the following copyrighted works.

American Philosophical Society. From *Age and Achievement* by Harvey C. Lehman, Memoirs American Philosophical Society 33 (1953). Reprinted with permission from Harvey C. Lehman.

Appleton-Century-Crofts, Inc. From *Great Experiments in Psychology 3rd Edition* by Henry E. Garrett. Copyright 1951, Appleton-Century-Crofts, Inc. From *Psychology of Thought* by H. L. Hollingworth. Copyright 1925, D. Appleton and Company. Both reprinted by permission of Appleton-Century-Crofts, Inc.

Houghton Mifflin Company. From *The Revision of the Stanford-Binet Scale* by Quinn McNemar. Reprinted by permission of Houghton Mifflin Company.

McGraw-Hill Book Company. From *The Analysis of Behavior* by James G. Holland and B. F. Skinner. Copyright © 1961 McGraw-Hill Book Company. Reprinted by permission of the publisher.

Professor Herbert Woodrow. From *Brightness and Dullness in Children* by Herbert Woodrow. Reprinted by permission of the author.

PREFACE TO THE REVISED EDITION

Like the original edition, this book introduces the reader to the whole field of Psychology by describing the work of the psychologists who have made the most significant contributions to the development of the science. Written primarily for persons who have not taken courses in psychology but who are interested in the subject, the revised edition, like the first edition, is well suited to use as a review book for undergraduate majors in psychology. And it may also appeal to former psychology students who would like a brief refresher course.

Each of the seventeen chapters takes up an important aspect of the study of human behavior, such as the testing of intelligence or of personality, individual development, learning, perceiving, thinking and imagery, motivation, mental illness, mental hygiene, social behavior, and applications of psychology to daily living. Included also are more specific topics, like the measurement of mechanical and other aptitudes; the study of retarded and of gifted children, of feral children, of identical twins reared apart; the effect of reward upon learning; electrical stimulation of the brain; the relation of body type to personality; the nature of psychosis and neurosis; psychoanalysis and other types of psychotherapy; the rise of group dynamics; the development of teaching machines and programed learning; the advent of the age of electronic computers and of cybernetics. The material in each chapter or major division of a chapter is presented in approximately chronological order, from early discoveries and theories to the most recent research and application.

Among the leading psychologists whose work is broad in scope and whose names appear prominently throughout the book are (in alphabetical order) G. W. Allport, Binet, Freud, Galton, Hollingworth, James, Lewin, Murphy, Thorndike,

Thurstone, Watson, and Woodworth. Others, whose work is more specialized, include Adler, James McKeen Cattell, Ebbinghaus, Gesell, Goddard, Guilford, Hebb, Helmholtz, Jung, Klineberg, Koffka, Köhler, Murray, Newcomb, Osgood, Pavlov, Rogers, Rorschach, Sherif, Skinner, Terman, Titchener, and Wechsler. The viewpoints of various schools of psychological thought are described and contrasted. The contributions of biologists, physiologists, psychiatrists, sociologists, and anthropologists who have markedly influenced psychology are mentioned in the relevant sections.

The combined name and subject matter index makes possible ready reference to the contributions of each psychologist and to a large number of specific items not named in chapter headings. The appendix of biographical notes gives brief sketches of more than two hundred of the men and women whose work is dealt with in the book.

To several publishers I am grateful for permission to quote brief passages from psychologists' writings, as follows: APPLETON-CENTURY-CROFTS, from *Psychology of Thought* by H. L. Hollingworth, and *Animal Intelligence* by G. J. Romanes; HARCOURT, BRACE & WORLD, INC., from *Middletown* by Robert S. and Helen Merrell Lynd; HOLT, RINEHART & WINSTON, INC., from *Principles of Psychology* by William James, and *Intelligence Testing* by Rudolf Pintner; HOUGHTON MIFFLIN COMPANY, from *The Revision of the Stanford-Binet Scale* by Quinn McNemar, and from *Psychology of Adjustment* by L. F. Shaffer; ALFRED A. KNOPF, INC., from *The Human Mind* by Karl A. Menninger; J. B. LIPPINCOTT COMPANY, from *Brightness and Dullness in Children* by Herbert Woodrow; LIVERIGHT PUBLISHING CORPORATION, from *A General Introduction to Psychoanalysis* by Sigmund Freud; McGRAW-HILL BOOK COMPANY for permission to redraw an illustration from *Infant Behavior* by Gesell and Thompson, and for permission to use the Simple Reflexes example from *The Analysis of Behavior* by James G. Holland and B. F. Skinner; WILLIAM MORROW & COMPANY, INC., from *Sex and Temperament* by Margaret Mead; W. W. NORTON & COMPANY, INC., from *Behaviorism* by J. B. Watson; and to the AMERICAN PSYCHIATRIC ASSOCIATION, from its *Diagnostic and Statistical Manual: Mental Disorders*, 1952 edition.

Since the publication of the original edition in 1944, my work has become somewhat more specialized—first, in the area of personality and social psychology, later in clinical psychology. In preparing the revised edition I have been fortunate, therefore, to have the collaboration of Professor Kenneth R. Stafford of the College of Education, Arizona State University. Professor Stafford's background and primary interest are in the psychology of learning and measurement, and in educational psychology. I feel sure that the present volume is better rounded and more comprehensive as a result of this collaboration.

Both of us are indebted to a large number of psychologists whose lectures, research, writings, and practical applications have contributed to our knowledge of, interest in, and experience with psychology. I wish to express once more my gratitude to two former colleagues, then of Barnard College, Columbia University, Dr. Tom Gaylord Andrews and Dr. Gelolo McHugh, who read and criticized portions of the original manuscript. We are likewise indebted to several psychologists who gave critical and bibliographic assistance during the preparation of the revision. Most of these are on the staff of the Neuropsychiatric Service of the Veterans Administration Hospital in Phoenix: Dr. and Mrs. Aaron H. Canter, Dr. Albert D. Annis, Dr. Virginia K. Maresca, Dr. Albert R. Hahn, and Dr. Stephen J. Kimler. For his suggestions and criticisms we also express thanks to Mr. Everett Davis of the College of Education at Arizona State University. We are grateful to Mrs. Ruth Rezab for frequent secretarial assistance. We wish particularly to thank Lila M. Stafford for her willing, efficient typing and proofreading, and Virginia M. Sargent for her constructive editing, in both editions, always in the direction of readability.

S. Stansfeld Sargent

CONTENTS

Chapter I

THE SCIENCE OF PSYCHOLOGY

WEBER   FECHNER   HELMHOLTZ   HERING
PEARSON   WUNDT   TITCHENER   HÖFFDING
JAMES   DEWEY   ANGELL   WATSON
FREUD   KÖHLER   KOFFKA

What is psychology? How did the science of psychology develop? What methods do psychologists use in their research? How is a psychological experiment performed? What is meant by "schools" of psychology? What are the important fields or subdivisions of psychology?

Psychology is the science of behavior. It aims to understand, predict, and when necessary, to change behavior.

How Psychology Developed

Until the late nineteenth century psychology was not considered a science. Its subject matter fell in the realm of philosophy, like most other knowledge in ancient and medieval times. Many great philosophers, including Plato and Aristotle, speculated about human nature and proposed theories, some of which lasted until modern times. But careful and systematic observation of human behavior, let alone experimentation, was unknown.

In the sixteenth and seventeenth centuries astronomy, physics, and chemistry broke away from philosophy to become separate sciences. Biology, less exact because it dealt with living things, became independent in the eighteenth century. Psychology hung on to its parent, philosophy, until nearly the end of the next century.

With the pioneer work of German physiologists like Ernst Heinrich Weber, Gustav Theodor Fechner, Hermann von Helmholtz, and Ewald Hering, it became apparent that human behavior is closely related to bodily functions. It was hard to know where physiologists left off and psychologists began. This was true of studies of the eye, ear, and other sense organs of the nervous system, or reflexes and muscular reactions. Gradually it became clear that the physiologist studies the functions of organs *within* the organism—respiration, circulation, digestion, and so on—while the psychologist studies the functioning of the *whole organism* as it responds to outside stimuli.

In the 1880's and 1890's a new group of psychologists, trained in both philosophy and physiology, founded laboratories in Germany and America, and psychology began its career as an experimental science.

Two major scientific trends led to the emergence of experimental psychology: 1. the increasing concern for measurement, and 2. the use of controlled laboratory methods. For centuries philosophers speculated as to whether mind and body are related, but not until the nineteenth century did they try systematically to relate the physical and the mental. From these efforts the science of psychophysics developed, chiefly from the work of Ernst Heinrich Weber and Gustav Theodor Fechner. With great precision they measured *just noticeable differences* in sensation. The success of their controlled experiments pointed up the importance of the laboratory in dealing systematically with human behavior.

Late in the nineteenth century the trends toward measurement and laboratory control of human behavior were strengthened even more by the work of Sir Francis Galton, James McKeen Cattell, and the experimentalists Wilhelm Wundt and Edward Bradford Titchener. Darwin had shown that marked variations occur within species. Galton extended this notion to human intelligence. He suggested ways of measuring these variations.

In 1879 Wundt established the first laboratory devoted to psychological experimentation. Impressed by the successes of physical science and wishing to break away from the endless speculation of philosophy, Wundt and his students led the way for the entry of psychology into the fold of laboratory sciences. His students spread over the Western world. In America, Cattell elaborated these techniques around 1900.

PRINCIPAL SCHOOLS IN PSYCHOLOGY

In a young and growing science internal disputes often occur. Psychology is no exception. Psychologists have differed about what psychology should or should not include, about what it should emphasize, about what research methods are best. When a large number of psychologists strongly support a certain viewpoint they are called a "school." In the early days of psychology, schools were more clearly defined than they are today; between 1900 and 1930 five important schools developed.

Structuralism traces back to two men, Wilhelm Wundt and Edward Bradford Titchener. Wundt is regarded as the father of experimental psychology since he established in 1879 at Leipzig, Germany, the first psychological laboratory. To study with Wundt came young and eager psychologists from many countries. One of these was Titchener, an Englishman, who later came to America to head the psychology department at Cornell University for many years.

Following out Wundt's basic ideas, Titchener established the school known as structuralism. Psychology is concerned with studying images, thoughts, and feelings, the three elements forming the structure of consciousness. The proper research method is introspection, performed by trained observers. Learning, intelligence, motivation, personality, or abnormal and social behavior Titchener ruled out of psychology. He and his students did notable laboratory studies, some of which are described in the chapters on Perceiving and Cognition.

Functionalism is a less systematic and unified school. It grew out of the protests of many psychologists against analyzing consciousness into ideas, images, and feelings. The Danish psychologist Harald Höffding, and the American William James both emphasized the dynamic, changing nature of mental activity and questioned whether it could be analyzed into structural elements. Shortly after 1900 John Dewey and James Rowland Angell at the University of Chicago began to stress the ways in which an organism adjusts to environment. Their aim in studying mental functions was to discover how thinking, emotion, and other processes fulfilled the organism's needs. The views of the functionalists helped to align psychology with biology and to bring about a genetic approach to psychological problems.

Behaviorism was founded about 1914 by John B. Watson, then an animal psychologist at Johns Hopkins University. He too was impatient with the narrowness of structuralism, but he did not feel that the functionalists went far enough in their criticisms. Watson objected particularly to introspection, which he considered unscientific. Psychology's real concern, he said, is to study *behavior*, not consciousness. Expose an animal or a human being to a stimulus and see how he responds; record this behavior objectively and you have real scientific evidence. Watson and his fellow behaviorists experimented on learning, motivation, emotion, and individual development.

Gestalt Psychology was a reaction against both structuralism and behaviorism. Wolfgang Köhler and Kurt Koffka, the leading Gestaltists, said experience and behavior cannot be analyzed into elements of consciousness, as claimed by the structuralists. Nor can they be broken down into stimulus-response units, as the behaviorists seemed to think. Behavior and experience are unanalyzable wholes, though certain relationships between the whole and its parts can be discerned. The Gestalt experiments are described in our chapters on perception, learning, and thinking.

Psychoanalysis stood apart from the other schools. Founded by a physician, Sigmund Freud, it grew out of his effort to cure persons suffering from mental and nervous disorders. Psychoanalysis presents amazingly fruitful and provocative theories of motivation, of personality development, and of abnormal behavior. Unlike other founders of schools, Freud made no effort to verify his theories by scientific experiment. Freud's major interpretations, and also those of his associates and followers who developed approaches of their own, are presented in Chapters XIV and XV.

THE NATURE OF SCIENCE

The Quest for Understanding. Throughout man's long history he has unceasingly sought explanations of his world and his place in it. It has been held by such social philosophers as Auguste Comte, Sir James Frazer, and Ernst Cassirer, that belief systems progress from the primitive to the sophisticated, from the animistic to the scientific. Primitive man, who must have been driven by fear and loneliness, quite naturally concocted anthropomorphic explanations of natural events. If a stone fell on him, he imputed life to it; when a volcano erupted, he viewed it as an angry organism; when a person became ill he was believed possessed by demons. Later this demonological or animistic view gave way to a more systematic "religious" explanation in which gods were believed to shape events in man's destiny. The early Greeks in particular developed this system.

Slowly and painfully man learned to use reason and observation in coping with natural phenomena. This new "naturalistic" approach ultimately led to modern science, beginning with the empiricism (determining truth by experimental methods) of Galileo, and Francis Bacon's inductive philosophy (making generalizations from known facts).

Two criteria that have served man well in his search for truth are: 1. When predictions can be made from information and can be confirmed empirically again and again, the information is probably true, and 2. When one event can be controlled by information about another event, the information probably is true.

Psychology as a Science. We have called psychology a science. Is this correct? Astronomy, chemistry, and physics are readily recognized as sciences; they involve careful laboratory work, exact measurement, rigid laws, and sure-fire predictability. Psychology is concerned with something less definite and tangible; exactitude is hard to obtain and exceptionless laws almost never occur.

However, it is not the definiteness of its material which determines whether a subject is a science. (If it were, biology might be excluded since it studies the great unknown—life.) Karl Pearson, an English mathematician and scientist, insisted fifty years ago that the criterion of science is not subject matter but the methods of investigation used. If scientific method is used systematically, we may properly speak of a science, whether the object of study is minerals, bacteria, human thoughts and feelings, or social institutions.

Scientific method is no mystery. It is a definite procedure used in trying to answer a question or solve a problem. The problem may be a practical one like "What causes malaria?", "What causes mental disease?", "How does alcohol affect behavior?" Or the problem may be inspired by mere curiosity: "Why do objects fall to the earth?", "How does heredity work?", "Can animals learn?"

The first step is to discover what other attempts have been made to answer the question. Why did they fail? Out of this knowledge emerges a new hypothesis or theory which can be tested by experiment.

Experimentation is the crucial step in scientific work. Essentially it is asking a question of nature. It means setting the stage in such a way that the events which follow will provide a meaningful answer.

Medical research into the cause of yellow fever furnishes a good example of hypothesis and experimentation. According to one theory, it is a contagious disease; this was shown to be wrong. According to another theory, the disease is carried by rats; this too was found to be incorrect. A new hypothesis attributed the cause to mosquitoes.

To test this hypothesis a group of men were exposed to mosquitoes known to have bitten yellow fever patients. Most of the men became ill. As a check a "control" group was used for comparison—men exposed to all other possible causes of the disease, except mosquitoes. None in the control group contracted yellow fever. The evidence was clear: yellow fever is transmitted by mosquitoes.

As a precaution against chance errors experiments are often repeated, using different groups of subjects. If the results agree, the proof is doubly sure.

The ultimate test of scientific discovery is prediction. A principle in chemistry or physics has a predictability of practically 100%. In biology it is not as high; we cannot say, for example, that everyone bitten by a mosquito carrying malarial germs will get the disease; a few don't. In psychology and the social sciences predictability is almost never perfect because of the complexity of human behavior. If an experimental finding enables us to make a prediction that is substantially better than a mere guess, it is considered worthwhile.

A PSYCHOLOGICAL EXPERIMENT

Few psychological experiments are as clear-cut as the precise laboratory studies of physicists, chemists, and biologists. They are more difficult to plan, execute, and interpret. But they follow the same principles of scientific method: studying the data, forming hypotheses, testing them by experiment, checking and verifying, and predicting.

Some years ago, when benzedrine appeared on the market as a new drug which was found to give a certain exhilarating effect over short periods, college students began to take benzedrine before exams, reporting it kept them awake and made them think more clearly. Psychologists looked into the subject and decided to see whether benzedrine actually steps up mental ability.

Many subjects were used. Two equivalent forms of a comprehensive intelligence test were given, one before and one shortly after the drug was administered. To eliminate possible influences of suggestion or expectation (like one's expectation that coffee will keep one awake at night) another group of subjects was used; these persons took a "placebo"— a flour-and-water tablet identical in appearance with a benzedrine tablet. In this way differences between performance of the benzedrine and placebo groups could be attributed to genuine effects of the drug.

Results showed that, despite many subjects' reports of feeling "pepped up," benzedrine failed to affect mental ability significantly. The results of several independent investigations verified this finding. It is possible to predict, therefore, that benzedrine will not have a noticeable effect on the mental performance of most persons.

In all sciences, unfortunately, scientific procedure sometimes is violated. An investigator's bias occasionally creeps in to prejudice results. Too few subjects to justify conclusions may be used. Careless measurements and calculations have been known to occur. On the other hand, scientists keep errors at a minimum by checking each other's work constantly and by repeating experiments whose results seem doubtful.

Certain studies are called "pseudo-sciences" because validity is claimed for their findings but no effort is made to use scientific procedures. For example, the astrologist says ability and personality are determined by planetary conditions. But he produces no proof. The proof, of course, would be to show that persons born at the same time have similar personalities, in contrast to persons born at different times. This has never been demonstrated. Until it is, astrology cannot be considered a legitimate science. The same is true of phrenology, which interprets personality by bumps on the head; of physiognomy, which reads character from facial features; and of graphology, which bases its interpretations upon certain characteristics of a person's handwriting.

PSYCHOLOGICAL METHODS

When scientists work, they strive to find relationships between observable variables. For example, Robert Boyle found a direct relationship between the temperature (variable 1) of a gas and its volume (variable 2) under certain conditions. By knowing one, the other can be predicted. By manipulating one, the other can be controlled. This is true in psychology, but psychologists use several methods of relating variables to predict, control, and understand behavior.

Typically one or more of the following four methods can be used:

1. *Experimental.* This involves a carefully planned and controlled arrangement. One variable is deliberately

manipulated while the other variable is observed and measured. The benzedrine experiment described on page 7 illustrates this method. The variable controlled by the scientist was the administration of benzedrine. The variable observed by him was performance on mental ability tests.

2. *Survey* (statistical or causal-comparative). Where it is impractical to contrive a controlled situation, survey techniques may be used. The scientific goal is the same —to relate variables. The real trick is to determine which is cause and which is effect, or whether either is sufficient cause. By survey methods a positive relationship is found to exist between mental health and marriage. But this correlation alone doesn't show whether mental health determines or is the result of a successful marriage.

3. *Case study or clinical.* Some psychologists deal directly with individuals, usually in a clinical setting. Here variables often can be less formally related. Facts are gathered into a "case study," or life story of the subject. Knowing the subject's background helps the psychologist understand influences and forces that shaped the former's development.

4. *Introspection.* Here a subject reports his own inner experience. If shown two designs and asked which he prefers, he gives his own subjective report. Probably he tells the truth, but verification is impossible. His word must be accepted. Or he may be asked to solve a problem, then told to describe how he solved it. This too is introspection. Despite its subjective nature, introspection yields evidence that can be obtained in no other way.

It is not always possible to use the experimental method or to have access to the many cases required by the survey method. Often a combination of methods is used, as we shall see in the following chapters. In experiments on thinking, for instance, objective data may be obtained and these results supplemented by introspection. The use of both objective and statistical procedures in an investigation is also common.

The Fields of Psychology

The study of human behavior includes a broad area. Research on eye, ear, or brain functions relates closely to physiology and neurology. Studies of attitudes, opinions, and propaganda are akin to sociology and other social sciences. Between these extremes the majority of psychologists work away at understanding the abilities, emotions, motives, memories, and whole personalities of children, adolescents, and adults, both normal and abnormal. Because psychology includes such varied material, several specialized subdivisions have developed.

In some of these fields emphasis falls on facts, principles, and theories rather than on applications. Fields that stress the solving of practical problems are included in "applied psychology." Actually no sharp distinction can be made between "pure" and "applied" psychology. All theoretical discoveries have possibilities for future usefulness. The most practical branches, like industrial and clinical psychology, owe a debt to theoretical psychologists who searched out new knowledge purely for its own sake.

Clinical Psychology is at present the largest field of specialization. This field deals primarily with diagnosis, therapy, and research in connection with mental illness. The clinical psychologist has a Ph.D. degree in psychology. (*Psychiatry* is the branch of medicine which deals with the study, diagnosis, and treatment of mental disorders. The psychiatrist has an M.D. degree, including specialization in psychiatry and several years of training working with mentally disordered patients.) Important aspects of the clinical psychologist's work are described in Chapters II, XII, XIV, and XV.

Counseling Psychology deals with relatively minor emotional problems and vocational-educational guidance. Schools and colleges employ the greatest proportion of these psychologists. The psychologists working in this field are called counseling psychologists; their work is very close to that of clinical psychologists.

Educational Psychology is concerned with psychology as it relates to education. Primary interests are in learning and mental testing. Closely akin to educational psychology is *School Psychology*, which, however, is more concerned with psychological applications in specific school settings. Chapters II, IV, VI, and IX are concerned, in part, with the work of educational and school psychologists.

Industrial Psychology deals with applications of psychology to industrial problems, for example: selection, placement, and training of personnel; supervision of human relations within a firm; surveying the effectiveness of advertising.

Experimental Psychology is devoted to the development of the science of psychology. Basic principles are developed through laboratory experimentation. These principles, when feasible, are used by other branches of psychology. Most experimental psychologists are employed by universities and research institutes. Their work is referred to at many points throughout the book.

Social Psychology deals with the ways a person influences others and is influenced by others. Government, private agencies and foundations, and universities employ specialists in this field. The field of social psychology is described in Chapter XVI.

Chapter II

HUMAN ABILITIES
AND THEIR MEASUREMENT

BINET   EBBINGHAUS   CATTELL   GODDARD
STERN   TERMAN   PINTNER   PATERSON
YERKES   THORNDIKE   SPEARMAN   THURSTONE
GUILFORD   MILES   WECHSLER   SEASHORE   MEIER

What is an I.Q. and how is it measured? Do intelligence tests give a valid measure of a person's ability? What are the components of mental ability? How does intelligence change with age? Can special aptitudes be measured? Can future occupational success be predicted on the basis of test results?

At school or at our work most of us take at least one intelligence test. The test reveals something about our capacity to learn, our adaptability, retentiveness, and ability to apply knowledge in solving problems. Intelligence is not identical with book learning, yet most educated men and women are intelligent. Intelligence is not a guarantee of success, but unsuccessful persons often are unintelligent.

To a psychologist the word "intelligence" has a somewhat different meaning from that given it in general usage. Until the nineteenth century "intelligent" and "intellectual" were used almost interchangeably, and both referred to the ability of human beings to think, as opposed to animals which were considered creatures of instinct.

Darwin's momentous theory of evolution changed all this. It closed the gap between man and animal; the two were seen to be related. Darwin and his successors pointed out similarities between the behavior of man and that of lower animals. Instincts were discovered in human beings, and signs of intelligence in animals. Intelligence came to be regarded as a certain kind of behavior, not necessarily synonymous with intellect.

The first "mental tests" did not measure intelligence, but gauged an individual's performance in simpler sensory and motor processes. James McKeen Cattell went to Germany in the 1880's to study under the famous Wilhelm Wundt. At Leipzig, Cattell became interested in individual differences. Returning to America he devised several mental tests which he gave to his students at Columbia University. These included strength of grip, rate of tapping, reaction time to sound, speed of naming colors, and memory span for letters. Hugo Münsterberg at Harvard and Joseph Jastrow at the University of Wisconsin also devised and administered similar tests. Though not called intelligence tests, all were supposed to measure the mind in some way; they were the first step toward valid measures of ability.

THE BINET TESTS

Shortly before 1900 Hermann Ebbinghaus, a German noted for his work on memory, brought forth a theory that intelligence is the ability to combine and integrate, and that it could be tested with sentences containing blanks which must be filled in to complete the sense. "The —— rises —— the morning and —— at night" illustrates the kind of test sentence he recommended. Evidence supported his theory; when he gave such tests to school children, older ones did better than younger, good students better than poor ones.

The father of intelligence testing, however, is not Ebbinghaus but a Frenchman, Alfred Binet. Binet disagreed with those who sought to measure general ability by testing speed of reaction, rote memory, sensory acuity, or muscular movements. Intelligence can be estimated, said Binet, only by tests of higher faculties like reasoning, comprehension, judgment, adaptability, persistence, and self-criticism.

In 1904 Binet, appointed to a national educators' committee to investigate retardation in French schools, put his ideas into concrete form. Collaborating with Théophile Simon, he published the first intelligence test. In it were thirty items arranged in order of increasing difficulty. Among them were: following a moving object with the eyes, recognizing food and simple objects in a picture, comparing two lines of different lengths, repeating spoken sentences, memorizing things in a picture, finding rhymes for a given word, completing sentences, and defining abstract terms.

Binet tried out these tests on children, and in 1908 published a revised scale which divided the tests into age groups from 3 to 11 years. At some age levels only three questions were asked; at others, 5 or 6. For example:

Age 3: Point to nose, eyes, mouth.
Age 5: Copy square; count four coins.
Age 7: Tell what is missing in unfinished picture.
Age 10: Repeat months of year.
Age 13: State differences between pairs of abstract terms.

With this scale Binet introduced the concept of mental age. A child who passed all or all but one of the tests for, say, age 7 was given a basal mental age of 7. If he passed five or six tests at higher age levels he was credited with another year of mental age.

In 1911, shortly before he died, Binet published a second revision of his scale. It omitted certain test items previously included, added others, and brought the scale up to the adult level. In this edition Binet included five tests for each age, except the 4-year level. The 1911 scale, validated and standardized, represented a great improvement over the earlier two series.

Henry H. Goddard, psychologist at the Vineland Training School for Feebleminded, began to use Binet's test soon after it first appeared in France. He found it useful in detecting mental deficiency in children and also in distinguishing between various degrees of feeblemindedness. However, the Binet test had to be slightly adapted and modified for American use. This adaptation and modification Goddard accomplished by trying out the 1908 scale on many hundreds of school children. He published his revision in 1910, translating

Binet's scale into English and changing the wording and order of several test items.

Goddard's revision was used widely during the next few years, though chiefly to detect mental deficiency rather than to study the intelligence of normal or superior children.

TERMAN AND THE STANFORD REVISION

A tremendous advance in intelligence testing came with the work of Lewis M. Terman, psychologist at Stanford University. For several years before publishing his book, *The Measurement of Intelligence* (1916), Terman and his colleagues worked at standardizing and validating the Binet test.

Terman tested 2,000 school children to discover just what a normal child at any given age can do. He chose six tests for each year from 3 to 10 inclusive, also for ages 12, 14, 16, and 18. His calculations indicated that an average adult has a mental age of 16 years while a superior adult has one of 18 years. By using six tests for each year he was able to give two months mental age credit for each test passed. Many of Binet's items were included, though some were shifted to higher or lower age levels, according to Terman's findings on normal children. Several new test items were added, so that the Stanford revision (including alternate items) totaled ninety tests, compared with fifty-four in Binet's 1911 scale.

Binet had introduced the idea of mental age. A German psychologist, William Stern, suggested in 1912 that a child's relative superiority or inferiority could be calculated by dividing his mental age by his chronological age. Stern called this the "Intelligence Quotient." Terman adopted the idea, and the abbreviation "I.Q." was accepted to designate a child's mental ability.

It is calculated thus: If a child to be tested is 7 years 1 month old, the tester might start by giving tests at the 6-year level. Suppose the child passes all the tests for age 6, four for age 7, three for age 8, one for age 9, and none for age 10. The child's mental age (abbreviated "M.A.") is obtained by crediting him with 72 months for passing all tests at age 6 (and presumably all under age 6), plus 8 months at age 7 (4 out of 6 tests), 6 months at age 8, and 2 months at age 9.

His total M.A. in months is 88. His chronological age in months is 85. His I.Q. therefore is 88/85. To remove the decimal point, the result is multiplied by 100; therefore this child's I.Q. is 104.

Suppose the child's chronological age (abbreviated "C.A.") were 8 years 6 months; and his mental age the same as above— 88 months. His I.Q. then would be 88/102, or 86. I.Q.'s near 100 are considered normal because mental age corresponds with chronological age. As we shall see presently, I.Q.'s below 70 definitely are inferior; those above 130, quite superior.

Terman's "Stanford-Binet" test is given by a trained tester to one person at a time. It is important that the tester learn to give and score tests in a uniform, standardized fashion, so I.Q.'s are comparable. The tester must also be trained in the ways of gaining a child's cooperation, so the test represents the child's best effort. The decade following 1920 saw hundreds of testers trained and thousands of children's and adults' I.Q.'s computed.

After twenty years' experience Terman, assisted by Maud A. Merrill, issued the 1937 revision of the Stanford-Binet test, extending the scale down to 2 years, and including many more items at upper levels. Two equivalent versions of the test—Form L and Form M—were devised so a child could be re-tested without using the same material. The test was revised again in 1959 into one standard scale, which combined the most valid items of Forms L and M.

Thanks to Terman's work the I.Q. is accepted as a measure of general mental ability, though not without criticisms. These criticisms will be discussed later.

Performance Tests

Given to one person at a time, the Binet type of test depends for its validity upon normal vision, hearing, muscular control, and comprehension of language. For testing blind or deaf persons, illiterates, or those who speak very little English, it is unsuitable. Performance tests were devised to meet these special conditions.

About 1850 a great French physician, Édouard Seguin, constructed a kind of test for feebleminded children. It consisted of fitting blocks of various shapes, such as a star, triangle, cross, square, or circle, into corresponding cut-outs in a board. By pantomime the child could be shown how to put each block in its proper hole. Later, Dr. William Healy of the Judge Baker Foundation in Boston arranged a completion test. In this the child was shown a farmyard scene out of which were cut several square holes. From many pieces that would fit the holes he had to choose those that made best sense in completing the picture.

Two psychologists, then at Ohio State University, Rudolf Pintner and Donald Paterson, taking over the Seguin, Healy, and similar tests, prepared the first performance scale in 1917. In this series all the tests call for a motor response (that is, responses involving movement), such as putting together a puzzle, fitting blocks into place, or imitating the tester in tapping cubes. Verbal directions are unnecessary. Tests are scored in terms of time taken and moves or errors made. A few years later Grace Arthur produced a revision, including the Seguin, Healy, and other performance items, which is used as a non-verbal test for subjects ranging in age from five all the way to the superior adult level.

While performance tests are useful with persons having sensory or language handicaps, they do not test quite the same thing as verbal tests. In actual practice, if a child is considered unfairly judged by the Binet test it is wise to give a performance test. If his M.A. shows a pronounced rise in the latter, probably the verbal test did not measure his ability accurately.

ARMY ALPHA AND BETA

The year after Terman's Stanford-Binet test appeared, the United States entered World War I. A critical need arose to sift out from the thousands of draftees those mentally unfit and, at the other extreme, to discover men best qualified for officer training. At once the American Psychological Association appointed a committee of experts to draw up a test that could be taken by many persons simultaneously. Professor Robert M. Yerkes of Yale was named chairman; members were Lewis M. Terman, Arthur S. Otis, Henry H. Goddard,

Frederic L. Wells, Walter V. Bingham, Guy M. Whipple, and T. H. Haines.

In framing the new group test the committee made every effort to keep it (so far as possible) independent of education or other training. Two tests resulted, Army Alpha for literates, and Army Beta for illiterates or persons with meager knowledge of English.

Army Alpha consisted of eight sections, each containing 12 to 40 questions. Every section began with easy questions and progressed to harder ones, so all persons could answer some but few could answer all. The subtests involved such tasks as following directions, solving arithmetic problems, making common sense judgments, identifying pairs of words as "same" or "opposite," rearranging jumbled sentences, and supplying general information. One item required completion of a number series:

$$3-4-6-9-13-18-\_\_-\_\_$$

A verbal analogy test, involving the seeing of relationships, asked for choice of the correct item at the right:

skirts—girl : : trousers—boy hat vest coat
mayor—city : : general—private navy army soldier

Maximum score on Army Alpha was 212 points. Over 135 was considered excellent, 105–134 good, and 45–104 fair. Nearly all officers rated above 105; enlisted men averaged a little below 60.

Army Beta also was a paper and pencil test, but directions were given by pantomime or demonstration. It included tracing a line through mazes, counting blocks in given piles, completing patterns of X's and O's, substituting symbols for numbers, noting similarities and differences in two sets of figures, completing pictures by supplying parts omitted, and solving simple geometrical puzzles. While Army Beta did not test exactly the same abilities as the verbal Alpha test, it helped discover men of good intelligence whose Alpha performance was bad because they lacked schooling or command of the English language.

More than a million and a half recruits took the Alpha test in 1918 and several thousand took the Beta. The tests helped enormously to separate satisfactory from unsatisfactory soldiers. At the same time they supplied psychologists with valuable information about intelligence and its testing. Shortly after the war many other group tests were devised; they have come to be used widely in schools and in business and industry.

When the draft began just prior to World War II, a new measuring device, the Army General Classification Test (AGCT), superseded Army Alpha and Beta. It consisted of only three types of problems: vocabulary, to measure verbal comprehension; arithmetic problems, to indicate quantitative reasoning powers; and block counting, to show spatial thinking ability. AGCT was used as a screening device, to classify recruits into five grades according to their ability to learn the kinds of tasks required in military life. A similar test was prepared by the Navy (NGCT) with material adapted to Navy life. The armed services also produced a large number of special ability tests for pilots, bombardiers, radio operators, and many other types of specialists.

WECHSLER'S SCALES

In 1939 David Wechsler published an individual test for adults which came to be known as the Wechsler-Bellevue Intelligence Scale. Six of the component subtests were verbal, measuring information, comprehension, arithmetic, vocabulary, and so forth. These yielded a Verbal I.Q.

Five other subtests sampled performance, and gave a Performance I.Q. based on picture arrangement, block design, object assembly, etc. All the subtests combined entered into a Full Scale I.Q. An alternate form was published later, and the whole scale was revised in 1955 as the Wechsler Adult Intelligence Scale (WAIS). The Wechsler Intelligence Scale for Children (WISC) was also developed, for ages five to fifteen; it consists of similar types of subtests adapted to the younger age levels.

The Wechsler Scales have provided a better measure of adult intelligence than the Stanford-Binet, since their items and norms are more appropriate for the adult population. Another advantage of the Wechsler is that the separate scores on the component subtests—arithmetic, comprehension, block design, etc.—reveal to the examiner or clinician the subject's pattern of mental abilities, which is difficult to obtain from the Stanford-Binet. Inclusion of the two broad categories of items, verbal and performance, provides greater diagnostic utility, especially when atypical persons are tested—for example, the poorly educated, those lacking in language mastery, and even brain-injured persons. In fact, Wechsler originally suggested that by noting the disparity between certain verbal and performance scores one could detect mental deterioration, since organic impairment affects motor activities more, on the whole, than it does verbal behavior.

How Good Are Intelligence Tests?

Whether or not intelligence tests really measure mental ability was hotly disputed in the years just after Binet's tests appeared. Scores of psychologists checked the validity of I.Q. ratings by looking for answers to these questions: Do teachers' estimates of students' ability agree with test scores? Do children who excel in school work also rate high in tests? Do those whose behavior shows them to be deficient rate low? Do more older than younger children answer a given test question correctly, since a child's mental ability can be assumed to increase with chronological age? And finally, do results of several different intelligence tests agree in ranking an individual's ability high, medium, or low?

All such check-ups show intelligence tests to be valid. Teachers' ratings and I.Q. scores agree rather well. Children doing good school work generally have high I.Q.'s. Goddard and his successors, working with the feebleminded, found that the tests discriminate well between normals and deficients. Binet and Terman found their tests passed by increasingly greater percentages of older than of younger children. For example, a Terman test at the 7-year level asked the child to repeat after the tester five digits. Children between 5 and 9 years passed the test in the following percentages:

Age	5	6	7	8	9
Percent	34	59	74	83	93

Comparing I.Q.'s obtained from several verbal type (e.g. Stanford-Binet) tests reveals that the scores agree significantly. Agreement between the scores of verbal and of performance (e.g., Pintner-Paterson) tests, though positive, is less striking.

All of these check-up methods, taken singly, are subject to error; but their consistently positive results indicate that intelligence tests do measure mental ability fairly accurately.

Intelligence tests have been criticized severely. Minor criticisms, as of certain test items and procedures, often resulted in revisions and improvements of the tests. For example, Terman twice revised his Stanford-Binet test and put out new forms of the scale, which are greatly superior to the 1916 edition.

Other criticisms are more fundamental. It is said that the tests fail to get at native, inborn ability, that a child's performance and resulting I.Q. are affected greatly by his home background and other social factors. This is true; many comparisons between individuals or between groups are invalid because of their differences in backgrounds and experiences. On the other hand, when children having reasonably similar environments are tested together, such as pupils in a small town school, intelligence test ratings give a fair measure of the children's relative abilities.

Another approach to the problems raised by environmental differences has been the "culture-free" intelligence test. Several interesting efforts of this sort have been made, including scales by Raymond B. Cattell, Russell G. Leiter, Allison Davis, and Kenneth Eells. All are basically performance rather than verbal tests and rely on pictures and form content, which is supposedly common to all cultures. While many psychologists doubt that this goal can be achieved, the fact remains that differences between ethnic groups decrease when this type of test is used.

The Factoring of Mental Ability

Edward L. Thorndike, of Columbia University, and others objected to the assumption that any test can measure "general intelligence." In his *Educational Psychology*, published in 1914, Thorndike questions the existence of general ability, stressing rather the "singularity and relative independence of every mental process." Instead of general ability there are many special or grouped abilities, he insists, such as mathematical or mechanical ability.

After making statistical studies of performance on many tests, an English psychologist, Charles Spearman, concluded that each individual has a certain amount of general ability which enters everything he does, but that special abilities which vary for each task undertaken also exist. Performance on a mathematics test, for instance, depends on both a person's general ability and on his specific aptitude and training in mathematics.

Truman L. Kelley, however, found the general factor to be relatively unimportant. The most significant differences, he maintained, depend upon broad group factors such as numerical, spatial, and verbal ability. Since about 1940 improved methods of "factor analysis" have been applied to batteries of test results. Louis L. Thurstone isolated a number of "primary mental abilities," notably visualizing, speed in perceiving, facility with numbers, memory, word fluency, verbal comprehension and, less clearly, reasoning. In later large-scale studies of Air Force cadets, J. P. Guilford confirmed the existence of such factors. He extended his research into the areas of reasoning and creativity, and isolated factors such as sensitivity to problems, associational fluency, and originality. These abilities are found to be relatively independent; a person proficient in one is not necessarily so in another.

Despite our continued use of the I.Q. as an indicator of a "general ability" which enters into all our activities, clusters of abilities clearly exist. In time we may cease to use a single index of ability such as the I.Q., but will speak instead of separate abilities in mathematics, language, memory, reasoning, and the like. Already generalized aptitude tests have been developed, as we shall see, for use in educational and vocational guidance. Before turning to this, however, let us examine the intelligence of the American population, and the correlation between mental ability and age.

Intelligence of the American Population

Terman revised Binet's test so that the average person, having a mental age equal to his chronological age, would obtain an I.Q. of about 100. By the 1920's it had become customary to consider those with I.Q.'s below 70 as mentally deficient, the large middle group clustering around 100 as normal or average, and those above 130 as very superior. The intelligence classification used by Wechsler is as follows:

I.Q.	CLASSIFICATION	PERCENT INCLUDED
130 and above	Very Superior	2.2
120–129	Superior	6.7
110–119	Bright normal	16.1
90–109	Average	50.0
80–89	Dull normal	16.1
70–79	Borderline	6.7
69 and below	Mental defective	2.2

Of course, no hard and fast lines divide the categories. No real difference can be noted between persons having I.Q.'s of 109 and those scoring 110 or between those having 69 and those of 70. Every degree of intelligence from the lowest defective to the most gifted person is found among our population.

How Does Mental Ability Change with Age?

Many persons were shocked when Terman announced that the average adult intelligence is equal to that of a 16-year-old. Even more shocking was the fact that Army Alpha tests placed the level at 14 years. (Terman's revised estimate was 15 years.) People forget that psychologists define intelligence as capacity to learn, adaptability, and mental alertness. In the tests, knowledge, information, and experience are kept at a minimum, though these factors are bound to affect performance.

Mental ability, as measured by intelligence tests, hits its

peak for most persons somewhere between ages 14 and 20. The newborn child progresses very quickly. In the first 4 or 5 years he gains more than at any other period in his life. After reaching its peak level mental ability declines slowly until old age, according to investigations by Thorndike and by Walter R. and Catharine C. Miles. More recent studies, by David Wechsler and others, locate the peak of mental ability somewhat after, rather than before, age 20. Graphically the curve of mental growth appears thus:

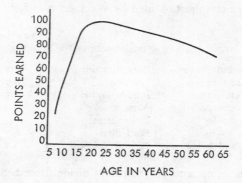

Note that no great decline appears in the curve before age 50; even then it is not marked. This curve represents an average individual. For superior persons it rises higher and drops off a little more gradually. For persons below average in ability it reaches a lower peak and declines somewhat faster.

Harold E. Jones and Herbert S. Conrad, of the University of California, revealed a great discrepancy in the performance of different age groups on tests depending largely on knowledge (e.g., vocabulary) and tests primarily measuring alertness (e.g., following directions). The *knowledge* curve remains almost level between ages 20 and 60, while the *alertness* curve declines gradually after age 17.

In these studies of the relation between age and mental ability it is comforting to note that alertness decreases very slowly until after middle age. A parent of 40, though past his own peak of mental alertness, can learn new things about as well as his youngster of 13 who has not yet reached his maximum. In fact the adult can learn them better if he is motivated strongly enough to make up for his slight inferiority in alertness and adaptability.

Irving Lorge has shown that the greatest difference in mental ability between younger and older persons lies in speed rather than accuracy or "power." A group of persons under 25 and a group over 40 did equally well on a test that had no time limit. When tests with a time limit, like Army Alpha, were used, the younger group showed a clear superiority because its members could work faster.

SPECIAL ABILITIES OR APTITUDES

Apart from our "general intelligence" all of us have certain special aptitudes that affect what we do in our personal or business lives. These specialized abilities have little relationship to I.Q. While a person of superior general ability usually has some particular talents, he may well be devoid of mechanical, musical, or artistic aptitude. While a majority of those having artistic talent are above average in intelligence, some of them are below par. It is impossible to predict general intelligence from a knowledge of special aptitudes, and vice versa.

Special abilities depend on both native capacity and training. Tests now exist which measure mechanical, musical, and artistic ability; also aptitude for clerical work, engineering, law, medicine, teaching, nursing, and science. Persons taking the tests are asked questions and given problems to solve that relate importantly to the field being considered.

MECHANICAL ABILITY

Tests of mechanical aptitude seek to measure skill and speed in perceiving mechanical relationships and in dealing with machines. John L. Stenquist, an American educational psychologist working on mechanical ability, devised a test that involves assembling the parts of ten small devices, among them a bicycle bell, a push button, and a mouse trap. He found a high correlation between success in this test and success in shop work, which suggests that the test is a valid indicator. Performance on the test was largely independent of general intelligence.

Stenquist later drew up a paper-and-pencil form of his test, showing pictures of common mechanical devices, instead of presenting the gadgets themselves in a box. This group test measures mechanical ability almost as well as the individual assembly test.

T. W. MacQuarrie prepared a test of mechanical ability with three subtests (tracing, tapping, dotting) to indicate manual dexterity, three to show spatial visualization (copying, location, blocks), and a "pursuit" test for perceptual speed and accuracy. This test has been useful in selecting trainees for mechanical occupations.

Donald G. Paterson, Richard M. Elliot, and colleagues, using many measures, constructed the Minnesota mechanical ability tests. They set up four criteria for mechanical aptitude: 1. quality of work done, 2. quantity done well, 3. creativeness in construction, and 4. critical appreciation, evaluation, and interest. The tests include assembling parts of gadgets, as in the Stenquist test, fitting cut-outs into corresponding holes in a board, and analyzing geometrical figures. The last-named test has several equivalent forms, in each of which the testee is asked to draw lines in the left-hand figure dividing it into the parts shown at the right.

The Minnesota psychologists found the tests most indicative when supplemented with ratings on interest and intelligence tests, with academic grades, and information about mechanical performance in the home, such as fixing light connections or leaky faucets. Performance on the tests was affected only slightly, they discovered, by environmental influences encouraging mechanical skill. However, older boys did better than younger ones, indicating that experience does affect ability. The popular notion that boys are natively superior to girls in mechanical ability finds no very definite support in the test results. Boys did better than girls in the assembly tests, but not in spatial relations or card sorting.

A somewhat different approach to mechanical aptitude was taken by George K. Bennett and his colleagues of the Psychological Corporation. Here the attempt was made to measure a person's ability to understand everyday physical and mechanical relationships. Familiar objects are shown—wheels, pulleys, gears, levers, etc.—to test the subject's comprehension of principles and relationships. Several forms of the test were devised, suitable for high school boys, engineering students, and women and girls. The Bennett Test of Mechanical Comprehension, focusing on a higher order of mechanical ability, has proved useful for both vocational guidance and selection.

Of course, not all persons who do well in mechanical aptitude tests would be happy in mechanical or construction work; they might excel also in other types of activity. Furthermore, occupational interests do not always coincide with aptitudes. But one who does badly in the tests is not likely to succeed in these fields.

Musical Aptitude

One of the earliest special ability measures was the musical aptitude test, designed in 1919 by Carl E. Seashore, of the University of Iowa. It involves the use of six phonograph records, which test, respectively, the senses of pitch, intensity, time, rhythm, consonance and dissonance, and tonal memory.

On each record, subjects have to make from 50 to 100 comparisons between two notes or patterns of notes. The differences sometimes are great, sometimes exceedingly small. In each test, except that involving consonance, a judgment is either right or wrong. Correctness in the matter of consonance is determined by musical experts. Seashore later substituted a more objective measure, "timbre," for consonance. Timbre refers to a tone's complexity in number and kind of overtones present.

Music teachers disagree about the value of Seashore's test. Some say it helps select satisfactory students for music schools and predicts their success rather accurately. Others contend that it overstresses mere sensory discrimination and fails to touch the essence of musical talent.

For eight years Hazel M. Stanton studied 600 college music students. Entering college, all were given a musical aptitude and a general intelligence test. From the resulting scores they were classified into five groups: of the group scoring highest, 60% eventually received music degrees from the school; of the next highest group, 42%; of the third group, 33%; of the fourth, 23%; and of the lowest group, 17%. Though not based entirely on musical tests, these percentages show that success in music school can be rather accurately predicted before the student enters.

For predicting success in a music career (which depends on many factors besides aptitude) Seashore's test has not proved particularly reliable. However, it is safe to say that a poor score on the Seashore test argues strongly against taking up music professionally. A good score means that one has potentialities for creditable musical performance, at least as an avocation.

A British psychologist, Herbert D. Wing, has tried to improve upon the Seashore test with his "Standardized Tests of Musical Intelligence." He has seven subtests, including chord analysis, pitch change, memory, rhythmic accent, harmony, intensity, and phrasing. On the whole, the Wing test is for a musically sophisticated group; the Seashore test is more useful and interesting for an unselected group of subjects.

Several music appreciation and accomplishment tests have been brought out. The Oregon Music Discrimination Test, devised by Kate Hevner, utilizes phonograph records of 48 short piano selections, arranged in pairs. One in each pair is part of a classic composition. The other is a changed version of the same in which melody, harmony, or rhythm has been altered. The person tested must choose the better composition (i.e., the original) and show how it was altered. Almost invariably those who do well on this test have a good deal of musical experience. However, some persons sensitive to melody may fail to discriminate subtleties of rhythm or harmony. The test gives a fair estimate of musical experience and appreciation.

Artistic Aptitude

Probably the best-known test of ability in pictorial art was designed by Norman C. Meier and Carl E. Seashore in 1929. Its revised form, the "Meier Art Judgment Test," consists of 100 pairs of black and white pictures. One of each pair is a copy of a masterpiece—landscape, portrait, pottery, woodcut, or mural. The other, an altered version of the same, includes some change in position, shading, or perspective. Told how the pictures differ, the subject is asked which one pleases him more. A key gives the right answers, based on opinions of several art experts.

Other procedures have been used in art tests. Margaret McAdory, for example, devised a measure of artistic feeling or appreciation. She presented four variations in design of furniture, textiles, clothing, architecture, etc. and the subject was asked to choose the most pleasing design in each group. Similarly, Maitland Graves prepared a "design judgment test" centering about the basic aesthetic principles of unity, dominance, variety, balance, continuity, symmetry, proportion, and rhythm. Charles C. Horn used a different approach; he asked his subjects to make drawings of objects and geometric figures, then to draw imaginative compositions. In all these tests, scores are determined by extent of agreement with criteria supplied by art experts.

Persons trained in art usually score higher on these tests than those who are untrained. Women surpass men, on the average, by a small but significant amount. Scores seem to depend partly on age as well as on art training. In a research study Meier isolated six ingredients of artistic ability: manual skill, energy output, intelligence, perceptual facility, creative imagination, and aesthetic judgment. The first three he considered mainly inherited, and the last three definitely influenced by heredity. Other psychologists stress the importance of environment, especially training, in producing artistic ability. As with all aptitudes the relative weights of training and inheritance are hard to evaluate. But whatever the answer to this question, tests of musical and artistic talent are helpful, if used with caution, in curricular and vocational guidance.

CLERICAL ABILITY

In his book *Aptitudes and Aptitude Testing*, Walter V. Bingham found four kinds of ability underlying clerical aptitude: perceptual (ability to observe quickly and correctly), intellectual (ability to grasp meanings and make correct decisions), motor (ability to manipulate office equipment), and skills like arithmetic, spelling, punctuation, and good English usage.

Clerical tests measure one or more of these abilities. For example, L. L. Thurstone in 1922 published a group paper-and-pencil test, later revised and lengthened, which included comparing and checking errors, solving arithmetic problems, spotting misspelled words, listing names alphabetically, grasping meanings, and using English correctly. It also tests one's vocabulary and business information.

Many similar tests exist. Lawrence J. O'Rourke, director of research of the U. S. Civil Service Commission, issued a junior grade clerical aptitude test. Divided into two parts—a reasoning test and clerical problems—it contains items like those described above. Donald Paterson and a student devised the Minnesota Vocational Test for Clerical Workers (later revised as the Minnesota Clerical Test) using only two kinds of problems, comparing numbers and comparing names. Persons tested are instructed thus: "If the two names or the two numbers of a pair are *exactly* the same, make a check mark on the line between them; if they are different, make no mark on that line." Then follow 200 pairs of numbers and names, such as:

John C. Linder _____ John C. Lender
5794367 _____ 5794367

Score is determined by the number of items answered correctly. The whole test takes only about 35 minutes.

Recent years have seen many other tests of clerical aptitude. Some, like the Clerical Battery of the Personnel Research Institute of Western Reserve University, have many subtests: name comparison, number comparison, tabulation, filing, alphabetizing, arithmetic reasoning, and spelling. Other tests have fewer subtests, such as the SRA Clerical Aptitudes test, which includes office vocabulary, office arithmetic, and number checking. The Psychological Corporation General Clerical test has nine parts, but only three differential scores: clerical speed and accuracy, numerical ability, and verbal facility.

Persons holding clerical jobs generally score higher than others in these tests, which suggests that the tests do measure abilities important in clerical work. Employers seldom rely entirely on them in selecting clerical help, however. Many give a general intelligence test also, and require a transcript of school grades besides a personal interview with the applicant. In recent years, clerical aptitude tests have been quite useful.

VOCATIONAL OR OCCUPATIONAL TESTS

Tests of mechanical, musical, artistic, and clerical aptitude are useful in connection with vocational guidance and selection. Since World War II, however, a broader type of aptitude test has become popular. They are similar to the Thurstone test of "primary mental abilities" described earlier in this chapter. Donald E. Super, an authority on vocational testing, calls them "standard batteries with norms for specific occupations." One of the most widely used of these is the Differential Aptitude Test, constructed by George K. Bennett, Harold G. Seashore, and Alexander G. Wesman of the Psychological Corporation. Included are measures of verbal reasoning, numerical ability, abstract reasoning, space relations, mechanical reasoning, clerical speed and accuracy, and language usage. The General Aptitude Test Battery (GATB) was developed by the U. S. Employment Service for use in its occupational counseling services. Along with its verbal, numerical, and spatial measures, its ten scores include eye-hand coordination, motor speed, finger dexterity, and manual dexterity. Research is continuing in an effort to find the "occupational aptitude profile" which correlates most closely with the demands of each vocation. Progress is made difficult by the overlapping of job analyses and the changing character of job demands. And, like all aptitude tests, they tell only a part of the story: tests of general intelligence, interest, and achievement are an important supplement.

PROFESSIONAL APTITUDES

The abilities one needs in order to make good as a court lawyer differ strikingly from those necessary for a corporation attorney. Similarly in the medical profession, a surgeon must have exceptional manual skill, while ability for detailed observation is necessary to the research man. These wide differences of talent required within any of the professions complicate the problem of measuring professional aptitudes. However, tests exist for law, medicine, teaching, nursing, science, and engineering, and while not infallible they are usually helpful to college students in choosing their vocations. These tests are best used along with general intelligence and interest tests.

George D. Stoddard, with M. L. Ferson, constructed a law aptitude examination. Taken in an hour, it measures capacity for accurate recall, comprehension of difficult passages, reasoning by analogy and by analysis, and skill in logic. It has forecast success in law school rather well. Of students in the highest quarter of test scores, more than half received A or B in their first year law school work. Of the poorest half in test scores a large proportion failed on their courses.

Just after the war a revised Iowa Legal Aptitude Test was published by Michael Adams and Dewey B. Stuit. Of the eight subtests five were legal in content, testing such things as memory of judicial opinions, judgments of relevance, and legal information. This type of test was found to be a good predictor of success in law school.

Teaching demands general intelligence, a good grasp of subject matter, and certain desirable personality traits. To predict teaching success it is best to use one's I.Q. test score, school record, results of achievement tests in subjects to be taught, vocational interest findings, and a test of teaching ability.

The Stanford educational aptitude test, devised by Milton B. Jensen, estimates fitness for teaching, school administration, or educational research. In questionnaire form it presents problems for which the student chooses one of several solutions, and rates his confidence in his own judgment.

Three types of material are included: position preference ratings (in which the more attractive of two hypothetical positions is chosen), discipline problems, and high school activities.

Another widely used measure of teaching aptitude is the Coxe-Orleans prognosis test of teaching ability, designed by two educational psychologists, Warren W. Coxe and Jacob S. Orleans, to select the most promising candidates for teachers' colleges. A three-hour test, it consists of five parts: general information, knowledge of teaching methods and practices, grasp of professional material, reading comprehension, and solution of educational problems.

Perhaps the most widely used current educational aptitude tests are the National Teacher Examinations put out annually by the Educational Testing Service. These are objective-type written tests designed to evaluate grasp of subject matter, reasoning, and judgment, but not interest or personality characteristics. They are found to be valuable in the selection of teachers.

Professor Fred A. Moss, of George Washington University, developed a scholastic aptitude test for medical schools. A paper-and-pencil test, it consists of six parts: comprehension and retention, visual memory, memory for content, logical reasoning, scientific vocabulary, and understanding printed material. Members of the Association of American Medical Colleges use this test or the more recent Minnesota Medical Aptitude Test. Applicants who score high in these tests tend to succeed in their medical training and as interns, while those who make low scores are not likely to succeed.

Aptitude for nursing somewhat resembles that for medicine. Catharine C. Miles found that to be a good nurse one should like people, have tact, good general intelligence, broad interests, emotional stability, patience, sound health, and resourcefulness. Moss, with Thelma Hunt, developed an aptitude test for nursing. It does not pretend to diagnose the total personality, but measures abilities required in nurses' training. It tests scientific vocabulary, general information, understanding printed material, memory, and ability to follow directions. As in the medical and other professional tests, this test deals mainly with general mental ability.

The Stanford Scientific Aptitude Test, constructed by D. L. Zyve, attempts to bring out aptitudes essential to success in scientific fields, irrespective of previous knowledge and training. It is designed to reveal experimental bent and ability to think and observe accurately. The questions deal with mathematics, choice of the best approach to common scientific problems, analysis of the motion of gears, inconsistencies in statements relating to chemistry and physics, approval or disapproval of proposed technical projects, comparison of heights and lengths of lines, procedures in several types of laboratory investigation, noting and checking the details of complex geometrical figures. Sometimes the subject is asked whether or not he likes this type of problem. This test has proved helpful, especially to students who are thinking of entering the fields of engineering, chemistry, physics, or biology.

During World War II Westinghouse Electric Co. and Science Service cooperated to initiate the Science Talent Search, an ambitious attempt to identify potential scientists among high school students. Harold Edgerton and Steuart H. Britt found that the best selection procedure was to supplement their Science Aptitude Test with an analysis of high school grades, teachers' ratings, written essays, and personal interviews.

Engineering has its own special tests. In 1922 Louis L. Thurstone devised a vocational guidance test for engineers, consisting of sections on arithmetic, algebra, geometry, physics, and technical information. From results of 6500 high school graduates taking the test Thurstone was able to predict that students in the highest quarter had 93 chances out of 100 of passing in engineering school. Those in the second and third quarters had 89 and 81 chances respectively out of 100. Those in the lowest quarter had only 53 chances.

More recently Henry Borow, Charles H. Griffin, and their colleagues drew upon earlier tests to construct the "Engineering and Physical Science Aptitude Test." It includes scores for mathematics, arithmetic reasoning, and mechanical and verbal comprehension. This scale has been valuable for measuring aptitude for engineering training, as has the "Pre-Engineering Inventory" developed by the Educational Testing Service.

Aptitude tests have also been developed for other specialized fields. One of the most extensive of these efforts was the program for selection of American aircraft pilots in World War II, under the direction of John Flanagan and reported by Philip H. DuBois. The battery of tests included general information, reading comprehension, interpreting serial photographs and maps, and a number of apparatus tests such as discrimination reaction time, rudder control, and two-hand coordination. The validity of such tests is shown by comparing the training record of those who received the lowest and the highest scores. Of those in the lowest category or "stanine," 76% were eliminated in their pilot training, while of those in the highest stanine only 4% failed their training. Using the whole group, those in the 5 highest stanines showed only 17% failure as compared with 44% for the lowest 4 stanines. A comparable program of selective aptitude tests for Navy personnel was developed by psychologist John G. Jenkins.

ACHIEVEMENT TESTS

While *aptitude tests* theoretically measure special ability apart from training, *achievement tests* measure learned performance regardless of ability. Achievement tests indicate how much knowledge or skill a person possesses in a particular field. Actually, no clear line divides the two. It is impossible for one's mechanical aptitude, as revealed in a test, not to be affected by experience and training. Likewise one's achievement in reading, algebra, or bricklaying necessarily is influenced by one's ability. Aptitude and achievement tests emphasize somewhat different things, both important in vocational guidance, employment, and personnel work. Achievement tests chiefly measure knowledge of school subjects or occupational proficiency. The occupational or trade tests include examinations for carpenters, plumbers, electricians, butchers, radio operators, etc., and performance tests for patternmakers, sheet-metal workers, lathe operators, and typists and stenographers. A good example is the Stenographic Proficiency Test put out by Harold G. Seashore and George K. Bennett of the Psychological Corporation.

Educational achievement tests have existed for many years, largely to measure the effects of school instruction, but also, to some extent, for the purpose of predicting later educational and vocational success. The Cooperative Achievement Tests were initiated in the 1930's under the leadership of Ben D. Wood and John C. Flanagan. These consist of annual editions of tests in natural sciences, social studies, mathematics, fine arts, and many other specialized fields. The Iowa Tests of Educational Development, produced under the direction of E. F. Lindquist, combine features of both achievement and intelligence tests. They include tests on understanding of social concepts, background in natural sciences, quantitative thinking, interpreting reading materials, and general vocabulary. These tests followed the example set by the Air Force Tests of General Educational Development, and were used extensively to evaluate the readiness of veterans for college education following their discharge. Other well-known scales in this area are the Metropolitan Achievement Tests developed by Gertrude H. Hildreth, the Modern School Achievement Tests (Arthur I. Gates, Paul R. Mort, and Ralph B. Spence), and the Stanford Achievement Test (Truman L. Kelley, Giles M. Ruch, and Lewis M. Terman). The Graduate Record Examination, used widely for selecting applicants to graduate schools, is a combination of achievement and aptitude tests.

Many criticisms have been made of psychological tests, including tests of ability and aptitude. Some critics charge that intelligence tests leave untouched many important aspects of personality, like interests, motives, attitudes, or social adaptability. One must, however, recall that these tests do not pretend to measure personality. In fact, no one test ever has been devised—and perhaps never will be devised—that measures all aspects of personality. The best procedure, when a complete personality picture is desired, is to make a case study of an individual's background and experience, and to supplement it with a variety of tests, not only those measuring intelligence, but also those measuring special aptitudes, achievements, interests, attitudes, and other phases of personality. We shall consider these tests in later chapters.

Whatever may be said for or against intelligence tests in the future, they now have practical value in several fields. Employers use them to help choose the ablest applicants for jobs. The army, navy, and air force give a comprehensive intelligence test to every new recruit. Teachers use tests to classify pupils in advanced, average, or retarded sections, and to arrange courses of study suited to individual abilities. Vocational guidance and personnel workers find them helpful in determining occupations for which students or employees are best fitted. Probably their use can be extended still further. As Pintner pointed out, even today thousands of workers are misfits in their jobs, some bogging down under work they are incapable of handling, others dissatisfied with tasks far below their capacities. Through the use of intelligence tests some of these situations could be avoided.

Aptitude tests, as we have seen, measure the special abilities not closely related to "general intelligence." They may help students in the choice of a vocation and may aid an employer in determining an applicant's fitness for a specific job. But they yield nothing on occupational interests or personality traits such as honesty or persistence. Previous knowledge or experience affects them to some extent, but not as much as in the case of achievement tests. We may conclude that both aptitude and achievement tests have their place in the whole process of evaluation, along with general intelligence and interest tests, and assessments of personality by tests, ratings, or interviews.

Chapter III

DETERMINANTS OF BEHAVIOR

MENDEL   GALTON   ITARD   THORNDIKE
NEWMAN   FREEMAN   HOLZINGER
GOODENOUGH   MC NEMAR   PINTNER   WATSON

*What is meant by heredity and by environment?
How are they related? Why are they important to
psychology? Is it possible to study the effects of one
independently of the other? What aspects of human
behavior are chiefly determined by heredity?
What by environment?*

Each of us enters the world with a certain heredity, the characteristics transmitted to us through our parents' germ plasm, itself the product of a long line of ancestors. We grow up in certain environments, our material and social surroundings. Everything we do, as a child or adult, in the last analysis results from the complex interacting of our heredity and our environment. To understand and control human behavior we must know something about the nature and function of each.

HEREDITY AND ENVIRONMENT

In 1900 an astonishing discovery was made almost simultaneously by three biologists working independently on problems of heredity. The discovery did not result from their own experimenting, but from that of an Austrian monk named Gregor Mendel, whose work they found in an obscure scientific journal which had been published 34 years earlier and promptly forgotten. Mendel had puttered in his garden, cross-breeding peas. When he mated white-flowered peas with red-flowered peas he found that certain intangible factors, which he called merely "elements" for want of a better term, determined whether the offspring would be red or white. The "elements" produced consistent ratios between red and white offspring, not only for one generation, but in successive generations. These rules for hereditary transmission became known as Mendel's laws.

At once biologists the world over followed up Mendel's study. In America Thomas Hunt Morgan and Raymond Pearl, among others, developed the theory of heredity according to *genes* and *chromosomes*, terms that replaced Mendel's "elements." Genes, so far as can be determined, are submicroscopic protein molecules existing in germ cells. Linked together in definite patterns, the genes form chromosomes. These complicated patterns of genes, unique for each person, determine his heredity. A human germ cell contains 24 pairs of chromosomes, each made up of probably thousands of genes. When a male sperm and a female ovum unite at the time of conception, each releases one of each of its chromosome pairs, which then combine in the cell nucleus of the new individual formed and thus determine his whole physical heritage.

What traits do we inherit? Amram Scheinfeld summarizes: we inherit the color of our eyes, hair, and skin, shape of skull, and a tendency to be short or to be tall. Certain physical defects like color-blindness, stub fingers, and some forms of baldness also are inherited. No common diseases except diabetes are hereditary, though inherited predispositions toward cancer, tuberculosis, and allergies may exist. Only a few mental abnormalities are inherited—notably certain types of mental deficiency, and Huntington's chorea, a rare malady characterized by physical and mental disintegration. Authorities disagree about the role of heredity in several other mental diseases. The degree of intelligence we possess is probably inherited, according to the majority of psychologists.

In one brief instant at the moment of conception when genes from the father and mother unite, heredity is determined. Whatever else shapes an individual is environment. As embryo and fetus he develops in a uterine environment; then after birth in a complex physical and social setting. Among other influences, he is affected by food, climate, geographical location, kind of home and neighborhood, school, community, and nation. This environment determines what a person sees, hears, touches, smells, and tastes. It can speed up or retard growth and development. It provides what one learns and remembers; it furnishes the stimuli to which one reacts emotionally. Other human beings, who influence and in turn are influenced by the individual, are a significant aspect of environment.

During every living moment every person is the product of his heredity and environment. Always the two forces interact. Psychologically speaking, the one cannot exist without the other. To ask "Which is more important, heredity or environment?" is like asking "Which is more essential to running a car, the motor or the gasoline?" Obviously both are essential.

This interdependence of heredity and environment presents a difficult problem to the scientist. He cannot, by studying a person directly, learn whether heredity or whether environment mainly determines his hair color, his I.Q., or his disposition. However, he can measure the mental or physical characteristics of two individuals and note the differences between them. By carefully studying their backgrounds and experiences he can frequently tell whether heredity or environment is the more powerful determiner of these *differences*.

Traits which heredity largely determines can be changed very little in this generation, though possibly in future generations they can be modified by a program of eugenics, through sterilization or selective breeding. Traits determined by environment can be changed by educational, social, and political improvements like better schools, more playgrounds, slum clearance, or higher standards of living.

For about a century, and especially since 1920, psychologists have been working on this problem of separating the strands of heredity and environment. The earliest research efforts consisted of tracing genealogies.

FAMILY TREES

A book called *Hereditary Genius* was published in 1869 by Francis Galton, a brilliant free-lance British scientist who helped launch psychology on its scientific career. Besides studying heredity and founding the eugenics movement, he devised many mental and physical tests and statistical methods for interpreting differences between individuals.

Galton believed genius is inherited and undertook to prove it. He selected names of nearly a thousand of the most eminent statesmen, military and naval leaders, and professional persons, who had lived in the British Isles during the preceding several generations. To see whether they had more distinguished relatives than would be expected by chance, he studied their genealogies carefully. For comparative purposes he calculated that among all the relatives of any thousand unselected garden-variety Britishers, one would expect to find only four eminent persons. In the family trees of his selected thousand, however, he found well over 500 distinguished relatives. Galton believed these results proved that genius is inherited.

Encouraged by his findings in the study of genius he began research into heredity and art. This showed that of the children in 30 families of artistic parents, 64% were artistic, whereas only 21% of the children in 150 families of nonartistic parents revealed artistic ability. Children resemble their parents, Galton concluded; heredity's influence far outweighs that of environment.

As later psychologists pointed out, however, Galton overlooked, or possibly in his enthusiasm ignored, several important items. In the first place, to identify eminence with genius is fallacious. Eminence implies achievement and social recognition. Some persons attain eminence at least partially through political favor, good name, or just plain luck. Genius connotes exceptional talent, which shows itself in creative achievement. Eminence and genius are related, but scientifically cannot be considered synonymous. Secondly, Galton judged eminence by his own personal standards. Probably he chose well, but any one person almost certainly shows bias, if only in betraying preference for certain professions.

The most significant oversight, however, lay in Galton's slighting the role of environment. He attached little importance to the various non-hereditary factors influencing the lives of his eminent men. Indeed, this oversight was noted by A. de Candolle, a Swiss, who published in 1873 a reply to Galton's *Hereditary Genius*. De Candolle, studying genius in the field of science, compiled a list of environmental influences affecting over 500 eminent European scientists. Among the influences which foster scientific creativeness he found wealth, leisure, scientific traditions, good education, available libraries and laboratories, freedom to express opinion and follow a chosen profession, and geographical location in the temperate zone. From his evidence De Candolle concluded that environment is the chief factor producing scientific genius—an unwarranted deduction because he overlooked hereditary influences.

To point out Galton's errors in the light of newer scientific findings is not to discount his great contribution in stimulating research on heredity. Unfortunately, difficulty in controlling variables has also led other investigators astray.

Consider, for example, the fabulous history of the Kallikak family. Henry H. Goddard noticed that several derelicts in the community (including one inmate of the Training School) bore the same surname as a well-known and respected family. Tracing the genealogy, he found that both groups stemmed from a common ancestor, a soldier in the Revolutionary War. In order not to reveal the family name, Goddard called this man Martin Kallikak. (The word "Kallikak" in Greek means "good-bad.") The records showed that Martin had had an affair with a retarded girl, which resulted in a mentally deficient illegitimate son. From this son (known as "Old Horror") 480 descendants were traced. Of them 143 were reputed to be defective and only 46 known to have normal mentality. The rest were of doubtful intelligence. The clan included 24 confirmed alcoholics, 3 epileptics, 3 criminals, 35 sexually immoral persons, mostly prostitutes, and 8 brothel keepers.

After the war Martin settled down to marriage with a woman of normal intelligence and of solid Quaker parentage. In striking contrast to the other strain, all but three of the

496 descendants traced from this legitimate union were mentally and morally fit. This branch of the family included only respectable and prominent citizens—doctors, lawyers, judges, businessmen. Several New Jersey towns, Goddard noted, are named for families into which these people married. No traces of defect were found, no illegitimacy, no epilepsy, no crime, and only one case of bad morals and two of alcoholism were found among all the descendants. Goddard concluded that Kallikak degeneracy resulted from defective mentality caused by infusion of "bad blood."

As with Galton, however, the conclusion can be questioned. One possible error centers around the paternity of Martin Kallikak, junior. His subnormal mother firmly fixed the paternity on Martin, senior, but the evidence rests on her questionable testimony. Without proof the case loses much of its force.

Goddard, moreover, minimized the effects of environment. Although he said that criminals are made rather than born, he did not consider the ill effects of poverty, filth, and deplorable home conditions on children born into the bad side of the family. Nor did he comment on effects of favorable influences such as the educational, cultural, and financial advantages enjoyed by the good side. That both branches lived in the same geographical locale in no way implies that their actual environments were the same.

In short, while *The Kallikak Family* may have indicated the inheritance of mental defect through six generations, it failed to prove that pauperism, drunkenness, and delinquency result primarily from bad family stock.

Jungle or "Feral" Children

Dramatic stories of infants abandoned in the wilds and reared by animals show strikingly environment's influence, which the genealogical studies neglected. Though such cases are rare and their data incomplete, they deserve mention.

In 1799 some hunters discovered a wild boy roaming the forests of Aveyron in southern France. He appeared about 11 years old and grubbed his living from roots and acorns, animal fashion. Captured and brought to Paris, he was put in the care of a Dr. Jean Itard, who undertook to civilize him. The task seemed hopeless. The boy seemed feebleminded. He was shaken with spasms and convulsions. His senses were dull. He uttered only occasional grunts and showed no social behavior or powers of attention or observation. In Itard's own words, "his whole life was a completely animal existence."

For five years the doctor tried to train him. The boy progressed but never became normal. His sense of discrimination improved. He learned to respond to his name "Victor," and to speak, read, and recall a few simple words. His highest achievement was to learn the meaning of *lait* (milk) and to arrange the word's letters in proper order. Toward Itard and the others who cared for him he developed strong affection, but he did not learn to play or behave like a normal youngster.

This case has two conflicting interpretations. One calls the wild boy a mental defective, probably an imbecile, suggesting that he was abandoned for this reason and explaining thus his lack of progress. The other attributes the boy's apparent defectiveness to his early non-human environment, an experience affecting him so profoundly that later training brought few results. Though he progressed somewhat he could not attain normality because his most impressionable years were grossly abnormal. The fact that he coped successfully enough with a wild environment to survive for a time is pointed out as evidence that he was not mentally defective.

Each view may be partially correct. Perhaps the boy began life with low mentality; both heredity and environment may well have produced the backward child on whom Dr. Itard spent so many patient months. One cannot interpret Victor's case accurately from the sketchy data recorded.

The amazing story of India's wolf children was first told by Paul C. Squires and was documented later in a book by the anthropologist Robert M. Zingg. In 1920 two little girls, later named Kamala and Amala, were found living with wolves in the Bengal province of India. The older child, Kamala, seemed about 9 and her sister about 2 years of age. Placed in a nearby orphanage, they were trained by the director, Rev. J. A. L. Singh, and his wife. At first the children behaved like animals. They moved about on all fours, standing upright only occasionally. Their senses of hearing and smell were acute, and

Kamala apparently saw better by night than by day. A picture of her taken soon after she entered the orphanage shows her lapping up food from a pan on the ground, like a dog or a cat. She ate ravenously, particularly meat, which she stole without compunction, and growled when approached while eating. Almost two years after her capture she found a dead chicken in the yard, seized it in her jaws, ran on hands and feet to the bushes, and emerged some minutes later with bloody telltale feathers clinging to her lips. She was also found devouring the entrails of a fowl.

Amala died after a short time, but Kamala lived nine years. She learned to wear clothes, eat from a plate using both hands, and walk upright, although she descended to all fours when running. Gradually her animal ways were abandoned. Instead of baring her teeth at other youngsters, she took part in their activities and moped if not included. At night she slept on a bed beside her playmates instead of roaming the fields as before. She ran errands, cared for children, used about 100 words, and showed responsibility, initiative, and self-reliance. In short, she developed an essentially human mode of life.

Unfortunately psychologists were not called to examine and train the wolf children. A journal kept by Rev. and Mrs. Singh records the only data we have of their progress. Though not scientific, it is extensive and includes 22 photographs; it is reproduced in full in Zingg's book, *Wolf-children and Feral Man*.

A more recently reported feral child is Tamasha, the "wild boy of Salvador," who was captured by police after a struggle and put in the care of a psychologist named Jorge Ramirez Chulo. Tamasha, named for the one word, meaning "village," that he could speak when found, apparently was lost or abandoned when very young and lived with animals in the jungle. He could throw stones with astonishing precision and swing skillfully from limb to limb of the jungle trees. At first he refused cooked foods, lapped up liquids from a dish, and preferred curling up on the floor to sleeping in a bed. Under Chulo's supervision he progressed rapidly. With good grace he accepted clothes, baths, and barber shops. He acquired a considerable vocabulary and described eating with animals in the jungle, but he could not recall human parents.

What, if any, conclusions can be drawn from these cases of feral children? Information on many important points is too scant; for example, an exact account of behavior when first discovered, precise data about training, or degree of success in learning. From the evidence on record one can say merely this: It is possible, though uncommon, for human children to survive in a non-human (animal) environment. Such children develop some means of locomotion, speech sounds of a sort, emotional reactions, and various habit patterns adapted to their environment. On the other hand, many kinds of usual human behavior are absent—chiefly reasoning, language, and social conduct. Feral children can be re-trained, but the longer they have been isolated from human influences the harder it is to teach them and the less likely they are to become normal. For a child to develop a human personality, he must have the usual social contacts. Environment is shown to play a vital part in the process.

CASES OF ISOLATION AND DEPRIVATION

Feral cases are very uncommon, and the descriptions of them somewhat untrustworthy. Data on isolated children are more reliable. In 1832, Anselm von Feuerbach, a prominent Bavarian lawyer, told the story of Kaspar Hauser. This was a child who, for reasons political or otherwise, was kept in a dungeon, separated from all communication with the world, from early childhood to about the age of seventeen. He was not even allowed to see his attendant. When set free, according to his biographer, he could walk only with difficulty, could understand no human speech, and was socially helpless. With friendly guidance, however, he learned rapidly, and later wrote the story of his experiences.

Sociologist Kingsley Davis has reported on two cases of children isolated for several years. When discovered, both seemed mentally defective and one, indeed, improved very little after two years of training. The other, however, progressed rapidly with intensive training; by the time she was fourteen, she had completed sixth grade and behaved like a normal child.

Effects of isolation have also been demonstrated in experiments on sensory deprivation. Three Canadian psychologists, W. H. Bexton, Woodburn Heron, and T. H. Scott, studied the behavior of individuals confined to a small soundproof room and cut off from normal sensory stimulation. Eyes, ears, and hands were covered to limit perception. The subjects soon became bored, and unable to concentrate and solve problems. As isolation proceeded, they became disturbed, confused, and began to have hallucinations. This experiment suggests that considerable contact with the outer world is necessary for us to function normally.

Similar findings are indicated by animal studies. Donald O. Hebb and his associates blinded rats at two stages of development to discover how this sensory deprivation affects adaptability. The rats in one group were blinded in infancy; those in a matched group at maturity. When tested for problem-solving ability the group blinded at maturity did better. In another experiment, the young rats of one group were placed singly in a bare cage which gave no opportunity for problem-solving. The rats in a matched group were placed in a large cage with many objects, barriers, paths, etc., which provided problem-solving experiences. When tested at maturity the rats raised in isolation were less adaptable to new situations. Isolation and sensory deprivation experiments performed on dogs and chimpanzees further corroborate the findings that deprivation causes retardation in ability to learn later in life.

The Ape and the Child

Children cannot be thrust arbitrarily into a non-human environment for experimental purposes. The opposite is quite possible, however; an animal can be reared in a human environment to see how far it can be humanized within the limitations of its structure or heredity. The story of how an ape and a child were brought up together reveals the astonishing capacity for human achievement shown by a young chimpanzee.

Professor and Mrs. Winthrop N. Kellogg, psychologists at

the University of Indiana, brought into their home a seven-and-a-half-months-old ape to be reared for about a year with their ten-months-old son, Donald. Like the boy, the ape, Gua, was dressed in diapers, rompers, shoes, and stockings. She was given a crib, high chair, cup and spoon of her own. She was bathed and fondled, just as the child was, by her foster parents. After a few weeks Gua and Donald became friends. The ape, more demonstratively affectionate than Donald, kissed the boy, held his hand, and assumed a protective attitude toward him. When he was given attention she showed obvious jealousy. They learned to play ball and other games together, like two children.

Gua learned to walk in an upright position, to shake hands, drink from a glass and eat with a spoon, to unlatch a door, and scribble with a pencil. In learning to switch on a light she outdid Donald. Although Gua failed to learn "pat-a-cake" she was more apt than Donald in solving problems such as moving a chair into position to reach a cookie hung from the ceiling. In mental growth ape and boy showed equal progress as measured by the Gesell tests for pre-school children, consisting of standardized norms by which to judge development.

The most striking differences between the two lay in the realm of language. Human articulation Gua never mastered, whereas Donald progressed normally through "ma-ma," "da-da," and the usual infant sounds. On the other hand, in responding to spoken words, Gua at first surpassed Donald. At about 16½ months she responded properly to fifty-eight phrases, like "don't do that," "hug Donald," "show me your nose," "blow the horn." In comparison the child responded to sixty-eight phrases, though it must be remembered he was nearly 3 months older.

Contrasts between ape and child are somewhat hard to make because their rates of physical and mental development differ. In general the ape progressed faster at first and reached her best performance sooner. The child developed more slowly but attained a higher level. However, the experiment did not continue long enough to determine whether or not the ape had reached her maximum capacity in all respects.

In a more recent experiment, Keith and Cathy Hayes reared

a chimpanzee, Vicki, as a child for over three years. Vicki's most remarkable achievement was learning to utter three words, "mama," "papa," and "cup," and apparently to use them with meaning. On her third birthday, for example, Vicki drank her cup of coffee, then asked Mrs. Hayes for a refill by holding her cup up to the coffee pot saying "Mama," then "Cup." Of course Vicki's progress in language was slower than her progress in perceiving and manipulating objects; it has been suggested that she functioned like a "language defective" child.

Thus strikingly unusual environments can greatly alter the behavior of both humans and animals—up to the point where hereditary structures impose limitations. Heredity sets limits that cannot be transcended; but within these limits widely varied behavior is possible, and the details of this behavior result from experience and training—that is, from environment.

Studies of Twins

How can psychologists disentangle the strands of heredity and environment in studying human beings? One good way is to compare persons having the same heredity (identical twins) but different environments. If the twins have been separated at birth or shortly after, and reared in different surroundings, the differences appearing in their physical and mental traits can be assumed to result from environment, since their heredities are identical. Another way is to compare persons having different heredities but the same environment, such as a foster child reared by parents with their own child of the same age, the two being treated just alike. Differences found here may be attributed to heredity since environment remains constant. Naturally such cases are hard to find, but approximate situations yield fairly conclusive results.

Twins may be *identical* or they may be *fraternal*. Identical twins stem from one ovum and are of the same sex and genetic constitution. Their eyes are alike, also their hair color, facial features, head shape, fingerprints, and even their brain waves. The twins we cannot tell apart generally are identicals. Fraternal twins, on the other hand, come from different ova and spermatozoa, though conceived and born at the same time. Their physical traits and genetic makeup are similar, but no more so than "siblings," the term applied to non-twin children of the same parents. Fraternal twins may be of the same or opposite sexes. For psychological studies identical twins are more useful, though often it is important to use fraternal twins for comparative purposes.

The indefatigable Galton, discussed in connection with heredity and genius, was the first to realize that twins could be valuable to science. He assembled information, mostly in the form of anecdotes, about eighty pairs of twins, both identical and fraternal. His data indicated amazing similarities between identical twins even when they were reared apart. On the contrary, twins dissimilar at birth, though brought up together and treated alike, differed widely in their behavior. Galton's conclusions again stressed the overwhelming importance of heredity. Unfortunately the accuracy of the data he secured was not checked, so the study hardly can be called scientific. For example, Galton includes a statement from a mother of twins in which she speaks of "an interchangeable likeness of expression that often gave to each the effect of being more like his brother than himself!"

The first really experimental twin study was made in 1905 by Edward L. Thorndike, of Columbia University. Thorndike, a pioneer experimental psychologist, contributed to practically every branch of the science and became famous for his work in learning and intelligence testing. Interested in heredity's effects on human ability, he gave fifty pairs of twins six mental tests which involved problems in addition, naming opposites of given words, canceling all "a's" on a printed page, and the like. With the same material he tested pairs of siblings, i.e., ordinary non-twin brothers and sisters. A striking similarity showed up between the test scores of the twin pairs as compared to scores of the sibling pairs. Twin scores were two or three times more similar than were sibling scores. Thorndike concluded that heredity dominated in determining the abilities tested, since the environments of twins and siblings were the same.

More recent studies, such as one by A. H. Wingfield, have used all three types—identical twins, fraternal twins, and siblings. Mainly tests of intelligence have been given, but physical traits and motor abilities (steadiness, rate of tapping, etc.) have been checked in some cases, as, for example, by Karl J. Holzinger and Quinn McNemar. The results are clear-cut. Identical twins resemble each other so markedly that by knowing how one performs on various tests we can predict quite accurately the other's performance. Fraternal twins resemble each other less, but more than do siblings. Apparently, then, heredity largely determines intelligence and motor performance as well as physique.

The question often arises: why are not measurements and scores of identical twins *exactly* alike? Their slight differences may trace back to minute differences in heredity; we never can be sure that twins' genetic patterns are identical in every detail. Or, as John B. Watson, the behaviorist, pointed out, the cause may be differences in environment which can occur even when identical twins grow up in the same home and are treated alike.

The last point is important. Even identical twins are separated at times, if only to visit the dentist or recover in isolation from mumps. One breaks a leg and the other goes to school alone. In some cases they make different friends. At home they work out a division of labor; one dusts and the other wipes dishes. One comes to act as spokesman for both in talking with strangers. This different behavior is even more marked with triplets.

Interesting differences in the Dionne quintuplets' behavior were reported by William E. Blatz, a Canadian psychologist. Yvonne was serene, self-confident, and liked best by her sisters. Annette assumed social leadership. Emilie seemed most self-sufficient. Cécile was capricious and unpredictable. Marie, who had physical handicaps and seemed the baby of the group, appeared least popular with the others and made most demands upon nurses. Genetically the "quints" were identical, though slight physical differences between them appeared at birth. According to Blatz, environment produced these personality and behavior differences, since each quint came to have a unique role and status in relation to the others.

To test the effect of different environments upon persons of the same heredity, three University of Chicago professors, Horatio H. Newman, Frank N. Freeman, and Karl J. Holzinger, scoured the country for cases of identical twins who had been raised apart. Finally they located nineteen pairs who had been separated when very young and adopted by different families. Their physical measurements were taken and they were given mental tests. The resulting average differences between these twins, compared to differences between identicals reared together, are shown in the following table*:

| | DIFFERENCES BETWEEN IDENTICAL TWINS | |
	REARED TOGETHER	REARED APART
Stature	1.7 cm.	1.8 cm.
Weight	4.1 lbs.	9.9 lbs.
I.Q. (2 tests)	5 or 6 points	8 or 9 points

A change in environment seems to affect stature very little, though, as might be expected, it can cause variations in weight. The effect on intelligence shown in the table is further borne out by dividing the 19 cases into those pairs where both were placed in similar homes (such as families of professional men) and those pairs where the twins went to dissimilar homes. It was then found that twins in the first group, like twins reared together, differed from each other in intelligence by only 5 or 6 points, whereas in the latter group the difference was 10 or 11 points. The greater the environmental difference, the greater the intelligence difference, though the amounts are small.

Education appeared to be the most important single factor affecting intelligence. One girl, for example, grew up in a good farming section and attended college; her I.Q. was 116. Her twin sister, who lived in a backwoods community and went to school only two or three years, revealed an I.Q. of 92. This was the greatest I.Q. difference found in the study.

* Adapted from *Twins*, by Newman, Freeman, and Holzinger.

STUDIES OF FOSTER CHILDREN

A question that doubtless enters the mind of many a foster parent captured the interest of Barbara S. Burks. The question was this: does the intelligence of adopted children tend to resemble that of the foster parents, or does it carry over as a heritage from the true parents? She took 214 cases of children placed in good homes at an average age of 3 months and compared them with 105 children living with their own parents. Results of intelligence tests given when the youngsters were 5 to 11 years old showed that adopted children only slightly resemble their foster parents. On the other hand, children reared in their own homes showed noticeable similarity to their parents.* A child's heredity, then, affects his intelligence more than does the home in which he lives. From her findings Dr. Burks ventured to conclude that heredity is four or five times as important as environment in determining how individuals differ on intelligence tests.

Alice M. Leahy performed a similar study in Minnesota, in which she matched each of 200 adopted children with an "own" child in the same home. Like Burks, she found the "own" children's I.Q.'s were much more like the I.Q.'s of their parents than were the I.Q.'s of the adopted children.

Another aspect of the same problem concerned Freeman and his two associates: how much can a foster home change the intelligence of an adopted child? He found that children given tests both before and after adoption showed an average increase of 7.5 I.Q. points after four years in a foster home. The youngsters placed in better homes gained about 10 points. Freeman tested also the intelligence of separated siblings who had lived in different foster homes more than five

* Correlation coefficients were .25 and .50 respectively. Correlation means the degree of relationship between two variables. A correlation coefficient having a value between .70 and 1.00 in this case would mean that the intelligence of any child agreed quite closely with that of his parents. A correlation between .40 and .60 means a moderate degree of relationship, while one of .30 or less indicates relatively little relationship.

years. The separated brothers and sisters resembled each other far less than brothers and sisters who grew up together.* Again it was found that where environments differed widely a greater gap between the I.Q.'s appeared. To complete the picture, unrelated children living in the same home were shown to resemble each other in I.Q. somewhat more than related children in different homes.

Several other studies have been concerned with the effects of major environmental change. George S. Speer investigated the intelligence of children of mentally defective mothers; these children had been removed to foster homes. The I.Q.'s of children who had lived with their mothers for 12–15 years averaged 53; for 6–8 years, 75; for two years or less, 101. Similarly, Marie Skodak and Harold Skeels studied a group of children who had spent about 10 years in superior foster homes. The I.Q.'s of their true mothers averaged 91, but the children's I.Q.'s had a mean of 109, which again suggests the facilitating effect of a good environment.

THE INFLUENCE OF EDUCATION AND CULTURE

Many psychologists regard education as the most important aspect of environmental influence. Newman, Freeman, and Holzinger, as already mentioned, found that the greatest I.Q. difference among separated identical twins was caused by education. Beth Wellman and associates discovered that children's attendance at a university nursery school resulted in a gain of about five points in I.Q., compared with control groups.

Read Tuddenham compared test scores of World War I and World War II soldiers. A revised form of the Army Alpha intelligence test was given to almost 800 World War II enlisted men. The average score of the latter was better than approximately 83% of the scores of World War I soldiers. This may well reflect educational differences; the average educational level in World War I was eighth grade, while in World War II it was two years of high school.

* Correlation coefficients were .25 and .50 respectively.

In general, city children do better than country children on intelligence tests. Lewis Terman and Maud A. Merrill in their book, *Measuring Intelligence*, reported an average I.Q. difference of 6½ points in favor of urban children. Other psychologists have found greater differences. It is signficant that the rural child's inferiority is greatest where the school system is poorest. In Scotland, where the rural schools are good, country children show no inferiority.

Besides differences in educational opportunity, another factor enters into the poorer performance of country children. Usually the materials used in test questions are more familiar to city children, giving them an advantage. Thus, discovered differences may result from failure of the tests to provide a fair measure of ability in both cases.

Such differences underscore earlier findings on the effects of socio-economic and cultural factors upon I.Q. An English school inspector, Hugh Gordon, studied canal-boat and gypsy children, who had only two or three months of schooling a year. Their I.Q.'s averaged about 70. The youngest children, however, were only slightly below normal; as they grew older, their unstimulating home environments and lack of education operated to lower their I.Q.'s—sometimes so far that they were classed as mentally deficient.

Mandel Sherman studied the intelligence of children in four primitive mountain hollows of Virginia, comparing them with children in a typical small town nearby. On every test, both verbal and performance, the children of the hollows were clearly inferior. As with the canal-boat and gypsy children, I.Q.'s went consistently down as the children grew older. At ages 6 to 8, the hollows children had I.Q.'s between 80 and 85; after age 12, their I.Q.'s averaged about 50.

The most likely explanation is this: children in isolated and backward environments do not get the kind of experience in their homes, schools, and communities that normal American children get. Tests are standardized upon the performance of these normal children. Since experience plays an increasingly greater part in the tests for children of higher age levels, the deprived children are at an increasingly greater disadvantage.

OCCUPATION AND ABILITY

Persons in different occupations vary markedly in intelligence test performance. In the Army Alpha tests, professional men—engineers, doctors, lawyers, teachers, and business executives—ranked highest. Next were bookkeepers, clerks, photographers, and skilled tradesmen. Then came carpenters, policemen, printers, farmers, and shopkeepers. In the lowest group were store clerks, cooks, fishermen, firemen, barbers, and day laborers.

Similar findings were reported by T. W. and M. S. Harrell, in a World War II study of Army General Classification Test scores achieved by air force enlisted men. Accountants, lawyers, engineers, and teachers were highest; clerks, salesmen, and toolmakers next; then came butchers, plumbers, carpenters, and mechanics; and farmhands, miners, and teamsters were in the lowest category.

All these rankings, of course, are based on averages; there is much overlapping among groups. Some miners are more intelligent than some clerks, and some teachers are less intelligent than some carpenters. Hence, knowing only a person's occupation does not enable us to predict his ability very accurately.

With children of persons in different occupations the same is true. Studying almost 3,000 children, Terman and Merrill found the following results:

FATHER'S OCCUPATIONAL LEVEL	CHILDREN'S MEAN I.Q.
I. Professional	116.2
II. Semi-professional and managerial	111.9
III. Clerical, skilled trades, retail business	107.5
IV. Semi-skilled, minor clerical, and business	105.0
V. Slightly skilled and unskilled	97.2

Florence L. Goodenough, investigating younger children, reported slightly higher I.Q.'s, but found the same relationship between I.Q. and parental occupation.

Average intelligence in children of professional parents is high. I.Q. decreases as one moves down the occupational scale to unskilled labor. There is, however, much overlapping; i.e., some children of professional parents are lower than some children of semi-skilled and unskilled parents.

But the question still remains as to whether these occupational differences in intelligence are chiefly hereditary or environmental. Are professional people inherently superior, hence having brighter children? Or are their children about the same as all children at birth, but with a better environment to grow up in?

A study by Nancy Bayley suggests that superior environment plays an important part. The intelligence of children under two, she found, is not related to the income, occupation, or socio-economic status of parents. From age 2 to 10 there is an increasing tendency for high intelligence to be correlated with high income and superior social and economic status.

Later research by Quinn McNemar showed average I.Q.'s according to the father's occupation and age of the child, in the following table*:

Age	2–5½	6–9	10–14	15–18
Professional	115	115	118	116
Semi-professional and managerial	112	107	112	117
Clerical, skilled trades, retail	108	105	107	110
Rural owners	98	95	92	94
Semi-skilled, minor clerical and business	104	105	103	107
Slightly skilled	97	100	101	96
Day laborers, urban and rural	94	96	97	98

McNemar's results indicate that the I.Q. differences among occupational groups are about the same for infants as for teenagers. In contrast to Bayley's study, this points to the

* From *The Revision of the Stanford-Binet Scale* by Quinn McNemar.

significance of heredity or to very early environmental conditioning or both. The precise influence of each factor is still difficult to evaluate.

Thus considerable controversy among psychologists has centered about the "constancy of the I.Q."—the degree to which the I.Q. can be changed by environmental influences. Some leaders, like Lewis M. Terman, Florence Goodenough, and John E. Anderson have leaned toward a hereditary interpretation and have questioned the studies showing large changes in I.Q. Others, such as George D. Stoddard and Paul A. Witty, believe the environment can raise or lower the I.Q. considerably. Most psychologists would probably take a middle view: major changes in a child's environment may produce sizable changes in I.Q.—up to, say, 20 or 30 points. But these variations are small compared to the differences between a defective child with I.Q. 30 and a gifted child with I.Q. 175, such differences being presumably genetic in origin. Even the most extreme environmental changes would hardly account for more than a fraction of this wide variation. Of course, from a purely practical standpoint, the environmental changes are more interesting, whatever their scope, since environment can be modified and controlled so much more easily than heredity.

INFLUENCES UPON PERSONALITY

In this chapter we have been dealing almost exclusively with the effects of heredity and environment upon ability. What about their effects upon other aspects of personality and behavior?

"Personality" is a very broad concept. Its comprehensive nature is portrayed in volumes by Gordon W. Allport and by Gardner Murphy, and its many theories are described in a book by Calvin S. Hall and Gardner Lindzey. (We shall discuss personality at greater length in Chapters XI and XII.)

From the standpoint of heredity and environment, the particular aspect of personality we are considering makes a great deal of difference. Are we talking about intelligence, "temperament," or perhaps mental illness? Or are we concerned with attitudes, interests, ego structure, or some phase of social behavior?

We need to be specific because different aspects of the total personality have varied determinants. Intelligence, for example, depends primarily upon the functioning of the brain and nervous system. Temperament and some aspects of mental disease are closely related to energy level and mood, which seem to be rooted in endocrine glands and other organic conditions. Many studies show that heredity bulks large in these areas. Robert C. Tryon separated laboratory rats according to their ability to run mazes. He then inbred the "maze-bright" and "maze-dull" rats for several generations until he had a clearly superior and a clearly inferior group, thus indicating the effect of heredity on maze-running ability, which is a good index of intelligence in the rat. Allport has noted that traits of temperament, such as activity level and restlessness, change very little over the years, suggesting a constitutional basis. Franz J. Kallmann found that identical twins (genetically alike) are far more likely to develop the same mental disease than are fraternal (non-identical) twins. If one identical twin becomes schizophrenic, the chances are 86 in 100 the other will do the same. With fraternal twins, the figure drops to 14 in 100. H. J. Eysenck, a British psychologist, finds that even the neuroses (milder types of personality disorder) may have a genetic basis. The correlation between identical twins on neuroticism was .85, and for fraternal twins only .22. Newman, Freeman, and Holzinger concluded in their studies of twins that temperament and the "deeper aspects of personality" depend upon heredity, while many other aspects of personality, such as social attitudes, do not.

Let us turn now to some studies showing the effect of environment. Carl R. Rogers has summarized the effects of foster homes. More than 80% of children having personality and behavior problems like bed wetting, masturbation, lying, and insecurity make a good adjustment in foster homes. Influenced by the new environment, their personalities improve. Young delinquents usually benefit less, though 60% or 70% commonly change for the better. Children classed as abnormal show still less improvement. A famous Boston psychiatrist, Dr. William Healy, found that only 40% of these change enough to be considered well adjusted to their foster homes. Where a child has some hereditary defect like mental deficiency, or an organic injury like a brain lesion, chances of success in a foster home decline further. If a child is under eight when adopted, if the home and parents are carefully chosen and he remains with the family for several years, he is likely to adjust well.

Without question, social attitudes are learned, as has been amply documented by Allport, Muzafer Sherif, and others. They rise from daily experiences in the family, play group, neighborhood, school, and other groups that are significant to the growing child and adolescent. We shall return to the subject of attitudes and of prejudices in Chapter XVI.

CONCLUSIONS

The relation between heredity and environment continues to be a source of controversy and misunderstanding. The disparity of viewpoints between prominent psychologists is shown by these two statements:

The potency of environment is not nearly so great as commonly supposed. . . . A child's abilities are determined by his ancestors, and all that environment can do is to give the opportunity for the development of his potentialities. It cannot create new powers or additional abilities. [Rudolf Pintner, 1920]

Give me a dozen healthy infants, well-informed, and my own specified world to bring them up in, and I'll guarantee to take any one at random and train him to become any type of specialist I might select—doctor, lawyer, artist, merchant-chief and yes, even beggarman and thief—regardless of his talents, penchants, tendencies, abilities, vocations and race of his ancestors. [J. B. Watson, 1925]

However, few psychologists today would subscribe to either of these extremes. The field of psychology extends from the domain of biology (including genetics) on the one side to that of sociology, anthropology, and kindred social sciences on the other. Hence, the psychologist is in a favorable position (even if unpopular!) to evaluate hereditary-environmental relationships.

As already indicated, many answers can be given if specific questions are asked. We cannot say that "human traits" are entirely inherited or entirely acquired. But we can say that physique and traits closely related to it, like motor abilities, are predominantly determined by heredity and are little affected by environment. Furthermore, many psychologists agree that heredity is largely responsible for one's level of intelligence. About the extent to which one's I.Q. can be affected by environment, they disagree. Personality is hardest to assign either to heredity or environment. Undoubtedly environment affects many personality traits, including attitudes and interests, more than heredity. But how much environment influences underlying "temperament," if at all, remains a question.

This we can say: heredity provides the raw material from which a person is made. What he becomes, how the material is molded, depends chiefly on environment. Good materials placed in good hands result in a fine finished product. Poor material, no matter how carefully fashioned, never becomes a first-rate product.

Chapter IV

DEVELOPMENT OF THE INDIVIDUAL

PREYER   HALL   MINKOWSKI   WATSON
CARMICHAEL   PIAGET   ALLPORT   GESELL   BÜHLER
BRIDGES   DOLL   HAVIGHURST   ERIKSON

How does a child develop before birth? Is a new-born baby helpless? How can one tell if a child is "normal"? At what ages does a youngster walk and talk? When does a child first become "socialized"? How are maturation and training related in child development?

For each of us there is a general life cycle—conception, birth, infancy, adolescence, maturity, senescence, and death. As we progress from stage to stage we change almost miraculously, though so gradually we scarcely notice it. We change not only in physical ways, but in behavior and personality too. The changes result mainly from physical development, yet experience and training affect our behavior and personality growth considerably.

Until late in the nineteenth century no very scientific study was made of just how our behavior changes as we grow up. Among the first to make such a study was Wilhelm Preyer, a German physiologist and pioneer experimental psychologist, who kept a complete diary of his son's growth from birth to three years. He noted how the child's senses of taste, touch, smell, seeing, and hearing developed. He studied reflexes, muscular movements, impulses, and will. From these data Preyer wrote a book, *The Mind of the Child*, which became a classic for child psychology.

Attacking earlier theories that a child's mind at birth is a blank on which experiences later are grooved, Preyer stresses the importance of certain "inherited endowments" that determine a child's mind.

Though later psychologists questioned his findings, his method encouraged scientific procedure.

In America the earliest great child psychologist was G. Stanley Hall, who founded the first magazine and national organization for child study, and published the first extensive book on adolescence. His "theory of recapitulation" holds that a child passes through stages of development comparable to those in social evolution. In the child's play Hall noted a hunting period, a building period, and other periods like those in mankind's history. Though later discredited, the theory was popular and stimulated much research in genetic and child psychology.

PRENATAL DEVELOPMENT

Between conception and birth a human organism spends 280 days in the mother's uterus. The organism develops structurally in that period from the first cell division until the fetus achieves human form at 5 or 6 months.

Behavior beginnings show up less definitely. Action is present in the fetus, as the mother knows, from about 5 months after conception when she feels the first faint thump of arms and legs.

An astonishing experiment on human fetuses was made about 1920 by a Swiss doctor named M. Minkowski. He found that he could keep fetuses alive in a saline solution for a short time after their removal from the mother's uterus. Each time he removed a fetus from a mother for health reasons he kept it alive and observed its reaction to various stimuli. He found that unborn babies move their heads from side to side, flex and extend their hands and feet. A touch on the skin causes movement throughout the body, including opening and closing the mouth or contracting the eyelid. When the fetus is shifted from a vertical to a horizontal position or otherwise moved, several symmetrical hand and foot movements appear, indicating the presence of a sense of balance.

An important discovery was that older fetuses show more clear-cut specific responses than young ones. A two- or three-months-old fetus (about 3 inches long) reacts to stimulation by moving its whole body. A four- or five-months-old fetus (about 7 to 10 inches long) responds more specifically by moving the parts stimulated. For example, a touch on the lip or tongue elicits a kind of sucking reaction. As the fetus has no chance to learn in the uterus, Minkowski concluded that behavior develops naturally from a primitive, poorly coordinated mass action to more precise and coordinated responses.

This view was confirmed in later studies by the biologist G. E. Coghill, who studied behavior development in the salamander tadpole, and by the psychologist Leonard Carmichael, observing behavior in the fetal guinea pig.

THE NEWBORN CHILD

John B. Watson, leader of the behaviorist school and a harsh critic of speculative psychology, attacked a problem over which scientists had wrangled for years. Studying newborn children, he tried to discover which, if any, of the many alleged human "instincts" are found in babies. Their presence would support the theory that instincts exist. Their absence, while in no sense conclusive, at least would open the possibility that the so-called instincts are in reality learned reactions, resulting not from any innate tendencies but from experience.

At the Harriet Lane Children's Hospital and Phipps Clinic of the Johns Hopkins Hospital, he observed hundreds of babies almost daily. Like earlier observers, he found many reflexes, or simple unlearned responses, present at birth. Among them are sneezing, hiccoughing, crying, sucking, urination, and defecation; responses of head, eyes, hands, and feet, including grasping and blinking. He detected no preference for the right hand, contrary to popular belief that right-handedness or left-handedness is inherited. Instead of complex instincts he discovered only three innate emotional patterns: fear, anger, and love. The fear reaction, marked by giving a start, catching the breath, crying, and clutching with the hands, was provoked by loud noises or loss of support. Rage or anger appeared when the child's head was held, or the arms pressed close to the sides; the child stiffened, struggled to escape, and screamed or held his breath. Love reactions like gurgling, cooing, and smiling were elicited by stroking, tickling, rocking, or patting.

Watson concluded that the only innate behavior items in a newborn child are the above reflexes and emotional reaction patterns. Other responses of children, including the so-called "instincts" of imitation, rivalry, sympathy, jealousy, or cleanliness must be learned. To show how new emotional reactions can be learned, Watson performed his famous experiments establishing "conditioned fears," described on page 204.

The newborn child's behavior repertoire now is quite fully catalogued, thanks to studies by Karl C. Pratt, Amalie K. Nelson, K. H. Sun, and Orvis C. Irwin.

About the sense of vision, they agree that a few hours after birth the pupillary reflex regulates the amount of light entering the eye.

At birth hearing is poorly developed, partly because of liquid in the ears. In the first week, however, most babies respond to sounds like a bell, snapper, tuning fork, or the human voice. Shortly afterwards they respond differently to high and low sounds. Infants awake but inactive seem most sensitive to sound.

Even in the first day of life most babies react favorably when they taste something sweet, and unfavorably when they taste something bitter or sour. Some react to unpleasant smells an hour after birth. In others, the sense of smell develops more slowly.

The skin of a newborn baby responds to heat, cold, and to touch, though some parts of the body are more sensitive than others. Apparently pain is felt very little at first, but sensitivity develops within two or three days, especially in the face and head.

The newborn child is said to sleep about four-fifths of the time, though many investigators estimate less. When awake, an infant is active, especially as feeding time approaches. Pratt and his colleagues, using special apparatus, found that from 11 to 43 movements are made per minute, on an average, though only a small percentage could be recorded. Babies twist, turn, stretch, and wave their arms and legs in generalized or "mass" activity. More specific behavior includes the reflexes of sucking, swallowing, grasping a rod or finger, sneezing, yawning, and hiccoughing.

A major infant activity is vocalization. From the "birth cry," when breathing begins, a baby cries when he is hungry, wet, or otherwise uncomfortable. At first one cannot distinguish between cries of hunger, pain, and anger, though some mothers say they can as the child grows older. A baby also coos, gurgles, and grunts. In the first month many speech sounds are made, including ow, oo, the short a, yah, m, ng, the hard g, r, and a few others.

Having developed for nine months, an infant at birth stands by no means at the zero of behavior. To various stimuli he makes many responses, some very highly adaptive. More important, his organism is plastic, capable of much development and modification.

NORMS OF DEVELOPMENT

For parents eager to know how their child compares in accomplishments with other youngsters of the same age, ample criteria are available. Thousands of babies have been studied by psychologists to determine norms for physical growth, motor development, speech, intelligence, and emotional and social behavior.

It is important to recall that these norms are only averages. Children differ greatly. Most babies are advanced in some respects, retarded in others. A lag of several weeks or months should cause no anxiety, especially if little training in that activity has been given. Only a definite lag in all types of development should concern parents. Conversely, only if a child ranks significantly above average in all respects can parents consider him an infant prodigy. Even then, unfortunately, they cannot be certain.

Probably the best-known norms are those issued by Dr. Arnold Gesell, director for many years of the Yale Child Development Clinic. Only when we know typical development patterns can we interpret individual deviations. For many years he and his associates studied children, seeking typical patterns. His procedures were thorough and ingenious. A complete record was kept for each child, including a family case history, results of interviews with the mother, physical measurements, moving pictures of the child's behavior while being tested, and data on a follow-up test. Only normal infants from a homogeneous selection of families were examined. Babies up to six weeks old were examined at home, with portable apparatus. Older babies, brought to the clinic at their longest waking period, usually in the afternoon, were placed in a special crib in a photographic dome. A one-way vision screen surrounded the dome, so the child's behavior could be observed and photographed from outside, without his being aware of observers.

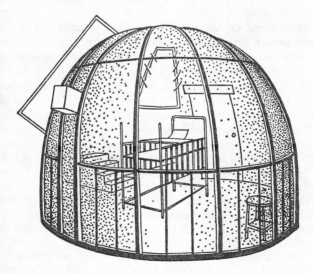

Observation Dome

The most important behavior milestones passed in a child's first five years, Dr. Gesell finds, are these, as described in his book *The First Five Years of Life:*

At 16 weeks, having gained control of his eye muscles, the infant focuses on a dangling ring, a cube, possibly even an 8 mm. pellet. He may turn his head on hearing a voice. He recognizes his mother, can smile broadly when pleased, and likes being held in a sitting position.

At 28 weeks he sits alone, reaches for and grasps a cube promptly, and passes it from hand to hand. He can see a string, though he fumbles in reaching for it, also a small pellet which he puts his hand over crudely but usually fails to get. From cooing he progresses to squealing, uttering vowels, consonants, and syllables. Self-sufficiently he explores the possibilities of toys, perhaps a single toy, oblivious to distractions.

By 40 weeks he stands alone, uses his fingers to poke and pluck, reveals a dim sense of relationships like top and bottom, or cause and effect (the first step toward intellect), imitates facial expressions, gestures, and sounds. Socially he tends toward shyness in presence of strangers, but in general likes to have people around. Nursery tricks like pat-a-cake can be trotted out for admiring friends.

One year finds him almost, but not quite, walking alone, using a spoon, talking in jargon, placing one block atop another. He creeps with skill, sometimes with speed, throws a ball using his newly acquired ability to release grasped objects, repeats familiar words, and sometimes follows commands. Emotions like anger, fear, affection, jealousy, anxiety, or sympathy appear. Occasionally he seems aware of these feelings in others.

The second year finds him walking, running, speaking words and phrases. He learns bowel and bladder control. A vague awareness of who he is and what belongs to him develops.

When three years old he uses sentences to express his thoughts. A desire to please prompts him to run errands, accept suggestions, heed admonitions. A future exists; he will postpone present pleasure for future satisfaction.

At four he asks endless questions, sees analogies, tries to generalize from his experiences. He tends to be bossy and dogmatic. With little assistance he can dress and undress himself, lace his shoes (but not tie them), and brush his teeth.

By five his motor control is good. He hops and skips. He speaks plainly and lengthily. He prefers playmates to playing alone. Socially he is sensitive, taking pride in clothes and in his appearance. He is self-assured and conforming.

Gesell and his associates have extended their studies of childhood development to age sixteen since completion of the famous norms for the first five years of life.

Norms for physical growth in the form of height-weight-age tables were set up by Bird T. Baldwin, educational psychologist, and Thomas D. Wood, physical educator. From them we see that the average child weighs about seven pounds at birth, and measures 20½ inches. In 6 months he doubles his weight. In one year he triples it. Boys are slightly heavier and taller at birth than girls. Children grow rapidly for the first two years, then more and more gradually until adolescence. Great individual differences in height and weight appear among normal children, depending mainly on physical characteristics of parents, somewhat on race and nationality.

One difficulty in the use of developmental norms is that they are based on averages, and it may be wrongly assumed that what is average is optimal. To make interpretations of individual physical growth rates more realistic, predictive charts or graphs based on a child's past growth and body type have been developed by Norman Wetzel and M. Massler.

Psyche Cattell, a practicing psychologist and daughter of James McKeen Cattell, has drawn up a "dental age scale," showing when teeth erupt and which teeth erupt in the average child between ages 5 and 13. At every age girls are more advanced than boys.

MOTOR DEVELOPMENT

After examining babies from birth to two years, Mary M. Shirley made a schedule of ages at which new motor achievements occur. At 1 month a child raises his chin when lying on the stomach; at 2 months, the chest. At 4 months he sits with support, alone at 7. He stands with help at 8 or 9 months, creeps at 10, walks when led at 11. At 1 year he pulls himself to a standing position by grasping furniture. Fourteen months finds him climbing stairs and standing alone; 15, walking.

Although the age at which these steps occur varies with individuals, the above sequence generally is followed. Nancy Bayley found the average age of walking alone is 13 instead of 15 months. Between 50% and 75% of children walk at or before reaching 15 months. Failure to walk by this time does not indicate mental retardation, however; possibly the delay results from lack of exercise or walking practice. Wayne Dennis found that babies prevented from exercising normally learn to sit, stand, and walk considerably later.

LANGUAGE DEVELOPMENT

Although a baby vocalizes from birth, he must *learn* to speak words and know their meaning.

The well-known social psychologist Floyd H. Allport proposed the "circular reflex" as a key to learning. It works thus: A baby makes random noises, like "da." Hearing himself utter the sound, he is stimulated to repeat it. Later an adult saying "doll" causes him to respond "da." Showing a doll to the child while repeating the word establishes a conditioned response, and he learns to say "da" on merely seeing the doll.

While a baby babbles incomprehensible jargon he learns at the same time to comprehend spoken words. Gesell found that 9-months-old babies normally respond to questions like "Where is the kitty?" or "How big is the baby?" At 18 months they pick out a dog in a picture, or throw a ball on command. Comprehension grows rapidly and is an important index of development.

At one year, according to Madorah E. Smith, the average infant uses only two or three words. After 18 months his vocabulary increases pheonomenally, as the following table indicates:

AGE IN YEARS	WORDS IN VOCABULARY
1	2 or 3
1½	22
2	272
3	896
4	1,540
5	2,072
6	2,562
18	15,000

Dorothea A. McCarthy found that half of a child's vocabulary at 18 months consists of nouns. This proportion decreases speedily, favoring verbs and adjectives between 18 and 36 months. She found also that girls' vocabularies exceed those of boys throughout the pre-school period.

Combining words into simple sentences occurs usually around the age of 2. Gesell noted the following samples at 18 months: *see that, bad girl, I do it, open door, gimme cracker.* At 24 months: *Papa gone, I want my cup, you get it for me, I want some more, I don't want to go to bed.* Dr. McCarthy estimated the average sentence length at age 2½ is three words, at 3½ is four words, at 4½ is four-and-a-half words. She found that when a child reaches 3 or 4 his baby pronunciations disappear.

Present-day psychologists are not as concerned as they formerly were with making word counts and descriptive studies of verbal behavior. Those who study language behavior generally attempt to do so within the context of existing learning theory. B. F. Skinner and O. H. Mowrer (see Chapter VI) have made notable contributions in this manner.

MENTAL DEVELOPMENT

Mental tests for very young children parallel closely development norms. Frederick Kuhlmann and Lewis Terman tried out and standardized tests for age 3 and above. For example, a 3-year-old is asked to name common objects like shoe, watch, or jackknife, and to repeat three digits like 6-4-9 spoken slowly by the tester. At 4, the child selects the longer of two lines, is asked to discriminate common geometrical forms. At 5, he counts four objects, defines common object like table, fork, hat. The 6-year test includes finding missing parts of pictures and noting differences such as between wood and glass. The 7-year child is asked to detect absurdities in pictures and repeat five digits after the examiner. At 8, he names days of the week, gives similarities between mosquito and sparrow, window and door. The 10-year-old is asked to name twelve animals in one minute and to repeat six digits. At 12, the child can define abstract words like pity, curiosity, grief, surprise, and repeat five digits backwards.

Florence Goodenough and colleagues constructed the "Minnesota Pre-School Tests" for ages 12 to 71 months, utilizing many of the test items from Kuhlmann-Binet. Rachel Stutsman Ball in 1931 brought out the Merrill Palmer Scale, another widely used pre-school test. This was a performance-type test consisting largely of motor-type items and standardized for children from about 2 to 6 years.

From the performance of individuals on items such as these, mental development can be plotted. When Stanford-Binet (see Chapter II) results are used, mental development is shown to increase for the average person until sixteen years of age. However, as might be expected, this gradually increasing curve of mental development reaches its maximum level at different ages as a function of the types of items used. It levels off early when performance and timed items are used; but when vocabulary items are used, the peak of mental growth comes at a later period of life, as was noted in Chapter II.

Jean Piaget, the famous developmental psychologist of Geneva, has described stages of intellectual development centering on ideas about cause and effect, space and time, and number. Piaget thinks the child uses different levels of explanation as he develops; for example, a child goes through a primitive stage of animistic explanation of events and later reaches a more objective, naturalistic one. That is, the very young child may explain thunder as being the voice of a living being, but at a later time he may explain it as resulting from the impact of air masses which were separated by lightning.

Viewing the adult life cycle, Harvey C. Lehman in 1953 studied the relationship between age and creativity as shown by superior contributions. He surveyed bibliographies and historical summaries in various fields with the assistance of experts. For most fields the age of maximum productivity ranged from 30 to 40. Some of the findings are shown in the table on page 74.

EMOTIONAL DEVELOPMENT

Disputing Watson's report that fear, anger, and love reactions appear in a newborn child, Mandel Sherman at the University of Chicago found that even experienced judges could not identify hunger, anger, pain, or fear reactions in young babies. Neither could they correctly identify the emotion on hearing the infants' cries.

A Canadian psychologist, Katharine M. B. Bridges, studying 60 babies daily for several months, discovered only one identifiable emotion in the new infant—a general agitation or excitement. After a month or two, "distress" and "delight" were distinguished. At 4 or 5 months fear, disgust, and anger appeared. At 8 or 10 months came elation and affection, still later jealousy and joy. When a child reaches 2, his emotional responses are many and varied. Emotional development becomes more and more complex as he grows older and reacts emotionally to countless situations.

Rene Spitz studied the effects of restricted environment on development during infancy. At the end of two years of institutional care many children were found to be retarded in height, weight, physical skills, speech, adaptability, and emotional development. Spitz explained this retardation as traceable to lack of "maternal" love and attention.

The consequences of child-training practices have been investigated in various ways. John Whiting and Irvin L. Child used a "cross-cultural" approach to determine the relationship between harsh training in feeding, cleanliness, sex, aggression, etc. and later anxiety in these areas. They sorted cultures according to their child-rearing practices and compared them with adult behavior. The evidence in general shows a high correlation between early restrictive rearing practices and

AGES AT WHICH GREAT CONTRIBUTIONS WERE MADE

FIELD	AGE AT MAXIMUM RATE OF CONTRIBUTION			
	25–30	30–35	35–40	40–45
Sciences	Chemistry	Mathematics Physics Surgery	Geology Astronomy Bacteriology Pathology Psychology Genetics	
Philosophy and Social Sciences			Political Science Ethics Education Logic	Metaphysics
Literature	Lyric Poetry	Short Stories Comedies	Tragedies	Novels Best Sellers
Music		Symphonies	Chamber Music Opera	Cantatas Light Opera
Art		Paintings		Paintings Architecture

(Table adapted from Harvey C. Lehman, *Age and Achievement*, Princeton University Press, 1953.)

later problem behavior; for example, early weaning was associated with adolescent or adult emotional disturbance.

SOCIAL DEVELOPMENT

The Viennese psychologist Karl Bühler found that very young wailing infants can be quieted as well by contacts with a hot water bottle or soft cushion as by the mother's caresses. Thus early behavior appears mainly non-social. At about the third month the baby becomes socialized, and thenceforth definitely responds to people.

Charlotte Bühler (Karl Bühler's wife), observed the ages at which babies respond to other babies. She found this: At 4 or 5 months an infant notes and smiles at other infants; at 8 or 9 months offers a toy and pays attention to another child's cries. At 9 or 10 months he imitates another's movements but objects to giving up a toy to him.

She noticed also great variation in the social behavior of young children. Some babies between 6 and 18 months appeared "socially blind," paying little or no attention to other children. Others were "socially dependent," highly sensitive to the presence of other children and affected by their behavior. Still others appeared "socially independent," being aware of playmates and often responding to them, but in no way dependent on them. Dr. Bühler believed that these personality differences are independent of previous social experience, home conditions, or nationality.

On the other hand, Spitz's work, as we have just seen, points to the significance of environment as affecting development. So do the provocative studies of Harry Harlow. During the course of extensive work with monkeys in the primate laboratory, Harlow observed that infant monkeys developed strong attachments for diapers which covered the floors of their cages. When kept on the bare floors of their cages, infant monkeys survive only with greatest difficulty. The monkey survives better when a wire mesh cone is provided to which it can cling, and even better when the cone is covered with terry cloth. Ultimately several "mother substitutes" or surrogates of various types were constructed, one of wire mesh with nipples to dispense milk, one of soft terry cloth without nipples but warmed with a light bulb inside, etc. It was found that infant monkeys preferred the soft, warm mother surrogate to the wire one, even though milk was given by the latter. For the young monkey "contact comfort" seems to be more important than a food dispenser.

In follow-up studies Harlow has found that monkeys raised alone with mother surrogates do not exhibit normal social behavior. For example, when a monkey raised this way becomes a mother, she does not respond like a normal mother, but neglects or abandons her offspring. Sexual behavior of surrogate-raised monkeys is atypical also. When raised by a real mother or with only other young monkeys, sexual development appears to be normal.

Ruth W. Washburn and Arthur T. Jersild, two noted child psychologists, working independently in their study of social reactions, found that followers, leaders, solitary, timid, impulsive, or outgoing children tend to remain the same through the pre-school or nursery school years.

The age of puberty has changed, according to James Tanner, who summarized evidence from a number of Western countries. In 1940 puberty occurred at an average of two years earlier than in 1880—at 14½ compared with 16½ for boys, and 12½ compared with 14½ for girls.

Mary C. Jones and Nancy Bayley studied the consequences of delayed puberty in boys. They found that early maturing boys become more adept socially, and apparently develop a sense of responsibility and self-control sooner. Every difference observed by these investigators favors the early maturer.

The years around puberty are stressful for girls, particularly a year or so before menarche. Jean W. Macfarlane has pointed out that there is a prepubertal peak of irritability, shyness, and emotional dependence.

Though social behavior cannot be measured by definite criteria, K. M. B. Bridges submitted a rough scale for estimating a child's progress. The items include speaking to other children, joining their play, asking another child for help, waiting his own turn, trying to help others, comforting a child in distress, making friendly advances, not claiming others' toys or interfering in their work, not pushing or pulling or hitting or pinching, sharing toys and candy, defending the rights of smaller children, and initiating group activities. From these norms, the normal child appears to mature socially during the pre-school years.

Edgar A. Doll devised a more formal scale, the Vineland Social Maturity Scale, which measures the level of social development or "social age." For example, at the 3- to 5-year levels such things are included as: "performs for others," "helps at little household tasks," or "plays competitive exercising games." This test is primarily used in the evaluation of the mentally deficient.

Robert J. Havighurst isolated stages of development from infancy through adulthood into what he calls "developmental tasks." These are increasingly complex tasks required of a normal individual as he grows up: learning to feed one's self, learning to dress, to read, to dance, etc. Educators use this concept extensively when they talk about "readiness levels." "Readiness" is a term that describes whether an individual is ready to perform certain functions. It is based on previously mastered developmental tasks.

Following a psychoanalytic orientation, Erik Erikson lists eight stages of life through which an individual passes. Erikson relates these stages to the development of personality characteristics: (1) the "oral-sensory" stage is the period when a sense of "basic trust" normally develops; (2) the "muscular-anal" stage is the period when a sense of "autonomous will" normally develops; (3) the "locomotor-genital" stage, when a sense of "initiative" normally develops; (4) "latency," a sense of "industry"; (5) "adolescence," a sense of "identity"; (6) "young adulthood," a sense of "intimacy"; (7) "adulthood," a sense of "generativity" or reproductivity; (8) "maturity," a sense of "integrity."

MATURATION OR TRAINING?

Whether behavior changes are a natural unfolding or maturing of the organism, or whether they result from training, is an important point in understanding human development.

In 1872 an English scientist, D. A. Spalding, tried to determine whether birds fly by instinct or by learning. He confined newly hatched swallows in small cages where they could not see other birds. At the normal flying age they were released. Some flew at once. The rest learned very soon. Spalding concluded that learning has little influence compared with innate maturation.

In 1926 Leonard Carmichael tried a similar experiment. Dividing several frog and salamander embryos into two groups, he allowed one group to develop normally. The other he put in an anesthetizing solution that prevented swimming but permitted internal neuromuscular maturation. After the normal tadpoles could swim expertly, the drugged tadpoles were placed in fresh water. In half an hour the latter swam as well as the former. This suggests that motor development depends on physiological maturation, not practice.

Less conclusive results emerged from a study of pecking in chicks. John F. Shepard and Frederick S. Breed discovered that a baby chick, permitted to peck freely from birth, requires a week or more to learn accurate pecking. Chicks isolated at birth and fed with a dropper for five days learned to peak accurately in about half the time required by a newborn chick. Again maturation appears important, though practice helps achieve maximum skill.

In studying the roles of maturation and training, Wayne Dennis was able to compare the development of walking in Hopi Indian children who had been bound to cradle boards, with walking behavior of those who had been removed from their boards at a much earlier age. He found that both groups learned to walk at approximately the same time.

The method of "co-twin control" has been used to study the nature of maturation by a number of investigators. This involves selecting a pair of identical twins (who are, of course, genetically alike), subjecting one to learning experiences while using the other as the control, and finally comparing the performances of each so that any differences due to training may be observed.

Arnold Gesell was among the first to use this method. With Helen Thompson and L. C. Strayer, he studied maturation and training in a pair of identical twins. At 46 weeks one twin was trained to climb stairs and build with blocks. The other twin, left to her own random efforts, climbed stairs as well as her sister in two weeks, acquired equal block-building skill in six weeks. The importance of maturation again appeared in acquiring vocabulary. At 84 weeks one twin was trained for five weeks to use words and name objects. At 89 weeks the other twin was trained for four weeks. In four weeks the latter achieved more than her sister did in five, presumably because of her greater maturity.

Josephine Hilgard performed a similar experiment. She trained one twin in certain motor skills, then waited three months and trained both twins in these skills. It was concluded that the early training period was of little value, for the twin who was not exposed to training quickly caught up with the one who was.

Myrtle McGraw has studied intensively the neuromuscular maturation of children in the well-known experiments on "Johnny and Jimmy." She was able to train one twin to swim, roller skate, climb slides, and jump at the very young age of 12 or 15 months. But the other twin made up for lost time and learned faster when he was older. In some areas training produced little effect; for example, Dr. McGraw found toilet training to be futile until the child was about two years of age. She believed in steering a middle course between constantly egging the child on, and sitting back to let nature take its course. At a certain time nerves and muscles are ready for each new activity; at this stage training and practice are beneficial. Practice given too early is useless.

Both maturation and training are essential processes in individual development. Maturation controls physical growth and the time of appearance of simple motor activities like reflexes, grasping, or crawling. Though psychologists differ about the importance of training in bringing about sitting and walking, they agree that in more complex activities like stair-climbing or talking, specific practice must occur. But only when an organism reaches a certain stage of physical development will training be fully effective.

Chapter V

PHYSIOLOGICAL BASES OF BEHAVIOR

DESCARTES BELL WEBER FECHNER
HELMHOLTZ HERING MÜLLER LADD-FRANKLIN
FLOURENS BROCA FRANZ LASHLEY
DONDERS WUNDT CATTELL KRAEPELIN
HOLLINGWORTH CANNON MOSSO

*By what mechanisms do we see colors and hear
sound? How does the nervous system work? Are our
various functions localized in certain parts of the
brain? What is a reflex? Upon what does our reaction time depend? How do alcohol and caffeine affect efficiency? In what ways may endocrine disorders
affect personality?*

We behave normally only when our senses, muscles, glands,
brain, and nervous system are intact and functioning well,
and when we are free from fatigue and the effects of drugs.
By studying our bodily states physiological psychologists have
contributed much to the understanding of human behavior.

PIONEERS OF PSYCHOPHYSICS

Ernst Heinrich Weber, a professor of anatomy and physiology at the University of Leipzig, was the first to make an extensive study of sensation as it relates to behavior. His discoveries about the skin and muscle senses have become
famous.

He placed one hand in a bowl of hot water, the other in a
bowl of cold water, then both in lukewarm water. In the luke-

warm water the first hand felt cold, the second hot. From this he concluded that the sensation of cold results from a drop in skin temperature, while hot results from a rise. The theory holds for moderate, though not extreme temperatures. Weber distinguished between the sense of touch, whose receptors (end-organs for receiving stimuli) lie in the skin, and the muscle sense whose nerve endings lie within the body. That the kinesthetic or muscle sense is important he showed by demonstrating how much more accurately subjects can judge weights when they "heft" them than when the weights are merely placed on the skin surface.

Weber is best known for initiating "psychophysics" (a name applied later), which deals with the cause-effect relation between physical stimuli and resulting sensations. Particularly he wanted to know how much a given stimulus must be increased or decreased to bring about a "just noticeable difference." With lifted weights Weber found that an increase of about $\frac{1}{30}$ can be just barely felt, on the average. Thirty ounces can be distinguished from 29, as can 15 from $14\frac{1}{2}$. The ratio remains constant. In judging lengths of lines the ratio is $\frac{1}{100}$; a line 101 mm. in length is judged longer than one of 100 mm. This principle that we notice relative rather than absolute changes in stimuli later was called "Weber's Law."

A colleague of Weber, Gustav Theodor Fechner, a professor of physics at Leipzig, tried to bridge the gap between mind and body. In Weber's work he saw possibilities for discovering a mathematical relationship between the mental and the physical. After years of labor he gave the world a significant but difficult book called *Elements of Psychophysics*. Its value lies mainly in presenting ingenious methods of testing sensitivity thresholds. The methods have been used ever since to devise aptitude tests and other measures of individual differences. In his experiments Fechner used lifted weights, light intensities, and various tactual and visual situations. His conclusions elaborated Weber's Law thus: "When stimuli increase by a constant ratio, the sensations aroused by them increase by equal increments or steps." As stimuli increase in geometrical ratio, sensations follow in arithmetical ratio, that is, by one sensation unit or "just noticeable difference."

Harry Helson's theory of adaptation level is a notable attempt to improve earlier psychophysical formulations. Sensory judgments are made with reference not only to the physical stimulus but also to the effects of previous stimuli of the same class. We judge according to prevailing norms, says Helson. Thus a 4-ounce fountain pen is heavy, but a baseball bat to be heavy must weigh over 40 ounces.

HELMHOLTZ ON EYES AND EARS

The dominant figure in nineteenth-century German science was Hermann Ludwig von Helmholtz, a physicist, physiologist, and psychologist. Trained in medicine, he turned to teaching and research. While still in his thirties he began to publish brilliant findings on vision and hearing. To facilitate more accurate study of the eye, he invented the ophthalmoscope, which permits direct observation of the retina. Experimenting on the external eye muscles, he showed how the lens focuses to accommodate vision at different distances.

A famous Helmholtz theory explains how we distinguish colors. Elaborating work of an English physicist, Thomas Young, he developed the "Young-Helmholtz" theory that three kinds of receptors, or end-organs, exist in the eye, one reacting to red, one to green, and one to blue-violet. Color is determined by light of a certain wave length. A wave length corresponding to saturated green arouses only the green receptor. Yellow arouses both red and green receptors, but to a lesser degree because its wave length lies between green and red. White light, synthesizing all colors, arouses all three receptors at once. The usual forms of color blindness result from a lack of red or green or both these end-organs. Though it fails to account for all the facts, Helmholtz's theory remains one of three notable attempts to explain color vision. His remarkable *Physiological Optics*, published in 1861, was translated into English and used in this country as a text as late as 1924.

Turning his attention to hearing, Helmholtz studied both structure and function of the ear, and issued the classic "piano theory." It accounts for our ability to hear different tones by the presence of fibers on a membrane of the inner ear, each of which corresponds to a different pitch and vibrates sympathetically with it, like a piano string.

Interested in music, Helmholtz helped solve the mystery of tone qualities and tonal relationships. He explained why the same note sounds different when played on different instruments like piano, violin, and flute, though the number of vibrations, or sound waves per second, is identical in each case. Differing patterns of overtones, or partial vibrations determined by the structure of a musical instrument, cause variations of quality or "timbre," he said. In fact he actually changed overtones by using resonators that artificially produced notes resembling various musical instruments.

Helmholtz also developed theories of discord and harmony in terms of overtones. Notes near each other in pitch seem dissonant because their overtones cause pulsating "beats." Harmony depends largely on simple ratios of vibration. Some pleasant combinations are notes an octave apart having a vibration ratio of 1 : 2 ; a major fifth having 2 : 3 ; a major third having 4 : 5 . Harmony, however, is not merely pleasing vibrations. Mature stages of both individual and cultural development bring a preference for more complex tonal intervals and combinations, Helmholtz pointed out.

TEMPERATURE AND COLOR ACCORDING TO HERING

Ewald Hering, a professor of physiology at Prague, modified Weber's theory for warm and cold sensations. The skin of a hand placed in cold water adapts to the water temperature, Hering said. Any stimulus warmer than the newly established skin temperature is felt as warm, though actually it may be cold. Likewise anything lower in temperature is experienced as cold. Hering thus dismissed the notion of an absolute zero and substituted a relative zero point dependent upon existing skin temperature.

Hering found four primary colors—red, green, blue, and yellow—as against Helmholtz's three. He noted that certain pairs of colors, mixed together, give gray. This is true for red and green, blue and yellow, white and black. The colors forming such pairs are "complementary." Also, Hering knew that after looking at red a person gets a green sensation or after-image, and that blue gives a yellow after-image. To account for these phenomena, he proposed three kinds of receptors in the retina, the most sensitive part of the eye. One responds to red-green, one to yellow-blue, one to white-black. Red, yellow, and white cause a "tearing down," or *catabolic*, process in their respective receptors. Green, blue, and black cause a "building up," or *anabolic*, process. When both processes occur together, as when complementary hues are seen simultaneously, a neutral, medium gray results. When we stare at red for several seconds, excess breakdown of that receptor occurs, which subsequent building up offsets. The building up gives the green after-image.

Color blindness, according to Hering, results from impaired or destroyed red-green substance in the eye. Color-blind persons usually can distinguish yellow and blue, indicating that their yellow-blue substance is unimpaired.

An interesting elaboration of Hering's theory was proposed by Christine Ladd-Franklin. Assuming that the vision of primitive man was colorless, capable of distinguishing only white, gray, and black, she suggested that the white receptor in time separated into yellow and blue, and the yellow later subdivided into red and green. If this is true, possibly in some distant future—thousands or millions of years hence—the red or green molecule will break down and yield two completely new colors!

OTHER PHYSIOLOGISTS' RESEARCHES ON SENSATION

Among other notable findings on the sensations is Johannes von Kries' "duplicity theory" of vision. He showed that, of the retina's two types of end-organs, the "cones" discriminate color and the finer kinds of form. The more widely distributed "rods" respond only to the light intensities, white, gray, and black. Ragnar Granit, a Scandinavian physiologist, has found support for the duplicity theory and for color receptors by experimenting on the eyes of animals possessing various combinations of rods and cones.

Selig Hecht has formulated precise quantitative laws of vision, based on his notion of a reversible photochemical process. Upon exposure to light his postulated photosensitive substance decomposes; in darkness the elements recombine. Like the Hering theory, Hecht's theory accounts for many of the phenomena of vision.

Two American psychologists, Ernest Glen Wever and Charles W. Bray, elaborated the Helmholtz theory of hearing. Their "volley theory" suggests that the auditory nerve fibers work together in groups, supplementing each other in such a way that the combination makes possible the transmission of complex sounds which could not be done by one fiber or even a few fibers alone.

Max von Frey found that the four skin senses—pressure, pain, warmth, and cold—have different end-organs. Neither he nor later investigators, however, have been able to show just which of the skin's tiny cells, bulbs, and corpuscles act as receptors for which senses.

That only four taste qualities exist—sweet, salt, sour, and bitter—was proved by Friedrich Kiesow. On the other hand, smell was classified by Hendrik Zwaardemaker under nine categories, each having several subdivisions. Later Hans Henning, admitting countless specific smells, reduced Zwaardemaker's list to six main qualities: fragrant, fruity, resinous, spicy, putrid, and burned.

Instead of five senses the physiological psychologists have shown that there are no less than ten or twelve distinct kinds of sensation. We have mentioned: the four cutaneous senses (pressure, pain, warmth, and cold); the kinesthetic or muscle sense; as well as the familiar senses—vision, hearing, taste, and smell. Early physiologists also demonstrated the existence of a sense of position, or equilibrium (balance), or of movement of the body as a whole, sometimes called the "labyrinthine sense," with end-organs in the semicircular canals of the inner ear. In addition some authorities now refer to various "organic senses," including hunger and thirst. Hence one may properly speak of at least ten senses, each having its own end-organs and each yielding a different kind of experience.

EARLY STUDIES OF BRAIN AND NERVOUS SYSTEM

An important discovery about the action of the nervous system was made by Sir Charles Bell, a British doctor and physiologist of the early nineteenth century. He found that nerves differ in function. Some are sensory, connecting receptors in the skin, ear, or eye with the spinal cord. These nerves enter the cord on the dorsal (back) side. Others are motor nerves, leaving the spinal cord on the ventral (front) side, and going to the muscles. This principle often is called the Bell-Magendie law, because a Frenchman, François Magendie, discovered the same thing independently a few years later. Bell also suggested though he did not actually prove, that each sensory nerve serves only one sense, like vision or hearing, not several senses at once.

Carrying Bell's idea further, Johannes Müller, professor of physiology at Berlin, elaborated the famous doctrine of specific energy of nerves. He proved what Bell offered as theory, that each nerve has its own special sensory or motor function. It was not clear in his mind whether sensory experience like seeing or hearing results solely from stimulation of the visual or auditory nerves, or from stimulation of a specialized brain center. Later he inclined toward the first explanation, possibly because the second smacks too much of phrenology, which already was suspect in scientific circles.

Thanks to Franz Josef Gall and an associate named Johann Gaspar Spurzheim, the so-called "science" of phrenology had soared to popularity shortly after 1800. A person's intellectual and emotional faculties can be estimated, said these men, by the bumps on his head. A bump in a certain place indicates conscientiousness, another shows conjugal love, another suavity, another self-esteem. The bigger the bump, the more pronounced the characteristic. Imposing charts locating all the faculties were drawn up. Though phrenology won the support of a few prominent scientists, most opposed it. Actually it served a purpose by stimulating its opponents to make scientific studies of brain functions.

While phrenology flourished, a French anatomist, Pierre Flourens, was performing operations on the brains of pigeons. He discovered that removing the cerebral lobes, or upper parts of the brain, impaired hearing, seeing, remembering, and "volition." Removing a lower part, the cerebellum, caused loss of coordination. Two other parts of the brain showed special functions. But Flourens also noted a unity of action in the brain and nervous system, and found that a function lost on removal of its brain center can be reacquired—a principle corroborated almost a century later by Lashley.

A significant discovery about the human brain was made in 1861 by a Paris physician named Paul Broca. He became interested in a patient who could not talk, though mentally fit and in no way paralyzed. When the patient died, Broca found a lesion in the third left frontal convolution of his brain. Broca concluded that this area is the speech center. In fact it is now called "Broca's area."

After studying soldiers with head wounds from the Franco-Prussian war, two German surgeons, G. Fritsch and E. Hitzig, turned to brain experiments on animals. They found that a weak electrical current applied to certain parts of exposed brains calls forth specific body movements. Brain centers controlling muscles of the face, neck, and legs were located. Other researchers quickly adopted the same technique. Using monkeys mainly, they soon mapped out the chief sensory and motor areas of the brain. Thus many functions were found to depend upon specific parts of the brain, but this was a very different kind of localization from that claimed by phrenologists.

After World War II Walter R. Hess and others devised more precise ways of studying the effects of electrical stimulation of the brain. The most successful method involves implanting tiny electrodes in certain areas of the brain; it is described in more detail in Chapter X.

BRAIN FUNCTIONS

A new look at brain functions derived from the work of Shepherd I. Franz and Karl S. Lashley. Franz taught cats and monkeys to escape from problem boxes by pushing a button on the door. Removing parts of their frontal brain lobes, he found that the new accomplishment was lost, though older habits like eating and scratching persisted. After checking his results, Franz concluded that the frontal lobes are brain centers for new activities though these functions may later transfer to other parts of the brain.

Lashley experimented similarly on white rats. After they

learned how to escape a problem box, he removed various sections and amounts of the cerebral cortex, the sensitive outside layer of the brain. An astonishing fact emerged. Not the specific area, but the *amount* of cortex removed determined how much of the habit was lost. In other words, retention of a new habit depends on the amount of brain tissue left intact. Furthermore, rats that lost their new habits when operated on were successful in relearning them in proportion to the amount of cerebral cortex remaining.

The experiments of Franz and Lashley do not disprove the location or "localization" in the brain of simple sensory and motor functions. They merely show that no one part of the brain is essential to learn fairly complex activities. Even when an operation disturbs an existing habit, another part of the brain takes over the work of the destroyed section and the habit can be relearned.

Transferring these principles to human psychology, Franz re-educated persons whose behavior was disturbed by brain lesions. Other cortical areas apparently "pinch hit" for the damaged parts.

Human brain operations often yield interesting results. To remove a brain tumor Dr. Richard M. Brickner of New York had to remove most of a certain patient's frontal lobes. No apparent injury to the sensori-motor functions resulted. But the patient's behavior changed astonishingly. He became restless, distracted, jittery. He shouted, sang in a loud voice, danced about, and boasted without restraint. Brickner concluded that the man had lost his ability to combine or synthesize, thus could not think out a problem, plan ahead, or restrain his impulses.

Reflexes

The great seventeenth-century French philosopher, René Descartes, distinguished between animals' automatic mechanical acts and the voluntary rational behavior of human beings. However, even man showed much automatic non-rational activity that depended on mechanical action of the nervous system. To this activity the name "reflex" was applied a century later.

During the French Revolution Dr. P. J. G. Cabanis wondered whether the guillotine caused pain in those it decapitated. His grim speculations led to research and later a theory that human activity occurs at three neural levels. According to Cabanis, the lowest or spinal cord level serves in reflex acts. A middle level functions in semi-conscious, semi-integrated activities. The highest level commands thought, volition, and other complicated functions.

Thirty years later a Scottish doctor named Marshall Hall, studying blood circulation in animals, noted that beheaded animals make muscular responses to stimuli. Studying beheaded animals further, he formed the first clear-cut definition of reflex action: unconscious movement that depends on the spinal cord and is independent of the brain.

Shortly afterwards Hall's work was elaborated in Johannes Müller's tremendous *Handbook of Physiology.* Müller himself studied reflexes in frogs and defined the reflex in neurological terms: stimulating a sense organ sends an impulse along the sensory nerve to the spinal cord, where it connects with a motor nerve, and travels to a muscle, resulting in action. Müller's book cleared up much that had not been understood about reflex action, though cataloguing human reflexes and studying their interaction was left to later neurologists and psychologists.

REACTION TIME

Interest in reaction time dates from 1795, when the astronomer of Greenwich Observatory near London dismissed his assistant for being slow to observe the exact time a star crossed the telescopic field. Astronomers thereafter noted great individual differences in speed of observing. This they called "the personal equation."

One theory held that the speed of nervous impulse varies with individuals. Helmholtz actually measured how fast it travels in human sensory nerves. He found it 200 or 300 feet a second. Measuring the complete time that elapses between stimulation of a sense organ and muscular response, he got such varying, inconsistent results that he gave up the experiment. Nevertheless, it was the first scientific study of reaction time.

Soon afterwards F. C. Donders, a Dutch physiologist, considered the psychological steps occurring between a stimulus and response. He found a "simple" reaction time, wherein a subject makes a prearranged response immediately upon perceiving the stimulus. A "discrimination," or "choice," reaction time appeared also, in which the subject differentiated stimuli before responding. The "choice" reaction time was one-tenth to one-twentieth of a second slower than the "simple" reaction time. This fraction of a second, Donders concluded, measures the time required to discriminate.

Wilhelm Wundt attacked the same problem. Like Donders he measured the speed of complex reactions involving discrimination, will, and association. From the time they required he deducted the time taken for simple reactions. His project struck a snag when Oswald Külpe and James McKeen Cattell showed that the two reactions involve different mental processes. Hence one cannot be subtracted from the other. They further pointed out that the attitude, or mental "set," of a subject just before stimulation occurs greatly affects the speed of reaction time.

James McKeen Cattell and Ludwig Lange revealed the interesting fact that when a subject concentrates on the stimulus he reacts more slowly than when he concentrates on his response. The former attitude they called "sensorial"; the latter, "muscular." An example may make this distinction clearer. A motorist, stopped at a traffic light, exhibits the sensorial type of reaction, because he concentrates on the stimulus and makes his response automatically. In contrast, a runner, all set to leap forward at the sound of the starting gun, fixes his attention upon getting away as quickly as possible. His mental set helps facilitate his reaction, but he may respond to wrong stimuli such as an onlooker's shout of "Go!"

Cattell and his students probed every aspect of the reaction-time problem. They found that we react faster to touches, electric shocks, and sounds than to lights or other types of stimuli. Practice and fatigue affect reaction speed very little, though distraction slows it considerably.

How drugs affect reaction time was first studied by Emil Kraepelin, a colleague of Cattell at Leipzig. Coffee and tea shorten the time slightly, he found, but anesthetic drugs lengthen it. Alcohol first speeds up reaction time, then, taken in larger quantities, slows it down.

Wide individual differences appear in reaction speed, also in susceptibility to stimulants and drugs. To Cattell goes credit for arousing interest in these individual differences—an interest which grew to have important applications later in aptitude testing.

DRUGS AND TOXIC PRODUCTS

In the association experiment, where a subject says the first word that comes to mind when he hears a stimulus word, Kraepelin found that alcohol induces a less direct, more superficial type of association. That alcohol actually does not stimulate, but depresses was shown by Raymond Dodge and Francis G. Benedict. Using moderate doses of alcohol (30 and 45cc.—about 2 or 3 cubic inches), they noted uniform decreases in sensitivity, in reflexes, and in reaction time.

Harry L. Hollingworth studied the effects of alcohol on mental and motor efficiency. Even the small quantity found in three or four bottles of beer caused a loss in hand steadiness, tapping speed, in eye-hand coordination, memory, naming opposites, and adding. Only the pulse rate speeded up with alcohol.

Caffeine, on the other hand, proved a real stimulant, according to Hollingworth. Two cups of coffee speeded up motor activity by about 4%, but decreased muscular steadiness. Larger doses taking effect within two hours and lasting until the next day increased speed of response in simple mental tests like naming colors, though small doses retarded the rate. Typing speed improved with small doses, but not with large ones. To disturb sleep more than two cups were required by most of Hollingworth's subjects.

Clark Hull of Yale studied the effect of pipe smoking on mental efficiency. The pulse rate rose, and subjects were shakier after smoking. Except that non-smokers, after smoking, lost accuracy in adding, no appreciable effects appeared.

It has long been known that psychological effects are produced by certain substances, such as some kinds of mushrooms, marijuana, and the peyote cactus. Not until Albert Hoffman, a Swiss pharmacologist, sampled a derivative of lysergic acid (LSD) which he had compounded was the potential fully realized. Effects of these chemicals have been variously described as producing intense euphoria, vivid imagery, kaleidoscopic colors, escape from material reality. Aldous Huxley and other artists have suggested the utility of these compounds for inducing creative activity. Psychochemical research has been responsible also for the development of tranquilizers and anti-depressants, which will be described in Chapter XV.

Some investigators believe that these discoveries open new vistas in mental health. B. F. Skinner, for example, proposes that in the not too distant future the motivational and emotional condition of normal daily life will probably be maintained in any desired state through the use of drugs.

EFFECTS OF FATIGUE

In recent years workers' rest periods have become a part of the program of every efficiently run industrial plant. Efficiency experts find that carefully planned rest periods can increase daily output by a sizable percentage.

Early proof that fatigue reduces efficiency was cited by Kraepelin. He had subjects add columns of figures, giving them rest periods at various intervals. Checking the amount of work done, he drew up a "work curve," which showed changes in output due to fatigue, practice, "warming up," and voluntary spurts. Almost all later research on fatigue follows Kraepelin's procedure.

In 1890 an Italian scientist, Angelo Mosso, invented the "ergograph," an apparatus which measures efficiency changes accompanying fatigue of finger and hand muscles from lifting a weight. He found that a finger, exhausted from lifting a weight 30 times, requires two hours' rest to recover completely. After only 15 lifts, recovery occurs in half an hour. In other words, the recovery from muscular work takes place much faster when the muscle is not completely exhausted.

This important principle applies directly to industry, where maximum production is sought.

Output loss from fatigue, though varying with individuals and with the nature of the task, was estimated by Tsuru Arai, Japanese physiological psychologist, to be 5% at the end of an hour. Loss increases in rough proportion to the amount of time worked, up to 100% at the end of eleven hours' continuous work.

That mental work causes bodily changes similar to those accompanying physical work was an astonishing fact revealed by Francis G. Benedict, chemist, and T. M. Carpenter, physiologist. In taking a written examination, subjects eliminated more than normal water vapor and carbon dioxide, absorbed more oxygen and gave off more heat, just as in physical activity.

With some types of work, on the other hand, feelings of fatigue do not indicate lowered efficiency. Albert T. Poffenberger discovered that when subjects completed unfinished sentences, working continuously for five hours, output did not change. Nor did it change when they judged the merit of compositions. On intelligence tests their performance actually improved after five hours. Presumably fatigue effects were offset by the facilitation of practice. Yet in all cases increasing feelings of fatigue were reported.

ENDOCRINE GLANDS

Just before 1900 physiologists began to report amazing facts about the endocrine, or ductless, glands. These glands, called by Claude Bernard "glands of internal secretion," discharge their secretion, known as a "hormone," into the blood stream. In this they differ from the duct glands, like salivary, tear, and sweat glands, which pour out their secretions at or near the body surface.

For some time psychologists did not realize the connection between endocrine glands and human behavior. Then in 1915 Walter B. Cannon, the Harvard physiologist, wrote *Bodily Changes in Pain, Hunger, Fear and Rage*. Psychologists sat up and took notice. Cannon showed that during intense emotional states the adrenal glands, located near the kidneys, discharge a hormone into the blood stream. This adrenal hormone, called adrenin, energizes the whole organism, preparing it for emergency action by stepping up blood pressure, increasing sugar content in the blood, sending blood to the extremities and causing it to coagulate faster if exposed to air, and the like. Knowledge of adrenal functions opened up new possibilities for understanding the emotions.

As endocrinologists reported on other glands, psychologists noted their profound effects on human behavior. The thyroid, located in the neck near the windpipe, influences physical and mental growth. As we are to describe in Chapter XIII, undersecretion of the thyroid in an infant causes "cretinism," a condition of serious physical and mental retardation. Deficient thyroid functioning in adults, called "myxedema," causes inactivity, listlessness, increased weight, puffy skin, and loss of hair. On the other hand, oversecretion of the thyroid produces restlessness, nervousness, and increased metabolism or energy consumption.

An interesting case of thyroid malfunction is presented by Florence Mateer. A 4-year-old boy deficient in thyroid had an I.Q. between 50 and 60, was overweight, had dry skin and hair, and showed other physical symptoms of "hypothyroidism." When glandular extract called "thyroxin" was given he began to improve. After 5 years his I.Q. reached 90; his appearance and general behavior were normal. Then through family negligence the thyroid treatments were dropped. Soon his school work became worse, and his intelligence quotient fell off. Before long he became a behavior problem. Other factors than glandular ones doubtless complicated the case, but it suggests how seriously an abnormal glandular condition can affect behavior.

Improper functioning of other endocrine glands also interest the psychologist. Oversecretion of a hormone from the pituitary, located at the base of the brain, causes giantism. Robert Wadlow, an Illinois lad almost nine feet tall at 22, was a hyperpituitary case. Undersecretion of the same hormone produces one type of dwarfism. The pituitary gland also helps regulate sexual development, as do, in all probability, two other glands: the pineal in the brain and the thymus in the upper chest. Dysfunction of the parathyroids, four small pea-like bodies found near the thyroid, causes severe cramps and spasms.

Other organs also have endocrine functions. The so-called "Islands of Langerhans" in the pancreas secrete the important hormone, insulin, the lack of which causes diabetes. Hormones from the liver, largely a duct gland, serve to regulate the chemical content of the blood. The sex glands are duct glands, but related cells have endocrine functions which produce at adolescence the physical changes called "secondary sexual characteristics." These include distribution of bodily hair, development of mammary glands and of fatty tissue, and changes in voice.

Much is still to be learned about the functioning of endocrine glands. They operate as an interconnected system, which makes it difficult to isolate the functions of each gland. Their importance, psychologically, lies in their effect upon energy level, upon physical and mental development, and upon emotional behavior.

In this chapter we have described some of the most important contributions of the physiological psychologists. The research upon sensation, brain function, and the nervous and glandular systems; upon reflexes, reaction time, and the effects of drugs, have shown how solidly our behavior is based upon the biological organism. Let us turn now to the study of learning, to see how behavior is modified by experience.

Chapter VI

LEARNING AND MEMORY

LOCKE   HARTLEY   HERBART   SPENCER   BAIN
JAMES   THORNDIKE   PAVLOV   BEKHTEREV   WATSON
KÖHLER   GUTHRIE   WOODWORTH   HULL   TOLMAN
SKINNER   MOWRER   HEBB   MILL   HAMILTON
EBBINGHAUS   MÜLLER   FREUD   JOST

*How is learning studied in the laboratory? What is
a learning curve? How do the various types of learning differ? What methods are used in studying
memory? What are the most effective ways for retaining what we have learned?*

Learning involves modifying behavior and forming habits.
"Learning" is almost synonymous with "living." Consciously
or unconsciously all of us learn something new every day—
persons, names and faces, news events, where to shop for
bargains, or how to use new gadgets. Individual differences,
of course, exist; some people learn more in their lifetime
and learn it faster than others. The biologist Herbert S. Jen-
nings in a book called the *Behavior of Lower Organisms*, published in 1906, shows that all animals learn, from the lowly
amoeba up to man. The amoeba may learn only to avoid eating dangerous food particles, while man learns to extract cube
roots, fly in airplanes, or dance the rumba. But both are learning. They differ mainly in degree of complexity.

EARLY STUDIES OF LEARNING

Early philosophers, despite their interest in education, said
little about the learning process itself. Several discussed "as-

sociation of ideas," but their concern lay more with memory and thinking than with learning as habit formation. An exception was John Locke, who noted in the seventeenth century how we tend to associate ideas or objects, a phenomenon similar to what is now called conditioning. He analyzed in remarkably modern fashion how dislikes and fears are inculcated by being associated in one's mind with unfortunate early experiences. For Locke a newborn child's mind is a *tabula rasa*, or clean slate, which receives impressions as he experiences the world about him.

Johann Friedrich Herbart, the first actually to write a textbook in psychology (in 1816), made an important contribution to early learning theories. Previously the associationists, as they were called, had treated the human being as a passive creature on whom certain impressions are made. Herbart maintained that one's past experiences, or "apperceptive mass" as he termed it, have much to do with making new associations and with memories. He also held that most things a person learns tend to cross into his "subconscious," from which they may reappear later. (This was the first foundation of a theory of the unconscious.)

Being a practical philosopher, Herbart applied his theories. He had met Johann Heinrich Pestalozzi, the pioneer Swiss educator, and became interested in his plan of building the curriculum around the child's capacities and interests. Herbart established a school at Königsberg and demonstrated among other things that a child can become interested in anything if the necessary preliminary experience (apperceptive mass) is present. For example, he can understand and interpret a map of Europe if he has learned already how the land, water, and mountains of his own neighborhood are shown on a map. Herbart therefore insisted that school subjects, to be learned effectively and to hold a pupil's interest, should be arranged and presented so that a child can relate new material to material already learned. Notably by attaching importance to interest and motivation in learning, Herbart tremendously influenced education throughout the nineteenth century and gave impetus to founding present-day progressive education.

In 1855 Herbert Spencer published his *Principles of Psychology*, introducing evolutionary ideas into psychology even before Darwin's books appeared. Spencer held a biological view. For him life is "the continuous adjustment of internal to external relations." Mind and behavior arise from and depend upon a person's adaptation to his environment. Learning Spencer explains physiologically as an organism's tendency to repeat pleasant acts and avoid painful ones. Increased nervous activity accompanies pleasure, he says; movements that heighten nervous activity and thus increase pleasure are reinforced and repeated. Painful acts, decreasing nervous activity, are eliminated.

Spencer's contemporary, Alexander Bain, propounded similar ideas on learning and habit, foreshadowing the interpretations of William James and Edward L. Thorndike. In fact, Bain introduced "trial and error," a term still widely used to describe early stages of learning. When we start to form a habit, spontaneous movements or trial-and-error activity occur. Movements having pleasant results are retained and those with unpleasant ones tend to drop out. We learn by repetition: "A few repetitions of the fortuitous concurrence of pleasure and a certain movement will lead to the forging of an acquired connection."

William James published his two-volume *Principles of Psychology* in 1890. Probably the most quoted chapter is that on habit. Impressed with the importance of habits in human life, James discusses their neurological aspects, offers several striking examples of their strength, and says:

Habit is thus the enormous flywheel of society, its most precious conservative agent. . . . It keeps the fisherman and deckhand at sea through the winter; it holds the miner in his darkness; . . . it protects us from invasion by the natives of the desert and the frozen zone . . . It keeps different social strata from mixing. Already at the age of twenty-five you see the professional mannerism settling down on the young commercial traveler, on the young doctor, on the young minister, on the young counsellor-at-law. You see the little lines of cleavage running through the character, the tricks of thought, the prejudices, the ways of the shop, in a word, from which the man can by-and-by no more escape than his coat-sleeve can suddenly fall into a new set of folds.

Though more philosophical than scientific, James was nevertheless strong for practical applications. The great thing in all education, he insists, is to "make our nervous system our ally instead of our enemy. . . . For this we must make automatic and habitual, as early as possible, as many useful actions as we can." He gives several maxims to help acquire new habits and break old ones. One advises us, when planning to change our behavior, to "launch ourselves with as strong and decided an initiative as possible." Another cautions thus: "Never suffer an exception to occur until the new habit is securely rooted in your life."

James' *Principles* became the standard psychology text, a brilliant finale to the speculative and philosophical tradition. Actually the new experimental movement already had begun. Even before James' book appeared, Ebbinghaus published his pioneer studies of memory. Shortly thereafter the scientific study of learning processes began in earnest.

ACQUIRING SKILL

In the closing years of the nineteenth century William L. Bryan and N. Harter studied how telegraphy is learned. Testing weekly the progress of students learning to receive and send code, they found that learning takes place in stages. First the dots and dashes for each letter are mastered. Then the student begins to think of common words as units, without having to spell out each letter. This stage lasts quite a while, then is succeeded by the "sentence habit," in which whole phrases or short sentences are grasped. While one of these so-called "higher units" is developing, a student may seem not to progress, but a period of rapid advancement follows. Apparently in the stand-still period the lower order habits can develop.

A few years later William F. Book studied how persons learn to type by the touch method. A sequence of stages similar to those for telegraphy was found. First, the letter position and proper striking are learned. Later, syllables and short word units appear, followed by phrase units. In the copying of skilled typists, however, Book found little evidence of phrase and sentence units. Their eyes looked ahead and they "copied behind" at a regular rate.

Book also confirmed a fact noted earlier by James and Ebbinghaus—that when students dropped their typing for a period of four months, they picked it up again very rapidly, and without various interfering habits that were present earlier. The typing habits had been established firmly, and therefore persisted, while the annoying practices, accidentally acquired, faded away quickly during the interval.

In recent years, acquiring skills have been described by many psychologists as "response differentiation." When learning a response or series of responses, an organism's behavior gradually improves (differentiates) with practice. This has been explained, notably by B. F. Skinner, by "differential reinforcement"; that is, desirable responses or those that make for a smooth pattern of behavior are reinforced (see pp. 105-8) either by automatic feedback or deliberately by a teacher or trainer, while inappropriate responses are not reinforced or are punished. The responses of a skilled dancer, speaker, or artist have been well differentiated; the skilled responses have been reinforced, while the unskilled ones have not.

ANIMAL LEARNING

After Darwin published his theory of evolution, animal behavior received more attention than ever before. Many physiologists studied animal reflex actions. Other scientists, notably George Romanes and Lloyd Morgan, observed the "instincts" and "intelligence" of animals. Unfortunately much of their data is anecdotal and cannot be considered strictly scientific.

Edward L. Thorndike pioneered in animal psychology, which compares human with subhuman organisms. While studying under James at Harvard in 1897, Thorndike began experiments on learning in chicks. The next year he set up a laboratory at Columbia and continued the work. Not only chicks, but cats, dogs, and monkeys were studied. A hungry cat, for example, was shut in a barred wooden box, and a dish of food placed outside. To get the food the cat had to turn

a button or pull a wire loop that opened a do
cat clawed, bit, scratched, and tried to reach t
bars—behavior called "trial and error" by Lloyd Morga
took over the term coined by Alexander Bain. In its hit-or-n
struggle, the cat accidentally struck the button and got to
the food. Next time, when placed in the box, it found the
button sooner. In each successive trial fewer random movements were made, until finally the cat went straight to the
button. Graphically, its learning is pictured thus:

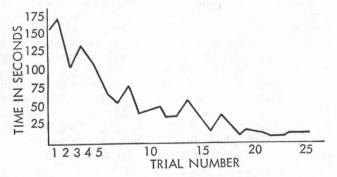

While the cat does not improve with perfect consistency, the
curve in general declines, rapidly at first, then gradually until
it reaches a level at 8 or 10 seconds. Experiments with other
animals showed similar results, though monkeys learned faster
than dogs and cats.

Thorndike drew important conclusions about animal learning: When driven by hunger, thirst, or other bodily urge, an
animal first shows trial-and-error behavior. After some successes learning occurs, and the useless movements are abandoned. To solve a problem an animal may use movements, or
responses, as they are called, that were successful in similar
situations. In other words, responses are shifted from one to
another stimulus, in the same fashion that an animal learns
to do tricks. Thorndike called this behavior "associative shifting." It resembles Pavlov's "conditioned response," described
later in this chapter.

Two fundamental laws of learning were postulated by
Thorndike—the laws of exercise and effect. The law of exer-

certain act strengthens the bond
sponse, hence makes the response
e weakens the bond. The law of ef-
sults in satisfaction or reward, the act
followed by no reward or by punish-
be repeated.

ard S. Small began studying how white
rats, com̄ maze, learned to find their way out. He
initiated what h. become one of the most popular methods
of studying animal learning. Motivated by hunger, a rat first
makes trial-and-error efforts to reach a food box. Once having
found the way, the rat on successive trials enters fewer blind
alleys, wanders less aimlessly, and finds the box more and
more quickly, until the maze is learned. Learning curves
similar to those for Thorndike's cats are obtained.

Other psychologists have used the maze to study many
problems. John B. Watson, founder of behaviorism, tried to
discover what senses a rat uses in its learning. He concluded
that the most essential is the kinesthetic, or muscle, sense.
Walter S. Hunter, Norman R. F. Maier, and Isadore Krechev-
sky built special kinds of mazes to test the higher limits of
animal learning and reasoning. Karl S. Lashley used the
maze, with other devices, to study the effects of brain operations on rat behavior. William McDougall tried (unsuccess-
fully) to show that maze learning ability can be passed by
heredity to successive generations of rats, which would prove
the inheritance of acquired characteristics.

Robert Tryon in 1940 developed strains of "maze-bright"
and "maze-dull" rats by repeated inbreeding, but this behavior was limited to maze learning.

How humans learn a maze was studied by Harvey Carr, of
the University of Chicago, and an associate. They found that
blindfolded adults and children do about as well as rats in
learning mazes of similar pattern. Fleming A. C. Perrin observed human performance in both outdoor mazes, of the
amusement park variety, and stylus mazes, where a blindfolded subject pushes a small rod through grooves in a board.
Learning such mazes turned out to be no blind hit-or-miss
process; his subjects reported visualizing, planning, and reasoning to find their way out. Somewhat later Carl J. Warden,

of Columbia University, and Richard W. Husband, of the University of Wisconsin, determined that human beings use any of three methods in learning a maze: 1. verbal formula ("left one, right three, left two," etc.); 2. forming a visual image of the maze; 3. motor learning, similar to ordinary trial and error. Most effective was the verbal method; least successful, the motor method.

Patterning a test after one of the Army Beta questions, Stanley D. Porteus, of the University of Hawaii, devised several "visible mazes," wherein one traces with a pencil the correct path through a printed maze. To succeed one must look ahead and plan, avoiding impulsive trial-and-error efforts. Porteus and others found that a good performance on these maze tests correlates somewhat with intelligence and "social adaptability."

THE CONDITIONED RESPONSE

In 1901 a Russian physiologist, Ivan Petrovich Pavlov, discovered something of enormous import to psychology—the conditioned reflex. In effect it is this: If each time a dog is given food a bell is rung simultaneously, the dog becomes "conditioned" to the sound of the bell and in time salivates on hearing the bell, even though no food accompanies it. Not only sounds, but light, smell, or touch stimuli may condition dogs to salivate when no food is present.

The careful experimental methods of Pavlov enabled him to discover many interesting facts. The conditioned reflex results if the conditioning stimulus occurs before or simultaneously with the original stimulus (food). If, for example, the bell sounds two minutes before food is given, a conditioned reflex is set up, the dog inhibiting salivation until two minutes after hearing the bell.

Moreover, a conditioned reflex can be "extinguished" as well as established. Keep on ringing the bell without presenting food, and the dog ceases to salivate, naturally enough. The conditioned reflex can be brought back in two ways: by "spontaneous recovery" after a lapse of time, and by "reinforcement"—that is, by again presenting food with the bell.

Using the Pavlovian technique psychologists have investigated fineness of sensory discrimination in animals and young children. Pavlov's significant study of "experimental neurosis" by breaking down powers of discrimination is discussed in Chapter X in connection with conflict.

Working with children, N. Krasnogorski, a student of Pavlov, found that the salivary reflex, normally occurring when food enters the mouth, can be conditioned to the mere sight of food and also to sounds or even to touches on the skin. An American, Florence Mateer, following up Krasnogorski's lead, in 1916 experimented with many children up to seven years old. By touching a child's arm when a chocolate candy was put in his mouth, she built up a conditioned reflex; in time the child opened his mouth as soon as the arm was touched. Dr. Mateer found that normal children learn to establish and extinguish the response about twice as fast as mental deficients. She decided that conditioning speed is an important indicator of intelligence.

Another American psychologist, Hulsey Cason, conditioned the pupillary reflex. By flashing a light into a subject's eye and ringing a bell simultaneously, he found, after about 400 trials, that the eye pupil contracted to the sound alone. Raymond S. Dodge conditioned the winking reflex to the knee jerk by making subjects blink, with a light or a gesture, each time their knees were tapped; eventually subjects winked to the knee jerk alone.

Other investigators showed that it is possible, by appropriate techniques of conditioning, to bring involuntary responses like blushing and the pupillary reflex under voluntary control. Such experiments suggest that there is no hard and fast distinction between voluntary and involuntary action, as is generally supposed.

American psychologists did not learn the details of Pavlov's experimentation until after 1909. Actually it was through the work of another Russian, Vladimir M. Bekhterev, that conditioning was introduced into this country. Bekhterev's book, *Objective Psychology*, was translated in 1913 and made conditioning the center of his new "reflexology." The foremost American sponsor was John B. Watson, the behaviorist.

Watson at Chicago and Johns Hopkins had insisted for

some time that psychology must be hard-boiled
Stimulated by the work of Thorndike and by a
man biologists known as the "objectivists," Wa
making intensive studies of animal learning. H
comed the work of Pavlov and Bekhterev and seized upon
the conditioned reflex as the most satisfactory explanation of
learning and habit formation. He also discussed its importance in relation to emotion, language, and even mental
disease. His best-known experimental work was concerned
with the establishing of fears through conditioning, as will be
described in Chapter X.

By 1920 conditioning was widely accepted as an important
psychological principle. The Pavlovian "conditioned reflex"
was too narrow a concept, however, as not only reflexes but all
kinds of responses can be conditioned. Two University of
Washington psychologists, Stevenson Smith and Edwin R.
Guthrie, suggested instead "conditioned response." They
pointed out that this term would then be applicable to all
learning by association.

Actually the principle of learning Guthrie emphasized was
"contiguity" or closeness, not conditioning *per se*. When an
act occurs in the presence of a stimulus, there is a tendency
for the act to recur in the presence of that same stimulus.

Literally hundreds of experiments have been done upon
the "CR," as it is commonly called. Our learning of spoken
and written language, our gestures, most of our emotional
reactions, responses to various signals—all these are examples
of conditioning. Much of our waking lives is given over to
making responses which have been conditioned in the course
of our past experience.

REINFORCEMENT

Are conditioning and trial-and-error really different kinds
of learning? Psychologists since Watson and Thorndike have
sought to harmonize them. Prominent among these was Clark
L. Hull, who clarified and intricately developed Thorndike's
law of effect. He thought "reinforcement" to be the basic
cause of learning. In Pavlovian or "classical" conditioning,
reinforcement occurs when the unconditioned stimulus (for

mple, food) is paired with the conditioned stimulus (for example, the sound of a bell). In trial-and-error learning, such as a rat in a maze, reinforcement of an act (taking the right path) results from a successful outcome (getting to food at the exit). According to Hull, learning in both instances probably traces to reinforcement.

There are several theoretical points about which psychologists disagree. The phenomenon of reinforcement is one of these. Hull, Neal Miller, and Kenneth Spence, for example, hold that reinforcement operates because needs or drives are reduced. They believe learning takes place when stimulus and response occur at approximately the same time and is accompanied by the reduction of a drive. When a lever (stimulus) is inadvertently pushed (response) by a hungry (drive) animal and he is fed, the animal learns to push the lever because a drive is reduced by this action. Guthrie's position maintains that reinforcement merely serves to remove the learner from extraneous stimuli: learning occurs when a response is contiguous to a stimulus and there are no interfering stimuli. Learning to push a lever happens because the act of eating removes the animal from other stimuli and prevents other responses—only the lever (S) and the push (R) are thus contiguous. Still another interpretation was made by Edward C. Tolman, who believed reinforcement to be the confirmation of expectancies. In the process of learning, a learner sets up expectations or hypotheses, the confirmation of which reinforces behavior. For example, the lever becomes the sign for the expectation of food when pushed—if this expectation is fulfilled, learning occurs. Skinner avoids the whole controversy by defining reinforcement as any stimulus event which increases the probability of a response.

OPERANT LEARNING

Two-factor learning theories, which have been essentially based upon classical conditioning and trial-and-error learning, are being developed by several psychologists, notably O. Hobart Mowrer and B. F. Skinner. According to Skinner there are basically two kinds of responses, which he calls "respondent" and "operant." Respondent responses are automatic (reflexive), *elicited* by definite stimuli—for example, salivation, the knee jerk, the eye-blink, fear, anger, withdrawal of hand from a hot stove. These responses are involved in emotional behavior and are apparently controlled by the autonomic nervous system. Classical conditioning starts with such automatic responses.

Operant responses are *emitted* when an organism must adapt to environmental conditions or solve problems. "Operant conditioning or learning" occurs when an operant response is reinforced. For example, when an animal is placed in a cage, it typically makes responses to escape (operant responses). The response that leads to freedom is reinforced by escape and is likely to be made whenever the animal is replaced in the cage.

Most complex learning is of operant type. William S. Verplanck observed an increase in the frequency of opinion statements ("I think," "I believe," etc.) when they were reinforced by agreement of the listener ("You're right," "I agree," etc.). There is even evidence that creativity (novel operant responses) can be facilitated by reinforcement of unusual responses. For example, Irving Maltzman found that atypical responses apparently increased in a word association test when these responses were reinforced.

Keller Breland has shown that animal behavior can be shaped, almost as a sculptor shapes clay, by reinforcing every operant response which leads to the desired behavior. Animal trainers have used this method of "successive approximation" for years. For example, when a seal is being trained to sit on a stool, every movement toward the stool is reinforced with a fish; when a response to mount the stool is made, it is reinforced; ultimately the seal is led to do the trick by reinforcing responses which approximate the goal. In several experiments Verplanck gradually shaped human behavior by the process of successive approximation. For example, people can be led to talk about their relatives by reinforcing 1. just talking, 2. talking about people in general, 3. talking about well-liked people, and so on until the topic of relatives is reached.

Charles B. Ferster and B. F. Skinner have extensively studied the influence of what they call "reinforcement schedules" or patterns of reinforcement. When responses of an organism are reinforced intermittently (not continuously), the learned behavior lasts longer. For example, a pigeon trained to peck a spot will stop pecking behavior sooner if it has been trained by reinforcing every spot-pecking response instead of reinforcing only some of the spot-pecking responses.

LEARNING BY INSIGHT

Three German psychologists, Max Wertheimer, Wolfgang Köhler, and Kurt Koffka, best known as the founders of Gestalt psychology, objected to Thorndike's and Watson's interpretations of animal learning. Given the right kind of problem, said Köhler, an animal does not necessarily learn by trial and error. If a problem involves "getting the point" or grasping relationships, an animal may solve it as fast as a human being "catches on" to solving a mechanical puzzle. Köhler further argued that learning does not involve merely forming simple stimulus-response bonds, as Watson and the behaviorists implied. It is total reaction to a total situation.

While interned on the Canary Islands during World War I Köhler did several famous experiments on apes. He hung a banana from the roof of a large pen, too high for an ape to reach by jumping. In one corner of the pen he left a box. The question was: would the apes get the point of standing on the box to reach the food? Some did. After much leaping, flouncing about, and whining, they would drag the box underneath the banana, mount it, and capture the prize. In another experiment apes used sticks to reach for food. Sultan, the cleverest of the lot, did even better. He tore a branch from a tree, and with it raked in food through the bars of his cage. Another time he joined two bamboo rods to form one long stick, with which he maneuvered food.

While Köhler's animals made trial-and-error efforts, obviously they also perceived relationships, often quite suddenly. Köhler called this quick grasping of relations, or seeing the point, "insight."

More about insight and how it occurs is given in Chapter VIII. That insight constitutes learning is best shown by the fact that when a person solves a problem by grasping a principle, he can solve similar problems immediately.

Transfer of Training

Having discussed the principal kinds of learning—trial-and-error, classical conditioning, and insight—we now turn to the very important question: can learning carry over or transfer to performance in another activity? How much does one kind of training or practice improve another?

In athletics considerable transfer takes place. Coaches insist on calisthenics, gymnasium work, and running to help train their football players. A discus thrower or shot putter develops his arm muscles by lifting weights and swinging Indian clubs.

It is often said that one's mind can be improved through certain studies, much as a muscle is strengthened by exercise. In fact, this argument still is used by those who believe particular subjects, such as Latin or mathematics, are good "mental discipline." The question has important implications for education.

As early as 1890 William James and his students tried memorizing verses from Hugo and Tennyson, then practicing other poets to see whether such training improved their memory for Hugo and Tennyson. Three of the subjects improved slightly; the other two became worse. James concluded that practice does not affect one's power of retention, though better memory methods may be cultivated.

Edward L. Thorndike and Robert S. Woodworth conducted a rather elaborate experiment to test the validity of "mental discipline" in education. They tested subjects' ability to estimate areas of rectangles, triangles, and other geometrical figures. The subjects were then given training that improved their ability to estimate areas of smaller rectangles. This training did not carry over at all consistently when the subjects again turned to triangles and large rectangles. Essentially the same thing resulted when the tasks consisted of guessing weights and lengths of lines, or canceling certain letters and words on a printed page. Sometimes, indeed, practice hindered more than it helped performance in similar activities. Thorndike and Woodworth concluded that training in one kind of activity transfers to aid performance in another only if the two have identical or common elements, such a material worked with, methods used, or attitudes assume by the subjects.

These findings give small comfort to those who conten that training in one subject improves the mind generally.

Shortly after 1920 Thorndike studied by an ingeniou method more than 13,000 high school pupils to see hov much each school subject improved their learning powei Mathematics and the social and physical sciences improved i most. Latin, French, and physical training had a slightly pos itive effect, while stenography, biology, and dramatic ai helped not at all. Thorndike points out that the general gair from any subject amounts to little, compared with improve ment resulting from the student's own ability.

No one subject can "train the mind" in general. On th other hand, specific transfer value attaches to almost any sub ject if specified applications are stressed. For example, wher the value of neatness is emphasized as students are trainee to write neat arithmetic papers, their neatness training carrie over to other subjects. Students in a Latin class where specia attention was given to word meanings and derivations im proved perceptibly in English vocabulary, compared to Latii students taught in the usual manner. Similarly, if principle of scientific method are stressed in a Chemistry course, ther is a positive transfer to Physics or Biology.

Negative transfer may also occur. That is, training ma interfere with subsequent learning. Linus W. Kline, educa tional psychologist, found that subjects trained to cancel e and t's on a printed page had trouble later canceling part of speech. Negative transfer appears also when subjects, hav ing learned to sort playing cards into one arrangement c boxes, are made to change and sort them in a different ai rangement.

Albert T. Poffenberger has shown that if a second task dif fers greatly from the first, no transfer of any kind results. I responses already learned can be used in the new problem positive transfer occurs. But if the new problem require changing previously formed habits, negative transfer or inter ference follows.

THE NEUROLOGY OF LEARNING

Two hundred years ago David Hartley, the first physiological psychologist, suspected that association, learning, and memory have a neural basis. He suggested that when several sensations arouse a certain pattern of "brain vibrations," if one of the sensations recurs later, it calls forth lesser vibrations or memory images of the others. Like John Locke, Hartley believed a child begins life without associations. Through continuous sensory experience, complex connections and associations occur in the nervous system, ultimately making possible the subtleties of adult human behavior.

William James' view, appearing a century and a half later, differed little from Hartley's. The intervening years had seen progress in understanding the structure but not the function of the nervous system. According to James, when we see a person and hear his name, two nerve centers are excited. A neural connection occurs between them, which enables us later to recall the face if only the name is heard, or the name if the face is seen. But James, like the neurologists themselves, was vague about the specific details of neural action.

In 1891, the year after James' *Principles* appeared, W. Waldeyer formulated the "neurone theory" which held that nerve cells, or neurones as he called them, link together or almost together at points called "synapses." (Neurologists still are uncertain whether a synapse is a junction or a small gap.) Synapses retard the progress of neural impulses, which follow the path of least resistance. Learning, Waldeyer said, consists of lowering resistance at some synapses and raising it at others, resulting in new neural pathways or patterns.

A few neurologists have expanded Waldeyer's neurone theory, notably Sir Charles S. Sherrington, whose *Integrative Action of the Nervous System* in 1906 described many details of neural function at the synapse. But essentially the theory has not changed for fifty years. The real nature of the neural impulse and of the specific processes occurring at the synapse remain a mystery.

James Olds and Peter Milner, under the guidance of D. O.

Hebb, implanted electrodes in the brains of rats to study the effects of electrical stimulation. They found an area of the brain where electrical stimulation was apparently pleasurable since rats continued to do that which gave them electrical brain stimulation. Neal E. Miller and others have been successful in using this kind of brain stimulation as reinforcement in learning experiments.

MEANING OF MEMORY

Memory is a phase of learning. Broadly speaking, learning has three stages: 1. acquiring, wherein one masters a new activity like driving a car, or memorizes verbal material such as a poem; 2. retaining the new acquisition for a period of time, and 3. remembering, which enables one to reproduce the learned act or memorized material. The commonest forms of remembering are recalling and recognizing. Forgetting signifies either failure to retain or inability to recall or recognize.

In a narrower sense learning merely means acquiring skill, as with mazes, problem boxes, and conditioned responses. Most of these are muscular, non-verbal activities. With remembering and forgetting we deal mainly with verbal activities.

HISTORICAL BACKGROUND OF MEMORY STUDY

Many philosophers have considered memory in discussing association of ideas. Plato noted that we associate by contiguity. The sight or sound of a lyre may call to mind the instrument's player or his friend, because previously they were experienced together. Plato mentioned also that a person or object may recall a like person or object, a process later called association by similarity. Aristotle wrote that recall takes place through suggestion. One item causes us to recall another because the two once were contiguous, or because they are similar to or opposite from each other. David Hartley, an eighteenth-century Englishman, stated that there are two sorts of association, the synchronous and the successive, according to whether impressions are made at the same instant or in successive instants. We already have mentioned Herbart's theory that association and memory are influenced by a person's "apperceptive mass" or sum total of past experience.

Thomas Brown, a noted Scottish philosopher, drew up in 1820 several principles of association that contributed significantly to existing theories of memory. We associate and remember, said Brown, according to the relative duration, liveliness, frequency, and recency of original experiences. He suggested also that temporary abnormal conditions like intoxication or delirium affect the way we associate and remember. Brown's principles antedated theories of learning that appeared nearly a century later.

In his *Analysis of the Phenomena of the Human Mind*, published in 1829, James Mill reduced all the laws of association to one—contiguity in experience. Memory in the form of recognition is an idea or image of an object plus awareness of our earlier experience with it. Mill's contemporary, Sir William Hamilton, protesting against oversimplified theories of association, introduced "redintegration." One impression, he said, evokes not a *single* associated idea but the *whole situation* of which both formerly were a part. Our experiences are complex and contain many elements; any one element later may redintegrate or recall the total earlier experience. Almost a century later Hamilton's theory of redintegration was developed and expanded by Harry L. Hollingworth.

Ewald Hering, a great nineteenth-century German physiologist, stressed the physical and neurological basis of memory. Any perception causes a certain neural process or path in the brain. Recurring, this perception follows the same neural path, bringing about the experience of memory.

William James held that each person has a certain power of retentiveness, its quality depending on his brain structure. Agreeing with Hering that any act of memory involves a certain neural pathway, James doubted that learning one thing can aid in learning another because the two neural bases differ. After studying transfer in memorizing poems, he concluded as we have seen, that one's retentiveness cannot improve by training.

The Work of Ebbinghaus

An amazing monograph called *Memory* revealed in 1885 what Hermann Ebbinghaus, a brilliant German, learned from studying himself for five years. Few pieces of research are as original. Influenced by Fechner's psychophysics and by new statistical methods, Ebbinghaus devised new materials and procedures and explored aspects of memory never touched before. For a generation afterwards few students found a memory problem not already investigated by Ebbinghaus.

The sections which follow contain the more significant findings of Ebbinghaus and his successors in each of the major areas of memory research. They are presented in an order which emphasizes first, memorizing; second, retaining and forgetting; third, reproducing or remembering.

Importance of Meaning and Rhythm

To get memory material free from past associations Ebbinghaus invented and used nonsense syllables. These are meaningless—or almost meaningless—combinations of three letters, such as rof, bap, tid, guk. Over 2000 such syllables exist in German and almost as many in English. By this means it is possible to make accurate study of rote learning; also to compare the ability of different individuals, since none are familiar with the materials.

Ebbinghaus compared his speed in memorizing lists of nonsense syllables with his speed for meaningful material. Certain stanzas of Byron's *Don Juan*, each having 80 syllables, took him about 9 readings each to learn. Eighty nonsense syllables required almost 80 repetitions. In other words meaningless material was nine times as hard to learn as meaningful.

Ebbinghaus thought that rhythmic grouping of syllables might affect his memorizing. Hence he used a constant rhythm in all his learning, though he did not study the effects of rhythm. Georg E. Müller, a German contemporary of Ebbinghaus, found that grouping syllables into units of two and three or even six helped learning considerably. However, one type of rhythm is not necessarily best for all persons, because individual differences are great.

George Katona found that recall of number sequences (581215192226) after three weeks' delay was greater when a principle was used ($5 + 3 = 8$, $8 + 4 = 12$, $12 + 3 = 15$) than when learned by rote. There was no difference in immediate recall.

LENGTH OF LISTS

If a memory task is made longer, does its learning time increase proportionately? Does it take twice as long to learn 20 lines of poetry as to learn 10 lines? Ebbinghaus found he could learn seven or eight nonsense syllables by reading them once. To learn 10 syllables required 13 readings. The time required for each new item and for the whole list increased disproportionately. His findings appear in the following table:*

LENGTH OF LIST	NUMBER OF READINGS	TIME FOR LISTS	AVERAGE TIME PER SYLLABLE
7	1	3 seconds	.4 seconds
10	13	52	5.2
12	17	82	6.8
16	30	196	12.0
24	44	422	17.6
36	55	792	22.0

Later studies report the same general results, though time taken usually is longer. No very consistent mathematical relation between length of list and learning time is found. Clearly, more associations require much more time per unit. Often, however, familiarity with the material compensates for increased length.

OVERLEARNING

Is a selection learned when we first recite it once correctly, or when we "know it by heart"? Ebbinghaus's criterion of

* From Garrett, Henry E.; *Great Experiments in Psychology*, 1941, p. 262.

learning was one perfect recitation of the list. To test over learning, i.e., learning more than is required for one correct recitation, he varied the number of readings given to lists of 16 nonsense syllables. Some lists he went over 8 times, some 16, and so on up to 64. At the end of 24 hours he relearned the lists up to one correct repetition, and found that the percentage *saved* corresponded almost exactly with the number of times he had originally read the material. Where he read a list 8 times he found 8% saving; 24 times, 23% saving; and 64 times, 64% saving. Undoubtedly a point of diminishing returns would have been encountered if Ebbinghaus had continued above 64 repetitions.

Other studies have on the whole substantiated Ebbinghaus's results, though there is doubt about the amount of overlearning which is profitable in terms of savings later. The consensus of opinion seems to be that retention is increased by overlearning up to 50%; that is, spending 50% more time memorizing material than is required for one correct repetition. Overlearning beyond that point, except when spaced over several days, may involve inefficiency due to wandering attention, boredom, and fatigue.

SPACED AND UNSPACED LEARNING

As might be expected, Ebbinghaus found that memorizing a large amount of material all in one day took considerably more effort than memorizing it over several days. Others report the same. William F. Book, studying how we learn typing, found it better to distribute his practice periods. Karl S. Lashley discovered that best results came from spacing the learning trials. He found also that rats learning a maze repeat errors more frequently when trials are bunched than when they occur a day apart. Robert M. Yerkes, the animal psychologist, noted that his dancing mouse learned to discriminate white from black faster when few rather than many trials were given the same day.

Two factors are involved in spacing learning periods: length of learning period, and the interval between periods. C. J. Warden studied both in animal maze learning. He gave his rats 1, 3, or 5 trials at a time; the intervals between varied from 6 hours to 3 days. Results showed clearly that one trial at a time, given at intervals of 12 hours, made for best acquisition of the habit.

Clearly, distributed learning is better than concentrated learning, but no general optimum length of practice period or interval between periods is found. Warden's findings do not hold for a pupil studying French. There are not only differences between the animal and human species, but also among individuals. Likewise, considerable variation in kind and difficulty of learning material is encountered. When material is easy, and when interest and motivation are high, massed learning is more effective. Where the task is difficult, when interest lags and boredom or fatigue sets in, distributed learning periods are best. Practically, a student must experiment on himself to find the most effective length for his study periods and for rest intervals between.

WHOLE VERSUS PART METHODS

Is it better to learn a poem one stanza at a time, or to go through it at each reading from beginning to end? Most persons prefer the stanza-by-stanza method, yet the majority of experiments show the other to be more efficient. One study showed that the whole method took 12% less time; another found it had a 15% advantage over the part method. Nonsense syllables, prose, poetry and vocabulary generally are learned best by the whole method. Mazes are not, either by animals or humans; sometimes the part method is better, though more often the two approaches seem about equally effective. In his *Psychology of Human Learning* John A. McGeoch says if a subject's level of mental development is high, the whole method probably is better. When practice periods are massed, the part method wins; when distributed, the whole method. Meaning and unity in the material, as in poetry or connected prose, favor the whole procedure.

Variations of whole and part methods are possible. In the "progressive part method," a subject learns part 1, then part 2, then ties them together; next part 3, then connects 1, 2, and 3, and so on. Louis A. Pechstein found this technique best in memorizing nonsense syllables.

Robert S. Woodworth says that a learner prefers working with parts and may gain skill with them which carries over to other sections of the problem. But he still must put the parts together. If he can adjust himself to the whole method, it will serve him best in complex learning tasks. Probably it is best, concludes Woodworth, to start with the whole method, feeling free to concentrate at any time on the parts.

THE CURVE OF FORGETTING

How fast does forgetting occur?

Ebbinghaus memorized lists of nonsense syllables, waited for a certain period of time, then tested his retention by the "savings method." This method, one of his ingenious inventions, consists of relearning material and calculating the percentage saving of time as compared with original learning time. In this experiment, for example, it took him about 24 minutes to learn 16 lists (up to a standard of two correct repetitions). An hour later he took only 13½ minutes to relearn the same lists. The difference between 24 and 13½, expressed as a percent, is the saving—in this case 44%.

Ebbinghaus found that most of the loss comes in the first few hours; after that forgetting proceeds very gradually. After one hour he forgot 56%, after nine hours, 64%, after two days, 72% and after 31 days, 79%. In graphical form, the curve of forgetting (or, more accurately, the "curve of *retention*") looks like this:

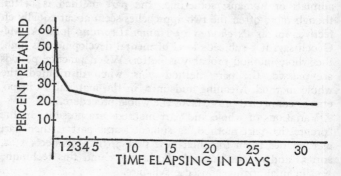

Results of many similar experiments, with materials ranging from nonsense syllables to high school Latin and algebra, agree with those of Ebbinghaus, though the precise form of the curve of forgetting depends largely upon the method used for testing retention. The savings method, as shown above, shows a quick drop at first, then a very gradual decline. When memory is tested by making the subject *recall* material, rather than *relearn* it, the curve of forgetting is found to fall off sharply for two days or more before it flattens out. But whatever the method used for testing memory, it still holds true that most of our forgetting takes place in the first day or two after we learn.

ATTITUDE OF THE LEARNER

Passage of time alone does not cause forgetting. Our retention of material is affected by a number of factors, which will be treated in this and the following sections.

To memorize efficiently and retain the memorized material, we need an active interested attitude, with intent to learn. Woodworth describes a student who seemed very slow at learning nonsense syllables. Asked if he was ready to recite the list, he exclaimed: "Oh! I didn't understand I was to learn them." He had noted the syllables separately, but made no effort to connect them.

Joseph Peterson found by experiment that a subject's intent to learn, compared with mere passive observation, caused a real advantage in retention two days later. Hermann H. Remmers and an associate discovered that a mental set to retain for three days, one week, and two weeks, consistently aided recall at each of these intervals.

Though learning occurs even without a "will to learn," it is sketchy and untrustworthy compared with learning where maximum attention and motivation are present.

An interesting theory of memory is proposed by Bluma W. Zeigarnik, a student of Kurt Lewin. She gave a large number of subjects 20 puzzles and similar problems to solve. They were allowed to work on half the problems until completed; in the other half they were interrupted before they could finish. When later asked to recall as many problems as possible, they remembered considerably more of the unfinished ones. Dr. Zeigarnik concluded that unfinished tasks leave a tension or dissatisfaction because a desire to solve the problem is frustrated. Hence we remember them better than the completed tasks where tensions are relieved.

EMOTION AND MEMORY

Emotion affects both learning and memory. Inaccuracies found in the testimony of witnesses result partly from emotional factors operating at the time of accidents or other dramatic incidents.

The best-known theory of how emotion influences memory is that of Sigmund Freud. Freud explains forgetting in terms of repression. Because we repress the unpleasant we forget ideas or incidents associated with it. He gives as an example forgetting the names of persons we dislike.

Two experiments to test Freud's theory were done by Hyman Meltzer and by Ross Stagner. They studied how well college students remember pleasant and unpleasant experiences. More pleasant than unpleasant items were retained, though the difference averaged only 10% or 15%. In fact, a good-sized minority of subjects forgot pleasant items more than unpleasant ones. In general, repressing the unpleasant probably explains some of our forgetting, as Freud believed, but by no means all of it. A more tenable theory, proposed by several psychologists, is that both pleasant and unpleasant emotional experiences are retained better than experiences having no emotional value.

SLEEP AND FORGETTING

A surprising discovery is that we do not forget something newly learned as quickly if we sleep right after learning it as we do if we remain awake. John G. Jenkins and Karl M. Dallenbach compared the effects of sleep and of waking activity on newly learned nonsense syllables. A much greater loss occurred during the waking interval than during sleep, particularly after four hours. After eight hours' sleep retention was as good as after two. Jenkins and Dallenbach interpreted this to mean that forgetting is caused largely by interference from new experiences, rather than by the mere passing of time.

RETROACTIVE INHIBITION

Remembering a newly learned poem may be interfered with if a second poem is learned right away. Forgetting caused by subsequent activities is called "retroactive inhibition."

In 1900 Georg E. Müller and Alfons Pilzecker, two German investigators, found that subjects recalled 56% of learned material after an interval of idleness, but only 26% when the interval was occupied by mental tasks.

If two learning tasks are similar they interfere with each other more than unlike tasks, John A. McGeoch reported. Students find this true when they study Spanish right after studying French. Learning and remembering the French is hindered more by the Spanish than it would be by Physics or Mathematics. Following a period of learning with sleep is best; next best is relaxation or complete diversion, such as listening to music. According to McGeoch, other ways to retain material despite retroactive inhibition are to learn it completely, and to widen the interval between the original and the interfering activity.

RELEARNING AND REVIEW

To see what effect periodic reviewing or relearning has on material to be remembered, Ebbinghaus learned lists of nonsense syllables and also stanzas of Byron's *Don Juan*. Then he relearned both every day for six days. Each successive day required less reviewing to repeat the lists perfectly once. This suggests that associations once formed become stronger as time goes on. The principle was formulated as a law by Adolph Jost, another student of memory. Jost's Law reads as follows: If two associations are of equal strength but of different ages, the older one will lose strength more slowly with the further passage of time.

For permanence of retention, then, frequent relearning and review are essential, as most actors and teachers well know. If we actually recite memorized items to ourselves, we remember them much better, Arthur I. Gates, of Teachers College, Columbia University, showed. In learning both nonsense syllables and material that made sense, one group of pupils studied by reading only. Another group read for 80% of the time and spent the remainder reviewing orally. With other groups the proportion of reading and recitation time was varied. Results showed clearly that the most efficient retention occurred when most of the time was given to review and recitation. In fact, the best proportion usually was 20% reading to 80% recitation. Students would profit by spending less study time in reading and more in reviewing and reciting to themselves.

Self-recitation has several advantages. It encourages concentration. It makes the learner notice his errors, which usually go undetected when he reads. It leads him to organize material for convenient use later, such as for an examination or oral classroom recitation.

REMINISCENCE

A mysterious quirk of memory is "reminiscence," the ability to recall *more* instead of *less* as time elapses. In 1913 an English psychologist, Philip B. Ballard, noted that a group of 6-year-olds who studied poems for 15 minutes recalled more several days later than they did immediately after learning! This was not true for adults, nor was reminiscence apparent for meaningless material. Horace B. English and associates at Ohio State University found reminiscence operating when subjects recalled substance or meaning, but not when they recalled material verbatim. Reminiscence occurred up to two months after the learning.

Reminiscence not only occurs when meaningful, cognitive material is learned, but when nonsense syllables or motor skills are learned. Lewis B. Ward found retention of nonsense syllables five minutes after learning to be greater than immediately after learning. Arthur L. Irion found that after twenty-five seconds of massed practice on a pursuit rotor (a device for studying hand skill learning), longer rest periods improved the scores on the next five trials more than did shorter ones. Reminiscence apparently is not due to review in the period between learning and recall; as yet no satisfactory explanation exists.

RECALL AND RECOGNITION

"Recall" and "recognition" are the best-known methods of testing retention. Recall means reproducing material as learned, as when one writes out or recites a poem. But a once-learned poem which cannot be recalled may be recognized when one comes across it in an anthology. Recognition means awareness of a previous experience, or a feeling of familiarity. Generally it is easier than recall. Edith M. Achilles found that two or three times as many nonsense syllables, words, and proverbs can be recognized as can be recalled.

Errors of both recognition and recall are common. Woodworth lists several names mistakenly recalled: McDonald for McDougall, Hennessy for Haggerty, Ernst for Stern, Barclay for Clayton, Underwood for Overstreet. Errors of recognition sometimes are puzzling: we feel certain we already have met a person to whom we are introduced. Walking in a strange city we suddenly have a conviction that we have been there before. Harry L. Hollingworth explains such instances by the principle of redintegration: a part of the new experience, having been present also in a past experience, calls to mind the past experience and with it a feeling of familiarity or recognition.

THE SAVINGS METHOD

Though not as well known as recognition and recall, the most accurate way to measure memory is the relearning or savings method, devised by Ebbinghaus. We may be unable to recall or even recognize poems learned years ago, but if we memorize the same poems now it takes less time than learning completely new poems of the same type. This happens because imperceptible memory traces have lasted over the years.

An almost unbelievable instance of these traces is evidenced in an experiment performed by Harold E. Burtt, of Ohio State University. When his son was about two years old, Burtt read him Greek passages daily for three months. When the boy was eight and a half years old, his father made him learn several Greek selections, including those which he had heard more than six years before. Between one-fourth and one-third *fewer* trials were needed to learn the passages heard by the two-year-old than to learn the completely new material! Never has an experiment shown so clearly both the impressionability of babyhood and the lasting character of memory traces.

MEMORY IMPROVEMENT

The many studies reviewed above bristle with practical implications. Remembering is aided by meaningfulness of material, by overlearning, by spacing periods of study, and sometimes by using the whole rather than the part method of attack. Most forgetting takes place in the first couple of days after learning. One's power of retention cannot be increased, but memory may be improved by active attention to the learning task and by adoption of a favorable, interested attitude. Retention is aided by sleep, relaxation, or change in activity right after learning. Frequent review and self-recitation helps to fix material firmly in mind. It may be true that every experience leaves a permanent memory trace, but these can seldom be detected by the usual methods of recall and recognition. They may be brought to light by the relearning or savings method.

Chapter VII

PERCEIVING

DA VINCI   BERKELEY   HAMILTON   HELMHOLTZ
TITCHENER   PILLSBURY   EHRENFELS   WOODWORTH
WERTHEIMER   KÖHLER   KOFFKA   BORING
MORGAN   BRUNER   MURPHY   GIBSON

What is attention? How is it attracted? Why is "mental set" important? How does perceiving differ from sensing? What is Gestalt psychology? What are optical illusions and how do they occur? How is it possible for us to perceive depth or distance? How do reward and punishment affect perception?

In a psychological sense the word *perception* means both the physical act of receiving sense impressions (seeing, hearing, smelling, etc.) and interpreting these impressions. To perceive accurately we must first of all have good sense organs. We must also "pay attention." Our past experience and present mood affect perception considerably. For example, different persons "perceive" symphonic music very differently. A deaf person hears only the loud instruments. A musically trained person hears intricate figures, counterpoint, subtle variations. To an unmusical person the performance is only a jumble of sounds. A weary person slumbers through many passages, while someone seated nearby is moved with deep emotion.

Though individuals vary greatly in what and how they perceive, several phenomena of perception are found to be much the same for most persons.

SPAN OF ATTENTION

Over a century ago Sir William Hamilton noted that six or seven separate objects, such as marbles, can be seen clearly at one time. William S. Jevons, well-known British economist and student of logic, shortly afterwards experimented on attention. He threw beans into a small flat box, trying to estimate how many were there as soon as they landed. With 3 or 4 beans he made no errors; with 5 only a few errors. Even with 8 or 10 beans his first glance gave the correct number about half the time.

These early studies of how many objects we can see clearly at a glance, called "attention span," later were confirmed by James McKeen Cattell and others, using more accurate laboratory techniques. Adults apprehend from 6 to 11 objects at a time, averaging 8. If items occur in groups of 3 or 4, many more than 8 can be caught in the immediate span of attention. Cattell found that a subject can note as many as 30 letters in a fraction of a second if the letters make up a meaningful short sentence. Apparently the number of units matters less than the organization of units.

FLUCTUATIONS AND LEVELS OF ATTENTION

A German scientist, V. Urbantschitsch, discovered that a watch, placed at a point where its ticking just barely can be heard, alternates between being heard and not heard. A similar oscillation or fluctuation of attention was noted by a Swiss

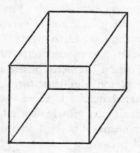

naturalist, L. A. Necker. Sometimes when he observed this diagram of a cube, one surface seemed to be the front; suddenly the cube appeared to shift and another side became the front.

Edgar J. Rubin, Danish psychologist, proved the same true of what he called an "ambiguous" figure:

Sometimes one sees a white goblet, then the figure becomes two faces.

Walter B. Pillsbury asked subjects to look at a small ink dot, and to press a key when their attention wandered or changed. Their attention fluctuated every second or two, on the average; apparently it could not remain absolutely unchanged for more than a very few seconds.

When we "pay attention" to something we bring it to the focus of our consciousness; everything else is relegated to the fringe or margin. Both William James and Edward B. Titchener stressed this contrast between focal and marginal consciousness. The focus, Titchener said, is a high level of attention, the fringe a low level. He illustrated the point with these figures:

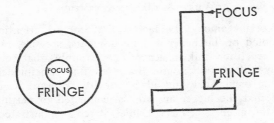

Titchener's pupil, Ludwig R. Geissler, found more than two levels of attention in many persons. Some of his subjects reported they could distinguish three or even more.

INTERFERENCE AND DISTRACTION

Alfred Binet and other early psychologists discovered that two simultaneous activities interfere with each other unless both are extremely easy, or very similar in nature, like patting the head with one hand and the stomach with the other. Apparently we can attend to but one thing at a time. Dictating several letters "at once," or playing ten chess games simultaneously, is possible because attention may alternate rapidly from one item to another.

The best-known distraction study was made by John J. B. Morgan. Subjects learned to punch keys, corresponding to a certain code, on a kind of typewriter. As the subjects punched, bells, buzzers, and other distractors were introduced. These slowed up work, but the subjects soon overcame the noise distractions. Later when the noises ceased, a slump resulted. Momentarily, quiet became a distractor! Morgan found also that during distraction the keys were struck harder, and that subjects tended to speak the letters as they worked, as if it aided them to overcome distraction.

How distractions affect business and industrial workers was studied by Donald Laird, Horace M. Vernon, and others. They showed that sudden or unexpected noises distract much more than continuous sounds; also that stimuli with meaning, like a radio speech, distract more than meaningless noises such as the subdued roar of street traffic.

WHAT ATTRACTS ATTENTION

Important among the factors that compel attention, as first noted by Titchener and his students, are size, motion, color, repetition and, in general, any stimulus that contrasts sharply with its background. These are first principles for advertising men. Analyzing advertisements, Howard K. Nixon found that the bigger an "ad" is, compared to neighboring ones, the more it attracts. Daniel Starch demonstrated that color pages of advertising draw almost twice as much attention as black-and-white pages. That ample white space surrounding an advertisement enhances, by contrast effect, its attention value was noted by Edward K. Strong.

Object Constancy

Individuals learn to perceive objects, regardless of the objects' distance or position, as constant in size, shape, color, and location. This perceptual constancy is learned. A child of three watching cars from a tall building may insist they are small toys; a few years later, he realizes that they are full size, although actually they still make a small image on his retina.

Jerome S. Bruner and Leo J. Postman demonstrated that color constancy develops through experience. They asked subjects to reproduce the colors of familiar shapes (banana, lemon, carrot, tomato) cut from a single piece of orange paper. Subjects reproduced colors of the real objects, not the orange of the paper cut-outs.

Adelbert Ames devised an interesting demonstration that seems to show an effect of learning shape constancy. A cardboard reproduction of a window in perspective (one end is smaller) is placed on a spindle which slowly rotates at 16 r.p.m. When this rotating trapezoidal window is viewed from a few feet away, it appears to oscillate, not turn. The reason is

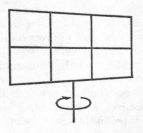

Rotating Trapezoidal Window

that rotation of the figure sometimes brings the small dimension nearest the viewer, which violates the way he is accustomed to seeing rectangles. Hence he tries, unconsciously, to put the figure back in its usual position, which results in the apparent oscillation. This experiment shows that one perceives familiar objects in a constant way; thus we see windows as windows, no matter what their position.

MENTAL SET

Cattell and others discovered that our attitude or expectation influences the speed of our reactions. If we concentrate on the response we must make when we see a light, we react faster than if we fix our attention on the light itself.

How our attitude or "mental set" affects behavior was observed by Narziss Ach, German psychologist. Studying reaction time, he found that subjects reported a period of preparation or "getting set" before the stimulus was given. When the light or bell signal was presented, the response followed almost automatically. Henry J. Watt, an English psychologist working in Germany, discovered that mental set operated similarly in the controlled association test. When a subject is told to "give the opposite" of each word named, he adjusts himself beforehand by thinking of a few examples or perhaps by making gestures. If the word "high" is then given, he responds "low" quickly and without effort. His mental set has prepared him for an efficient response.

Oswald Külpe, a graduate of Wundt's Leipzig laboratory, found that a specific intention to learn nonsense syllables resulted in twice as much actual learning as a mere general observation of the syllables; and subjects do not learn the serial order of nonsense syllables unless specifically directed to, Georg E. Müller and Friedrich Schumann, two other German experimenters, found.

Leonard Carmichael and two associates demonstrated how mental set influences perception. Subjects were shown, briefly, several figures like those in the center below. If told the figures resembled a beehive and eyeglasses, they tended to see those objects and reproduced them as shown on the left. If told they resembled a hat and a dumbbell, they reproduced what appears at the right.

Apparently a mental set can influence the way a subject perceives a stimulus and the way he remembers it.

Elsa Margareeta Siipola showed that mental set can influence the way ambiguous stimuli are interpreted. Two groups of subjects were shown short nonsense words (e.g., "chack," "sael," "wharl") flashed on a screen for about one-tenth of a second. One group was told that the words related to birds or animals; the other group, that the words related to travel or transportation. The group told that they would see terms related to animals or birds typically perceived "chick," "seal," and "whale" instead of "chack," "sael," and "wharl." Those told that the words related to travel perceived "check," "sail," and "wharf."

Bruner and Postman found that mental set can also affect subjects' perception of playing cards. For example, subjects called a red four of spades "spades" and a black four of hearts "hearts." When subjects became aware that the cards were incongruous, they made fewer errors in identification. The set to see cards as they had known them was modified to include unfamiliar cards.

Among American psychologists Robert S. Woodworth probably stressed most the importance of mental set in behavior. He considered "set" a highly selective and active process that favors some responses and prevents others. He distinguished between "preparatory set," in which we adjust ourselves beforehand to make a certain kind of response, and "continuing set," which steers activity already going. A runner awaiting a starting gun or a motorist at a stoplight show preparatory set. A speaker seeking the right words to express his thoughts illustrates continuing set. Attitudes of readiness doubtless have bases in the brain and nervous system, according to Woodworth, though such bases are hard to discover experimentally.

EARLY THEORIES OF PERCEPTION

An eighteenth-century Scottish philosopher, Thomas Reid, distinguished between sensation and perception. His distinction carried over into modern psychology. Sensation, he said, occurs when a sense organ like eyes or ears receives a stimulus. Perception involves sensation, but includes also knowledge of the object perceived and awareness of its existence. A certain stimulus produces *sensations* of redness, roundness, and pleasant odor. But what we *perceive* is a rose.

An important function of perception, Thomas Brown added, is grasping relationships. When two objects are observed together, we perceive similarities or differences between them in size, color, and quality.

Wilhelm Wundt believed that perceptions combine or fuse together a number of sensory elements. Each percept has unique characteristics. Just as hydrogen and oxygen combine to form water, which has properties not found in either component gas, so a percept resulting from several sensations is a new psychological product, or "creative synthesis." This theory resembles John Stuart Mill's earlier idea of "mental chemistry."

William James agreed with Wundt that a percept is more than its component sensations. But he went a step farther in insisting that it cannot be analyzed into them.

James' view was supported by Christian von Ehrenfels, German philosopher and psychologist, who introduced the idea of "form-quality." The form-quality of an object is, in effect, the relationship of all its parts which combine to make up the whole that we see or hear. For example, the form-quality *squareness* depends on the relationship or pattern of its four lines, not on any line separately. This again shows that perception is not a mere sum of sensations, but a new product. Ehrenfels noted temporal as well as spatial form-qualities. The best instance is a musical melody, a pattern of sounds made by combining many separate notes. If the notes are all transposed into another key, the melody remains, showing the same form-quality.

GESTALT PSYCHOLOGY

The notion that perception involves much more than sensation or even combined sensations was clarified and verified experimentally by Max Wertheimer, founder of the school of Gestalt psychology.

About 1910 he discovered that two slits in a screen, lighted up a fraction of a second apart, produced an effect of movement. The light seemed to move from one slit to the other, though no actual movement took place. (Moving pictures are based on this illusion of movement. Actually nothing moves on the screen; we see a rapid succession of slightly differing still pictures which our eyes interpret as movement.)

Impressed by this experimental evidence that perception includes more than is found in separate sensations, Wertheimer and his colleagues Wolfgang Köhler and Kurt Koffka continued experimenting and, as a result, built up the school of Gestalt psychology. "Gestalt" is one of those German words that defies translation. "Form," "figure," "pattern," and "configuration" have been suggested; none is quite right. So "Gestalt" carries over, as is, into English.

Gestalt psychologists hold that every experience is an unanalyzable whole that cannot be understood by breaking it down into parts. The whole is more than the sum of its parts. A landscape is not merely grass plus trees plus sky plus clouds plus other details. It is a distinct percept or experience, with a quality all its own. One may note parts of the whole, but the parts exist in definite relationships to each other. Disturb the relationships and the quality of the whole changes.

To show that perception of relationship is important, Köhler conducted an ingenious experiment with hens. Grain was placed on both white and gray pieces of paper. If a hen pecked at grain on the gray paper, she was permitted to eat. When she pecked at grain on the white paper she was shooed away. After several hundred trials the hens learned to peck only from gray paper. Then Köhler substituted black for the white paper. Would the hens still respond to the gray paper, to which they were conditioned? In almost three-quarters of the trials the animals approached the black rather than the gray paper. In other words they had learned to respond to the relation "darker than," not merely to the gray paper as such. Relationship between light and dark dominated the animals' perception.

Among other relationships commonly perceived, Köhler and Koffka noted that figure and background occur frequently. When we perceive a thing, some aspect of it stands out rather clearly. A figure emerges against a vaguer, more diffuse background. In a symphony the melody is the figure, the harmony and accompaniment are the ground. Sometimes the figure and ground alternate, as in the sketch on page 127 of a vase and two faces. A small boy at the zoo confused figure and ground when he looked at the zebra and said: "Mama, is that a white horse with black stripes, or a black horse with white stripes?"

An interesting principle found by Gestaltists is that we tend to close in or complete an incomplete figure. They call this

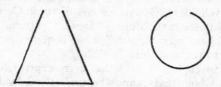

"closure." The figures above we perceive as a triangle and a circle, though actually they are not.

Unconsciously we fill in the gaps and perceive complete figures. We are likely also to establish groupings or patterns in a uniform series of items. Sounds, for instance, are heard in twos, threes, or fours. This grouping tendency, as Wertheimer showed, is helped by proximity, similarity, or other cues.

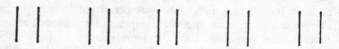

In the figure above we see five pairs of parallel lines. In the figure below, however, we are likely to see four boxes in the middle. The short horizontal lines give this effect:

In the following figure we probably see a diamond formed by the small crosses, and a large cross formed by the circles:

Gestalt psychologists demonstrate clearly that each of our perceptions is a unique pattern of relationships, a unitary experience with qualities and properties of its own. It is a whole greater than the sum of its parts; it cannot be broken up and analyzed without altering the nature of the experience. These principles are the Gestaltists' greatest contribution to psychology.

Optical Illusions

An illusion is a false or distorted perception. Psychologists of the late nineteenth century noted and tried to explain several common illusions.

Wilhelm Wundt observed that we tend to overestimate vertical compared with horizontal distances. In the following figure the vertical line seems longer than the baseline:

Actually they have the same length. Wundt explained this illusion by eye movements; eyes move vertically less often and with less ease than horizontally. Hence a one-inch vertical span seems longer than the same span horizontally.

J. C. Poggendorff and F. Zöllner designed figures to illustrate illusions of direction.

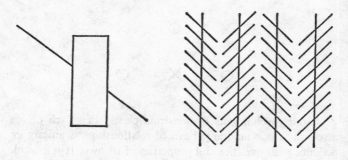

Poggendorff   *Zöllner*

In Poggendorff's figure the lower part of the diagonal line seems not to be a continuation of the upper part. Actually it is. In Zöllner's figure the verticals appear to converge or diverge. In reality they are parallel. A generally accepted explanation of these illusions is that we tend to overestimate the size of small angles and to underestimate the size of large ones. This affects the apparent direction of lines forming the angles.

The famous illusion of F. C. Müller-Lyer, another German psychologist, wherein the line of the right-hand figure appears longer than the line of the left-hand figure, is explained on a Gestalt basis.

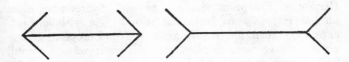

We cannot rid ourselves of the diagonal lines' effect as we observe the horizontals. Hence the line at the right, being part of a larger whole, seems longer. Other theories are proposed, but this has most support.

Other illustrations hinge on contrast effects. Geza Révész, a Hungarian psychologist teaching in Holland, noted a striking one. Which figure is larger?

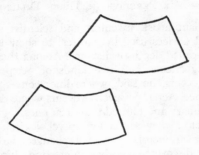

They are alike. The contrast between the long slow bottom curve of the upper figure and the smaller top curve of the lower figure creates the illusion.

Why does the moon look bigger when it is near the horizon than when it is overhead? This illusion has puzzled people for years, thousands of years probably. Not until the 1940's did a satisfactory answer emerge. Edwin G. Boring and A. H. Holway found that the illusion depends on viewing the moon with the eyes lifted. If one stoops over and looks at the moon between one's legs, the illusion disappears, and there is no difference between the appearance of the moon near the horizon and overhead. Evidently perception is affected by bodily orientation and muscular activity.

Evidence that a relationship exists between perception and the culture one lives in is shown by findings summarized by Marshall H. Segall, Donald T. Campbell, and Melville J.

Herskovits. Europeans viewing geometric figures gave more illusion responses to horizontal stimuli (e.g., Müller-Lyer, page 137) than did non-Europeans. Non-European groups generally gave more illusion responses when vertical stimuli were prominent than did Europeans. Half a century ago a famous English anthropologist, W. H. R. Rivers, made similar findings. One hypothesis to explain this unusual finding is that we moderns are used to a "horizontal" world—possibly due to our reading habits, to following moving vehicles with our eyes, and the like—and as a result are more subject to visual distortions in this direction.

How We Perceive in Three Dimensions

The brilliant artist, inventor, and scientist, Leonardo da Vinci, listed devices used by painters to show how far away objects are—called depth or distance. Among them were shadows, shading effects, and two kinds of perspective. Linear perspective occurs, he said, where lines converge to a point in the distance. Aerial perspective occurs where distant objects appear more hazy and blurred than near ones.

These factors now are called "psychological," in contrast to physiological factors or actual changes within the eye.

Leonardo discovered another interesting thing about perceiving depth. In effect it was this. He held a small object about six inches in front of his nose. He shut one eye and with the other looked at a picture on the wall beyond. Part of the picture was cut off from his vision by the object. He then looked at the picture with both eyes. He saw all of it. No part was cut off. In other words, using two eyes he actually *saw behind* an interposed object. Since each eye has a different line of vision, what is cut off from one eye is seen by the other. This revealed the importance of binocular vision.

René Descartes suggested that changes within the eye itself help us gauge the distance of objects. Also the curvature of the eye's lens changes when we shift our gaze from far to near or vice versa. These changes, known respectively as convergence and accommodation, are physiological factors which help us to see distances.

Bishop George Berkeley elaborated Descartes' theories early

in the eighteenth century. He noted three other things that occur when we perceive distance. When an object is near and the eyes converge, the sensation is more intense. When an object is very near, the image is blurred. When the curvature of the eye lens accommodates to close vision in regarding near objects, noticeable strain occurs on the eyes.

The great physicist and physiologist Hermann von Helmholtz added other items. When two distant objects are close together, the nearer object blots out the farther one. If we move the head from side to side or walk forward or backward to examine a distant object, we get a better idea of its distance than if we remain still.

Helmholtz believed that the main helps in judging distance are convergence and accommodation, in other words physiological factors. Present-day psychologists, notably Woodworth, disagree with Helmholtz. The stereoscope reveals the importance of unsuspected psychological factors, namely the three-dimensional effects produced by two-eye vision.

The Stereoscopic Effect

Though Leonardo da Vinci and other early writers noted that our two-eye vision enables us to see behind a nearby object, they overlooked the fact that each eye receives a different image of it. To a British physicist, Charles Whetstone, goes credit for first realizing the importance of this difference. Whetstone invented in 1838 an apparatus he called a "stereoscope." By using mirrors, he presented slightly different pictures to the right and left eyes. The pictures could be adjusted to give a vivid impression of depth. When identical instead of differing pictures were used, no depth effect resulted.

An improved stereoscope soon was devised by Sir David Brewster. The brilliant American poet and physician, Oliver Wendell Holmes, perfected the well-known hand stereoscope, which provided a popular parlor pastime of the '80's and '90's. The stereoscopic lenses, fusing the right and left eye pictures, proved the importance of two-eyed vision in perceiving distance. That the stereoscope does not give the perfect fused image the eyes themselves give suggests that other factors play a part in our ability to see objects in three dimensions.

Nowadays stereoscopic photography has become a popular hobby. With a twin lens camera which simulates the position of the human eyes, two photographs of the same object are taken simultaneously. Transparencies are then made and placed in a viewer, enabling one to see the photographed object as it originally appeared to both eyes.

Since World War II, stereophonic phonographs (and radios using AM-FM tuners) have been produced and widely distributed. The principle involved here is the same as that in stereoscopy. Sound which normally enters one ear is recorded so it can be conducted back to that same ear. For example, when symphonic music is recorded, a microphone on the left picks up the violins strongly for the left ear recording, while one on the right features the woodwinds for the right ear. The recordings are then played simultaneously through two speakers, and the fusion takes place in the brain of the listener.

CHANGES IN PERCEPTION

Since perception is greatly influenced by learning, it should be possible to change one's perception under appropriate laboratory conditions. Apparently hallucinations (perceptual responses that occur in the absence of perceptual stimuli— that is, seeing things that aren't actually there) can be conditioned. Douglas G. Ellson instructed subjects to press a key as soon as they heard a tone. A light preceded the tone as a signal. Soon subjects would press the key after the light, even though the tone was not given. Ellson reasoned that if merely conditioning had occurred, key pressing could be extinguished by repeatedly presenting the light signal without the tone. This did not happen, so he inferred that the tone was hallucinated.

About the turn of the century, G. M. Stratton performed an interesting experiment showing the effects of learning on perception. He wore a pair of inverting lenses, which made the world look upside down. At first, things were very confused as he moved about in this new world. After some days, however, he began to be able to localize objects and to harmonize sounds with observed movements, showing that new adjustments were being made. When the lenses were removed, Stratton again experienced confusion, but he reverted quickly to his original perceptual habits.

More recently, Ivo Kohler in Innsbruck wore half-prism eyeglasses which inverted the upper half of the visual field but not the lower half. After wearing the glasses for about fifty days, he reported only a slight distortion when he looked up, but a great deal when he looked down. It took about forty days after the prisms were removed before downward distortion disappeared.

Kohler also studied the effects of wearing glasses with a blue lens for the left eye and a yellow one for the right eye. Subjects wore these glasses for twenty to sixty days. For several days after they stopped wearing the glasses an eye movement to the left produced a blue color, and one to the right a yellow color. Apparently stimulation from these eye movements became conditioned stimuli for eliciting the perception of blue or yellow.

EFFECTS OF REWARD AND PUNISHMENT

When objects are associated with reward or punishment, perception of those objects is affected. Roy Schafer and Gardner Murphy performed a classic experiment. When a series of figures was presented to subjects, those figures associated with reward were more easily recognized when they were shown later than the unrewarded ones.

The effects of punishment on perception seem to vary with the situation. Charles M. Solley and Gardner Murphy point out that studies have involved two kinds of experimental situations. In one, the stimulus presages punishment from which there is no escape. In the other, the stimulus is a signal that punishment will occur unless the subject performs some appropriate act. If escape from punishment is possible, the stimulus comes to be more readily perceived. If there is no possibility of escape from the adversive stimulation, perceptual sensitivity to the stimulus decreases.

These phenomena make for survival of the organism. When an organism's association with an object or event leads to pleasure, its perception of object or event is enhanced. When pain is encountered in connection with an object, an organism is likely to become more perceptive of the pain producer. But if pain inevitably accompanies an object or event, perceptual discrimination of the pain producer decreases, as a kind of defense mechanism.

PERSONALITY AND PERCEPTION

Our needs, values, and personality characteristics are internal conditions ("intervening variables") that can influence our perception. David C. McClelland and John W. Atkinson studied the influence of hunger on perception. Subjects were divided into groups and given a perception test: one group took the test one hour after eating; a second group took it four hours after eating; and a third group, sixteen hours after eating. Ambiguous stimuli were projected on a screen, and subjects were given such information as "All the people in this picture are enjoying themselves. What are they doing?" The hungrier subjects saw more food-related objects, and perceived food objects as larger than non-food objects.

Jerome Bruner and C. C. Goodman found differences in size estimation of coins between children from poor homes and those from well-to-do homes. Children from poor homes overestimated the size of coins. Apparently money looks bigger if you don't have it.

Muzafer Sherif made a provocative discovery related to the "autokinetic effect." The autokinetic effect occurs when one looks at a pinpoint of light in a dark room. Although the light source is stationary, it seems to move. Every individual soon sees the light moving in a unique pattern. In Sherif's experiments, individuals compared their patterns. When they again looked at the pinpoint of light, it was found that they now saw patterns similar to each other's patterns, rather than those that they had previously seen. This shows how group norms affect an individual's perception. The implications of this are tremendous. Not only are understanding and concepts to a large extent a product of group membership, but so also is that which people actually *see* and *hear*.

Personality traits have been found to affect perception.

Some people must categorize things clearly and precisely. They cannot tolerate ambiguity or uncertainty. By means of personality and attitude studies, Else Frenkel-Brunswik picked out persons prejudiced toward relations with minority groups. She compared their reactions with those of unprejudiced persons to varied ambiguous stimuli. For example, a picture of a dog was followed by a series of other pictures which gradually made the transition to the picture of a cat. The prejudiced group tended to hold to the original perception (dog) longer than the other; they were inclined to make definite interpretations and adhere to them.

SUMMARY OF VIEWS OF PERCEPTION

Summarizing psychological studies, we see that perceiving has several characteristic features. It is selective; we react to but one aspect of the total environment. It involves meaning in terms both of past experience and of present mental set. And it depends upon experiences we have had in becoming familiar with, and adjusting to, our environment.

There have been three prominent points of view about perception: 1. the "copy" theory; 2. the Gestalt theory; and 3. the learning, or behavioristic, theory. The notion that what one perceives is a copy of reality is the oldest view, and has been reformulated in a sophisticated way by James J. and Eleanor J. Gibson. Perceptions are not created by the observer, either out of past experience or by innate preknowledge. Knowledge of the real world through perception is as complete as the incoming stimuli. Our responses improve as we are able to detect ever-smaller nuances of stimuli. Differences in perceptions can be explained by differences in attention of sense organs.

Some of the principles of Gestalt psychology already have been presented (page 133). These principles assume that the organism contributes something to perception—stimuli are automatically organized or categorized into assimilable form. Gestalt psychologists believe that there are basic innate determinants of perception.

Learning has been emphasized as a determinant of perception for many years. Perceptual constancies and differences can be explained as the result of one's experiences. We learn to see a circle as circular no matter what the angle of observation; we learn to see a cow as a large animal regardless of distance from the cow; and we learn to perceive differently as a result of experience (coins apparently look bigger to persons from poor families).

Chapter VIII

COGNITION AND SYMBOLIC BEHAVIOR

BINET   KÜLPE   BÜHLER   THORNDIKE
MORGAN   KÖHLER   HUNTER   DEWEY   HOBHOUSE
MAIER   HOLLINGWORTH   WATSON   CLAPARÈDE
GALTON   PIAGET   WHORF   HULL   SKINNER
JAENSCH   MOWRER   OSGOOD

*Does thinking go on in images? Do animals think?
How is reasoning related to thinking? What kinds of
images exist? What are the leading theories of
dream interpretation? Under what conditions does
creative thinking occur?*

Philosophers and the earliest psychologists assumed that
thinking, like remembering, occurs by means of association of
ideas and images. Late nineteenth-century psychologists began to study thinking experimentally. In connection with their
investigations of learning they experimented upon problem-
solving in animals and human beings. More recently psychologists have turned to the study of logical reasoning and to the
processes of creative thought.

The Nature of Thought Processes

Alfred Binet, later to become famous as the originator of
intelligence tests, pioneered in the investigation of thinking
and reasoning. Using his two daughters as subjects, he asked
them to describe their thought processes. He found very often
that no images or other sensory components were present.
Binet therefore concluded, contrary to tradition and to earlier

theories of his own, that images are not essential to thinking. The materials of thinking are simply *pensées,* or thoughts incapable of further analysis.

About the same time Oswald Külpe and several of his students at Würzburg began systematic study of thinking. Külpe doubted that thoughts go on in terms of sensations, images, and feelings, as had been claimed by the dean of German psychologists, Wilhelm Wundt.

The first of the Würzburg investigations was by Karl Marbe, who reported on the process of judgment. Subjects lifted two weights and judged which was heavier, then were asked to introspect. Though judgments were usually correct, the subjects often had no introspections to report; i.e., experienced no sensations or images. Marbe concluded that some kinds of experience must be present to account for the judgments; he called them, vaguely, "conscious attitudes."

A few years later Karl Bühler studied thought processes in more complex problems such as interpreting paradoxes and fables. He too concluded that thinking can occur without images and sensations. Almost simultaneously in America, Robert S. Woodworth published his findings on "imageless thought." Introspection often revealed images and sensations, but these seemed unimportant to the content or meaning of a thought. Woodworth emphasized consciousness of relationships as the core of thinking processes.

These findings were roundly attacked by Edward B. Titchener, who insisted there can be nothing in consciousness except sensations, images, and feelings. Conscious attitudes, feelings of relationship, and mental sets, he said, are actually kinesthetic (muscular) sensations or images, not new kinds of thought elements at all.

By the time of World War I, the controversy over imageless thought had quieted down, but experimental work continued. Thomas V. Moore, of the Catholic University of America, for example, studied the time relations between appearance of meaning and of images in thinking. He found that meanings generally came first, therefore must be independent of images.

One of Külpe's successors, Otto Selz, noted the presence in

thinking of a guiding principle or plan
called an "anticipatory schema." Suppose
name the capital of each country in a list t
instruction gives the subject a steer or an
facilitates his responses. Selz's "anticipatory sch
to Marbe's "conscious attitudes" and Woodwo.
of relationship.

The controversy over imageless thought has been decided.
The verdict is against Wundt and Titchener, who insisted
that thought consists only of sensations, images, and feelings.
Probably most psychologists nowadays would agree with Harry
L. Hollingworth, who stated that thinking goes on in terms
of all kinds of cues from our previous experience.

In his *Psychology of Thought*, Hollingworth said:

I think of objects and events which are not present—say of a number of people I have known. How can I do this? A simple way would
be for part of each person to be at hand—say each man's hat, or
perhaps his photograph, presenting his physiognomy. I may use
names which have been associated with the men, speaking, writing,
or looking at them. Or I may take attitudes in each case, characteristic of the way in which each person has affected me; I may experience what I call feelings, appropriate to each. Or if I have visual
imagery at my command, such imagery may also be employed.

Photograph, name, gesture, attitude, feeling, and image all
have meaning. Any one of these "redintegrates," or calls to
mind, the person or event it symbolizes. Any or all of these
varied items may function in the thinking processes.

BODILY BASES OF THINKING

The behaviorist John Watson thrust aside all introspective
interpretations of thinking. Thought, he said, is nothing but
talking to ourselves. Most of it occurs as subvocal speech, that
is as almost imperceptible movements of muscles in the
tongue, throat, and larynx. Evidence for this theory, according
to Watson, is found in the young child's tendency to think
out loud, a process which is discouraged by social pressure,
so the child learns to think, as it were, behind closed lips.
Watson believed that thinking might go on in terms of nearly

cle action. He cited deaf and dumb individuals who
k, just as they talk, in hand movements. Some have even
been observed to use finger language in their dreams.

Psychologists in general do not accept Watson's theory.
Experimental work has failed to reveal any correlation between thinking and movement of vocal muscles. Other objec-
tions have been advanced. Woodworth, for example, points
out that words sometimes cannot be found to express a meaning which is very clearly in mind. Or again, a well-known
poem can be recited while one thinks of something entirely
different. Finally, says Woodworth, thinking involves something new, the seeing of relationships; it is hard to account
for this solely on the basis of muscular activity.

Psychologists speak of two theories of thinking—the *central*
theory, and *motor* or *peripheral* theory. According to the *central* theory, thinking and reasoning depend on brain processes
alone. Adherents of the newer *motor* or *peripheral* theory,
like Watson, maintain that thinking is a function, very largely
at least, of muscular responses and of neural activity in outlying portions of the nervous system. Those supporting this
theory have shown that muscular activity often accompanies
thinking, but thus far they have not proved that it is essential
to or identical with the thinking process itself.

ANIMAL INTELLIGENCE

In accordance with his ideas on evolution, Charles Darwin
maintained that continuity exists between lower animals and
the highest humans. Both have similar senses, instincts, emotions, and mental processes. Human beings are of course superior, but, says Darwin, animals possess in lesser degree the
same traits as man. To prove his point he cited many anecdotes illustrating high animal intelligence. An apostle of Darwin, George J. Romanes, presented still more stories of the
same sort. In his book, *Animal Intelligence*, Romanes says
that fish display emotions of anger, pugnacity, fear, and jealousy; social, sexual, and parental feelings, and play and curiosity. He finds in birds signs of affection, sympathy, pride,
vindictiveness, and aesthetic emotions. Sagacity, slyness, and
keen reasoning power are credited to dogs. Cats and monkeys,

also highly intelligent, "delight in torturing for torture's sake." Many of Romanes' anecdotes, cited to back up his interpretations, are from pet lovers. A short illustration is the following:

One day the cat and the parrot had a quarrel. I think the cat had upset Polly's food, or something of that kind; however they seemed all right again. An hour or so after, Polly was standing on the edge of the table; she called out in a tone of extreme affection, 'Puss, puss, come then—come then, pussy.' Pussy went and looked up innocently enough. Polly with her beak seized a basin of milk standing by, and tipped the basin and all its contents over the cat; then chuckled diabolically, of course broke the basin, and half drowned the cat.

As a corrective for such unverified and unscientific anecdotes, an English psychologist named Lloyd Morgan insisted that no behavior should be interpreted as the product of higher mental faculties if it could result from simpler processes. This principle came to be known as "Morgan's Canon." When applied to the anecdotes of Darwin, Romanes, and others it showed that many human characteristics had been improperly read into animal behavior.

Animals can, however, learn to solve problems, as Morgan showed. He noted that his dog learned, after an hour or two, to pick up a knobbed stick near the knob end. The dog, said Morgan, did not reason or perceive relationships. "The process throughout was one of trial and error; gradually he found the most comfortable way of carrying the stick, and adopted it." Placed in new circumstances, an animal chances, through trial and error, to hit upon a solution.

The work of Edward L. Thorndike came shortly after that of Morgan. Thorndike studied the behavior of animals seeking escape from a puzzle box to obtain food outside. Escape could be accomplished in such ways as pulling a string or turning a catch on the door. Thorndike found much clawing, biting, mewing, and other signs of trial-and-error behavior, in the course of which "accidental success" typically occurs. With successive trials the animal gradually focuses its activity in the area of the string or catch until the trick is learned. Like Morgan, Thorndike believed that reasoning and the seeing of relationships do not characterize problem solving in animals.

But belief in the almost superhuman abilities of animals persisted. The tallest tales concerned "Clever Hans" and the Horses of Elberfeld. Hans, a stallion, was able to spell out names, count objects in the room, and solve problems in arithmetic. The Elberfeld horses could add and subtract, tapping out answers with their feet. One of the horses, Muhamed, learned to do problems of square root after only one lesson, according to his trainer!

Psychologists studied the performance of these amazing animals. Edouard Claparède noticed that the horses could not solve problems of which he himself did not know the answer. Others found the animals curiously at a loss when their trainer was out of the room. The psychologists concluded that the horses had learned to react to slight nods and other cues furnished—often quite unconsciously—by people present in the room. The animals' *perception* was developed to an incredible degree, but not their linguistic and mathematical ability!

INSIGHT IN ANIMALS

An English psychologist, Leonard T. Hobhouse, disagreed with Morgan and Thorndike. He believed animals, like human beings, can perceive relations, though in lesser degree. Hobhouse tested his theory on otters, apes, elephants, dogs, and cats. Animals can get food, he found, by pulling a string attached to it, by reaching it with a stick, by removing an obstacle, by pushing food out of a tube with a rod. For Hobhouse the secret of problem solving was seeing objects in relation to each other; he proved animals can do this.

Robert M. Yerkes discovered that a young orangutan could get the idea of stacking boxes and standing on them to reach food, after being shown how. He noted several steps which apes take in problem solving: they inspect the problem, attend to it, try out various responses, and sometimes solve it suddenly. After getting the solution apes can repeat it and transfer it to similar problems.

As we have already seen, Wolfgang Köhler, the Gestalt psychologist, introduced the term "insight" to describe solving problems by grasping relations, especially if the solution is

een suddenly. Köhler found many examples of insight in
pes. They got the point of piling up boxes to reach fruit hung
rom the ceiling. They knocked down fruit with sticks or small
ranches. With a small stick they reached for a large one to
ake in food outside the cage. Occasionally they could fit a
mall stick into a hole in the end of a larger one to make a
ong reaching tool.

Köhler contrasted insight with trial and error. Maze prob-
ems, or Thorndike's puzzle boxes, solved by trial and error,
e said, do not indicate animal problem-solving ability be-
ause they give no chance to see relations. They are solved by
hance; a better problem is one where the whole situation can
e surveyed, and the subject can see its relationships.

Köhler proved that apes have insight. Two University of
California experimenters, Edward C. Tolman and Charles
H. Honzik, wondered about insight in lower animals like rats.
They built an "elevated maze," without side walls, so the rat
could see the whole maze as he ran it. Of two possible paths
to the goal, one short and one long, the rats chose the short
path 90% of the time. When a barrier was put in that could
be passed only by taking the longer route, all but one of the
rats immediately chose the longer path. By observing the
whole maze problem they showed immediate insight.

An ingenious test of animal thinking was made by Walter
S. Hunter. He devised a "temporal maze," in which an animal
had to make, on successive trials, different responses to the
same situation. Rats learned to turn right on the first trial,
left on the second, right on the third, and so on. They did not
learn to go right on the first two trials, and left on the next
two. Some higher animals, including cats, dogs, raccoons, and
monkeys, did master this. Children and adults learn it easily,
of course. Generally they verbalize "twice to the right, then
twice to the left." Animals successful in this kind of problem
must have some ability to symbolize or to count; both are
important in thinking at the human level.

Norman R. F. Maier believes that animals which can combine in one act two or more reactions learned separately before, can be said to reason. He taught rats to get food on a
low table. He taught them also to run a maze. Then he put a
barrier around the food, but made it possible to reach the

food by a roundabout course via the maze. Some rats promptly combined the two kinds of experience and got the food.

In 1945 H. G. Birch presented chimpanzees with the hoe problem illustrated.

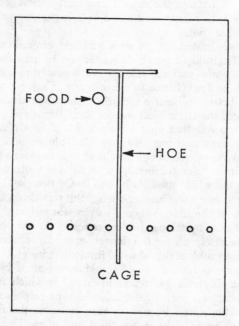

The Hoe Problem

The animal was simply required to rake the food in. Four out of six animals failed to solve the problem within the 30-minute time limit. Birch then provided sticks for his animals to play with. After experience with these the chimpanzees readily solved the hoe problem. This indicates that insight depends on a background of simple trial-and-error or operant habits.

Harry Harlow in 1951 argued that it is not necessary to postulate two distinct processes (trial-and-error and insight) to explain problem solving. Elementary habits are established by trial-and-error behavior. These habits, through *stimulus generalization* (transfer into other similar situations), make possible the more complex insightful behavior.

THINKING IN CHILDREN

Walter S. Hunter devised a "delayed reaction" apparatus to test simple thinking in animals and children. Through a door subjects see three boxes; one containing food is lighted momentarily.

Rats and dogs could not go to the correct box without remaining pointed toward it. Hunter proved that young children could be delayed and distracted a long time and still pick out the right box. Children able to talk may have said "middle one" or some similar phrase that became a cue. But even a child of 13 months, too young to talk, succeeded. Evidently some symbols or cues operated—a kind of rudimentary thinking.

Jean Piaget, a famous Swiss psychologist, showed that the thinking of children under 7 or 8 years of age is self-centered, and vague about relative judgments and cause and effect. A 5-year-old child, for instance, knows that Geneva and Switzerland go together, but has no notion of the part-whole relationship. A child of 8 begins to reflect, reason, and understand logical relationships.

On the other hand, very young children's thinking shows insight. Augusta Alpert gave 2- to 4-year-old children problems similar to Köhler's in studying apes. The youngsters showed immediate insights oftener than the apes in stacking boxes to reach a toy, or raking a toy into a play pen with a stick. Sometimes the insights were incomplete, or they arrived gradually, which occurs also in adult reasoning. Much trial and error was used, of course.

PROBLEM-SOLVING IN HUMAN BEINGS

Just what goes on in a person's mind while he works at solving mechanical puzzles interested Henry A. Ruger. Subjects were asked to take apart a variety of metal links. They used random trial and error, as animals did in the experiments of Hobhouse and Thorndike. But much of the human trial and error went on mentally; subjects thought out certain moves and their consequences without actually making the moves. Ruger found that his subjects often got the point in a flash. Such sudden solutions generally came from analyzing or locating a part of the puzzle that caused the difficulty. This analysis was helped by a carry-over from similar problems that the subject had solved. A favorable attitude toward the problem seemed to speed up its solution. Subjects did best when absorbed in the work, unaware they were being watched. They excelled when willing and able to discard unsuccessful leads and to try out new ones. Ruger showed that human problem-solving is not a single process. It may involve trial and error in the form of actual manipulation, mental trial and error, analyzing the problem, rapidly seeing the point, or hours later getting the solution in a flash.

Unwarranted assumptions or mental sets give subjects a good deal of trouble with thinking problems, M. E. Bulbrook and Norman R. F. Maier found. Bulbrook asked subjects to change the color pattern of a string of beads without unstringing them or breaking the thread. Few subjects thought of breaking the beads. They wrongly assumed it was forbidden.

Often subjects fail to solve problems because they cannot overcome habitual responses. In Maier's experiments one solution, for instance, involved tying pliers to a cord and swinging them like a pendulum. Half the subjects failed because pliers were firmly fixed in their minds as a tool, not as a weight.

Maier also showed that the problem-solving ability of subjects can be improved by teaching them to abandon unsuccessful leads and keep their minds open for new ideas.

Karl Duncker gave students several simple problems. One required subjects to mount three candles on a door. This could be solved by tacking three small cardboard boxes to the door in such a way that the candles could be fastened upright on the boxes. Materials were presented in two ways: 1. boxes, tacks, candles, and matches were scattered randomly on a table; 2. tacks, candles, and matches were placed separately in the three boxes. All subjects solved the problem when materials were presented the first way (scattered). Only about half succeeded when materials were presented the second way (in the boxes). In the second case, Duncker said, solution is interfered with by *mediating verbal responses*, or symbols which stand for something else. The filled boxes are likely to be regarded as "containers," not as a means to the solution. The symbol, "container" is a mediating response.

A. S. Luchins gave this type of problem to subjects: Given three jars of 21 quarts, 3 quarts, and 127 quarts, how would one measure out exactly 100 quarts? After the first six problems, subjects were given problems that could be more efficiently solved by using only two of the measures, though all three measures *could* be used. Subjects kept on working by the more complicated method, indicating that habits or fixations established by previous experience tend to persist.

How do these very important new ideas or "slants" arise? The French psychologist, Edouard Claparède, suggests a theory based on "resonance." The nature of a problem, he says, calls forth "as if by a kind of internal resonance" the items in our past experience which may be useful in satisfying the present need.

REASONING

Reasoning is thinking which follows an orderly logical sequence. In his book, *How We Think*, John Dewey gives a good example of reflective thinking, or reasoning. On a ferryboat he noticed a long white pole, with a ball at the tip, projecting nearly horizontally from an upper deck. He first thought it was a flagpole, but soon doubted this because it was horizontal and had no ropes attached to it. He then tried other possibilities. Perhaps it was an ornament. But even tugboats carried such poles, so this hypothesis was rejected. Possibly it was part of a wireless, except that wireless apparatus would be placed on top of the pilothouse, the highest point on the boat.

Still another hypothesis arose: the pole might be for the purpose of pointing out the direction in which the boat is moving. This idea seemed plausible since the pole was so placed a steersman could easily see the tip from his pilothouse. Such poles would also be useful on tugboats. The hypothesis was accepted since it fitted the facts and seemed more probable than any of the others.

Five distinct steps occur in reasoning, Dewey says. First, a problem, perplexity, or difficulty arises to start the process. Then comes locating and defining the difficulty—determining carefully what the problem really is. Next, a hypothetical solution is suggested. Next comes the essence of reasoning: developing each hypothesis until one emerges that meets all requirements. Verification completes the process; observation or, as in scientific work, experimentation provides this.

Dewey says his five steps generally, though not inevitably, occur in the order given. A trained mind best grasps what each case requires in observation, and in forming, developing, and testing ideas. It also profits most from past mistakes. "What is important," says Dewey, "is that the mind should be sensitive to problems and skilled in methods of attack and solution."

Psychologists, like philosophers, distinguish between deductive and inductive reasoning.

DEDUCTIVE REASONING

Deduction proceeds from the general to the particular, according to well-established rules of logic. It is well illustrated in geometry where from certain broad axioms and postulates all sorts of conclusions can be deduced about the nature of triangles, and squares, and circles. Deduction is the fundamental method of philosophy and mathematics.

The best example of deduction is the syllogism, which dates back to the ancient Greeks. A syllogism consists of three statements—a major premise, a minor premise, and a conclusion deduced from the premises. If the major and minor premises are:

> All men are mortal;
> Socrates is a man;

the inevitable conclusion then is "Socrates is mortal."

Diagrams often aid deductive reasoning. An eighteenth-century Swiss mathematician, L. Euler, first used them. He pictured syllogisms thus:

Since "all men are mortal," "men," shown by a small circle, fall within the larger category of "mortal." Since "Socrates is a man," "Socrates" belongs inside the "men" circle.

At a glance we now see Socrates must be included in the larger circle "mortal."

Euler diagrams help most with difficult syllogisms. For example, is the following reasoning correct?

> All P's are S's;
> Some P's are Q's;
> Therefore some Q's are S's.

It may help us if we see circle P included by circle S, and circle Q intersecting both of them:

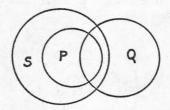

Since circle P must be entirely within circle S, and since some of circle Q must be within P, some of Q is bound to be found inside S. The conclusion, as stated, is correct.

Whether or not people tend to use diagrams when reasoning syllogistically was tested by Gustav Störring, a German psychologist. Though some subjects used diagrams, he found that often they did not. They reached conclusions directly from the premises, without visualizing.

A curious cause of *fallacies* (errors) in syllogistic reasoning was demonstrated by Robert S. Woodworth and S. B. Sells. They called it the "atmosphere effect." Take the syllogism:

> All x's are y's;
> All x's are z's;
> Therefore all y's are z's.

To most persons the conclusion sounds right. Actually it is wrong. The correct answer is "Some y's are z's." Why does the wrong one seem right? Because, says Woodworth, the word "all" in each premise builds up a general impression or atmosphere that makes "all" seem valid in the conclusion.

The atmosphere effect extends to speaking and writing, Woodworth discovered. We tend to make verbs agree with the singular or plural impression a sentence conveys, instead of with the grammatical subject. He cited examples from psychology books, "*Is* trial and error blind or not?" and "A series of experiments *were* conducted . . ." Apparently we respond to general impressions, instead of to the relationship of parts.

Many reasoning problems, of course, require deduction though not presented in syllogistic form. Cyril Burt, English psychologist, made up a test of reasoning ability for children. It consisted of items like these:

In our school a third of the school play football and a third play cricket. Are there any who play neither football nor cricket?
                    Yes   No   Can't tell

My brother writes: "I have walked over from Byford Wood today, where I had the misfortune, yesterday, to break a limb." Can you guess from this which limb he probably broke?
                Right arm   Left arm   Right leg   Left leg

Burt found the way a problem is worded greatly affects the ease of solution. About half the 8-year-olds figured out this one:

Edith is fairer than Olive, but she is darker than Lily. Who is darker, Olive or Lily?

Reworded thus, almost 75% got it:

Lily is fairer than Edith; Edith is fairer than Olive. Who is the fairest, Lily or Olive?

Complicated wording, or including irrelevant material, made reasoning hard even for older children and adults.

INDUCTIVE REASONING

Induction means drawing a generalization from a series of particular experiences. A child, for instance, forms the general concept "animal," after experience with dogs, cats, rabbits, squirrels, and so on. The law of gravity is a product of inductive reasoning. So are other scientific principles.

CONCEPT FORMATION

In time the "buzzing, blooming confusion" (as William James called it) of the newborn's world falls into meaningful categories through the formation of concepts. After a person responds a number of times to a class of experiences that have common characteristics, he develops a *concept*, or general notion about the characteristics of that class of experiences. For example, as a child has experiences with dogs he learns to respond "dog" in the presence of animals that have the common characteristics of four legs, a tail, fur, and a bark.

Psychologists differ about just what is meant by "common characteristics" that figure so prominently in concept formation. Three leading theories are worth noting:

1. *Identical elements.* In the 1920's Clark Hull began a classic study of concept formation by assuming that identical elements are abstracted from stimuli when concepts are formed. He paired complex Chinese characters with English words and presented them to subjects. The Chinese characters varied, but those having identical checkmark-like elements were paired with the same words. Although these elements varied in position within characters, subjects were able to associate the proper word with the correct element, even though many could not recognize or verbalize that element.

2. *Perceptual relations.* K. L. Smoke in 1932 gave experimental evidence to support the notion of common perceptual relations. He arranged stimulus objects that had perceptual relationships but not identical elements. For example, a ring, a ball, and the moon all have the characteristic of roundness and can be described by the concept "round"; they do not have identical elements. Given these stimuli, the subjects developed concepts on the basis of perceptual relations, indicating that identical elements are not necessary for concept formation.

3. *Mediating* or *symbolic processes.* A third group holds that common characteristics not classifiable either as identical elements or perceptual relations are found in groupings such as "vegetables." Vegetables may have neither identical elements nor perceptual relations. Still they have characteristics in common. These common characteristics are mediating responses (verbalizations such as "vegetable").

H. B. Reed in 1946 demonstrated how the last process works by a rather complicated experiment involving a special set of flash cards that he presented to subjects. He wanted to see whether students can learn faster by using verbal mediators.

EXAMPLES FROM REED'S FLASH CARDS

		CONCEPT TO BE
SYLLABLE	FOUR WORDS	FORMED
DAX	BOARD–BEAST–BLUE–BEHIND	} Color
DAX	ANYWHERE–GREEN–ALOUD–BUTTER	
YOF	PEN–HAT–CAT–MAIL	} Animal
YOF	LION–CLIP–GRASS–KNIFE	

One word on each card was in some way similar or related to one word on other cards. In the example above, "blue" and "green" are related; both belong to the concept "color." On the back of cards containing related words was printed the same nonsense syllable. For example, on the back of cards containing instances of "color" was the syllable DAX. On the back of cards containing instances of "animal" was the syllable YOF. Just after showing a card to his subjects, the experimenter spoke the nonsense syllable printed on the back. When he showed the card bearing the words BOARD–BEAST–BLUE–BEHIND, he said the syllable DAX. When he showed the card bearing the words PEN–HAT–CAT–MAIL, he said the syllable YOF. Subjects were to identify the concept (by finding the related words) and to associate it with the appropriate nonsense syllable.

Some subjects were told merely to learn the correct nonsense syllable for each card. Others were told that each nonsense syllable represented a certain concept (e.g., DAX cards contained words in the concept "color"). The subjects who were given the "concept" clues both learned and retained more than subjects who were not. Apparently the "clued" subjects actively tried out various *verbal mediators* (color, animal, etc.) to arrive at their concepts. This indicates that concepts are formed by means of common mediating symbols.

Edna Heidbreder had a group of subjects learn to attach names to groups of visual stimuli. Her subjects learned to form concepts with varying difficulty, ranging from the concepts readily formed from the most concrete stimuli to those slowly formed from the most abstract stimuli. She attributed this to a special factor, the "hierarchy of dominance." Concrete concepts (such as "dog") are easy to form since instances of them can be perceived directly, whereas concepts of number, for example, are difficult to attain because they cannot actually be perceived but are merely embodied in concrete objects. "Dog" is based on concrete stimuli (dogs); "three" is based on *threeness* (three dogs, three books, three words . . .).

VERBAL BEHAVIOR

Most people assume that reality as we know it is independent of language; that any idea expressed in one language can be translated into another language. Evidence to the contrary is given by B. L. Whorf, an engineer who extensively studied American Indian languages. Often he found direct translations impossible. For instance, the distinctions between past, present, and future are not even made in the Navajo Indian language. Whorf concluded that a people whose language differs markedly from other languages also conceives of the world very differently.

The premise that environmental conditions shape language structure is widely accepted. But whether and how language shapes conceptual and thinking processes is still controversial. Certain languages may be more efficient for the development of science or mystical philosophies than others.

Only recently have psychologists given serious attention to analyzing verbal behavior. Skinner uses operant principles (see pages 106–7) to explain language. He believes verbal responses developed in man because they led to more frequent reinforcement; when a person asks for a banana and gets it, this is easier than climbing a tree to get one; he then has more time available to seek other reinforcers (drive satisfiers). A child is taught to say a word by reinforcing—e.g., praising—babbling sounds that approximate the proper word sound in the presence of the object. For example, when a child utters a series of "da-da-da's" in the presence of the father, this is reinforced (praised) as it approximates "daddy." Conversation originates and continues because it is reinforcing (satisfying) to all involved: information is exchanged, recognition or compliments are given.

Sign or word learning is explained by O. Hobart Mowrer by a variation of the principle of classical conditioning. When the word "Tom" is paired with the man Tom repeatedly, "Tom" comes to elicit a response similar to that elicited by Tom the man. This kind of conditioning may show how sentences convey meaning. In the sentence "Tom is a thief," responses to thief have already been learned. When "thief" and "Tom" are paired, the response elicited by "thief" comes to be elicited by "Tom." Such work on syntax has just begun, but it promises to be more fruitful than either word or concept learning in understanding complex verbal behavior. Mowrer is a pioneer in this field.

Charles E. Osgood has gone far in developing the notion of *mediation*. If an individual screams "Ouch!" when he touches a hot stove and this is seen by another, the observer —provided the exclamation "Ouch!" has meaning for him— henceforth will avoid the hot stove. Thus the term "Ouch!" *mediates* avoidance behavior. This partly explains the vicarious function of verbal behavior.

MEASUREMENT OF MEANING

Connotative word meanings, or meanings suggested by a word rather than specifically denoted by it, vary with individuals according to what culture, social class, race, sex, or group they belong to. Osgood developed a scale for measuring connotative meaning; he calls it the *semantic differential*. Subjects are asked to rate words, such as "polite," using scales similar to the ones shown below. Subjects who think along similar lines tend to rate words similarly. Differences result from the variables named above—culture, social class, etc.

This technique, when refined by a statistical process known as *factor analysis*, makes possible the study of how human beings categorize or form concepts about their world. Possibly different semantic dimensions (conceptual structures) can be found for different groups of people. Thus far all concept formation appears to have at least three major dimensions: 1. an *evaluative* dimension (good-bad, clean-dirty, etc.), 2. a

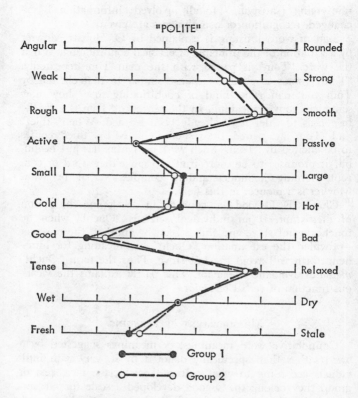

Semantic Differential Scale for the Word "Polite"

potency dimension (strong-weak, large-small), and 3. an *activity* dimension (fast-slow, active-passive, etc.).

NEUROPHYSIOLOGICAL INVESTIGATIONS

Using primates as subjects, C. F. Jacobsen and associates in the 1930's experimented to determine where the brain centers for various types of behavior are located. The technique usually involves determining an animal's performance capacity, destroying a portion of its brain, then testing its final performance capacity. Even when prefrontal lobes were removed (lobectomy) discrimination problems were solved successfully, also problem boxes with levers and cranks. Delayed reaction problems, on the other hand, could not be solved, indicating a marked lack of immediate memory. When the lobectomy was performed on only one side, few if any differences in performance were observed.

Robert B. Malmo found that monkeys with both frontal lobes removed could solve delayed reaction problems if kept in darkness during the delay. This indicates that organisms without frontal lobes are very susceptible to interference or immediate memory loss.

Norman R. F. Maier, using rats as subjects, found that removing critical tissue beyond 18 percent had harmful effects on "reasoning" behavior. Location of the removed tissue made no difference.

The use of electrical stimulation of various portions of the brain promises to be fruitful as a means of investigating relationships between brain areas and thought.

IMAGES

We have three kinds of mental images. One is the after-image, wherein we see, hear, or feel an object for a brief instant after it is removed. In vision there are positive and negative after-images. In the positive we see an object as it was just before disappearing. After a light is turned out, for example, we have a fleeting image of the bulb or lampshade. Negative after-images are an opposite or "complementary" sensation of color or brightness. If we gaze for half a minute at a spot of bluish green, then look a few inches to right or left, we see a red image of the same size and shape, which lasts for several seconds. The negative after-image of an electric light is a black image of the bulb. After-images result from a lag in our sensory receptors.

Memory images, less vivid and accurate than after-images, are duplicates of original sensations and perceptions which may occur when we recall previous experiences.

Eidetic images are amazingly vivid, almost photographic,

reproductions of objects recently seen. They are common among children but rare in adults.

Early research on imagery dealt with memory images almost exclusively.

EARLY THEORIES OF IMAGERY

In the eighteenth and early nineteenth centuries, psychologists used the term "image" synonymously with "idea," "association," and "thought." They assumed memory and thinking involved definite imagery. But they did not test their assumptions experimentally.

David Hume, a philosopher, distinguished between what he called "impression" on the one hand (later termed sensation or perception) and image or idea, on the other. Impressions, said Hume, occur in the presence of an object; images and ideas in its absence. Impressions are vivid; images are faint copies of original impressions. Today the distinction seems obvious. At that time (1739) it was a striking departure from traditional thinking.

David Hartley, a pioneer neurologist, believed images have a bodily basis. Sensations cause nerve vibrations and arouse miniature, feeble vibrations in the brain, causing images. To show the interdependence of sensations and images, Hartley cited the positive after-image, really a persistence of sensation after the stimulus ceases. Usually images are weaker than sensations, though not always. In dreams, for instance, images may be as vivid as actual sensations. Whether weak or strong, they originate in the brain, Hartley claimed. Though even now little is known about the neurology of images, they are still thought to result from brain processes.

James Mill, British psychologist, economist, and historian, believed images are "copies" of sensations. Though the two usually can be distinguished, sometimes they are confused. Sensation must occur first, however. After seeing the sun, said Mill, shutting one's eyes does not prevent one from thinking of it. A copy or image is still present, distinct from the sensation yet more like it than anything else can be.

Galton's Study

In 1860 Gustav Theodor Fechner, a German experimental psychologist, reported that many persons lack imagery. Twenty years later Francis Galton announced astonishing results of a questionnaire on mental imagery.

Galton's survey, the first large-scale questionnaire in psychology, began as follows:

> Before addressing yourself to any of the Questions, think of some definite object—suppose it is your breakfast-table as you sat down to it this morning—and consider carefully the picture that rises before your mind's eye.

(Questions)

1. *Illumination*—Is the image dim or fairly clear? Is its brightness comparable to that of the actual scene?

2. *Definition*—Are all the objects pretty well defined at the same time, or is the place of sharpest definition at any one moment more contracted than it is in a real scene?

3. *Colouring*—Are the colours of the china, of the toast, bread-crust, mustard, meat, parsley, or whatever may have been on the table, quite distinct and natural?

Many of Galton's subjects were scientific men, chosen as the most likely to give accurate answers. Curiously enough they were very deficient in imagery. They had no more notion of the true nature of imagery, says Galton, than a color-blind man has of the nature of color.

At the other extreme, non-scientific persons reported seeing the breakfast table as clearly as if it actually were present. Most subjects saw at least one or two items quite distinctly. Women and children had more distinct and vivid imagery than men. Galton attributed the scholars' and scientists' lack of imagery to their practice of abstract thinking carried on in symbols. "Our bookish and wordy education tends to repress this valuable gift of nature," he said. He found that many persons' imagery improved through practice.

Galton's survey did not show that persons belong to one or another sensory category according to their dominant imagery. Other investigators asserted this, however, and soon it was said that some persons were visualizers, meaning they were strong in visual imagery and weak in all other types. Other persons were "audiles," with dominant auditory imagery. Still others were "motiles," since their motor or kinesthetic imagery was keenest. A study of the French novelist Émile Zola called him the olfactory type because his thoughts and memories of persons or places occurred in terms of odors.

As usually happens with type theories, most persons did not fit neatly into one or another imagery category. Soon a "mixed type" was used to designate persons reporting imagery in several sense departments. An American psychologist, G. H. Betts, prepared an imagery questionnaire, more complete than Galton's. It called for visual images and also for images of voices, music, odors, tastes, the feel of velvet, of running, or of a headache. If imagery types exist, persons with one kind of vivid images should be weak in other kinds. Betts found the reverse true. Subjects reporting clearest imagery for one sense had also clearest imagery for other senses. Mixed imagery was the rule, and pure visual, auditory, or motor imagery very exceptional.

OBJECTIVE TESTS OF IMAGERY

Galton's and Betts' studies were criticized because each subject rated the quality of his own images. The reliability of such subjective data seemed dubious. Psychologists tried to devise really objective tests of imagery.

Several methods were tried by James Rowland Angell and by Mabel R. Fernald. But none determine exactly the subject's predominant type of imagery. For example, a subject is asked to name as many colored objects as possible in a given time. Then he does the same for objects having sounds. The longer list is supposed to tell which imagery is stronger. The trouble is, a subject may get a perfectly good visual image of a noisy object, or might have an auditory image for something colored, like a child's musical toy. Or again, a subject may be asked to visualize a long word, then read off the letters in it from right to left. While this seems a fair test for visual imagery, there is no assurance that auditory or motor imagery is excluded.

The best-known objective measure of imagery is the "Aussage" test, devised by the famous experimental psychologist, William Stern. Its name comes from the German word meaning "testimony." Originally the test was used to check memory accuracy. A picture is shown briefly. The subject recalls as many details as possible. Charles H. Judd found no subjects able to form an accurate visual image from which details could be read off, as from a photograph. Fernald found verbal as well as visual imagery employed; subjects named things to themselves as they looked at the picture.

Unfortunately the so-called objective imagery tests cannot limit subjects rigidly to visual, auditory, motor, or other types of imagery. Despite this weakness, however, their results agree, in general, with subjective reports from the same persons. Often a combination of subjective and objective methods is used in imagery studies.

SENSATIONS VERSUS IMAGES

The puzzling distinction between sensation and image, which had been noted by Hume, became the subject of some interesting experiments.

Oswald Külpe tested whether sensations and images can be distinguished. Subjects placed before a screen in a darkened room were told to judge whether or not dimly colored lights appeared on the screen. Though sometimes no stimulus was shown, the subjects thought they saw it. Thus images were assumed, wrongly, to be visual sensations. Occasionally the reverse occurred: subjects thought a patch of light was merely their own image.

Later C. W. Perky, a student of Titchener, did a similar experiment. Subjects were told to visualize a banana on a screen before them. Without their knowledge she projected a faint picture of a banana on the screen. Most subjects unwittingly believed the picture was their own visual image.

Edmund Jacobson, physiological psychologist, used delicate instruments to detect the electrical changes produced by muscular contractions. When subjects were asked to imagine raising a weight or pumping a tire, minute muscular contractions took place in the right arm. In fact, Jacobson found that muscular relaxation and motor imagery cannot occur together. Imagery always is accompanied by tension in the muscles involved.

Electrodes placed near the eyeball showed the eye muscles active during visual imagery. Tongue and lip muscles contracted slightly when subjects imagined talking to a friend or thought about abstract ideas like "eternity." According to Jacobson's results, imagery cannot occur without muscular activity.

NUMBER-FORMS AND SYNESTHESIA

Studying imagery, Francis Galton found that some persons visualize numbers in spatial patterns. Some of these patterns formed simple lines and columns; others were quite bizarre. The following is not at all extreme:

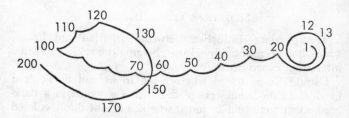

A clocklike circle from 1 to 12 often was used. Some persons visualized in three dimensions. Dates, letters, and months of the year frequently followed an original pattern.

Other psychologists confirm Galton's results. Carroll C. Pratt, of Rutgers University, found a subject who thinks of a point directly before his eyes when number 1 comes to mind. Five is higher and a little to the left. Twelve is farther away and still higher. Twenty is lower at the right. Thirty-nine is behind his right elbow. Parallel columns include 40 to 49, 50 to 59, up to 100, after which the number form tapers downward to the right of his body.

With colors, Galton's subjects noted many curious associations. One man saw his numerals this way: 1 was black; 2, yellow; 3, pale brick-red; 4, brown; 5, blackish gray; 6, reddish brown; 7, green; 8, bluish; 9, reddish brown somewhat like 6. A woman reported vowels having definite colors. A was pure white; E, red or vermilion; I, light bright yellow; O, a transparent black; U, purple; Y, a dingier color than I. Consonants were almost colorless, though M had some blackness.

A few persons see definite colors when they hear certain sounds. This is called *colored hearing.* One man reported seeing a different color for each orchestral instrument. Cases of colored odors and tastes occasionally occur. Such associations, when stimulation of one sense organ evokes a different sensory image, are termed synesthesia.

Herbert S. Langfeld studied a case of synesthesia and found that color images associated with each note of the scale remained remarkably constant for nearly eight years. The person experienced a fusion of colors when two notes were sounded together. And the fusion followed the laws of color mixture! The associated notes and colors were as follows:

C—Red	F♯—Green blue
D♭—Purple	G—Greener blue
D—Violet	G♯—Clear blue
E♭—Soft blue	A—Cold yellow
E—Golden yellow	B♭—Orange
F—Pink	B—Brilliant coppery

Most psychologists believe that number forms and synesthesia result from early forgotten associations that continue until they become habitual reactions.

EIDETIC IMAGERY

In 1907 V. Urbantschitsch, German investigator, described certain persons whose imagery was as clear-cut as though the object actually were present. A few years later, Erich R. Jaensch, of the University of Marburg, named this "eidetic imagery." Jaensch and his Marburg associates have done most of the research in this field.

An eidetic person, after looking at a picture for half a minute or so, has a clearer, more intense and detailed memory image than ordinary persons. Often an eidetic image includes details the person failed to note in his original observation. Certain details may be larger in the image or even may appear to move. Eidetic imagery is commonest among children. Studies of youngsters from six to fourteen show it in about two-thirds of the cases.

Tests for eidetic imagery can be devised easily. Gordon W. Allport showed 30 English children a picture for just over half a minute. It was a German street scene, with men, dogs, and a wagon, and over the door of a building the word *Gartenwirthschaft*. Projecting their image of the picture on a screen and describing it, the youngsters noted many small details when questioned about them. Some could read off the long German word, though they did not understand the language. A few even could spell it backwards!

Allport considered eidetic images a variety of memory image. Jaensch believed they belong in a category between after-images and memory images, being less realistic than the former but more so than the latter.

DREAMS

Most dreams consist of visual imagery. Less than half as many are auditory. Practically all are one or the other, or a combination of the two.

Joseph Jastrow has shown that dreams depend on past sensory experiences. Testing blind persons, he found that none blinded before age 5 had visual imagery. Of those becoming blind after age 7, all had visual dream-images.

What causes our dreams? How can they be interpreted? Sigmund Freud's theory is best known. He believed dreams symbolize, in disguised form, our repressed desires or conflicts. Freud's view is described in Chapter XIV.

Another theory suggests that they result from physiological causes, like sleeping in odd positions, or from sensory factors like smells or sounds that disturb sleep. Knight Dunlap suggested that dreams of nakedness arise from chilliness; dreams of falling possibly result from contraction of certain genito-urinary muscles that contract when we actually fall.

Lydiard H. W. Horton noted that dreams are misinterpretations of sensory impressions. He gave these examples: a person suffering from head noises caused by an ear disorder often dreamed about thunderstorms; a student with a toothache dreamed of boxing with a friend and getting several blows on the jaw.

Harry L. Hollingworth described an experiment in which a subject was stimulated several ways while asleep. When tickled on the lips and nose with a feather, he dreamed that the skin was being torn from his face. When made to breathe perfume he dreamed of entering a perfumer's shop in Cairo. When pinched on the neck he dreamed that a blister was there and his childhood doctor was treating it.

Another theory calls dreams a carry-over from our daily doings. Many persons have noted that they tend to dream about new or strenuous activities, like driving a car several hundred miles a day. F. Pierce compared the dreams of a writer, farmer, teacher, scientist, and others. He found their dreams closely tied up with their occupations and daily environment.

Related to Freud's theory is one that says dreams center about emotional states like aversion, fear, hope, and worry. Anticipation combined with an emotional state probably is the most effective background for producing dreams, according to Roy M. Dorcus and G. Wilson Shaffer. Often in dreams we re-live an intense emotional experience. Lowell S. Selling, a Detroit psychiatrist, found almost all the dreams of juvenile delinquents focus on their home life, about which they have strong emotional reactions.

A well-known dream theory is associated with the name of Alfred Adler, though actually he adopted it from earlier philosophers. It interprets dreams as turning over unsolved problems or anticipating new ones. The problems are portrayed symbolically. An imminent decision may be represented by an impending school examination, a strong opponent by an older brother, a danger by an abyss or a fall.

Gestalt psychologists hold a similar view. Any unfinished business sets up a tension and tends toward solution. One Gestaltist found that children dream more about unfinished activities than about those they have completed.

DREAM SYMBOLISM

Often dream symbolism can be interpreted with the dreamer's help. Laurance F. Shaffer gave an example:

I seem to be standing on a street in W———, near the principal corner, with a group of unidentified people. In the group are one or two familiar young women, and I am trying to speak to them without interrupting the others. One of the young women leaves the group. I identify her now as Peg G——— and follow her running. As I am nearing the corner, a cut-down Ford comes around the turn, loaded with young people from P———. Following the Ford are two street cars, also loaded with merrymakers. Then an ox-cart, drawn by five oxen, crowds between the cars, obstructing my passage. At the risk of being run down, I push past the ox-cart and try to overtake Peg, who is well down the street by this time.

Interpreting, Shaffer went on to say:

This dream is silly and meaningless to the dreamer and unintelligible to the psychologist, until by questioning, the background is ascertained. A crucial point is the identity of Peg G———. The subject remembers her as a girl whom he once invited to a college dance. He and Peg quarreled throughout this social function, and thereafter regarded each other with mutual dislike. Recently the student had heard that Peg was studying painting in New York. The student has recently been escorting another girl who was also an art student. The progress of this relationship has been unsatisfactory, the student feeling that he lacks the sophistication and social graces of this girl's other companions. In his own words, he is too "slow" for her. The meaning of the dream is now apparent. Peg G——— symbolizes the other girl because of two very obvious relationships, her course of study and the unpleasant social relationship. The ox-cart by a very commonplace figure of speech is a symbol of slowness. This personal defect keeps the dreamer from the girl and interrupts his pursuit of pleasure. The "slowness" gets in the way of the "merrymaking."

Shaffer did not believe dream symbols always can be understood. Nor did he think Freudian and other ready-made interpretations of symbols are valid.

Hollingworth sharply criticized Freud's "arbitrary symbols," calling them "fantastic dogmas . . . espoused by a zealous but uncritical group of disciples." Dream images and dream symbolism, he said, follow the laws of redintegration; incoming sensory stimuli, for example, arouse images and feelings related to them in a person's waking life. However, in states of sleep or drowsiness there is a lack of mental integration. Hence unusual associations and interpretations occur. Dreams are affected also by existing mental sets and emotional states.

Hollingworth believed dreams can be understood better by studying what takes place during drowsiness, a state between waking and sleep. He gave this illustration—a report made just after the individual recovered from his drowsiness:

On board an ocean liner, dressing for dinner in a suit purchased abroad, sitting drowsily on the edge of the berth and thinking that the suit had turned out to be a bad investment and had been forced upon me by a tricky salesman. Planning to buy cloth next time, to be made up in America, and wondering if it would pass the Customs. Suddenly the rush of water, heard through the port-holes, becomes transformed into the husky voice of the salesman trying to sell me the suit, and repeating his previous conversation. I fall to musing in the process, wondering, while he talks, at his husky voice and why he has no more inflection. Coming to, at the sound of the dinner bell, I still hear the husky monotonous swish of the water, and realise that this is all. The incoming sensory impression had substituted itself for the memory content, in my reflection.

In such states of drowsiness, Hollingworth noted, occur images and sensory substitutions unusual in the waking life. These experiences help to explain dreams.

Most psychologists agree that no one dream theory explains everything. Interpretations often conflict. With many dreams it is hard to evaluate the part played by sensory stimuli, organic states, recent experience, and hopes, wishes, anxieties, and other emotional factors.

Woodworth makes a good suggestion. The object of interpreting a dream, he says, is not to understand that particular dream but to discover something about the dreamer's personality. If we learn something genuine about him it is worthwhile, even if the dream itself has been misinterpreted.

DAYDREAMS

When we daydream we tend to satisfy desires unfulfilled in real life. Mandel Sherman divides daydreams, sometimes called fantasies, into the casual and the systematic. Most of us have casual daydreams about our momentary aspirations or conflicts. Systematic daydreams recur; they involve permanent underlying motives and their frustration. If a person fails to deal with his problems realistically and gets his major satisfactions by daydreaming, personality maladjustment may be on the way.

Eugen Bleuler calls daydreaming "autistic thinking," which implies its self-centered, illogical, and unrealistic nature. Most common is the "conquering hero" type, in which a person imagines himself performing feats of strength, achieving professional recognition and the like.

An English psychoanalyst, George Henry Green, suggests four types of daydreams. The "display" fantasy involves applause for daring or brilliant performance. The "saving" fantasy pictures a rescue or other act of bravery. In the daydream of "grandeur" a person imagines himself achieving great renown. The fantasy of "homage" occurs when the dreamer gives valuable aid to someone whose love or friendship is desired.

Two other types often are noted by clinical psychologists. In the fantasy of death or destruction, a person imagines the removal of someone who stands in his way or of whom he is jealous. In the "martyr" daydream, he pictures himself injured or dead, bringing remorse to those who wrong him.

Psychologists find daydreaming common among children. Though it commonly diminishes after adolescence, adults daydream occasionally. Of 200 college students questioned by Laurance Shaffer, nearly all admitted daydreaming, at some time, about wealth, vocational success, and attracting the opposite sex. On the average they reported indulging in five or six kinds of daydreams. That half the students admitted recurrent daydreams leads Shaffer to conclude that even systematic daydreaming cannot be considered pathological.

IMAGINATION OR CREATIVE THINKING

Sometimes we think of imagination as meaning mental imagery. It also can be applied to daydreaming, contrasted with logical, realistic thinking. Most psychologists use it to designate creative thinking, or invention. In this sense imagination means forming new combinations or patterns out of past experiences, resulting in an original product. In their book, *The Great Apes*, Robert and Ada Yerkes picture an imaginary creature that combines ape and human features. Other examples of this kind are the unicorn, centaur, mermaid, and most *Alice in Wonderland* characters.

The great German physiological psychologist, Hermann von Helmholtz, studied his own creative thought processes. His original ideas, he found, always followed considerable labor on the problem at hand. After a rest following the work, inspirations might come. They never appeared while his brain was fatigued or while he was drinking alcoholic liquors.

A French mathematician, Henri Poincaré, came to the same conclusion. His creative ideas did not arise while he worked at his desk. One came on an excursion, just as he stepped on a bus. Solutions of other problems flashed into his mind as he walked along the street or the seashore in a relaxed mood.

Joseph Rossman, an American patent lawyer, studied the creative thinking of several hundred inventors. Their "hunches" too, he discovered, appeared in relaxed moments following hard work. One inventor said that his productive ideas came while he was half asleep or daydreaming; another while he was dressing, shaving, or bathing. To another they came suddenly while he listened to a concert or sat in church. The inspirations of several inventors arrived just before they dropped off to sleep or when they awoke from a good night's rest.

In 1900 a leading French psychologist, Théodule Ribot, said that the inventive process springs from desire, which arouses images that the imagination arranges and combines. He observed four steps in mechanical invention: the germ, or first desire to solve a specific problem; the incubation, a long, painful period of work; the flowering, or sudden solution; and completion, by which the solution is made workable —often the hardest part of the whole process.

Graham Wallas, the British psychologist and political scientist, later named four similar stages of creative thought: preparation, incubation, illumination, and verification. They were verified in Catharine Patrick's experiments on creative work. She showed a mountain scene to several dozen poets and asked them to compose a poem, talking out all their thoughts as they progressed. The preparation period included first impressions and memories of earlier experiences. Next came incubation, best defined in this case as a recurring idea. Illumination or inspiration meant actually writing lines of the poem. Revision followed, a concluding stage corresponding roughly with the inventor's final checking or verifying.

J. P. Guilford found over forty "mental factors." He called two of these factors—discovered by a complex technique of intercorrelating many test scores—*convergent thinking* and *divergent thinking. Convergent thinking* refers to thought culminating in a definite outcome—solving a mathematics problem, for example. *Divergent thinking* moves in several apparently unpredictable directions and does not lead to a specific end. When individuals are requested to "paint any picture," their efforts represent divergent thinking. Guilford believes this aspect of mental functioning is creativity.

Summarizing, we see that imagery is intensely variable. Some people have rich imagery, while others are almost totally lacking. Some children have near-photographic "eidetic" imagery. Dreams are characterized by vivid images, though their precise meaning is often difficult to interpret. Daydreaming is a wish-fulfilling rather than creative type of imagination. The crux of real creative thinking is inspiration or illumination which follows, somewhat unpredictably, a period of concentrated work on a problem.

Chapter IX

MOTIVATION

DESCARTES   JAMES   THORNDIKE   MC DOUGALL
WOODWORTH   BERNARD   WATSON   DUNLAP
WARDEN   ALLPORT   MASLOW   MURRAY
KLINEBERG   MC CLELLAND

*Are there any instincts? How does the psychologist
classify human urges and desires? What is the difference between a drive and a motive? What are
the outstanding motives? The strongest motives?
How does an incentive operate?*

Tell almost any psychologist today that somebody does something "instinctively" and he is apt to rise in indignation and
point out that instincts were thrown overboard shortly after
the First World War. Little or no human behavior is instinctive, he will declare. Practically everything we do is
wholly or partially learned, not the unmodified expression of
an inborn urge.

René Descartes spoke of man's "intelligent" behavior as
against animals' "instinctive" behavior. This notion lost favor
after Darwin, when man's relation to animals was shown.
Human instincts began to be noted. By the late nineteenth
century philosophers and psychologists were drawing up elaborate lists.

"INSTINCT," A DISCARDED TERM

William James claimed that man has more instincts than
any other animal. He compiled a long list that includes suck-

ing, crying, locomotion, curiosity, sociability, shyness, cleanliness, pressing downward on the feet, imitation, pugnacity, sympathy, fear of dark places, acquisitiveness, love, jealousy, and many more. James added, however, that instincts can be modified by habit.

Instinct theories were furthered by William McDougall, who interpreted all behavior, even social behavior, as an expression of innate impulses. His list of major and minor instincts includes flight, repulsion, pugnacity, curiosity, mating, food-seeking, acquisitiveness, sneezing, and laughing. Instincts, he said, are the equipment by which man perceives certain stimuli, experiences emotion, and acts in a certain way. Perception and action can be modified, but emotions remain the core of instinct and change very little. This view found favor with many psychologists and others.

A few years later Edward L. Thorndike listed more instincts, giving examples. Gregariousness he illustrated with "restlessness when alone," "interest in the behavior of others," and "satisfaction in admiring glances," among others. He mentioned also sex behavior, maternal and paternal behavior, fighting, anger, mastery, submission, fear, disgust, food-getting, and acquisitive responses. Thorndike disagreed with McDougall's argument that instinct is mainly emotional. He preferred calling it simply unlearned behavior.

Just before and during World War I instinct theories flourished. The term instinct was not used by psychologists only. The economist Thorstein Veblen called one of his books *The Instinct of Workmanship*; Wilfred Trotter, a sociologist, wrote *Instincts of the Herd in Peace and War*. Ordway Tead, a personnel specialist, named a book *Instincts in Industry*. The psychoanalyst Sigmund Freud proposed two fundamental instincts: the sexual and the self-preservative. Freud's one-time associate, Carl G. Jung, founder of "analytical psychology," called the nutritional, sexual, and herd instincts primary.

In 1924 the sociologist, Luther L. Bernard, in a book called *Instinct*, surveyed the work of about 400 authors and showed the ridiculous extremes to which instinct theories were being carried. He found the terms "instinct" or "instinctive" applied to almost 6000 urges or activities! Some, like sex or social behavior, were generalized; others, astonishingly specific, like an "instinct to avoid eating the apples in one's own orchard" or "an instinct to insert the fingers into crannies to dislodge small animals hidden there."

Not all psychologists, however, believed that the activities called instinctive are innate. They might be learned. Robert M. Yerkes and Leonard Bloomfield showed that mouse-killing in kittens is at least partially learned. Others pointed to what pet-lovers often observe, that a puppy and kitten reared together do not show the alleged "instinctive hatred" between cats and dogs.

Two outspoken critics of the prevailing concept of instinct were Knight Dunlap and John B. Watson. Both insisted that most human behavior, especially adult behavior, is greatly affected by learning and therefore not innate. Watson showed from his studies of babies that fears and right- or left-handedness are acquired through experience, and that crawling, standing, walking, and numerous other activities are partially learned.

It began to dawn on psychologists that the term "instinct" was being used in two different ways. Sometimes it referred to a kind of behavior such as sucking, fighting, or fear of dark places; sometimes to impulses or urges like sex, hunger, or acquisitiveness, that lead to behavior. Robert S. Woodworth applied the term "mechanism" to behavior or activity, because it needs something to start it going. The impulse or urge prodding us to act he called "drive," likening it to the power that makes a machine operate. The two cannot be distinguished sharply, because a mechanism, once started, can furnish its own drive. For example, a child induced to learn singing, if musical, will be carried along by enthusiasm growing out of his singing. Any habit, says Woodworth, contains its own motivating power and exerts a drive toward being repeated. A person's drives naturally change as he forms new habits and behaves in new ways.

Similarly, Gordon W. Allport suggested that adult motives become "functionally autonomous"—that is, they come to operate independently of their origin. Thus a businessman goes on working years after he has achieved economic security, sometimes even to the detriment of his health. What was once an "instrumental technique," said Allport, becomes a master motive.

Bernard, Dunlap, Watson, and Woodworth began the overthrow of instinct doctrines in psychology. Anthropologists finished the job by showing that human urges and behavior differ the world over according to the cultures in which people live. Let us see what some noted anthropologists report.

Instead of an "instinctive love of one's own children," William H. R. Rivers found among the Murray Islanders in the Torres Straits indifference to the real parentage of a child. Adoption is common, and children do not know who their real parents are. Furthermore, among these people of Murray Island a child may be put to death if a family has too many of the same sex.

Ralph Linton reported an unusual custom in one Madagascar tribe. If a divorced woman remarries, her former husband receives the first three children from the new union; he treats them like his own.

Margaret Mead noted that the fathers, not the mothers, in the Manus tribe of New Guinea bring up the children. Perhaps for that reason she found that boys rather than girls liked the dolls she presented to them!

Fighting, which is supposedly a human instinct, is unknown in some primitive communities. Studying the Kwakiutl Indians of the Canadian Pacific region, Franz Boas found that quarrels were settled not by physical combat but by holding a "potlatch," or feast, at which possessions were given away. The one who gave away most property won. Alexander Goldenweiser discovered that disputes among persons in certain Eskimo tribes were settled by a singing contest, the victor being chosen by popular vote.

Most psychologists who have discussed instincts have included acquisitiveness in their lists. Yet anthropologists find incredibly different attitudes toward property among primitive peoples. In one community every rock and water hole may be privately owned. In another only a few items like ornaments and tools are private; everything else is owned in common.

Competitiveness varies greatly among cultures. Ruth Benedict noted that Zuni Indians frowned on a person who sought prestige or power. A man who consistently won races was prevented from entering contests. Individual initiative was discouraged. Otto Klineberg, a social psychologist, found it impossible to test accurately the intelligence of many Indian tribes because the members could not grasp the idea of competing to achieve a high score.

Thus many so-called instincts vary widely from group to group, depending on the customs in each culture. Instinct is defined as "innate, relatively unchangeable behavior that is universal to a species." Nest-building in birds, or web-spinning in spiders are true instincts. Because most forms of human behavior are so variable and modifiable, psychologists have generally dropped the term "instinct" when speaking of human beings.

Renewed interest in instincts is shown by "ethologists"—psychologists or naturalists who study behavior of species under natural conditions. Ethologists examine, among other things, three phenomena best described under the following headings:

1. *Species-specific* behavior is behavior unique to a certain species. The dance done by bees locating a honey source is a good example. K. von Frisch has demonstrated how this is done. When a bee finds honey it informs other members of the hive by performing a dance; the tempo of the dance reveals how far away the honey is, and the dancer's angle to the sun indicates in which direction the source lies.

2. *Releaser* is the term given to certain cues that evoke unlearned complex series of unlearned responses. A European psychologist, N. Tinbergen, found that the male three-spined stickleback fish will not exhibit courtship behavior in the presence of an almost perfect replica of a female, but will do so in the presence of an imperfect replica with a distended abdomen. The distended abdomen in this case is the releaser.

3. *Imprinting* is learning based on an instinctive tendency present only at a certain developmental stage. Eckhard H. Hess found that mallard ducklings betweeen 12 and 17 hours old will follow almost any moving object

that simulates a mother duck, and from that time on will forsake all others to follow this imprinted object.

Studies like these, however, reveal much variation in behavior—so much so that a leading animal psychologist, Frank A. Beach, advises against generalizing about behavior on the basis of experiments on one or a few species.

DRIVES

Human behavior obviously arises from some urge. If not from an instinct, then from some other kind of urge. Animal psychologists adopted Woodworth's term "drive," meaning the energy that sets things going. Later it was accepted generally to mean energy or action arising from physiological needs like hunger, thirst, sex, fatigue, elimination of bodily wastes, maintenance of constant temperature and barometric pressure.

Physiologists already had studied hunger. Just before World War I, Walter B. Cannon and Anton J. Carlson found that hunger pangs correlate with rhythmic contractions of the stomach walls. Later a Japanese psychologist named Tomi Wada showed that when a person is moderately hungry, general muscular activity and mental alertness increase.

Ging Hsi Wang, Chinese physiologist and psychologist, noted the effect of sex on the activity of the female white rat. Each day he checked the rat's runs in a revolving squirrel cage. Every four days, when the rat's heat, or oestrous periods, occurred, it made almost twice as many revolutions of the cage as normally. No such fluctuations of activity occur in the male, the prepubescent female, or in the female during pregnancy or lactation. Wang showed conclusively that the sexual cycle greatly affects a rat's energy.

The connection between glands and drive was demonstrated by Curt P. Richter, a physiologist. Castrated rats, or rats whose adrenal, pituitary, or thyroid glands are removed, show amazing loss of activity. From several thousand daily revolutions of the activity cage they drop to only a few hundred.

Curious tie-ups between the drives appear. Studying the effects of thirst on rats, Lucien H. Warner found that lack of water reduces the hunger drive. Hunger weakens the sex drive, Fred A. Moss discovered. Several young men who reduced their diet for an experiment reported their sex urge and sexual interest considerably lessened during that period, according to Walter R. Miles.

To calculate the strength of drives, Carl J. Warden devised an obstruction box. A rat motivated by hunger, thirst, or some other drive is placed in a compartment at one end of a long box. At the other end is food, water, or some other incentive. Between animal and incentive lies a narrow passage, the floor of which is an electric grid which gives a shock when touched. The stronger an animal's drive, the more shock it can take.

Warden's most famous experiment compared the relative strength of five major drives in the white rat. A hungry or thirsty rat was allowed to cross the grid and nibble food or sip water, briefly. Then it was put back in the end compartment. Each time it crossed the grid it was put back. The strength of its drive was measured by the number of times it crossed the grid in twenty minutes. With maximum drive operating, Warden found these averages, using many rats:

DRIVE	INCENTIVE	NUMBER OF CROSSINGS
Maternal	Litter of young	22.4
Thirst	Water	20.4
Hunger	Food	18.2
Sex	Rat of other sex	13.8
Exploratory	New location	6.0

Maternal, thirst, and hunger drives differed little in strength, but they were definitely stronger than the sex and exploratory drives.

Interested in human motivation, Floyd H. Allport in 1924 listed six "prepotent reflexes," or basic inherited activities of humans. They are: starting and withdrawing, rejecting, struggling, hunger reactions, "sensitive zone" reactions aroused in tickling, and sex reactions. The first four operate from birth. The sensitive zone reaction appears in early infancy; sex activities appear much later. These six primary activities, Allport said, can be modified and diversified greatly through learning. Thus, rejecting leads to cleanliness, struggling to pugnacity, sex to maternal and paternal habits. Cleanliness or pugnacity is not an "instinct" but a "social habit" acquired through individual experience.

More recently, psychologists have shown that not all drives are tied to organic need. For instance, Donald O. Hebb calls attention to several examples of innate fears: the fear of snakes among primates, the human fear of mutilated bodies, a chimpanzee's fear of a model chimp head. K. D. Montgomery shows visual exploratory behavior of the white rat to be a natural motive. Several psychologists, notably Harry F. Harlow, have demonstrated that the rhesus monkey is strongly motivated to explore and manipulate strange objects.

That humans seem to need stimulation is shown in the isolation experiment by Canadian psychologists W. H. Bexton, W. Heron, and T. H. Scott, already described in Chapter III. College students were paid to remain in bed in isolated cubicles with eyes, ears, and hands shielded to minimize perception of their environment. Few could endure these conditions more than two or three days. The need for stimulation became overwhelming.

MOTIVES

The word "drives" appeared inadequate to describe all of human motivation. Human beings are more complex than animals. They have physiological urges, but they have other powerful urges too that seem to spring from social sources. For instance, many persons seem driven by a desire to acquire and hold property or other possessions. Their urge is deep-rooted. Yet its absence in other persons, in fact its absence in whole cultures like the Kwakiutl Indians of British Columbia as shown by the anthropologist Franz Boas, indicates that it is acquired from the cultural pattern.

To include these social urges as well as the physiological drives found in human beings, the term "motive" came to be used.

William I. Thomas, a sociologist, prepared one of the best-known comprehensive short lists of human motives. In the normal adult, said Thomas, are four fundamental motives: desire for security, for response, for recognition, and for new experience. To get security we provide bodily necessities, work at jobs, and acquire property. To satisfy our response needs, we seek social and sexual contacts. For recognition we strive for prestige, admiration, the respect of our social group. For new experiences we lean toward adventure or any change from routine. All normal persons in our culture have these four motives, though seldom in the same degree. The well-adjusted person satisfies reasonably well each of his fundamental wishes.

Henry A. Murray lists over twenty needs, including activity, nurturance, succorance, harm-avoidance, autonomy, acquisition, affiliation, cognizance, construction, deference, dominance, recognition, achievement, and blame-avoidance. Like other psychologists he distinguishes between physiological drives, which he calls "viscerogenic," and socially acquired or "psychogenic" needs.

Contemporary behavioristic psychologists, opposing instincts and other theories of innate needs (e.g., Freud's "Eros" or life instinct and "Thanatos" or death wish), maintain that social drives or motives are learned. Love of money, for example, can be considered a "secondary drive" acquired through the association of money with basic need satisfaction.

L. F. Shaffer and E. J. Shoben, Jr., insist that motives are complex, socially learned patterns or sequences. To identify a motive one must specify the situation giving rise to it, the drive or tension operating, the behaviors resulting, and the adjustment which brings the sequence to a close. They mention social approval, conformity, mastery, and sex as important socially conditioned motives, but they believe no dependable list of motives can be compiled because of cultural and individual variations.

Looking at motivation from a cultural and national standpoint, the sociologist David Riesman believes that American thought has been dominated by the achievement orientation, characterized by individuality, self-assurance, and independence. Today the picture is changing, and we seem to be entering an era of affiliation orientation, or "other-directedness," marked by loss of individuality and a desire to conform. We shall return to Riesman's theories in Chapter XVI.

A. H. Maslow has formulated a hierarchical theory of human motivation, including five basic needs which develop as an individual grows and matures. In terms of strength, each one emerges only when the one above it in the list is satisfied: physiological needs, safety needs, belongingness and love needs, esteem needs, and last of all, self-actualization, a uniquely human need referring to one's desire for self-realization or fulfillment.

Otto Klineberg has presented a useful summary of motives, according to both origin and dependability:

1. Dependable motives, with a physiological basis; e.g., hunger, thirst, need for rest and sleep, need for activity.

2. Motives with a physiological basis, somewhat affected by social factors, and with some individual exceptions; e.g., sex, post-maternal drive, self-preservation.

3. Motives with an indirect physiological basis, and with both individual and group exceptions; e.g., aggressiveness, flight, self-assertiveness.

4. Motives which have no known physiological basis, growing out of social experience and demands; e.g., gregariousness, paternal, pre-maternal, filial, acquisitive, self-submissive.

How may human motives be measured? Murray devised a projective technique, the Thematic Apperception Test, which he used to estimate the strength of the various needs within the total personality. (This test is described in Chapter XII.) D. C. McClelland, J. W. Atkinson, and colleagues modified Murray's test in order to study the achievement motive. They had subjects write stories in response to the pictures; these were then scored in terms of "achievement imagery"—i.e., concern with accomplishment or some standard of excellence. McClelland later extended his investigations into the psychological basis for the achievements of ancient, medieval, and modern societies.

Older studies had used other methods. Daniel Starch asked 74 men and women to rate the importance of several dozen motives in determining their actions from day to day. The strongest were hunger, love of offspring, health, sex attraction, ambition, bodily comfort, possession, approval by others. Evaluation of one's own motives, of course, is a procedure that many would question. Trying for more objective data, Thorndike used figures on the annual amount of money spent by Americans on clothes, food, life insurance, shelter, and the like. Then impartial judges estimated which desires the various expenditures seemed to satisfy. Of 24 desires the following rated strongest: hunger, security, protection against the elements, approval of others, welfare of others.

Newer experimental approaches to motivation are often concerned with relationships among dynamic tendencies. Stanley Schachter, for example, investigated the relation between anxiety and affiliation. He introduced women college students into either a high or a low anxiety-inducing situation (expectation of electric shock) and gave them a choice to wait alone or with other students. He found that 63% of the high anxiety group wanted to be with others, as compared with only 33% of the low anxiety group. And the high anxiety group wanted to be with other high anxiety subjects; as Schachter put it: "Misery doesn't just love any kind of company; it loves only miserable company!"

Elizabeth French presented tasks to groups of airmen having either high achievement or high affiliation motivation. Half the groups were praised for efficiency, the other half for friendliness. When praised for efficiency, the achievement-oriented men made high scores; when praised for friendliness, they made relatively low scores. The reverse was true for the affiliation-motivated groups. What is rewarding for those with one orientation is not for those with different motives.

INCENTIVES

Our drives and motives are always with us. We cannot shake free from hunger or thirst, or from most of the social motives which we have learned. On the other hand, the inner push of motivation is by no means the whole story. Kurt Lewin and the Gestaltists have noted the importance of the individual's "psychological field"—i.e., of the objects and persons which attract and repel him. These are called *incentives*. Reward and punishment, or praise and reproof are everyday examples.

The magic effect of a chocolate bar promised to fifth-graders working multiplication problems was shown by Clarence J. Leuba. For a week he gave them ten-minute exercises in multiplying without reward. Then he promised each a chocolate bar for improving a certain amount. Performance shot up 52%. Combining incentives (rivalry, praise, and candy) he got a 62% improvement, compared with a group of children not similarly motivated.

Rats require a reward to learn a maze, Edward C. Tolman and associates found. A hungry rat learns little or nothing about finding its way through a maze until a food reward is produced. If the reward is given at the end of several trials, then removed, learning ceases and the rat may lose its previous progress.

Punishing kittens with an electric shock for erring in a problem box, Robert M. Yerkes and John D. Dodson discovered that with easy tasks learning improves in proportion to strength of punishment. With difficult problems only mild punishment brings improvement. Severe shocks disorganize behavior.

The same principle holds for blindfolded human beings learning to push a stylus through a maze, according to James Vaughn and Charles M. Diserens. Slight electric shocks step up progress, but bigger shocks disrupt rather than hasten learning.

Albert M. Johanson compared the effects of two incentives —knowledge of results, and punishment—on speed of reaction time. Subjects pressed a key as fast as possible on hearing a signal. When told their previous reaction times, they speeded up 6%. When given electric shocks for slowing down, they improved 15%.

Further proof that motivation increases when subjects know how they are getting along comes from William F. Book. With four different tasks of the intelligence test variety, subjects who knew how they were doing gained faster and more steadily than those who did not. When not told their results, the first group slumped badly. Book concluded that the "will to learn" is stimulated a good deal by telling a student his progress.

How praise and reproof affect our learning is demonstrated by Elizabeth Hurlock in an important experiment. She chose four groups of school children, equal in arithmetic ability. One group was praised before the class for doing excellent work. The second group was reproved severely for bad performance. The third was ignored, though it heard the other groups praised and reproved. In another room the fourth group heard nothing. Striking results appeared. Both the praised and reproved groups immediately improved 35% to 40%. The ignored group improved only half as much. Later the praised group climbed to a 79% improvement. The reproved and ignored groups fell off in performance. The isolated group lost slightly but not significantly throughout. Dr. Hurlock concluded that praise and reproof motivate about equally in the short run, but that over longer periods praise brings better results.

Industrialists, quick to see that whatever psychologists learned about incentive had practical value for them, launched experiments in their own plants. Bonuses for improvement, Harry D. Kitson found, upped by 35% in twenty weeks the output of hand compositors in a print shop.

The English industrial psychologist Stanley Wyatt compared three wage plans. For nine weeks girls received a fixed wage. Then for a time a bonus system was used. Finally a piece rate was adopted. The bonus increased output more than 50% over the fixed wage production. An extra 40% rise accompanied the piece rate system.

Financial incentives are not always stronger than other factors. Wyatt found that when workers did disagreeable jobs the bonus or piece rate failed to increase output. With interesting jobs, on the other hand, improvement soared as much as 200%.

Probably the most extensive industrial motivation study was made for Western Electric by several Harvard University experts, including Elton Mayo and T. N. Whitehead. For several years six girls assembling telephone relays were studied under various types of work periods, rest pauses, atmospheric conditions, and wage plans. Curiously enough, output in general rose steadily, even when unfavorable conditions were introduced—a result that surprised the investigators. Both the long run improvement and most of the temporary lags or spurts turned out to result not from physical factors like hours and wages, but from social factors like the girls' attitudes toward each other. Approval, antagonism, or indifference directly affected production. A feeling of importance at being selected for the study, a sense of responsibility for the project, and growing congeniality among themselves caused the general improvement. In other words, human relationships motivated the workers more strongly than financial incentives or good working conditions.

Clearly, motivation is a fascinating and significant area of psychology, but one in which definite answers are extremely difficult to obtain. At least, progress has been made since the days when the dynamics of human behavior were considered innate and were compressed into one or another list of instincts. We now know that the subject of motivation is closely involved not only with physiological drives, but with learning and the social scene, with incentives, and with emotions. We turn now to a more detailed consideration of emotions.

Chapter X

EMOTION

DARWIN   JAMES   LANGE
SHERRINGTON   CANNON   BARD   LANDIS
BENUSSI   JUNG   HESS   WATSON   JONES
PAVLOV   LINDSLEY   DOLLARD   MILLER
MAIER   WOLFF   SELYE

Is emotion physical or mental or both? To what extent do facial expressions and gestures reveal emotional states? What happens to our bodily functions when we experience emotions? What is a lie detector and how does it work? Do emotions just develop or do we learn them? What are psychosomatic disorders?

Charles Darwin published a little book in 1872 entitled *Expression of the Emotions in Man and Animals*. He said that facial expressions and postural movements trace back to once useful actions. Showing the teeth in anger, for example, is a relic of primitive combat when man fought his battles by clawing and biting. Closing the mouth firmly in determination comes from physical effort and straining, which with our ancestors generally accompanied determination. Social tradition plays a part too; clasping the hands in supplication originated in the early custom of raising the hands to be bound.

SCIENTIFIC VIEWS OF EMOTION

Darwin did the first experiment on emotions. He showed

pictures of posed emotional expressions to several judges. They disagreed surprisingly in identifying the emotions.

Differing with Darwin, a German anatomist named Theodor Piderit believed that facial expressions actually help or hinder reception of stimuli by the sense organs. Wrinkling the nose helps shut out bad smells. Pressing tongue and lips against the teeth gives maximum sweet taste. Dropping the tongue from the roof of the mouth helps avoid bitter tastes. We make these grimaces when smells or tastes are recalled though actually absent. With unpleasant thoughts the mouth screws up as though avoiding bitter tastes.

A puzzling aspect of emotion is the relation between our feeling and our accompanying physiological changes, like facial expression, heart beat, or breathing rate. Formerly it was assumed that when we feel afraid the fear causes the heart to pound and we then run away.

William James and a Danish physiologist, Karl G. Lange, independently advanced an interpretation later called the James-Lange theory. It reversed the old idea. Bodily changes cause emotion, it said. If there are no changes, there is no emotion. Instead of the sequence, "man sees bear, feels frightened, runs away," James and Lange offered this sequence: "man sees bear, starts to run, and as a result feels afraid." Though backed by little real proof, the theory, having a physiological basis, seemed at the time more scientific than others.

Wilhelm Wundt objected to the traditional classification of emotions into pleasant or unpleasant. He proposed a "tridimensional theory." Every feeling, he said, has three aspects: pleasantness or unpleasantness, excitement or quiet, and tension or relaxation. A feeling may be pleasant, relaxed, and quiet, or it may be unpleasant, excited, and tense. If none of these six experiences is present, there is no emotion.

Experimenting on the problem, Edward B. Titchener, who had studied with Wundt, found that his subjects often had difficulty in identifying these three "dimensions" of feeling, in distinguishing between excitement and tension, for example, or between quiet and pleasantness. The only real dimension, Titchener found, was pleasant-unpleasant. His research led him to suspect that experiences like "tenseness" or "excitement" really are organic or muscular sensations, not feelings.

More recently several psychologists, including Donald Lindsley and Elizabeth Duffy, have espoused the "activation theory" of emotions, which holds that emotion varies in intensity, from sleep at one extreme to excitement at the other. Activation implies the utilization of energy which makes emotions seem very much like motives or drives, as Robert Leeper has suggested. For him, fear, anger, elation, and other emotions are motives in the sense that they arouse an organic activity and channel it into a particular direction.

EXPRESSING EMOTIONS

We judge others' emotions largely by their facial expressions and their gestures. It seems easy to recognize anger in a person's face, or astonishment; yet experiments show that we are often mistaken.

Herbert S. Langfeld of Princeton University asked subjects to identify emotions portrayed in 105 photographs posed by an actor. The best subjects judged 58% correctly, the worst, 17%. Correctness meant agreement with the actor's intended emotion. Langfeld found that his subjects not only judged emotions wrongly; they were uncertain of their judgments, and were easy to lead astray by suggestion.

Edwin G. Boring and Titchener also proved that subjects are suggestible when judging facial expressions. They prepared different expressions of the mouth, eyes, nose, and brow that could be combined various ways into profiles. Practically all of the composite faces, when shown to subjects, were judged to portray actual emotional states, even when the parts, arbitrarily assembled, were inconsistent.

Whether the eyes or mouth express more emotion was studied by Knight Dunlap. He cut portrait photographs in half, crosswise, then combined the parts so that the eyes of a face expressing pain, let us say, were put with the mouth of the same face showing pleasure. Contrary to a general, perhaps literary, notion that eyes are "mirrors of the soul," subjects proved more influenced by mouths than by eyes in judging emotions.

A woman psychologist named Antoinette Feleky asked a hundred persons to identify the emotions in 86 pictures, posed by an actress. Judgments varied. The highest agreement was 52%. One picture was identified in 39 different ways. However, Robert S. Woodworth later showed that the judges were not in great disagreement. Although only 52% judged "surprise" correctly, another 31% called it "wonder," "astonishment," or "amazement," synonymous terms. By grouping similar poses and judgments, Woodworth found 60 or more percent agreement on happiness, surprise, fear, anger, disgust, and contempt.

Harold Schlosberg later schematized Woodworth's group of emotions by arranging them along the circumference of a surface which had two perpendicular axes: pleasant-unpleasant and attention-rejection, demonstrating that while love is clearly pleasant, for example, disgust represents a combination of rejection and unpleasantness.

To avoid the chance that posed pictures fail to express genuine emotions, Carney Landis photographed faces in real emotional situations. He shot off guns unexpectedly, gave electric shocks, showed bawdy pictures, made subjects decapitate a rat with a blunt knife, or watch the decapitation.

His pictures revealed no characteristic facial expression for pain, surprise, disgust, or other emotional states. The only response common to many persons was a smile. The same subject showed similar expressions in various situations, but Landis proved conclusively that no specific facial reaction characterizes a given emotional state.

Studying vocal expression, Mandel Sherman showed that in newborn babies cries of pain, hunger, fear, and anger cannot be distinguished, contrary to what young parents are told. Older children and adults tend to reveal their stronger emotions, like excitement or anger, by speaking loudly in high-pitched tones.

Hand gestures seem more specifically expressive. Leonard Carmichael and associates had an actress portray emotions solely by movements of the hands. College students, interpreting them, agreed fairly well. Imitating the gesture and trying to think of situations wherein it occurred helped them name the expression, they said.

Physiological Aspects

Ingenious experimental operations on animals' nervous systems, performed about 1900, discredited the James-Lange theory that emotion follows physiological changes.

Sir Charles Sherrington cut the spinal cords of several dogs just below the brain. They then had no sensations from the viscera or skeletal muscles. According to the James-Lange theory the animals should not experience emotion because the bodily basis was removed. Yet the dogs continued to show anger and affection. They also revealed disgust, rejecting unsavory meat. Though the evidence is inconclusive because we cannot know how a dog really feels, the outward expression resembled true emotion.

The American physiologist Walter B. Cannon revealed the relation between emotions and the autonomic nervous system, which regulates circulation, breathing, digestion, and glandular action. He proved that the sympathetic or central division of the autonomic system controls bodily changes occurring in strong emotions like fear and rage. It speeds up blood pressure, heart beat, and breathing rate, and inhibits digestion.

Cannon operated on cats, severing the sympathetic from the central nervous system. This eliminated visceral sensations during emotional states. Yet he found, like Sherrington, that the cats showed all the signs of genuine emotion when given an electric shock or approached by a barking dog.

Cannon showed also the adrenal gland's importance in emotion. During intense pain, fear, or anger, the adrenal hormone is injected into the blood stream. This hormone releases sugar from the liver into the blood stream, increasing muscular energy. It counteracts muscular fatigue, raises blood pressure and heart rate. It supplies more blood to arm and leg muscles. It also hastens blood clotting in case abrasions occur. These functions, said Cannon, help deal effectively with emergencies. They have survival value in situations that endanger existence, because they prepare us for more intense effort. Sometimes a person chased by an angry bull finds he has scrambled over a high fence that he could not have scaled without the help of his adrenal hormone.

Studying brain action, Cannon found that a lower brain center, the thalamus, controls emotions. Intact, the thalamus permits normal emotional reactions. If areas near the thalamus are cut away, a more intense emotion generally occurs. This suggests that other brain centers inhibit the thalamus. Cannon worked out a "thalamic theory" of emotions as an alternative to the James-Lange theory. The thalamus, he said, sends impulses directly to the cortex and to the muscles, and to the viscera by way of the autonomic nervous system. The feeling of emotion does not cause bodily changes, nor is it caused by them. But it is intensified by pronounced, prolonged muscular and visceral activities. Cannon's theory assigns emotions to a brain function instead of to widespread bodily changes.

Philip Bard, and later Jules H. Masserman, stimulated the hypothalamus in cats and obtained overt manifestations of rage and fear. But something was lacking; the animals did not seem to "feel" really angry or afraid or anxious to fight or escape. Masserman concluded that the hypothalamus produces a certain dramatic appearance of emotion, but not the complete expression.

Other theorists, notably Donald O. Hebb, have supported a neurological explanation of emotion. Hebb thinks of emotions such as anger or fear as a disruption of cellular activities, especially "phase sequences," in the brain. But such explanations are not satisfactory *psychologically*, as Magda Arnold indicates. A theory of emotion, she insists, needs to include an ingredient of perception or appraisal of the situation which underlies the felt tendencies and the physiological changes, if one is to have a complete explanation of emotional experience.

BREATHING CHANGES

When we have an emotion, our breathing changes. Fiction writers often refer to this phenomenon. Men and women are said to "gasp with amazement," "sigh with relief," "catch the breath in fear." Early this century psychologists began actually to measure breathing changes.

Gustav Störring, a German psychologist, suggested that

noting the ratio between time taken for inspiration and for expiration would show the changes quantitatively. The pneumograph is used for this. Usually it consists of an air-filled rubber tube strapped about the chest, with an outlet at one end connected to a recording needle. The needle, moving up and down as the subject breathes, records on smoked paper a wavy line showing inspiration and expiration.

Dr. Feleky found a low ratio of inspiration to expiration during laughter (about .30), when inspiration is fast and expiration slow. On the other hand, she found it very high in wonder or surprise, inspiration taking two or three times as long as expiration. With fear, William E. Blatz discovered the ratio rose from normal (about .70) to 3.00 or 4.00.

In 1914 Vittoris Benussi, an outstanding Italian psychologist, proved that this ratio can be used to detect lying. He had almost 100% success in telling whether or not his subjects were lying, whereas persons trying to judge by observing the subject did no better than if merely guessing. The respiratory ratio decreased after truth-telling and increased after lying. This happens because a liar has a harder job making his story hang together, Benussi said. No other investigator has detected lying so successfully by breathing changes, though the pneumograph still is used as a part of most lie-detection systems.

Effect on Blood Pressure

Of circulatory changes caused by emotion, blood pressure is the best indicator. It is measured by the sphygmomanometer, an instrument used by doctors. William E. Blatz placed subjects in a special chair, which unexpectedly fell backwards. Fear and surprise raised their blood pressure about 20 beats a minute. Later, blood pressure rose again when subjects returned to the chair anticipating the fall. Landis found that a combination of hunger, fatigue, and pain raises blood pressure.

William M. Marston, physiological and consulting psychologist, studied blood pressure changes of ten men and ten women in several situations. Conversation with a new acquaintance of the opposite sex shot blood pressure up twice as much as did reading a story or newspaper, he discovered. Telling one's actions for the past day raised it somewhat, as did cross-examination on the same topic. Women's blood pressure increased twice as much as men's, though wide individual differences appeared.

Marston tried out blood pressure as an index of deception. Ten "witnesses," testifying before a jury, were instructed to tell the truth part of the time and to lie part of the time. Blood pressure changes enabled Marston to distinguish truth from falsehood in 96% of the cases. The jury relying on observation alone judged no better than if they had judged by chance (50%). Blood pressure increased slightly even when subjects told the truth; it went up three times as much when they lied. The rise Marston attributed to emotional excitement.

The Galvanic Skin Response

Several nineteenth-century physiologists noted electric phenomena of the skin. J. Tarchanoff discovered a weak current passing between electrodes placed at two points on the skin. He measured it by a delicate galvanometer. The amount of current, he found, varies with mental activity, due to changing action of the sweat glands.

This change in the skin's electrical conductivity is called the galvanic skin response (GSR), psychogalvanic reflex, or electrodermal response.

Carl G. Jung and an associate used the skin response to reveal personality "complexes." They read off, one at a time, a list of words asking the subject to respond to each by giving the first word that came to mind. A galvanometer was applied to the subject's hand during the word association test. When a word aroused emotion, the instrument registered a higher current. Analyzing the responses, Jung detected emotional tensions like love affairs, guilt or inferiority feelings, or thoughts of suicide.

To test whether skin responses really measure emotion, Frederic L. Wells and an associate gave subjects emotion-arousing stimulus words and noted the amount of current recorded by the galvanometer. The subjects then rated the emotional value of each word. In general the skin response corresponded closely to the estimated emotional intensity. Carney Landis and William A. Hunt proved that the galvanic response is greatest in states of "tension," startle, surprise, fear, and confusion.

Brain Potentials and Emotions

In 1929 Hans Berger, German neurologist, reported finding "brain waves" in human beings, when two electrodes were placed on the surface of the skull. The clearest of these, called alpha waves, have about ten oscillations per second. Alpha waves are most noticeable when a subject's eyes are closed. When he pays attention, reads, or tries to solve a problem, alpha waves diminish markedly while other types of waves appear. Alpha rhythms increase with mental age—at least during the first few years of life. They also have discernible patterns during sleep, after administration of drugs, and in certain abnormal mental states such as epilepsy and brain tumor.

The study of electrical brain waves, known as "electroencephalography" (EEG), has yielded additional information about emotions. Both Donald B. Lindsley and Chester W. Darrow have shown that the normal "alpha rhythm" is much affected by emotional states. Lindsley, for example, found that tension and worry reduced the alpha rhythm greatly; after the subject became relaxed, the EEG pattern returned to normal.

Since World War II many scientists have studied the effects of electrical stimulation of the brain. It had been known for almost a century, due to the pioneering work of two German surgeons, G. Fritsch and E. Hitzig, that body movements could be elicited by electrical stimulation of exposed brain cells. Following this, researchers had mapped out the chief sensory and motor areas of the brain. In the 1930's, a Swiss neurophysiologist, Walter R. Hess, perfected a technique by which a very fine electrode may be inserted into the brain in actual contact with nerve cells. (No pain is felt by the subject.) Appropriate amounts of current are discharged into the nerve cell just as if it were charged by natural internal stimulation. Further improvements have been made with the use of transistors and radio pickups.

Drs. Jose M. R. Delgado, Neal E. Miller, and Warren W. Roberts at Yale University have reported amazing results from electrical stimulation of the brain (ESB). Using animals as subjects, they have been able to produce not only motor and sensory responses, but emotional reactions as well. Rage and fighting responses have been induced in cats; also fear, anxiety, and submissiveness. The experimenters were able, through appropriate ESB, to change the dominant behavior of the leader, and thus alter the social relationships of a whole colony of monkeys.

James Olds and Joseph V. Brady have discovered pleasure centers in rats, the stimulation of which caused the animal to continue pleasurable behavior for days on end, with little or no apparent fatigue. A similar study was mentioned in Chapter V.

Can these techniques be used on human beings? Preliminary findings suggest that ESB can elicit feelings of happiness, anxiety, restlessness, and rage, and that it can suppress pain. Obviously, experiments on human beings will be performed cautiously, but a new vista of possibilities—presenting both benefits and dangers—may be opening up.

LIE DETECTION

In 1921 an enterprising young police officer, John A. Larson, devised a "lie detector," based on Benussi's and Marston's experiments. It recorded pulse rate, blood pressure, and breathing changes.

A few years later Leonarde Keeler, of Northwestern University's crime detection laboratory, brought out an instrument he called the "polygraph." It recorded changes in blood pressure, respiration, and galvanic skin response.

The polygraph technique helps detect guilt in many legal cases. It requires expert handling and a quiet atmosphere, typically. The subject is told that the instrument will show whether or not he answers questions truthfully; if he tells the truth he has nothing to fear. This relieves tension in an innocent person and intensifies it in a guilty one, which makes detection easier.

First several neutral questions are asked: Is your name John Doe? Did you drink coffee for breakfast? At intervals among irrelevant items come the key questions: Did you shoot Richard Roe? Do you know who shot him? Almost always a guilty person shows greater upset than an innocent person at crucial questions, compared with his reaction to irrelevant ones.

Good as it is, the method occasionally fails. Innocent persons also can be upset by key questions. Keeler and Fred E. Inbau improved lie detection by a so-called "peak of tension" test. It works this way. Suppose several suspects are picked up after the theft of two diamond rings from an Oak Street house, which was entered through a cellar window about eleven o'clock Tuesday night.

Six or eight street names are listed, like Walnut, Chestnut, or Pine. Oak Street appears about midway in the list. Each suspect, shown the list, is told he will be asked whether he knows about a robbery on any of these streets. Then the test proceeds. To each question the suspect answers no. Typically the guilty person's blood pressure rises gradually to the key words, Oak Street, then declines. Breathing usually slows perceptibly at the key question. If only one subject shows peaks of tension at all key items—Oak Street, cellar window, diamond rings—his guilt is apparent.

Often the lie detector induces guilty persons to confess. Innocent persons welcome the test, confident it will reveal their innocence.

However, the lie detector is by no means 100% accurate. In a study done by Douglas G. Ellson for the Office of Naval Research, liars were detected from 60% to 70% of the time. The best single indicator was the galvanic skin response, which was 79% successful. These figures are hardly surprising, since many persons are difficult to test, particularly defectives, psychopaths, and persons with abnormal physiological reactions. Almost always they can be identified, however, and the experimenter simply reports that a test is useless in such cases. When a test is given and inconclusive results occur, they are reported to the court, which then decides the case on the basis of other evidence.

Appellate courts do not recognize lie detector evidence, according to a survey made by Inbau. Suspects in trial court cases are often referred for the test, when both prosecuting and defense attorneys agree to it.

Business firms frequently make use of guilt detection methods. To test the honesty of their employees some companies send their whole personnel to a guilt detection laboratory. In one instance reported by Keeler, a big majority admitted stealing, from costly items right down to stamps, pencils, and stationery. Or, if they denied stealing, they were caught by the detector. No punishment was given, but the employees were told that another test would be given during the following year. On the re-test only 2% or 3% were found guilty; they were discharged.

How Emotions Develop

We now turn to the important question of how emotions originate. Do a child's emotions develop as he grows up, or does he learn them? Here again the old maturation or training question arises.

K. M. B. Bridges showed how emotional reactions develop from simple excitement in a newborn baby to a dozen or more distinct reactions in the 2-year-old, including fear, disgust, anger, jealousy, delight, and affection.

William E. Blatz and a colleague noted the ages at which new behavior appears during emotional states. Up to 4 months the baby cries, struggles, gives a start. Between 4 and 8 months he resists, holds out his arms, and throws things. Later he stiffens and clings. Between 1 and 2 years of age he runs away, hides his face, says no, and slumps.

An interesting case supporting maturation is described by Florence Goodenough. A 10-year-old girl, deaf and blind from infancy, was found to express fear, anger, disgust, and delight like normal children. As this child could not have learned from seeing or hearing others, Goodenough believes the case argues strongly for maturation.

To show how learning affects emotional reactions, John B. Watson gave a white rat to a year-old child having no fear of small animals. As the child reached for it, a loud noise was

made behind his head. He drew back, startled. This was repeated several times. After conditioning, the child cried at
seeing the rat alone. The acquired fear spread to similar objects, like a rabbit, dog, and fur coat. In accounting for fears
and other emotional reactions, Watson thereafter stressed
experience, especially in childhood.

A few years after Watson's experiment, Mary Cover Jones
showed that fears can be eliminated by conditioning. While a
child who feared rabbits was eating, she brought a caged rabbit into the room and kept it some distance away. During
subsequent meals the rabbit was brought closer and closer
until the youngster ventured to touch it, eventually to fondle
it. The procedure was very gradual. A too-hasty approach
might have brought back all the old fear, indeed might have
transferred it to the food instead of removing it from the
rabbit.

Dr. Jones found that most methods recommended to eliminate fears do not work. Fears, she learned, do not "die out"
with time, nor can they be argued away. Becoming familiar
with a feared object by constant exposure to it may reduce
fear, but even this seldom entirely removes the fear. Repressing fear because other children ridicule it only intensifies emotional reaction, she discovered.

A method called "social imitation," in which a child having
a fear is placed with others not having the fear, sometimes is
successful. Their reassurance helps him overcome his fright.
Social imitation and reconditioning, mainly the latter, are
the most effective ways of eliminating fear.

Neal Miller has shown in a study of rats that an acquired
fear may eventually function as a drive, such as hunger, thirst,
sex, or any other unlearned motive. At the human level, the
"phobia" is an acquired fear (of closed places, heights, thunder, etc.) which may have a tremendous effect upon a person's
life. Similarly, anxiety, which is related to fear but is a less
specific state of apprehension, is learned, and may become a
strong motive. According to psychiatrist Harry Stack Sullivan,
anxiety is basically a fear, stemming from insecurity, and is
learned in infancy due to deprivation and lack of affection
from the significant adults in the child's life.

Punishment, too, may have the power of a drive. B. F. Skinner found its initial effect was to reduce a rat's rate of responding (i.e., its activity), but his punished rats later caught up with the unpunished group. Later, William K. Estes explained the effect of punishment as conditioned emotional responses. Richard L. Solomon and L. C. Wynne discovered that when such responses are conditioned by extremely painful stimuli, they are highly resistant to extinction, becoming firm and lasting.

How we express our emotions, as well as what arouses them, depends a good deal on our training and experience. Otto Klineberg presented interesting anthropological evidence of this. The Chinese are "poker faced" largely because they are taught restraint. Chinese boys and girls learn not to laugh boisterously or show their anger. Yet in different environments with different culture patterns, like Hawaii, Chinese persons express their emotions more like Westerners.

Many emotional expressions differ the world over. In some societies the kiss as a sign of affection is unknown; instead, two persons may rub noses, touch the nose to the other's cheek, or touch the other's nose with the index finger. Weeping often is part of tribal ceremonies, yet once the ceremony ends, laughter and gaiety follow quite naturally. Certain peoples vent their anger in queer traditional ways; they break up their possessions or set fire to their own houses. Laughter, however, seems the universal expression of high spirits. Klineberg concluded that emotional expression, like language, must be at least partially learned.

EXPERIMENTAL NEUROSIS

Emotional upset is the primary ingredient in mental illness. Long ago, Ivan Pavlov found that he could produce emotional conflicts in dogs by means of conditioning. He called this "experimental neurosis." A dog was trained to salivate by being given food whenever a circle of light appeared. The same dog was shown an elliptical patch of light, but was not fed and did not salivate. After the dog clearly differentiated between the circle and the ellipse, the latter was made more and more circular. When the two became almost identical, the animal's powers of discrimination broke down. It salivated without restraint, barked, whined, and struggled to get out of its harness. The experimental conditions had placed so much strain upon the dog's ability to differentiate stimuli that it became a neurotic animal, according to Pavlov's interpretation.

Later investigators have followed Pavlov's lead. Howard S. Liddell, of Cornell University, produced nervous, disorganized behavior in sheep and pigs, using Pavlov's technique with some modifications. Norman R. F. Maier, of the University of Michigan, trained rats to discriminate between two cards of different brightness; then changed the conditions and forced the animals to act without having any appropriate response. The rats showed abnormal behavior. They jumped wildly, ran violently to and fro, went into epileptic-like convulsions, and became rigid or passive as if in a coma. The essential condition for such abnormal behavior, said Maier, seems to be the necessity of reacting in a situation in which all ordinary modes of behavior have been removed.

In another study, psychiatrist Jules Masserman trained cats to open small boxes containing food. He then punished them when they attempted to open the boxes. This produced markedly deviant behavior; some of the cats became fearful of the box; others went into cataleptic states and would not move or eat for long periods of time. Like Maier, Masserman considered such traumatically produced disturbances in animals to be analogous to neuroses in human beings.

In 1950 John Dollard and Neal Miller sought to bring laboratory and clinic closer together by reviewing studies of animal conflict and relating them to behavior disorders in humans. Their paradigm for conflict was the so-called "approach-avoidance" type, in which a conflict between desire and fear is produced. This scheme was carried out by training an animal to get food in a certain spot; then when he responded this way, an electric shock was administered. Dollard and Miller saw conflict as a learned reaction; they also interpreted psychotherapy as a process of learning and, following some earlier work by Robert R. Sears, attempted to explain psychoanalysis in terms of learning theory.

FRUSTRATION

Dollard and Miller, along with their colleagues Leonard W. Doob, O. Hobart Mowrer, and Robert R. Sears, published a book in 1939 entitled *Frustration and Aggression.* They proposed that frustration leads to aggression, and that the occurrence of aggression presupposes frustration. This theory stirred up interest, but proved difficult to defend *in toto*, though it is undeniable that frustration very often arouses anger and aggressive behavior. Somewhat earlier, Saul Rosenzweig had suggested that there are three types of reaction to frustration: the "extrapunitive," marked by anger and blaming of others; the "intropunitive," characterized by humiliation, guilt, and blaming oneself; and the "impunitive," involving embarrassment, shame, and the condoning of the situation. S. Stansfeld Sargent proposed that reaction to frustration involves four steps or stages: frustration, emotion, habit or mechanism, and overt behavior. Each stage is determined by the previous one, as well as by the individual's past experience and the present situation as he perceives it. If anger is the dominant emotion evoked, aggressive behavior is likely to follow; if fear or anxiety is aroused, the behavior will, in all probability, be different.

Many experimental studies of frustration have been performed. One of the best known was done by Roger G. Barker, Tamara Dembo, and Kurt Lewin. Several nursery school children were given toys to play with, while observers rated their performance on a scale of "constructiveness." The youngsters were then allowed to play for fifteen minutes with a number of much more interesting toys. Then, without explanation, the children were forced to return to their earlier, less desirable playthings, though they could still see the fine toys at the end of the room. They revealed their frustration in various ways, the most significant being a great decrease in the constructiveness of their play. In Freudian terms their frustration caused regression to a more infantile level of behavior.

Psychosomatic Disorders

Relevant to the topic of emotion are the effects of emotions upon bodily ills. For hundreds of years, the adverse effects of anger and fear upon the organism had been observed or at least suspected. Not until the early years of the present century, however, did we learn of the precise physiological changes produced by emotional upsets; this knowledge was derived largely from the work of Cannon, Carlson, and others. In the meantime, the pioneer French psychiatrists—Charcot, Liébeault, and Bernheim—had been describing hysteria as the outcome of emotional conflict (see Chapter XIV). This paved the way for Sigmund Freud's formulation of emotional conflict as the basis for the bodily symptoms found in hysteria and related neurotic disorders.

By the 1930's, psychosomatic research was well underway; extensive reports and interpretations were given by Drs. Flanders Dunbar, Franz Alexander, and others, and the journal *Psychosomatic Medicine* was founded. Researchers found, for example, that emotional conflicts and persisting hate or fear reactions are primary causes of stomach ulcers and colitis. Bela Mittelman and Harold G. Wolff showed that resentment and anger caused an increase in the secretion of acid gastric juice, in the number of stomach contractions, and in the degree of blood flow to the area. This was true for both ulcer and normal patients, and was, as Harold G. Wolff and Stewart Wolf found, different from the effect produced by fear and dejection, which is marked by a decrease in gastric juice and constriction of the blood vessels. Other medical studies have pointed to the significance of emotional factors in the causation of hypertension, asthma, dermatitis, headache, backache, and a large number of other somatic complaints.

The theory of stress elaborated by Hans Selye, a Canadian endocrinologist, offers another interpretation of psychosomatic disorders. Any injury to the organism, physical or psychological, provokes a stress reaction or "general adaptation syndrome," according to Selye. The first phase is an "alarm reaction" sparked by the pituitary and adrenal glands. This reaction produces changes like those associated with unpleasant emotion, along with common symptoms such as fatigue, fever, headache, loss of appetite, aching muscles and joints, and a feeling of malaise. If the stress-producing situation persists, a "state of resistance" ensues, in which the organism, aided by hormones, manages to adjust to the stress. With continuing stress, the organism enters the "state of exhaustion," during which its resistance breaks down and many of the earlier symptoms recur.

Selye subjected animals to a number of different stressful situations, and found that the resulting physiological reactions were not specific to the situation but were, to a considerable extent, a generalized pattern of changes. These findings do not, of course, rule out the possibility of individual variations in the type and severity of symptoms induced by stress. Thus Selye's "general adaptation syndrome" seems a very plausible theory of the origin and nature of psychosomatic illness.

Let us turn now to personality and its development.

Chapter XI

PERSONALITY AND INFLUENCES
ON ITS DEVELOPMENT

HIPPOCRATES THEOPHRASTUS BAIN NIETZSCHE
SPRANGER ALLPORT KRETSCHMER SHELDON
FREUD ADLER JUNG SULLIVAN
GOLDSTEIN MEAD BENEDICT KARDINER LINTON
BURT BETTELHEIM MURPHY NEWCOMB

*What is personality? Do personality types exist? To
what extent does personality have a physical basis?
How is personality development affected by the
family, school, community, and other cultural
influences?*

Each of us has a personality unique and distinct from every
other person. By personality we mean the sum total, the general pattern, of an individual's ways of thinking, feeling, and
behaving, especially with reference to other people. This pattern results from a combination of physiological and social
forces, though heredity and prenatal influences lay physical
foundations. Environment, including home and family,
friends, school, church, neighborhood community, and nation, also affect us indelibly. Whether physical or social forces
contribute more to personality is still the subject of considerable dispute, but as we saw in Chapter III, both are essential.

Personality is not an elusive quality which radiates from
certain fortunate persons and not from others. It is unbeliev-
ably complex, the result of a lifetime of experiences and influences. Superficial changes, like affecting a genial smile, adopt-

ing a new hairdo, or cultivating poise, fail to affect our true personalities, which go much deeper.

Until recent times the meaning of personality was not clearly defined. The word itself probably derived from the Latin *persona*, a mask through which an actor spoke his lines. In this sense it referred to external appearance, or the role one plays.

But the word "personality" has been used in many ways. Gordon W. Allport identified no less than fifty different usages with theological, philosophical, legal, psychological, and other connotations. Allport considers personality to be the pattern of habits, attitudes, and traits that determine an individual's characteristic behavior and thought. Gardner Murphy has stressed the "biosocial" nature of personality, and has surveyed it all the way from hereditary origins to social and cultural pressures which shape it. Let us examine some of the best-known ways of judging and categorizing personality.

THEORIES OF PERSONALITY TYPES

Almost everyone who has ever pondered the problem of personality has sooner or later classified people into types, generally on the basis of certain physical characteristics.

The first classification into types was the work of Hippocrates, famous Greek physician of the fifth century B.C. Human temperaments, he said, are divided into the *sanguine*, the *melancholic*, the *choleric*, and the *phlegmatic*, according to the dominance of the following bodily "humors": red blood, black bile, yellow bile, or phlegm respectively. This assigning of a bodily basis for personality has a very modern sound, and has an echo in recent attempts to explain personality through study of the endocrine glands or of biochemistry.

Theophrastus, a pupil of Aristotle, founded "characterology," a literary description of personality types. He described, skillfully and with striking examples of behavior, thirty extreme types of persons, such as the penurious man, the boor, the flatterer, or the loquacious man.

Two thousand years later character writing was resumed by the Frenchman Jean de la Bruyère and by numerous English writers, among them Ben Jonson, Joseph Addison, Richard

Steele, and Samuel Butler. Character writers have generally shown much psychological insight, though they seldom have probed deep enough to uncover the real origins of behavior.

The nineteenth century produced several interesting personality type theories. Alexander Bain, impressed with Plato's threefold division of the soul, suggested that men's energies go chiefly into intellectual, emotional, or volitional channels. This theory survives in the classification of people into intellectual, artistic, and practical types.

Friedrich Nietzsche proposed two contrasting philosophies of life, the Apollonian and Dionysian. The Apollonian signifies calm, reason, restraining the passions, and, in general, living by the rule of "nothing to excess." In the Dionysian way the senses and impulses dominate, free from reason's restraint.

William James suggested that people can be divided into the "tender minded" and the "tough minded," according to whether they are influenced more by ideas or by facts. Similarly William Stern divided them into subjective and objective.

Probably the best-known type theory is Carl G. Jung's introversion-extroversion. The *introvert* is preoccupied with his own impressions and psychological processes; for him subjective factors dominate. The *extrovert* leans toward objective facts, and activities in the outside world. Outward relations, not subjective values are important. Hermann Rorschach, originator of the famous inkblot test, arrived at somewhat similar categories. The introversive person has well-developed inner resources and is largely self-sufficient; he is not dependent upon other people but may enjoy social contacts. In contrast, the extroversive person responds readily to the outside environment either warmly and creatively, or with more passive acceptance. Neither Jung nor Rorschach suggested that people should be classified either as introverts or extroverts. Unfortunately this often is assumed. He said that everyone has tendencies toward both introversion and extroversion, though one generally predominates. In fact, the same person may alternate between introversion and extroversion.

One other type theory holds considerable interest. Edouard Spranger, a German psychologist, classified people according to what values they believed most important. He noted six types: theoretical, economic, political, esthetic, social, and religious. He admitted that people do not fit exclusively into one or another category. Allport and Vernon devised a test based on Spranger's six values. Their results showed that persons in various arts, professions, or in education do lean toward the values predominant in their own fields. Engineering and business students scored highest in economic values; language and literature students in esthetic values; persons preparing for the ministry in religious values. Men ranked higher in theoretical, economic, and political values, women in esthetic, social, and religious values. The differences in tendency were not large, however. People generally do not stress any one value to the exclusion of others.

Physical Characteristics and Personality

Physiognomy. Physiognomy interprets personality from physical features, particularly the face. It began before Aristotle's time and revived with the Renaissance. We review it here for its historical interest.

Johann Lavater, the best-known physiognomist, wrote late in the eighteenth century. He described the psychological significance of height of forehead, shape of nose or jaw, and other features. Though for the most part unscientific, he maintained that a person's features are consistent with each other. Gordon W. Allport and Philip E. Vernon show some evidence for this theory by demonstrating a consistency between such expressive features as voice and handwriting.

More modern writers have claimed that type of facial features reveals personality. The Italian criminologist, Cesare Lombroso, said that criminals have prominent cheekbones and jaw, oblique eyes, receding forehead, and large ears. Skeptical of this, the English scientists Charles Goring and Karl Pearson measured features of 3,000 criminals and compared results with measurements of college students and army men. No differences were found between the physiognomies of criminals and of Oxford or Cambridge men. Havelock Ellis, among others, claimed that skin and hair coloring tie up with personality traits. Studying portraits, he reported that thinkers and writers are brunet while men of action and ambition are blond.

In 1930 Donald G. Paterson published *Physique and Intellect*, which summarized the case against physiognomy. Absolutely no evidence exists that shape of nose, mouth, or ears, height of forehead, contour of skull, or any other feature has anything to do with personality. A cheery or sad facial expression may reveal a psychological state, but this is very different from what the physiognomists claim. As Gordon Allport says, our muscles—including those of the face—reflect life experiences to some extent, but our bony structures do not.

We shall next discuss the more important physical approach resulting from the studies of types of bodily constitution.

CONSTITUTIONAL TYPES

A persisting type theory centers about biological structure or body form. This stemmed primarily from the work of Ernst Kretschmer, a German psychiatrist. He distinguished three body types. The "pyknic" is short and stout or at least thickset. The "leptosome," or "asthenic," is tall and thin. The "athletic" is muscular and well proportioned. In mental hospitals Kretschmer examined manic-depressive and schizophrenic (dementia praecox) patients. (Manic-depressive persons show extreme elation, extreme depression, or alternate between the two. Schizophrenics show emotional apathy, introversion, and withdrawal from reality.) Manic-depressives, Kretschmer found, tend to be pyknic in type, while schizophrenics are leptosome and athletic. Kretschmer believed practically all persons of pyknic body build are "cyclothyme" in temperament, that is, they alternate in mood and are extroverted. Most leptosomes are "schizothyme"—inclined to be shy, serious, and introverted, he reported. Actually the body-form differences he notes between schizophrenics and manic-depressives may be due to their age differences, because schizophrenics average many years younger than manic-depressives; persons tend to become shorter and heavier as they grow older. Among normal individuals there is practically no evidence that a relation exists between body form and personality type.

An American psychologist and physician, W. H. Sheldon, has recently carried forward "constitutional psychology" with vigor and improved techniques. He proposes three basic "somatotypes":

> Endomorphy, meaning roundness and softness of body form, with relatively little development of bone and muscle
>
> Mesomorphy, referring to the strong, athletic physique, with well-developed muscles and bones
>
> Ectomorphy, indicating a linear and fragile build, flat-chested, thin, and delicate

These three components exist in all degrees, Sheldon concluded after studying several thousand photographs of male college students. He rated each component on a scale from 1 to 7; thus the extreme endomorph would be 7-1-1 and the most pronounced ectomorph 1-1-7. A 4-7-1 would be average in endomorphy, high in mesomorphy, and low in ectomorphy.

Sheldon reported a close correlation between each of his somatotypes and certain temperament patterns of personality. The endomorph, whose "digestive tract is king," is high in "viscerotonia"; that is, he loves food, comfort, and sociability and is relaxed, even-tempered, and tolerant. The mesomorph by contrast, is "somatotonic," which means that he needs vigorous muscular exercise, and is energetic, aggressive, and dominant. The ectomorph is "cerebrotonic," indicating inhibition, sensitivity, secretiveness, and preference for being alone.

Other investigators have questioned Sheldon's findings, and find lower, sometimes negligible correlations between physique and temperament. Some critics say that associations, when found, may not be due to an inherited, biological relationship, but to social factors. Thus athletes, who have high status in our culture, are encouraged by social expectation to be dominant and aggressive.

In any event, the scientific advance resulting from Sheldon's improved methods of somatotyping is undeniable.

BIOCHEMICAL BASES OF PERSONALITY

In 1928 Gilbert J. Rich measured the relation between body alkalinity and emotional excitability. College students and clinic patients were rated for excitability by persons well acquainted with them. Their alkalinity, as revealed in saliva or urine, showed a slight positive correlation with the degree of excitability assigned them on the ratings. Most other attempts to relate biochemical conditions with personality have failed.

On the other hand Roger J. Williams, a biochemist, believes that the great individual variations among people in anatomy and physiology—in the brain and nervous system, in the gastrointestinal tract, in blood groups, in the neuromuscular system—are of great significance to personality. He is aware of the profound effect of cultural factors, but it seems probable, he says, that a person's distinctive endocrine system and brain structure are more important influences than infant toilet training, which has been so much emphasized recently.

It may help the reader to recall our earlier discussion, toward the end of Chapter III, of the many ways in which the term "personality" is used. The studies of Rich and Williams, we suggest, seem very relevant to personality as temperament, but hardly to personality as attitudes, values, and interests.

NEUROLOGICAL CONDITIONS

A few researchers have been concerned with the effect of abnormal biochemical or neurological conditions upon personality. Kurt Goldstein, a German neuropsychiatrist, studied brain-injured soldiers following the First World War. His principal finding was that such "organic" cases have lost the power to abstract, which affects their behavior tremendously. For example, a brain-injured person cannot comprehend the idea—the concept—of a mirror or a clock, although he might make use of both correctly. He tends to be limited to the concrete; he cannot understand principles, directions, or logical relationships. However, to understand an organically injured person one must study his whole pattern of behavior as he seeks ways of adjusting to his environment; his attempts to realize himself—his "self-actualization"—became the keynote of Goldstein's "organismic" theory of personality.

FREUD AND PSYCHOANALYTIC INTERPRETATIONS

Sigmund Freud, developing psychoanalysis to cure neurotic persons, worked out his theory of personality. Every person has a fundamental drive or source of energy called *libido*. Broadly speaking it is a sexual drive. The libido springs from the vast unconscious part of our mental life. Our complete self includes the *Id, Ego,* and *Superego.* The Id is our primitive animal nature. Located in the unconscious, it constantly strives to satisfy the libido. Our rational self is the Ego, which controls the Id's animal urges and "represses" them into the unconscious, though it does permit some expression of Id impulses. Similar to conscience, the Superego is a repository of moral ideas. It works on the Ego to repress the Id's socially reprehensible tendencies. The Superego and Id are in continual conflict, which the Ego tries to resolve. In a normal person the conflict is resolved successfully.

Freud traces personality development. A baby's libido is undirected. In the Narcissistic period, named for the legendary youth who fell in love with his own image, a young child's libido turns toward himself. When four or five, a child's libido attaches to an external object—one of his parents.

Emphasizing the libido's sexual nature even in childhood, Freud introduced his famous concept, the "Oedipus complex." The male child has sexual love for his mother. Jealous of his father, he comes actually to hate him. Conversely, a little girl develops intense father love, with hostility toward the mother. Normally, says Freud, the Oedipus complex disappears at adolescence when the libido fixes on adolescents of the opposite sex.

Freud's emphasis on infant sexuality is confirmed in studies by Susan Isaacs, Gilbert V. Hamilton, and others. With regard to the Oedipus complex, however, experimental studies do not confirm Freud's view. Lewis Terman, for example, found no evidence that boys favor their mothers and girls their fathers, but rather that both boys and girls favor the mother slightly. Studies of the personality development of children agree roughly with Freud's theories of libido development, but with many exceptions.

Freud's successors have placed less stress on instinctual forces, including the sex drive, and more upon cultural and social influences. E. H. Erikson, for example, finds that the ego faces crucial problems at all stages of individual development. At the early "oral-sensory" stage, the child's feeding experience may lead to either trust or mistrust. At the later latency or pubertal periods, difficulties may result in inferiority reactions or failure of ego identity. Erikson believes that the stages of ego development form an orderly sequence but are much affected by social experiences, not only in the family but also in the community and larger settings. (See Chapter IV.)

Adler's Approach

The emphasis upon social influences in personality development is apparent in the writings of others inspired by psychoanalysis. Though he realized that personality traits do not depend upon body form or endocrine glands, Alfred Adler saw important connections between physique and personality. He noticed that "feelings of inferiority" often develop in persons having a physical handicap. Lame, undersized, ugly, or deformed children may feel inferior and attempt to compensate for their defects, real or imagined. Their whole personalities may be affected by the compensation. Actually the inferiority does not arise from the defect itself, but from the unfortunate comparison with normal persons. If everyone were crippled, none would feel inferior. If all women were homely, none would be concerned about her lack of beauty. Thus physical factors influence personality only because social factors make them important.

The Views of Sullivan

Harry Stack Sullivan, Karen Horney, and Erich Fromm are sometimes called "neo-analysts" because their theories and interpretations, while generally psychoanalytic, differ perceptibly from Freud's. (The theories of Horney and Fromm will be described in Chapter XIV.) Sullivan thought of personality as enmeshed in interpersonal behavior. He saw development as a series of stages which are not so much a biological unfolding as a sequence of interpersonal relationships with "significant others" in infancy, childhood, preadolescence, adolescence, and maturity. How a person thinks of himself (his self-image) depends upon his treatment by these significant persons, as does his view of the world and his attitude toward people. If he acquires distorted rather than realistic perceptions they may be corrected or validated by later communication and interaction with people.

Social Factors in Personality Development

William James, James M. Baldwin, and other early psychologists have noted how a child's early social contacts help to build his "self" or "social self"—later termed "personality." Charles H. Cooley, a sociologist, has stressed the influence of parents and others with whom a child associates constantly. Selfhood, or personality, including ideas, attitudes, and even intelligence, depends a good deal on what kind of persons they are and how they treat the child, Cooley says.

George H. Mead, a philosopher, believed that a child in his first social contacts assumes a role and plays a part. Early roles probably imitate the father or mother, later the policeman, cook, storekeeper, or cowboy. From these roles, both realistic and imaginative, emerges a generalized behavior pattern basic to his personality, according to Mead.

Sociologists and anthropologists stress the importance of environmental factors in personality development. William I. Thomas and Florian Znaniecki studied Polish peasant immigrants in the United States. They found that great changes occur, over a period of years, in personality, attitudes, and social organization because of the new environment. Thomas believed, as did his fellow sociologists Ernest W. Burgess and Ellsworth Faris, that the cultures in which people live and the cultural changes they experience affect their personalities in major ways.

Margaret Mead, well-known American anthropologist,

found that adolescent girls in Samoa do not suffer the "storm and stress" common among girls of our culture. Samoan customs permit early sexual experience. Adolescents have a specific station in society, whereas in our culture a girl's rights and privileges depend mostly on her parents' notion of what is good and proper. Some girls "date" freely at fourteen, others are shadowed by chaperones until nearly twenty. She concluded that Samoan adolescents pass through puberty free from conflict, which suggests that our so-called "typical" adolescent difficulties depend on social instead of biological factors.

Dr. Mead also studied psychological differences between men and women in three neighboring but culturally contrasting groups. Local customs, she discovered, can modify "masculine" and "feminine" temperament a good deal. In one of the cultures both men and women were mild and responsive; in another both were violent and aggressive. In the third she found "a genuine reversal of the sex-attitudes of our own culture, with the woman the dominant, impersonal, managing partner, the man the less responsible and the emotionally dependent person." Though there were some exceptions, Mead felt she was describing the great majority of men and women in each group. Thus, despite the physical differences between the sexes, their personalities and social behavior were found to be patterned primarily by their cultures.

Ruth Benedict, another noted American anthropologist, pointed out striking personality differences among peoples in various cultures that stressed different values. The Zuñi Indians of New Mexico, whose culture demanded conformity to tribal ritual, lacked initiative and individualism. In contrast, the Dobuan people of New Guinea were competitive, deceitful, and dominated by a belief in magical formulas and incantations. Kwakiutl customs emphasized striving for prestige, superiority, and self-glorification. Apparently tribal values influenced the personalities of all individuals in the group, though some exceptions doubtless existed.

Psychoanalyst Abram Kardiner and anthropologist Ralph Linton spoke of "basic personality structure" as those aspects of personality shared by most members of a society as a result of their common early experiences. Basic personality grows out of child care disciplines such as the kind of maternal care, affectional relations with parents, type of discipline, and relationships with siblings. These influences not only determine the child's attitudes, but through the process of projection account for institutions like religion, art, folklore, and so on, Kardiner concluded. Recently anthropologists have favored the term "modal personality" for the most characteristic patterns of personality appearing in a culture.

It is not necessary, however, to turn to so-called "primitive" peoples to see how environment affects personality; we can see it in isolated communities of our own country. Mandel Sherman discovered that children living in a remote mountain hollow of Virginia had little initiative or imagination. They did not even play. Practically no social organization existed. Nor did competition or frustration. The very young children resembled those in nearby villages. As they grew older they became listless, dull, and superstitious like their adult relatives.

John Dollard, of Yale University, believes certain social and cultural criteria must be applied in tracing personality development. The customs of a person's social group must be known. His family must be studied carefully because it affects his personality vitally. Special attention should be given to the relationship between biological factors like endocrines and all the social forces influencing him. Throughout his life his personality is shaped by and interwoven with his social environment.

Lawrence K. Frank says "culture is literally built into the organism." Custom determines even the intervals between meals, time of weaning, type of toilet training, and kinds of stimuli to which persons respond emotionally. All behavior patterns that parents teach their children are cultural products. Important among them are moral ideas, social attitudes, and interests. Frank concludes that culture is the ground from which personality emerges.

FAMILY INFLUENCES

Most psychologists would agree that social factors are the significant determiners of our personality traits, and first among these comes the family. A congenial home atmosphere, with good relations between the parents and between the parents and the child, is almost essential for development of a well-adjusted personality. Early studies of broken homes supported this theory. Cyril Burt, a British psychologist, found that 58% of the delinquents he observed came from families split by death, divorce, or other absence of one parent. Only 25% of non-delinquent children from comparable environments were products of broken homes. Later studies generally arrive at the same conclusion, though the results are not always as striking. Many investigators believe that the most harmful factor is not so much the loss of a parent as it is a disharmonious or hostile relationship between parents. Hornell Hart and E. B. Hart, sociologists, find that constant antagonism between parents can disrupt a child's personality. The child has a close emotional tie to each parent. Hence their quarrels cause serious conflict in his own personality. Often the conflict leads to abnormal or anti-social behavior.

A Viennese psychologist, August Aichhorn, reported that children in his institution for delinquents came almost entirely from disrupted or disharmonious homes. La Berta W. Hattwick, Winnetka child psychologist, found that pre-school children from calm, happy homes behaved cooperatively and showed good emotional adjustment. They were remarkably free from jealousy, nervous habits, sulking, and fears. In contrast, children from homes marked by tension and conflict between parents proved uncooperative, emotionally insecure, disturbed, and given to jealousy, crying, fears, and nervous habits.

Adults whose personalities were not warped in childhood by emotionally upset homes tend to have happier marriages. This was pointed out by Lewis M. Terman and by the sociologists Ernest W. Burgess and Leonard S. Cottrell. Happy marriages are commonest among persons whose parents were happily married.

The behaviorists, led by John B. Watson in the 1920's, insisted that child development is largely a matter of conditioning, which can be applied scientifically and objectively. This became the rationale for regimented feeding schedules and for a depersonalized and fairly strict discipline. A generation later, however, permissiveness was in the ascendant, and Dr. Benjamin Spock, in his popular *Pocket Book of Baby and Child Care,* urged parents to trust themselves and to play with and enjoy their children. Another wave of firmness and discipline may now be on the way, suggesting that child-rearing "fashions" tend to go in cycles.

Parent-child behavior has been categorized into three dimensions by Alfred L. Baldwin and his colleagues at the Fels Research Institute:

1. Acceptance-rejection, referring to the emotional relationship

2. Possessiveness-detachment, running the gamut from protectiveness and interference all the way to actual neglect

3. Democracy-autocracy, describing the general home atmosphere in terms of participation

These dimensions were found to be relatively independent. For example, rejection or lack of warmth might or might not be accompanied by a passive and detached kind of treatment or by autocratic and dictatorial methods.

Robert R. Sears, Eleanor Maccoby, and Harry Levin studied a representative group of mothers in New England. Data collected were analyzed statistically and several factors isolated. The most all-pervasive dimension to emerge was *permissiveness-strictness* of mothers. An interesting finding was that permissiveness regarding aggression results in a high level of aggressive behavior, not that general restriction produces aggression. Another dimension was *warmth* of mother-child relationship. Maternal coldness was found to be correlated with emotional difficulties centering about feeding and bladder control. In a similar study D. R. Miller and G. E. Swanson, emphasizing the powerful affect of child-training patterns, point out the futility of prescribing child-rearing practices until the nature of the society in which the child is to fit is known.

After extensive study of scientists, Anne Roe finds that many researchers are drawn toward the physical world because social relations are not particularly rewarding to them. She concludes that whether one has strong achievement needs, is aggressive, or is interested in social interaction apparently depends in large part on early training practices.

Many other psychological studies have shown a close correlation between the personality or behavior of children and the predominant type of parental behavior. Cyril Burt found defective home discipline among 61% of his delinquent children and among less than 12% of his comparable non-delinquent group. August Aichhorn showed that parental neglect causes behavior problems in children as much as overprotection does. Delinquency results mainly from parents rejecting a child, not from excessive love, which merely encourages childishness and immaturity, he pointed out.

Richard H. Paynter and Phyllis Blanchard, clinical psychologists, analyzed the backgrounds of delinquent and behavior problem children brought to clinics. Home training and discipline were found at fault in 90% of cases. Sheldon and Eleanor Glueck, psychiatrists, studied 500 delinquent boys, matched with non-delinquents for age, intelligence, and social background. They found great differences in home treatment. The delinquents were typically rejected or treated with indifference, and their disciplining was lax, overstrict, or inconsistent.

David Levy reported on "maternal overprotection," which he found to be either "dominating" or "indulgent." The former tended to produce submissiveness or dependency and the latter aggressiveness or even delinquency. Another psychiatrist, Edward A. Strecker, described the evils of "momism"—the mother's clinging to her offspring and refusing to grant them emotional emancipation. He found it produces serious immaturity in later life. (Philip Wylie, the writer who coined the term "momism," wrote interestingly on the problem in his book, *Generation of Vipers*.)

Probably rejection of the child has been regarded as the most harmful parental practice, since the days of William Healy, pioneer student of delinquency in the United States. But it is easy to oversimplify. Love, for example, is the opposite of rejection, but love can turn into indulgence or overprotection, as Bruno Bettelheim notes in his book *Love Is Not Enough*. Percival Symonds compared children from families having dominant parents with those having submissive parents. He found some bad and some good results in each case, and concluded that a golden mean somewhere between parental dominance and submission is best.

The effect upon personality of a child's position in the family has interested several psychologists. Younger children in a family, said Alfred Adler, feel inferior to their older brothers and sisters. They compensate by developing a great drive for superiority. A child's personality pattern depends a good deal on his family position—whether he is an oldest, middle, youngest, or only child, according to Adler.

However, results of studies that compare the personalities of older, younger, and only children are inconclusive and contradictory. Summarizing 50 of them, Gardner Murphy, Lois Murphy, and Theodore Newcomb, in their *Experimental Social Psychology*, noted that little evidence supports the claim that a certain ordinal position in the family affects personality. "Psychological" position in the family, on the other hand, is important, they pointed out. This depends on the child's emotional relationships with his parents and with brothers and sisters. Similarly, ordinal position such as "oldest child" might have great importance in certain cultures, and this particular social role could affect personality significantly.

Stanley Schachter, in a recent study of affiliative tendencies, found that when they are anxious, first-born persons are more likely than are the later-born to seek out social means of handling their anxieties—for example, through talking with others, joining a group, or asking for psychotherapy. This interesting finding is likely to evoke further research.

SCHOOL AND PERSONALITY

Compared to the home, the school seems to play a small part in shaping a child's personality. But since the advent of progressive education, inspired by John Dewey, in the 1920's, teachers became more interested in educating the "whole child." Not just training in skills, but developing the personality became more and more the concern of educators. Starting at age six, the child spends ten or twelve of his formative years in school. During these years he becomes increasingly socialized and emotionally controlled, in addition to learning essential skills and information.

Children of less than average ability have a difficult time in school. Ira S. Wile, well-known New York psychiatrist, showed how hard a time the dull child has trying to meet school standards. Unless given personal attention or placed in a special group, he probably reacts to his inadequacy by open rebellion or passive daydreaming. Both have bad consequences in personality development.

Teachers face a difficult job coping with pupils' personality problems. The child psychologists John J. B. Morgan and Carolyn Zachry, in their books on children's personality maladjustments, frequently noted aggressiveness, insecurity, daydreaming, glandular difficulties, overdependence, or anxiety. Unfortunately most teachers are not trained to deal adequately with pupils' problems. E. K. Wickman found that teachers considered sex offenses, lying, cheating, impertinence, and truancy the major problems. They rated as rather inconsequential seclusiveness and withdrawal. Several clinical psychologists, on the other hand, believed the unsocial behavior more serious and symptomatic of maladjustment.

Teachers influence their pupils a good deal, directly or indirectly. Studying honesty, Mark A. May and Hugh Hartshorne found that pupils of certain admired teachers cheated very little, while those of disliked teachers cheated often. Robert J. Havighurst showed how a teacher may influence a child's adjustment by helping him select friends and by rearranging play groups in order to improve social relationships.

Despite the crucial importance of the teaching profession, it is not held in very high esteem in the United States. Whether or not a result of this, both sociologist Willard Waller and psychologist Robert Challman find that many teachers suffer from frustrations, complexes, and personality problems that militate against their effectiveness and personal adjustment.

Education affects student attitudes, especially at the college level. Daniel Katz and Floyd H. Allport, testing college students, discovered more liberal religious attitudes in upperclassmen than in lowerclassmen. Theodore Newcomb found an increasingly liberal viewpoint on socioeconomic matters in a liberal arts women's college as the students progressed from freshman year to senior year. This change he attributed both to liberal faculty attitudes and to curricular emphasis upon contemporary problems. In a recent volume on the American college, Nevitt Sanford brings together a number of reports which shows a variety of trends in attitude and personality change, depending in large measure upon the intellectual atmosphere of the college involved.

All in all, the school does exert an influence upon child personality. Here youngsters learn many of the prevalent values, attitudes, and forms of social behavior of their culture. H. H. Anderson found that teachers displayed more "dominative" than "integrative" or democratic behavior, which seems poor preparation for living in a democracy. Cooperativeness is stressed as a virtue by teacher and textbook, but the basic pattern of life in school is competitive. This inconsistency, as the psychoanalyst Karen Horney noted, is the source of much conflict and maladjustment.

COMPANIONS AND THE COMMUNITY

Since World War II we have learned about the significance of "peer groups" in the child's preadolescent and adolescent periods. Havighurst points out that peer groups help socialize, sensitize, and indoctrinate the youngster and prepare him for independence. Chicago sociologists studied these influences as they relate to juvenile delinquency. Clifford Shaw found almost perfect correlation between the kind of neighborhood and its delinquency rate. Near Chicago's downtown "loop," slum areas lie among railroad yards, vacant lots, factories, and broken-down warehouses. Here delinquency is high. As one goes toward outlying residential areas, delinquency drops. Cyril Burt found the same situation in London, and later studies confirmed it for Philadelphia, Boston, Cleveland, and other cities.

William Healy noted how a child's companions affect his morals and conduct. Almost two-thirds of child delinquencies in Chicago and Boston trace directly to bad companions, he learned.

Another sociologist, Frederick M. Thrasher, studied more

than 1300 Chicago gangs. Not all of them influenced their members badly. The gang, he discovered, gives a youngster important social contacts. He gains status by taking a role in his gang. On the other hand, gangs flourish in bad neighborhoods. Often they lead children to become truants, then hoodlums, delinquents, and even criminals. William F. Whyte became a member of an Italian neighborhood gang in Boston in order to study its structure and function. The definite hierarchy and close-knit social relationships he found suggest the paramount significance of the adolescent gang to its members.

Effects of community on personality are sometimes striking. Sherman's study, mentioned earlier, of a backward, isolated, mountain community showed how this type of community fostered lack of initiative, lack of competitiveness, and lack of responsiveness. The well-known *Middletown* by Robert and Helen Lynd depicted a medium-sized Midwestern city. The authors focused on major aspects of community life such as earning a living, making a home, training the young, and using leisure. They felt that these community activities, especially their economic aspects, had most to do with determining the major values, attitudes, and opinions of the residents, though in many ways the community merely reflected the broader American culture pattern.

ECONOMIC AND GROUP STATUS FACTORS

Economic influences, as already suggested, have a tremendous effect on the developing personality. Poverty and the conditions accompanying it (poor neighborhood, overcrowding at home, parental discord, etc.) make up a major cause of juvenile delinquency.

James S. Plant, psychiatrist and director of New Jersey's Essex County Juvenile Clinic, found that overcrowded living conditions influence personality in unfortunate ways. Overcrowding, Plant noted, means little or no personal privacy, no chance to develop a sense of individuality or to look objectively at oneself. It involves also the strain of constantly having to get along with others.

Some investigators have found that children of low socioeconomic status may be toughened and strengthened by it. Arnold Gesell, for example, reported that poor children are better able to care for themselves than upper-class children of the same age. However, Ross Stagner found that college students from such backgrounds were handicapped by lack of confidence and by more frequent emotional upsets. Similarly, Paul Lazarsfeld discovered that continued unemployment had a demoralizing effect upon personality, including loss of confidence, loss of status, and a feeling of futility.

In their study of Middletown, the Lynds graphically summarized the influence of economic status on behavior:

It is after all this division into working class and business class that constitutes the outstanding cleavage in Middletown. The mere fact of being born upon one or the other side of the watershed roughly formed by these two groups is the most significant single cultural factor tending to influence what one does all day long throughout one's life; whom one marries; when one gets up in the morning; whether one belongs to the Holy Roller or Presbyterian church; or drives a Ford or a Buick; whether or not one's daughter makes the desirable high school Violet Club; or one's wife meets with the Sew We Do Club or with the Art Students' League; whether one belongs to the Odd Fellows or to the Masonic Shrine; whether one sits about evenings with one's necktie off; and so on indefinitely throughout the daily comings and goings of a Middletown man, woman, or child.

Still another social influence may affect personality importantly: belonging to an unfavored ethnic group. We shall consider this in our discussion of prejudice in Chapter XVI.

THE PERSONALITY PATTERN

It is clear that personality development results from many influences that operate in and upon a child. The temperament of an individual—that is, his underlying energy and emotional tone—apparently are affected by his endocrine glands, nervous system, and other physical or physiological conditions. But these factors by no means determine what Gordon Allport calls "the finished portrait" of personality. An individual's personality pattern, which includes traits, attitudes, interests, values, and ideals, is largely a product of his environment. The quality of a child's home and family is of paramount importance, but his school experience, his friends, his community, his socioeconomic status, and the whole culture pattern in which he lives also are significant. Evaluating the relative importance of these forces is a most difficult job for the psychologist; thus far only the surface has been scratched.

Chapter XII

EVALUATING PERSONALITY

WOODWORTH   ALLPORT   MURRAY
HARTSHORNE   MAY   MAC KINNON   FRANK
RORSCHACH   STRONG   KUDER   GUILFORD   TERMAN
MILES   EYSENCK   CATTELL

How is personality measured? Can personality be judged from performance? How do projective techniques differ from other types of tests? What is the chief value of interest tests? Do psychologists agree on the major dimensions of personality?

Assuming that the term "personality" is fairly well defined and understood from our discussion in the preceding chapter, there remains the problem of measuring and evaluating personality, and of differentiating among the personalities of various individuals.

PERSONALITY QUESTIONNAIRES

The measurement of personality began very shortly after psychologists succeeded in measuring intelligence. Personality questionnaires started when Robert S. Woodworth devised a "Personal Data Sheet" in 1918 to determine emotional instability or neurotic tendency among soldiers. It had 116 questions, each answered by yes or no. Woodworth chose items relating to various physical symptoms, fears, worries, feelings, and attitudes known to indicate mental and nervous disorders. Some of the questions are: Do you usually feel well and strong? Do you have nightmares? Have you often fainted away? Does liquor make you quarrelsome? Are you troubled with the idea that people are watching you on the street? Did you ever have the habit of wetting the bed? Did you ever have a nervous breakdown?

Following World War I many psychologists drew up personality questionnaires to measure introversion-extroversion, ascendance-submission, and many other traits. Robert G. Bernreuter prepared a "Personality Inventory" of 125 questions to be answered by encircling "Yes," "No," or "?." By scoring the answers four different ways, Bernreuter obtained measures of neurotic tendency, self-sufficiency, introversion-extroversion, and dominance-submission. For example, the question, Do athletics interest you more than intellectual affairs? relates significantly to introversion-extroversion. The question, Are people sometimes successful in taking advantage of you? relates most closely to dominance-submission.

John C. Flanagan, specialist in mental measurement, analyzed Bernreuter's test statistically and found it had two important components: self-confidence and sociability. Bernreuter then added these to his original four so that his test measured six personality traits.

Probably the best-known and most widely used of the personality inventories is the Minnesota Multiphasic Personality Inventory (MMPI), developed by Starke R. Hathaway and J. C. McKinley. This test contains several hundred items chosen with a view to differentiating "normal" persons from those who are hypochondriacal, depressed, psychopathic, schizophrenic, and the like. The test's reliability and validity are high enough to make it a valuable tool for the clinical and counseling psychologist, for both research and diagnostic purposes.

Unfortunately, people may answer questionnaires incorrectly, especially if they assume some answers are "right" and others are "wrong," or that certain responses will be regarded more favorably than others. One attempt to avoid this difficulty was made by Allen L. Edwards in his "Personality Preference Schedule," which yields information on a subject's needs such as achievement, dominance, aggression, deference, and so forth. Here the subject responds by choosing between two statements which have been matched for "social desirability." On the whole, however, psychologists have felt that the errors of personality questionnaires are avoided best by the use of performance tests. In performance tests the subject is not asked to tell about himself but is given the opportunity to perform or behave, and his behavior is used as an index or key to his personality.

PERFORMANCE TESTS

Among the earliest performance tests was June E. Downey's "will temperament" test, based mainly on handwriting. It purported to measure persistence, decisiveness, speed, flexibility, and other traits. A subject writes "United States of America" at his usual speed, then writes it as fast as he can. The difference between his two speeds indicates freedom from inhibition. His ability to change writing speed shows how flexible his personality is. His success in writing several words on a line slightly over an inch long demonstrates his coordination of impulses.

Dr. Downey's test was popular during the 1920's. But it proved a poor measure of personality, chiefly because psychologists showed that no one type of expression like handwriting indicates personality trends adequately.

On the other hand, Gordon W. Allport and Hadley Cantril showed that judges could identify personality characteristics somewhat better than chance simply by hearing a person's voice. Allport and Philip Vernon found that a person's handwriting, walking, reading, and other forms of expressive behavior also fit into a fairly consistent personality pattern. Werner Wolff studied a large variety of expressions of personality and found them to be congruent within the individual, though the latter was often unaware of this pattern. Nevertheless, the matching of expressive material such as handwriting specimens with personality sketches of the writers yields results which are closer to chance than to perfection, as Allport and Vernon point out. So we must conclude that expressive movements do not furnish a reliable index of personality in the broader sense.

Leslie R. Marston estimated introversion-extroversion in children by observing their behavior in a toy room and in a museum. He found their actions in these situations correlated fairly well with their teachers' ratings on introversion-extroversion. A more elaborate performance study of personality was an honesty test devised by Hugh Hartshorne and Mark A. May. They gave children many natural situations wherein they easily could cheat. They could copy from a neighbor's paper, change answers when scoring their own tests, "peep" in a blindfold game. Other situations tested stealing and lying impulses.

A general trait of honesty or dishonesty does not exist, Hartshorne and May found. Almost all children were dishonest in at least one situation, but many cheaters did not steal, and many who lied did not cheat. A child's Sunday school attendance had negligible effect on his honesty. Older children cheated more than young ones, the retarded more than intelligent ones. Children who came from good homes and who respected or admired their teachers were more honest. But in general, honesty or dishonesty depended on a specific situation, not on a consistent personality trait.

During World War II the Office of Strategic Services faced the task of selecting and evaluating personnel for intelligence work and delicate overseas assignments such as espionage. Under the supervision of Henry A. Murray and Donald W. MacKinnon, a staff of psychologists set up an intensive series of interviews and performance tests designed to evaluate personality. For example, a group of men without a designated leader would be given a problem to solve; the observers noted which man showed leadership ability. Or a frustration-producing situation would be contrived in which a stooge had been instructed to needle the candidate, while the experimenters watched to see how well he could withstand the frustration and ridicule. Such selective procedures seemed effective in weeding out the weak candidates, though thorough validation of the testing methods was not possible. After the war MacKinnon and others extended these methods into the selection of persons for high-level positions.

Projective Techniques

About 1940 psychologists became interested in a new type of performance test, the so-called "projective technique." According to Lawrence K. Frank, an early sponsor of these tests, projective techniques give a person a chance to express his "private world of meanings, significances, patterns, and feelings." Standardized personality tests like questionnaires tell little about active and dynamic individual personality, said Frank. When a person tells what a cloud looks like to him, or gives his own interpretation of a picture containing people, he "projects" into it something of his own personality. If he interprets several items in the same general way, this may reveal important trends of thinking, attitude, interest, and emotion.

The "inkblot test" prepared by Hermann Rorschach, a Swiss psychiatrist, is the best-known projective technique. It consists of ten cards, each containing a rather elaborate inkblot. Five blots are in color, five in gray and black. Subjects study one blot at a time and tell what each resembles. They

A Simple Inkblot

can ruminate as long as they like over each card. The examiner records their responses, then shows the cards a second time, asking the subjects to elaborate ambiguous interpretations and explain which parts of the inkblots led to their responses.

The Rorschach test has had many exponents, of whom the best known in the United States are probably Samuel J. Beck,

Bruno Klopfer, and Zygmunt Piotrowski. These men and other test experts have systematized the scoring and interpreting of this essentially qualitative technique. Generally speaking, the test results are scored according to three main criteria:

Do subjects react to the whole blot, to a part, or to a small detail? Do their responses involve movement, form, color, or the three combined, and is the form clear or blurred? Do subjects see human or animal figures, or chiefly inanimate objects? The complete scoring is quite complex, involving many factors beyond mere counting of responses.

Seeing whole figures, generally speaking, indicates high intelligence and ability to synthesize. A predominance of forms in motion, especially human ones, suggests creativeness and empathy. Great response to color means impulsiveness, if not emotional instability. Seeing mostly animals, and giving unoriginal responses in general, suggest lower intelligence and stereotyped thinking. On the other hand, noting small unusual details indicates introversion and possible emotional conflicts. Noting third-dimensional shading effects signifies anxiety. A preponderance of responses determined by shape or form means good control, harmony between the intellectual and emotional aspects of personality.

Many other projective tests have been constructed, and are used by clinical psychologists in their diagnostic studies. Some of the best known are the Thematic Apperception Test, the Draw-a-Person Test, and the Bender-Gestalt Test.

The Thematic Apperception Test (TAT) was devised by Christiana D. Morgan and Henry A. Murray. It consists of a number of cards, each bearing a picture; some of these are vague, shadowy, and abstract, while others are more definite or "structured," like a magazine illustration. The pictures include quite a variety of persons and situations. Their object is to stimulate fantasy on the part of the subject, who is shown a picture and asked to make up a story about it. The examiner usually suggests that he tell what is going on at the moment, what led up to it, and how things are likely to turn out. Analysis of the records seeks to identify recurrent themes, such as rebellion against authority, fear of women, conflict over sex and so forth, then to translate these into personality trends.

The Draw-a-Person Test had been used since the 1920's by Florence Goodenough as a performance type of intelligence test (see Chapter II). Some twenty years later, Karen Machover showed that it can serve as a useful projective technique. The figure drawn is analyzed as to reality factors such as presence of eyes, nose, ears, mouth, limbs, etc. But other factors are also important, such as presence or absence of clothing, over- or underemphasis of various parts of the body, position and size of the drawing, "boldness" of the pencil strokes. The psychiatrist Paul Schilder had written on the significance of the "body image" in a person's self-concept; the drawing of human figures is one way to depict the body image, and perhaps even to present the person's image of himself.

The Bender-Gestalt Test, originated by psychiatrist Lauretta Bender, consists of nine designs chosen from a number of geometrical Gestalt figures originally devised by Max Wertheimer. A subject is shown each card for five seconds, then asked to copy it. The types of distortions found in the drawings give clues to the presence of such illnesses as organic brain disease and schizophrenia.

Since World War II several new projective techniques have appeared. Edwin S. Shneidman, for example, originated the "Make-a-Picture-Story Test" (MAPS). This is a fantasy test, similar to the TAT, but the subject first constructs his own scene or picture by selecting from a number of possible backgrounds and figures. He then tells a story about it. MAPS seems to provide considerable scope, action, and enjoyment, especially for youngsters. Saul Rosenzweig constructed a "Picture Frustration Test" from twenty-four cartoons, each depicting a scene in which one person frustrates another. The subject is asked what he thinks the frustrated person would say, thus projecting his own feelings of frustration into the pictures; and his responses are then analyzed. A somewhat different type of projective test was worked out by Lipot Szondi, a Hungarian geneticist. A person is presented with six sets of eight portraits, and in each set is asked to pick the two he likes best and the two he likes least. The eight pictures are of an epileptic, a hysteric, a homosexual, a sadistic murderer, and other similarly abnormal types. Supposedly a subject chooses and rejects the pictures according to his latent tendencies toward the personality pattern involved. While Szondi's idea is ingenious, many American psychologists feel the test has not yet been sufficiently validated to make it serviceable in clinical practice.

In the early days of projective techniques, psychological opinion was sharply divided as to their reliability and validity. Their acceptance has been increasing, in all probability, partly because scoring methods have become more systematic and precise. More important is the accumulating evidence indicating their usefulness in clinical diagnosis. In practice, clinicians seldom rely on any one test, but generally use a combination of qualitative and quantitative data in their evaluations and diagnoses.

TESTS OF INTERESTS

Another sector of personality is tapped by interest tests, which are used chiefly in vocational guidance. In 1922 Max Freyd made up a test listing 72 occupations to which a subject responded: Like, ?, or Dislike. Another part of the test listed over 100 items that a person might like or dislike; among them were fat men, nervous people, solitaire, picnics, football. Freyd found distinctly different interests in socially inclined persons and mechanically minded ones.

Edward K. Strong developed a "Vocational Interest Blank" that is used a good deal. Subjects record the comment, Like, Indifferent, or Dislike to each of 400 items. Several dozen occupations are scored separately to see how each subject's interests compare with interests of persons successful in each field. The women's test is scored for 30 occupations. Strong does not claim that his test will predict accurately a person's success in a given occupation. Vocational guidance psychologists report it the most useful test to direct students toward suitable occupations and—what is more important—to keep them out of fields for which they are unfit.

Louis L. Thurstone analyzed Strong's Interest Blank statistically and found four basic interests: science, language, people, and business. He showed also which interests are strongest in persons in various occupations. For example, engineers have much scientific interest; lawyers and advertising men lean toward language; teachers, preachers, and personnel workers are interested in people; while real estate men and accountants like business.

More recently G. F. Kuder devised a "Preference Record" which measures interests in ten broad areas: outdoor, mechanical, computational, scientific, persuasive, artistic, literary, musical, social service, and clerical. When an individual's pattern of preferences is identified, he considers the occupations most relevant to his major interests.

Although interests are determined largely by training, Thorndike and others find them remarkably consistent over long periods of time. Strong notes one exception: noticeable changes of interest occur between 15 and 25 years of age.

The biggest psychological differences between men and women, Lewis Terman and Catharine Cox Miles find, are their interests. Men incline toward adventure, physical activity, science, mechanics, and business. Women tend toward sedentary, domestic, aesthetic, and humanitarian interests.

A person's values and attitudes are closely related to his interests. We mentioned values and their testing in the last chapter. Later, in discussing social behavior, we shall describe attitudes and their measurement.

Conclusions on the Dimensions of Personality

Despite the dozens of personality tests and hundreds of research studies, psychologists have not agreed upon the basic personality traits or dimensions. Early testers simply assumed that introversion-extroversion or dominance-submission were important components of personality, and went ahead with their testing. Some tests, like the Minnesota Multiphasic, follow psychiatry and abnormal psychology in using pathological categories such as schizophrenic, depressive, hypochondriacal, and the like. Several psychologists turned to new statistical methods as a substitute for what they considered subjective or traditional approaches. Their chief weapon is factor analysis, based on complex operations with correlation coefficients, which seeks out the major patterns or "clusters" involved in many tests given to hundreds or even thousands of persons. Factor analysis had been used successfully by Spearman in England and by Thurstone in Chicago in their efforts to isolate the components of intelligence. Applying factor analysis to personality tests, J. P. Guilford and Ruth B. Guilford arrived at social introversion (shyness, withdrawal), thinking introversion (meditation, self-analysis), masculinity or dominance, emotionality (instability, fluctuations in mood), depression (including feelings of unworthiness and guilt), and rhathymia (a happy-go-lucky, carefree, impulsive disposition).

Unfortunately, the factor analysts of personality do not agree among themselves any more than the personality theorists. Consider the work of two leading postwar researchers in the field of personality. H. J. Eysenck, a German-born British psychologist, concluded there are three major dimensions of personality: introversion, neuroticism, and psychoticism. Raymond B. Cattell, a British-born American psychologist, has proposed anywhere from twelve to twenty "primary source traits of personality." Some of these are "General mental capacity versus mental defect," "surgency versus desurgency" (anxious melancholy), "socialized cultural mind versus boorishness," and "adventurous cyclothymia versus withdrawn schizophrenia."

Is there, then, hopeless disagreement among psychologists as to the basic dimensions of personality? Perhaps not. Solomon Diamond, for example, notes that some of the same factors keep appearing in different lists, such as the affiliative or sociable, the aggressive or dominant, the timid or depressed, and a dimension of soundness or maturity. Time may show a fair amount of agreement.

On the other hand, Gordon Allport, one of the best-known students of personality, believes that statistical analysis of personality does not do justice to the uniqueness of the individual person. He favors a new concept which he calls "personal dispositions," of which a small number (say five to ten) will describe the essential characteristics of a person. Allport does admit, however, that when comparing one person with another, common traits or factors have to be used.

It may well be that, despite all the work done, the assessment of personality is still in its infancy.

Chapter XIII

THE MENTALLY RETARDED
AND THE GIFTED

SEGUIN   BINET   SIMON   GODDARD
TERMAN   HOLLINGWORTH   TREDGOLD   PENROSE
GALTON   ELLIS   CATTELL   MILES
PRESSEY   MAC KINNON

*What is mental defect and how is it measured?
Can the retarded be trained? What is "genius" and
what produces it? Do our greatest leaders have the
highest I.Q.'s? How is creativity fostered?*

The terms "mental defect" and "mental illness" are often
confused. Mental defect, or mental retardation, formerly
called "feeblemindedness," involves limitation of intelligence so marked as to result in social and economic disability.
Mental disease, on the other hand, is primarily an emotional
illness, which in severe cases used to be designated "insanity"
and, before that, "lunacy." Its most noticeable effect is probably personal unhappiness and maladjustment; yet in very
severe cases there is disintegration of personality.

In this chapter we shall examine mental retardation; and
in the latter part of the chapter we shall turn to the excep-
tionally gifted, who are at the upper end of the intelligence
scale. We shall then devote Chapter XIV to Mental Illness
and Chapter XV to Mental Hygiene.

MENTAL RETARDATION

Mental defect or mental retardation exists in all degrees,
from the mildest to the most severe amount of retardation.

It is usually present from birth, though it cannot be detected accurately from outward appearance. Only when afflicted persons are required to make common-sense judgments or to learn new acts do they reveal their shortcomings in ability. Little can be done at present to remedy mental defect as such, though various kinds of worthwhile training have been developed.

Herbert Woodrow described a case of mild to moderate defect similar to many found in the special classes of city schools:

Admitted to the New Jersey Training School . . . at the age of eleven, Abbie was small for her age, left-handed and awkward. She always put the *same foot* forward when going up or down stairs; she knew her letters but could not read; she could count to ten; she knew some color and form; and she sang a number of hymns that she had learned at home. Her sight and hearing were normal, and she was fond of play. Among Abbie's more unfavorable characteristics were a bad memory and a poor power of imitation. She was gluttonous, untidy, untruthful, sly and profane.

Three months after her admission she could thread a needle and sew on buttons, could dust and rub floors a little, had learned to read *A man ran* and *I see a man* (sometimes), counted to twenty, and, with help, could do such number work as this:

$$
\begin{array}{ccc}
1 & 2 & 3 \\
1 & 1 & 1 \\
\hline
- & - & - \\
\end{array}
$$

For ten years she went to school. "For ten years," runs the report, "her teachers struggled heroically to give her mastery of *something*. Little less than marvelous is the optimism and faithfulness of those teachers! We see them struggling on month after month, not in that perfunctory way born of discouragement or conscious failure, but with that courage and cheerfulness which comes from grasping at every straw of encouragement, of progress, of fancied improvement. Had these teachers become discouraged, we would have to admit that perhaps the result might be due to that fact. But there is no sign of giving up in all these years. Within the last few months, however, there has appeared the feeling that Abbie has reached her limit. She will be twenty-two years old before long.

"To-day she is still small for her age. She can braid cornhusks a little; can make a bed; can iron an apron; cannot count the cost of three one-cent stamps and three two-cent stamps, with the stamps before her; cannot repeat five figures or a sentence of fifteen words; defines only in terms of use; can read a few sentences, spell a few words, and write about twenty-five words from memory; knows the days of the week, but not the months of the year; and does not know how many fingers she has on both hands."

CATEGORIES OF MENTAL RETARDATION

Until the nineteenth century little attention was given to training the retarded. Among the first to experiment on this was Édouard Seguin, a French doctor, who founded in 1837 a center for training mental defectives. Realizing he could not restore them to normal, Seguin tried to develop what capacities they had by what he called a "physiological method." He trained subjects in motor control by having them walk along lines, climb ladders, and the like, and taught them to respond to loud noises or bright colors. Treatment of mental defectives in general followed Seguin's system until the twentieth century, when intelligence tests and studies of heredity were introduced.

Alfred Binet and Théophile Simon, the originators of intelligence tests, suggested that mental defect be defined by mental age. This idea was adopted by the American pioneers in testing, notably H. H. Goddard, Lewis M. Terman, and Leta S. Hollingworth. As a result of their labors three grades or degrees of mental deficiency were agreed upon: "moron," "imbecile," and "idiot." As time passed, especially since World War II, these harsh terms have yielded to designations of degree: "mildly retarded," "moderately retarded," and "severely retarded."

Goddard coined the term "moron" to specify the highest level of mental defect, ranging in I.Q. from 50 to 70. An adult in this category has a mental age of 8 to 10 or 11 years. The men can learn to do many kinds of farm work, some carpentry, janitorial work, and even mechanical jobs like operating a lathe. The women can learn to knit, cook, wait on tables, do fancy laundry, and operate a sewing machine. But they are retarded and have to be supervised; they are at a loss when something goes wrong. They get along best on farms or in small towns where they are known and allowances are made for their dullness. In large cities life is difficult, and some drift into thievery, prostitution, and petty crime.

Some of the moderately retarded need institutional care. With an I.Q. of 25 to 50 the adults have a mental age equivalent to a child between 4 and 7 years. Most of them learn to dress, wash, and feed themselves. They can do many kinds of routine work, such as washing floors, digging holes, weeding, dishwashing, simple sewing, and laundry work. Their work has to be planned and carefully directed. The moderately retarded can talk a little, but seldom learn to read.

The severely retarded, smallest of the three groups, have a mental age of 3 years or less and must be treated like infants. With patient instruction they can learn to pick up stones, pile wood, polish flat surfaces, and perform similar tasks. After long periods of training some severely retarded persons can learn to dress and undress themselves. But they learn to speak and understand only a few words.

In general, psychologists use "mildly retarded" for the 50–70 I.Q. category, "moderately retarded" for the 25–50 I.Q. group, and "severely retarded" for the 25 or less in I.Q. Psychiatric usage is somewhat different. Psychiatrists think of mild defect as applying to I.Q.'s of 70 to 85, moderate defect from 50 to 70, and severe below 50. This is spelled out in the last *Diagnostic and Statistical Manual: Mental Disorders* of the American Psychiatric Association (1952).

Idiots Savants

Once in a while a person who is mentally defective shows singular skill in some special line; such a case has come to be known by the French term "idiot savant." Actually, as Edmund S. Conklin pointed out, such cases are nearly always moderately rather than severely retarded. Their special skills are generally in the fields of memory, mathematics, or mechanical ability.

Probably the most famous case of an idiot savant was the "Genius of Earlswood Asylum," described by A. F. Tredgold, British authority on mental defects. From 1850 to 1916 an inmate of Earlswood Asylum named Pullen astonished authorities by producing remarkable crayon drawings, carving expertly in ivory and wood, and constructing ship models so intricate and detailed that they are still displayed in the two large workrooms placed at his disposal in the asylum. His proudest accomplishment was a ten-foot model steamship that took more than three years to complete. Equipped with brass anchors, screws, pulley blocks, copper paddles, 5585 copper rivets, and 13 complete lifeboats, it also contains nearly a million and a quarter wooden pins fixing the planks to the ribs. Pullen made these with a special instrument of his own designing. The cabins are decorated and furnished with chairs, tables, beds, and bunks.

In other abilities Pullen was notably deficient. Until the age of 7 he did not speak and then for a long time uttered only the word "muvver." He learned to wash and dress himself and eventually to write the names of simple objects, but beyond these elementary accomplishments he failed to go. Probably it is significant that he was very deaf. At the asylum he behaved well usually, if left alone to work out his projects. Once he threatened to blow up the place because a request was refused, and at another time constructed a guillotine over his door, planning to behead an unfortunate steward whom he disliked violently. A crisis arose when he fell in love and determined to marry the lady against all arguments. In an inspired moment the committee procured an elaborate gold-braided uniform. Pullen was called to the board-room, told that his request to marry would be granted, although the asylum would deeply regret losing his valuable services, but that if he would reconsider, the committee proposed, as an alternative, to make him an admiral in the navy. The uniform was then produced. Pullen succumbed. He took the uniform and never again mentioned the subject of marriage. At the age of 81 he died, having worn the uniform often on special occasions.

Tredgold notes that Pullen's observation, attention, and memory were good, but he was emotionally unstable, childish, and lacking in mental balance. A brain defect which impaired hearing early in life cut him off from his fellows and made possible his tremendous absorption in carving and drawing. How much his striking achievements were due to this intense and single-minded preoccupation with mechanical things, and how much was due to innate special abilities, it is impossible to say.

CASES WITH PHYSICAL DEFECTS

Rudolf Pintner and Donald Paterson estimated in 1916 that about 3% of our population is mentally deficient. Later research confirms this estimate. Not more than 10% of mental defectives can be recognized as such from outward appearance, according to Harry L. Hollingworth. However, a few varieties are accompanied by physical defects. Four readily distinguishable types are described by A. F. Tredgold and Lionel S. Penrose:

The *cretin* is dwarfed in stature, with short, bent legs, dry skin, coarse hair, thick lips, and a large head. Cretins are moderately to severely retarded. Cretinism definitely results from underactivity of the thyroid gland, and can be relieved by giving thyroid extract if treatment begins early enough.

The *mongoloid,* so called from a supposed resemblance to the Mongolian race, has narrow, slanting eyes, an enlarged tongue with deep crosswise fissures, and a flattened face and skull. Mongoloids are usually moderately retarded. Mongolism always is congenital, not hereditary; the embryo seems to be affected by the eighth week of pregnancy.

The *microcephalic* is characterized by an extremely small skull, with receding forehead. They range through every degree of mental defect. Probably microcephaly results from damage to the fetus during gestation, caused by a diseased condition of the mother or fetal injury from mistreatment.

The *hydrocephalic* has an abnormally large skull, with high, protruding forehead, due to excessive fluid between his skull and brain or within the brain. Variations in mentality are great. Medical treatment seldom remedies the condition.

"Cerebral palsy" is the name given to nervous system damage which causes paralysis in the prenatal or early childhood periods. W. M. Phelps estimates that about 7 infants per 100,000 are afflicted with cerebral palsy, one-third of them being so retarded mentally as to require permanent hospitalization. The most frequent cause is birth injury. Edgar A. Doll found that the destruction of cerebral tissue through birth injury alone accounts for 5% to 10% of all cases of mental defect. Fortunately, some birth injury cases improve with maturity and special training.

Other diseased conditions which may cause mental defect are congenital syphilis of the brain and nervous system, epidemic encephalitis or "sleeping sickness," some forms of epilepsy, some endocrine disorders, malnutrition before or shortly after birth, and sensory defects such as partial deafness or blindness.

Training the Retarded

For the majority of cases of mental defect no clear-cut organic basis is known. Presumably the condition results from imperfect structure and function of the central nervous system. "Insufficiency of brain cells" is the way one authority summed it up. In by far the greatest number of cases medical treatment is ineffective. The best that can be done is to fit mentally retarded persons into the social order as well as possible.

Such persons are by no means hopeless, as was shown by Warren R. Baller, educational psychologist. He made a study of 200 persons who had, in elementary school many years before, I.Q.'s of less than 70. Though these persons completed, on the average, only four and one-half grades of school, 83% of them were wholly or partially self-supporting in their adult years. Baller concluded that mental deficiency does not make impossible a life of social usefulness. Similarly in 1948, Ruby Kennedy compared some 250 "morons" (I.Q.'s 45–75) with a control group of normals matched for everything except intelligence. As might be expected, many more of the control group graduated from high school and entered professional work, but most of the retarded were self-supporting, and the earning power of the two groups did not differ materially. Samuel Kirk has recently developed a diagnostic test of psycholinguistic abilities to reveal specific areas of retardation and indicate means of remediation.

For dull pupils special classes exist in the larger public school systems. Here extra drill is given; if they cannot be brought up to their grade they are taught that part of the curriculum they can grasp and are given vocational and industrial training. Experiments are constantly being tried out to discover the kind of training programs and working situations which will best fit mental defectives into our social and economic system.

STUDIES OF THE GIFTED

At the other end of the intelligence scale from the retarded are the gifted or exceptional children. Terman spoke of the brightest 1% of children, who have I.Q.'s of 140 or more, as possessing "genius." This turned out to be an unfortunate use of the term, since genius is a word commonly applied to persons who have made outstanding contributions of a specialized sort to society. Leta Hollingworth suggested using "gifted child" or "exceptional child" as a more appropriate designation. She considered a child with an I.Q. of 180 or better a potential genius, with one or two chances in ten of making a contribution which would justify the use of the word "genius."

Most psychologists agree that genius combines exceptional ability with outstanding achievement in certain fields. Anne Anastasi notes that we speak of genius only in science or the arts, not in, say, roller skating or cooking. In cultures having different standards a cook might well be called a genius, but not in ours.

Genius has been a topic of considerable interest for a century or more. Francis Galton, a cousin of Charles Darwin, published the first systematic study of genius in 1869. Making eminence his criterion for genius, he concluded that genius is hereditary. Shortly afterwards a Swiss writer named de Candolle disagreed with Galton, listing numerous environmental conditions that help to produce scientific genius.

The English philosopher scientist, Havelock Ellis, after investigating the backgrounds of prominent persons, reported in 1904 that the eminent come chiefly from professional families. Less than 2% of his group of over 1000 had either insane parents or insane offspring. Ellis also found that his eminent persons often were eldest children, born when their parents were on the average 37 years old. Noting that more males than females were found among geniuses, Ellis proposed that males tend to extremes more than females. Leta Hollingworth disagreed, pointing out that society never gave women an opportunity to manifest their genius.

James McKeen Cattell studied the backgrounds and birthplaces of outstanding American scientists. He found that more than half came from the most favorably situated 1% of the population. The son of a successful professional man, said Cattell, is fifty times as likely to become a leading scientist as an ordinary boy. Cattell also found that the cities, and the states with good educational systems, contributed a disproportionately large share of eminent scientists. These data suggest that environmental factors are important in fostering genius.

Sigmund Freud, founder of the school of psychoanalysis, was interested in the personality factors producing genius and talent. Believing that the libido, or sex drive, is man's strongest motive, he regarded the contributions of genius as substitute activities resulting from a frustrated sex urge. Alfred Adler, an early collaborator of Freud, best known for originating the term "inferiority complex," considered the achievements of genius to be overcompensation for inferiority feelings.

Other writers assert that genius is akin to insanity. This theory was advanced by the Italian criminologist Cesare Lombroso, and popularized about the turn of the century. Though psychological research justifies no such conclusion, the idea persists that insanity and emotional instability accompany genius. Some psychiatric interpretations of leadership have followed this line. C. S. Bluemel, for example, notes neurotic or psychotic trends in Columbus, Lindbergh, Gandhi, Oliver Cromwell, Stalin, Joan of Arc, Napoleon, and Hitler. While much is to be said for psychiatric interpretation of history and an understanding of the personality disorders of leaders, we must beware of overgeneralization and oversimplification. Napoleon, Hitler, Wagner, and Dostoyevsky may be good subjects for psychiatric interpretations; does this mean that

Churchill, Bach, Shakespeare, and Einstein are also? Outstanding leadership is a product of many forces, some emotional and personal, some social and cultural, all of which are difficult to evaluate.

THE I.Q.'S OF FAMOUS MEN

Catharine Cox, later Mrs. W. R. Miles, an associate of Terman, has studied carefully the biographies of 300 eminent persons born between 1450 and 1850. From her data three psychologists estimated that the I.Q.'s of these famous men and women ranged from 100 to 200, the average falling between 155 and 165. John Stuart Mill, Goethe, Macaulay, Pascal, Leibnitz, and Grotius were assigned I.Q.'s of more than 180. Previously Terman had placed Galton's I.Q. at close to 200.

Amazing early accomplishments of these men are reported. John Stuart Mill learned Greek from his father at the age of three. Before he was eight he had read many Greek classics, also English historians like Hume and Gibbon. Between eight and twelve he added Latin and mathematics, including algebra, geometry, and calculus. He started to write a history of Roman government, and became interested in science. Logic and political economy came next. Mill admitted reading some lighter books, like *Robinson Crusoe*, but usually his father kept him on sterner fare. In his autobiography Mill expresses doubts as to the wisdom of this kind of education. But the fact remains that his very superior ability plus a rigorous intellectual training produced one of Britain's greatest logicians and political economists.

Francis Galton learned to read at the age of two and a half, to sign his name at three, and to write a letter before he was four. At five he could recite long passages from Scott's *Marmion*. The day before his fifth birthday he wrote the following letter to his sister Adele, who had directed much of his training:

> My dear Adele, I am 4 years old and can read any English book. I can say all the Latin substantives and adjectives and active verbs besides 52 lines of Latin poetry. I can cast up any

sum in addition and multiply by 2, 3, 4, 5, 6, 7, 8, 10. I can also say the pence table. I can read French a little and I know the clock.

Francis Galton
Febuary [sic] 15, 1827.

Abraham Lincoln, on the other hand, is assigned only a moderately high I.Q. (125–140) in Mrs. Miles' genius study. Lincoln's mother took an active interest in his education because he seemed promising, though slower to comprehend than other boys. In childhood he was extraordinarily studious, and had an "investigating mind" that dug relentlessly into facts and ideas. Once learned, a fact was not forgotten. His power of concentration was intense. He studied long and hard, often at night by a log fire, as every school child has heard, and stood at the head of his class in grammar school. He became champion speller of the district and also something of an authority on astronomy. Farm work he did with equal thoroughness, though in every free moment he was inclined to pull a book out of his pocket and read. At 17 he dabbled in verse writing, a not unusual pastime for young men of that age, wrote essays on American government and on temperance, which won local praise, and continued to read everything available in print, from the Bible to a Louisville newspaper. In these early intellectual prowlings was laid the foundation of Lincoln's later career. Unlike many prodigies, he was a bootstrap genius who rose above his surroundings by independent effort and indefatigable study.

Benjamin Franklin's rise to fame shows certain similarities. In and out of school during early childhood, he read constantly anything and everything he could lay hands on, while learning the soap-making trade and serving as apprentice to a cutler. When his father recognized Franklin's ability as a scholar, the boy was sent regularly to school, where he leaped to the head of the class and promptly skipped a grade. He flunked arithmetic. Later, ashamed of his record in mathematics, he determined to master the subject, sped through an arithmetic text and two books on navigation, including their geometry. Like Lincoln, he excelled in intellectual argument and in physical feats. Where Lincoln split rails to the admiration of the countryside, Franklin won considerable acclaim as a swimming teacher. In the printing trade Franklin showed his inventiveness by making both type and ink, but for a time his talent turned chiefly toward writing. He became best known as a diplomat, statesman, and scientist. In Mrs. Miles' genius study his I.Q. is rated at 145.

Napoleon Bonaparte is given an I.Q. between 135 and 140. When very young he showed a passion for military things. Above all he liked playing with tin soldiers. He organized snow fights, led the village boys in raids against the shepherd boys, and later, in a Paris military school, spent his free hours studying military tactics and planning elaborate battles. To subdue his tempestuous nature, his mother first sent him to a girls' school. His first love affair is said to have occurred at the age of five. At later schools he showed unusual interest in mathematics, history, and the exact sciences. Repetition irked him. He never learned to spell correctly, wrote a deplorable hand, and limped along in languages. A professor of literature once described his flair for rhetoric as "granite heated by a volcano"—the rhetoric flowed mostly in patriotic torrents, eulogizing his native Corsica or military heroes. He was not slated for genius by his family, who looked at his misshapen head and foresaw no brilliant future. But the haughty, obstinate, egotistical schoolboy realized his ambitions. Over a century after his death his name remains synonymous with military genius.

The intelligence of these famous men, though high, is not always remarkable. (I.Q.'s of 140 to 160 are not uncommon among college students and professional persons.) Mrs. Miles notes also that the eminent persons she studied had many favorable personality traits like persistence, self-confidence, and great strength of character. In addition, she generally finds other advantages aiding their development, such as eminent relatives, cultured homes, and good schooling. Three factors—natural ability, personality traits, and environment— according to this investigation, combine to produce genius.

CHILD PRODIGIES

Present-day prodigies also have been studied and followed over a period of years. Leta S. Hollingworth, for example, reported on a youngster with an I.Q. of 187 who graduated from high school just before his twelfth birthday. He completed college in three years, and was elected to Phi Beta Kappa at the age of 14 years and 9 months. Entering graduate school, he obtained his Ph.D. degree at 18. Like many talented and gifted New York City children studied by Mrs. Hollingworth, he was somewhat healthier and better adjusted than the average child.

Another precocious child, a little girl described by L. M. Stedman, obtained an I.Q. of 214, probably the highest on record. This child spoke meaningful words when only 7 or 8 months old, and walked at 10 months. At 3 years her parents found she knew the alphabet, which she had learned by asking questions about printed signs. When 4½ she was permitted to sit in the first grade because her chum was there. In a few months she could read easily, so she was put in the second grade. At the end of the next year, when 5 years 9 months old, she was promoted to the fourth grade. She was an untiring reader; at 9 her favorite authors included Barrie, Dickens, Victor Hugo, and George Eliot. Her parents were professional people, and both they and the grandparents were of superior mentality.

Gertrude Hildreth, psychologist at the experimental Lincoln School of Teachers College, Columbia University, compared children having I.Q.'s over 130 with children having I.Q.'s around 100. In the superior group she found these traits: perseverence in the face of difficulty, alertness, interest in problems, great mental energy, good humor, sustained attention, and mature use of language. The gifted children also comprehended and responded more quickly than the normal group.

Terman, with several associates, surveyed more than 600 cases of California children whose I.Q.'s were 140 or more. Comparing these children with others of average ability, they made several important discoveries. The gifted children came from socially and culturally superior homes. They had many eminent relatives and ancestors, and their parents were well educated. Incidence of insanity was much lower than the average. The health and growth rate of gifted children was superior, as was their personality and character development.

'ollow-up studies made seven years later revealed very little ecrease in I.Q.'s; the gifted group still ranked far above verage in scholarship, health, leadership, and personality adustment.

In 1940, eighteen years after the first investigation, Terman made a second check-up to see how well these gifted hildren were succeeding in life. He found the death, inanity, suicide, and divorce rates for the group lower than verage. Ninety percent entered college, and of these 93% graduated; their scholarship and activity records considerably outranked those of average students. At age 30 their incomes vere substantially above the national average. A still later tudy of the group by Terman and Melita Oden compared hose most and those least successful as adults. Differences in ntelligence were negligible among the high and low achievers of the group; the main distinctions were in family background, motivation, and personality traits such as perseverance and self-confidence.

Thus very superior ability is associated, biologically and environmentally, with superior family background. High mental ability tends to remain high, and those having it show better-than-average health, physical strength, and general adustment. And outstanding achievement depends upon a combination of intellectual and personality factors.

CREATIVENESS

In the 1930's Robert M. Hutchins, then president of the University of Chicago, pleaded for liberalization of the high school and college curricula in order to permit faster and freer development of gifted youngsters. Even more recently, especially since the launching of the first Russian Sputnik, American educators have been seeking to encourage gifted youngsters and generally to foster the creative talent of our youth. S. L. Pressey, for example, notes that a practicing genius is produced by giving a precocious, able youngster early encouragement, intensive instruction, continuing opportunity as he advances, a congruent, stimulating social life, and cumulative success experiences. He proposed the providing of specialists in our school systems who would identify and sponsor gifted youngsters. Along with this should go adaptation of curricula to enable the gifted to accelerate and take advanced programs, with scholarships or other financial aid if necessary.

Donald W. MacKinnon studied creative people in the arts and sciences (novelists, essayists, poets, industrial scientists and mathematicians, and architects) to discover what constitutes creative ability. He found high intelligence, special aptitudes, interest in meanings and the broad implications of things, high esthetic and theoretical values, social awareness, and preference for independence. Both parents and schools, according to MacKinnon, need to nurture creative talent by de-emphasizing conformity while providing maximum opportunities within which able youngsters can develop. This is made somewhat difficult by the conformist and group-centered tendencies of the day.

Chapter XIV

MENTAL ILLNESS

KRAEPELIN BLEULER CHARCOT
LIÉBEAULT BERNHEIM MEYER JANET
FREUD ADLER JUNG RANK
SULLIVAN HORNEY FROMM

*How does mental disease differ from mental defect?
What is the difference between organic and functional disorders? How are mental diseases classified? What is a personality disorder? How are neuroses distinguished from psychoses? What is
Freud's theory of neurosis?*

As we mentioned at the beginning of Chapter XIII, mental
illness is primarily emotional malfunction and not intellectual
deficiency. At present mental illness exists to such an extent
that mental disease has become our most pressing medical
challenge. It has been estimated that one American in twenty
will at some period of his life spend time in a mental hospital. Just over half the beds in our hospitals are occupied by
patients who are mentally ill. One person in ten will at some
time consult a clinician about a problem, primarily emotional,
which is too great for him to handle by himself.

EARLY STUDIES OF MENTAL DISEASE

Apparently mental disease has always existed, but only in
the last few generations has it been handled scientifically. We
have progressed a long way from the days of narrow cells and

chains for the mentally ill. We still have far to go to reach a satisfactory solution.

Ancient records reveal cases of ravings, convulsions, and stupors. Evil spirits were believed to be the cause, and often persons "possessed" were put to death.

Occasionally a voice protested. Hippocrates, a keen-witted Greek doctor living in the Age of Pericles, struck out against traditional views. Writing of epilepsy, then called the "sacred disease," he said it had a natural cause and was no more sacred or divine than other diseases. He believed mental disease has a physiological basis, often a disorder of the yellow or black bile. "If you cut open the head," Hippocrates said, "you will find the brain humid, full of sweat and smelling badly. And in this way you may see that it is not a god which injures the body, but disease." He described many mental abnormalities, like phobias, loss of memory, and mental confusion. Classifying mental diseases he included epilepsy, mania (which he called "abnormal excitement"), extreme depression (termed melancholia), and paranoia (defined as mental deterioration). Hippocrates remained the chief medical authority for many centuries.

At the same time modern science was beginning, a few daring voices were beginning to be heard crying out against the stupid brutality practiced in the name of religion. In the sixteenth century a Dutch doctor, Johann Weyer, wrote a thorough refutation of witchcraft. He cited many cases of mental disease, explaining them in remarkably modern fashion. For example, he noted that suggestion helps bring about such disorders. Weyer was the first doctor to concern himself chiefly with mental diseases. Actually he foreshadowed psychiatry. But he was ahead of his times; his writings were banned by the Church and remained so until the twentieth century. Georg Ernst Stahl in two books published early in the 1700's carried forward the understanding of mental disease. He made a distinction between deliria which have a physical origin and those which have an emotional origin, thus foreshadowing the classification of organic and functional disorders.

By the nineteenth century, however, neurology and physiology had made great strides, and psychiatrists were gradually adopting the view that mental diseases have a physiological basis. Wilhelm Griesinger, for example, wrote in 1845 that insanity results from disorders of the brain and nervous system and is therefore a physician's problem. He saw no difference between organic and functional disorders; for him psychiatry and neuropathology are "but one field in which only one language is spoken and the same laws rule."

Griesinger had begun to classify the symptoms of mental disease and seems to have been the first to recognize that there are certain distinct categories of mental illness. But it remained for Emil Kraepelin, one of the two or three greatest figures in psychiatry, to make the first comprehensive classification of mental disease. This was in the 1880's, and despite some criticism, it was adopted the world over. He based his classification on causes of the disease, how much of the brain and nervous system it involved, the variety and course of symptoms, and methods of treatment. His fifteen major headings included disorders of infection, of exhaustion, of intoxication, brain diseases, paranoia (delusions), epilepsy (periodic convulsions), neuroses (milder mental and emotional disorders), and mental defect (imbecility and idiocy). Kraepelin believed mental diseases caused mainly by external conditions are curable; those caused by constitutional factors, incurable. A curable disease is manic-depressive psychosis, wherein the patient suffers from extreme elation, depression, or an alternation of the two. On the other hand, said Kraepelin, the severe mental deterioration called dementia praecox cannot be cured because its source is brain disease, defective metabolic processes, or some other bodily condition.

DISTINGUISHING ORGANIC FROM FUNCTIONAL DISORDERS

By the late nineteenth century most psychiatrists made a distinction between organic and functional disorders. It seemed clear that certain diseases, notably the neuroses, involve no known structural impairment; the difficulty is functional.

H. L. Hollingworth has clarified the distinction between organic and functional disorders by using the analogy of two types of automobile trouble. A car may balk because some part breaks down. A spark plug cracks, the gas line clogs, or the radiator freezes. Clearly these are "structural" causes. Replace the broken parts and the car runs again. On the other hand the car may stall though its "parts" are in good order, if some of them are *out of adjustment*. Perhaps the ignition points should be moved closer together, the fan belt tightened, or the gas mixture regulated. Here the trouble is not defective parts, but faults in organization or function. Hollingworth adds that the distinction between structure and function may be vague, but that it is useful to know whether one needs to buy new parts or just make a few adjustments.

The functional view of mental disease for the most part grew out of the work of Freud and of several French psychiatrists, whose contributions we shall examine shortly. After Kraepelin and his contemporary, Eugen Bleuler, Swiss psychiatrist, schizophrenia, manic-depressive psychosis, and paranoia were considered functional disorders because no definite organic bases could be found for them. When structural changes were absent, it was naturally assumed that the cause must be functional.

Organic Disorders

Senile dementia, general paresis, epilepsy, and other organic illnesses have been described in well-known psychiatric texts such as those written by C. Macfie Campbell, William Alanson White, and E. A. Strecker. They are now considered types of "chronic brain syndrome" according to the current classification of mental disorders by the American Psychiatric Association.

Senile dementia occurs in old age when mental changes follow increasing physical deterioration, notably cerebral arteriosclerosis. Critical capacity and general orientation decline, as does memory for recent events. Other symptoms are worry about health, suspiciousness, selfishness and, in cases of more extreme deterioration, delusions, hallucinations, and severe emotional upsets.

Epilepsy or convulsive disorder is marked by loss of consciousness, disturbed motor coordination, and convulsive spasms of greater or lesser extent. The severe form, "grand mal," involves violent convulsions and complete loss of consciousness. A patient suffering from the less drastic "petit mal" loses consciousness for only a few seconds, and seldom has a noticeable convulsion. Frequency of such attacks is variable, ranging from several per day to a number of years apart. The English psychiatrist, Hughlings Jackson, maintained that epilepsy results from a sudden explosion of nervous discharges in the motor area of the cerebral cortex. Others disagree on details but acknowledge that some kind of imperfect physiological and neural functioning must underlie the attacks. Evidence as to the inheritance of epilepsy is claimed by some researchers and denied by others. W. G. Lennox has presented evidence to show that a relationship exists between epilepsy and the severe headache known as migraine. The problem is complicated by the possibility that several forms of epilepsy exist, each of which may be caused by several factors.

Functional Disorders

Schizophrenia, formerly called "dementia praecox," is the commonest of the serious mental diseases or *psychoses*. According to Carney Landis and J. D. Page, almost half the mental hospital population and over 20% of first admissions are schizophrenic.

Kraepelin used the term "dementia praecox" to signify serious mental deterioration occurring early in life. He found its peak of incidence between ages 20 and 30, and attributed it to physiological causes. Bleuler noted that the disease often occurs earlier or later, and that some patients may be cured or may recover spontaneously. Bleuler doubted that it is constitutionally caused, and defined its chief symptom as emotional rather than intellectual disruption. He substituted "schizophrenia" as a more suitable name; literally this means a splitting of the personality, though technically it signifies a breaking away from reality.

The following illustrative case of schizophrenia is mentioned in Karl A. Menninger's *The Human Mind*:

A girl reared in the lap of luxury had been transferred from a finishing school to a coeducational college. She was very active socially, but owing to a technicality was not initiated into her sorority. Simultaneously she failed in one study, a unique experience for her. Finally there was "a poor young professor" with whom, out of sport at first, and then seriously, she began a flirtation. His financial incompetence and other such matters militated against a full development of the affair and she and her friend broke off over a misunderstanding, but with much distress and pain.

Suddenly, soon after, she leaped to her feet in the middle of the living-room and screamed at the top of her voice, assigning irrelevant explanations. She soon began to hear "voices" which told her that there had been a wedding at the college, that she and the professor had been married, that everyone was looking for Mrs. S., herself. . . .

Many other queernesses and delusions followed. She was pregnant; she had had a child. She was a queen or even an empress; . . . she was hypnotized, infected with syphilis, poisoned; gas was being shot into the keyhole, arrows were fired at her . . .

This is a sample of her writing:

> "The test therefore is this: that if in the past we have met with the glorious success of example and time we steadily acquire so law among men. To proceed, I am illegitimate, being an orphan in society I was taken at five years of age by England to be the subject of a hypnotic test most guards of Chicago are being brutally poisoned she's place so are my darling brothers the blue-eyed Congressmen."

The main symptom of schizophrenia is emotional abnormality, generally in the direction of apathy. Persons or situations which formerly aroused love or fear or sorrow are now met with indifference. Patients often become unaccountably happy or sad. Their mental ability, as shown by intelligence tests, does not deteriorate in most cases. But intellectual powers are divorced from other aspects of personality. For example, a patient may discuss current affairs very sensibly for a few minutes, then relapse into his world of daydreams or describe how people are trying to rob or poison him.

The characteristics of schizophrenia are well summarized in the American Psychiatric Association's classification:

A group of psychotic reactions characterized by fundamental disturbances in reality relationships and concept formations, with affective, behavioral, and intellectual disturbances in varying degrees and mixtures. The disorders are marked by strong tendency to retreat from reality, by emotional disharmony, unpredictable disturbances in stream of thought, regressive behavior, and in some, by a tendency to "deterioration." The predominant symptomatology will be the determining factor in classifying such patients into types.

Since Kraepelin's day, psychiatrists have spoken of four types of schizophrenia: *hebephrenic, catatonic, paranoid,* and *simple.* The *hebephrenic* form is marked by silliness and childishness of thought and action. The distinguishing sign of *catatonia* is either stupor and muscular rigidity or the opposite extreme of frenzied excitement and activity. *Paranoid* schizophrenics suffer from delusions and hallucinations and often from feelings of hostility. *Simple* schizophrenia is harder to describe than the other types as it has no clear-cut set of characteristics. Usually there is a pattern consisting of emotional blunting, withdrawal from reality, carelessness of personal appearance, lack of responsibility, and prevalence of fixed ideas (often relating to sex). As in the case cited above, foolish talk and signs of delusion and hallucination often appear. Many cases, however, do not fit any of these categories. The latest psychiatric classification lists two "undifferentiated types"—one acute and one chronic—and a new category, the "schizo-affective" type, which is a combination of schizophrenic symptoms along with pronounced elation or depression.

Manic-depressive psychosis is the second most common of the functional psychoses. It accounts for some 10% of admissions to mental hospitals. The term "manic-depressive" was introduced by Kraepelin, who noted that alternating periods of elation or depression may occur in the same individual, though many patients show only one form.

The *manic state* may be mild or acute. It is marked by activity and excitement. Manics are full of energy, restless, noisy, talkative, and have one bizarre idea after another. In hyperacute cases the patient becomes wild, delirious, and completely unmanageable.

The *depressed state*, by contrast, is characterized by inactivity and dejection, often with feelings of guilt and worry about health. In the extreme state, called depressive stupor, a patient is completely unresponsive—to an extent that he has to be fed by tube or injection.

A disorder commonly thought to be related to manic-depressive psychosis is *involutional melancholia*. This disease is most prevalent in women at the time of the menopause—between 40 and 55 years of age. Depression, agitation, irritability, anxiety, and guilty feelings typically occur, sometimes with delusions. In extreme cases there is danger of suicide. Fortunately, however, most involutional cases recover gradually over a period of two or three years, as the organism becomes adjusted to its new physiological status.

Another serious functional disorder is *paranoia*, a delusional condition without other personality disturbances. True paranoia is relatively rare, accounting for only about 2% of cases in mental hospitals. Formerly all patients having delusions were classed as paranoid; now delusions are known to be common in schizophrenia and other disorders.

Aaron J. Rosanoff, a psychiatrist, describes paranoids as having fixed suspicions, with delusions of grandeur and of persecution; otherwise they seem normal and rational. The paranoid is a victim of his delusions and may attempt to attack or even murder the person he believes is wronging him. Commoner than such extreme cases in the hospitals are the cranks or eccentrics who make wild complaints and accusations, or who plague friends and associates with their constant espousal of a single idea.

PSYCHOPATHY: CHARACTER OR PERSONALITY DISORDERS

Another type of mental illness has had a variety of names, from "constitutional psychopathic inferior," through "character disorder," to the contemporary term, "personality disorder." Originally the term was applied to persons having no discernible mental disorder except that they could not adjust themselves to society morally, socially, or legally. At about the turn of the century Adolf Meyer distinguished between psychoneuroses and behavior, or personality, disorders. Benjamin Karpman later stressed the psychopath's irresponsibility and inability to develop emotional attachments to others. Recently Hervey M. Cleckley summarized the characteristics of the typical psychopath. These include absence of neurotic anxiety, irresponsibility, disregard for truth, failure to learn by experience, incapacity for love, sexual promiscuity, lack of insight, and a persistent pattern of self-defeat.

Expert opinion has turned against a hereditary explanation for personality disorder, and only a few investigators find a neurological basis for it. Most students of psychopathy attribute it to unfortunate if not traumatic social experience, primarily within the family circle. Karpman and the late Robert Lindner reported successful treatment by means of psychotherapy; others are less optimistic, but admit that August Aichhorn, Fritz Redl, and a few of their colleagues have made progress in dealing with juvenile delinquents through "milieu therapy"—i.e., creation of a permissive environment.

CAUSES AND PREVENTION OF PSYCHOSIS

After discussing the neuroses, we shall turn to the treatment of mental illness. To conclude the present section we note that prevention of psychosis is a complicated medical, social, and psychological problem.

We know how some mental diseases can be prevented; if persons are kept away from drugs, alcohol, and syphilitic spirochetes they cannot develop toxic psychoses or general paresis! Other diseases are a puzzle. Their prevention hinges to a large extent on whether they are inherited or acquired.

Unfortunately research on the causes of schizophrenia and other functional disorders has resulted in a variety of conflicting interpretations. Kretschmer, as we have seen, finds that body-build is the important factor in the development of schizophrenia and manic-depressive psychosis. Franz Kallmann, of the College of Physicians and Surgeons at Columbia University, insists on a hereditary interpretation of those diseases. On the other hand, Don D. Jackson and his collaborators have accumulated considerable evidence showing the importance of parental, family, and other social influences in the development of schizophrenia.

Most psychiatrists probably agree with Adolf Meyer of Johns Hopkins that functional mental disorders result from years of faulty habit formation. According to Meyer, psy-

choses represent the culmination of failures to make successful adjustments to one's environment. The causes of such
failures may, of course, be hereditary or physiological, but are
not necessarily so.

In the opinion of most psychiatrists, "predisposing" and
"precipitating" factors cooperate to produce the functional
disorders. Heredity predisposes certain persons toward mental
disease, but disease does not actually appear unless precipi-
tated by unfortunate experiences. Since regulation of heredity
by eugenic measures is extremely difficult, the most practical
plan is to note our potentially unstable persons and keep them
away from the stress and strain of frustrating situations.

THE NEUROSES

Psychoneuroses, or as they are more commonly called, *neuroses*, are milder but more prevalent forms of disturbance
than the psychoses. While neurosis is a form of mental illness,
neurotic persons seldom are thought of as "insane" or mentally sick; they are just considered queer, eccentric, or difficult. In most respects they seem normal. They hold jobs and
go about their affairs like the rest of us. But they are shadowed
by fears, anxieties, or obsessions; they are nervous and often
have physical upsets like headaches, giddiness, indigestion, or
other aches and pains. Neuroses arise from severe emotional
conflicts not properly dealt with. Even now this fact is not
generally realized.

Since psychotherapy, the subject of our next chapter, is
largely concerned with treating neurotic symptoms, we shall
describe here the leading theories of neurosis and their origins.
Curiously enough our understanding of neurosis arose from
two very controversial curative practices—mesmerism and
hypnotism.

MESMERISM

About 1760 a young Austrian medical student, Anton Mesmer, became interested in the peculiar theories of Paracelsus.
This Paracelsus, a sixteenth-century doctor, believed that magnetic influences from the stars can cure human ills. Mesmer

hit upon the use of a magnet to "draw out" disease. He reported successfully curing cases of paralysis and convulsions. Soon he found that magnetic influences could be imparted by the human hand as well as by metal. This "animal magnetism" was labeled charlatanism by most doctors, though they had to admit it could effect cures. A royal commission was appointed that included the American Minister to France, Benjamin Franklin, as well as Lavoisier, the chemist, and other great figures. This group studied Mesmer's work and concluded that the cures came not from magnetism but from the patient's imagination. Mesmerism was discredited further in scientific circles and even branded dangerous to public morals, but popular interest in it continued for nearly a century.

About fifty years later an English surgeon named James Braid studied the trance-like state that mesmerists produced. He noted that the patient's expectation was the most important factor, that the trance resulted mostly from suggestion. Braid introduced the term "hypnotism."

Doctors began to show interest in hypnotism and suggestion. A French physician, Ambroise Auguste Liébeault, used hypnotism in his practice at Nancy. It proved successful in cases of hysteria, a nervous disorder whose chief symptom is a physical ailment. Hysterical patients were cured of paralysis, blindness, tics, or anesthesias by positive suggestion. During the trance Liébeault told patients that their ailments would disappear; they did! He and his colleague, Hippolyte Bernheim, after years of experience with hypnotism, concluded that all persons are suggestible, though in different degrees.

THEORIES OF CHARCOT AND JANET

While Liébeault and Bernheim were practicing in Nancy, Jean Martin Charcot began in Paris his studies of mental and nervous disorders. The greatest neurologist of his day, Charcot held that hysteria has a physiological basis. Opposing the Nancy view, he said that hypnosis is a symptom of hysteria—the hypnotic trance can be induced only in persons with hysterical tendencies. Charcot described three stages of the hypnotic state: lethargy or drowsiness, catalepsy or rigidity, and somnambulism or dissociation of personality. Liébeault and

Bernheim disputed the inevitability of three such stages. They said that hypnosis varies according to the patient. Mild hypnosis, which is merely a passive, receptive state, can be induced in more than 80% of normal subjects, they pointed out. Bernheim presented data on 10,000 cases to prove the statement. Subsequent studies seem to verify the views of the Nancy School, though it is clear that hysterical persons can be most easily and most deeply hypnotized.

Charcot studied carefully the characteristics of hysteria, noting that neurological changes occur during hypnosis. He described the hysterical personality, finding it as common in men as in women, contrary to previous beliefs. He insisted that faith cures, such as those at Lourdes, occur in persons with hysterical tendencies as a result of the hypnotic influence of the shrine. Thanks to his prestige he succeeded in convincing men of science that hypnosis is a psychological fact.

Charcot attracted many able doctors to his Paris hospital and school. The greatest of these were Pierre Janet and Sigmund Freud.

Janet found that hypnotized hysterical patients can recall events unremembered in the normal state. A forgotten emotional shock, for instance, would be revealed and thus give a clue to causes of the neurosis. By suggesting during the trance that the upsetting event was past and gone, Janet was able to make many symptoms disappear. He developed a theory that hysteria is a "dissociation," or imperfect integration, of personality. Normal personalities are well integrated. Hysterical personalities are split and subject to internal division.

Neuroses, Janet believed, arise from constitutional weakness and lack of energy, possibly with a hereditary basis. But he recommended psychological treatment, not drugs or other physiological therapy. He coined the term "psychasthenia" (meaning "weakness of the mind") to identify cases involving extreme fears, obsessions, and compulsions.

FREUD AND PSYCHOANALYSIS

What Charcot and Janet hinted obliquely, Sigmund Freud stated positively: that neuroses have a psychological origin.

His remarkable theories and his technique of therapy for neuroses stirred the world as no other psychologist before or since has stirred it.

Sigmund Freud was born in 1856 in a little Moravian town, then a part of Austria-Hungary. He studied medicine in Vienna and lived there until 1938 when the Nazi annexation of Austria forced him into exile. He died in London in 1939.

Interested in neurology, Freud went to Paris in 1885 to study under Charcot. There he learned the use of hypnosis to treat hysteria. Once he heard Charcot say, in discussing a young woman's neurosis, that sex is always at the bottom of the trouble. This remark impressed Freud greatly and had much to do with the subsequent development of psychoanalysis.

Returning to Vienna after a year, Freud began treating neurotic patients and working out psychoanalytic methods, which we shall discuss shortly. Here we shall enlarge on Freud's theory of personality and neurosis.

THE UNCONSCIOUS

As mentioned earlier, Freud proposed that the libido or life urge, basically sexual in nature, originates in the unconscious. This concept is central both to the theory and practice of psychoanalysis.

Existence of an unconscious, as opposed to conscious, mental life was not a new idea. Johann Friedrich Herbart, seventy-five years before Freud, had made the unconscious an important part of his system of psychology. Harald Höffding and William James, older contemporaries of Freud, both wrote of the influence of the "subconscious mind" on human behavior. But Freud developed the idea more systematically and more persistently.

Mental life, said Freud, is divided into three parts: the conscious, preconscious, and unconscious. The conscious is much smaller and less significant than generally supposed. It is made up only of ideas and feelings present in immediate awareness. But other mental content is easily recalled to consciousness; this is the preconscious—material only temporarily absent from central consciousness.

Quite different is the unconscious. It is the greatest segment of mind, a huge reservoir which contains all our primitive impulses and strivings. Though completely out of consciousness, it can and does influence mental life tremendously. Forbidden or socially disapproved impulses from the unconscious constantly strive to cross the threshold into consciousness and are restrained by the Ego, thus producing conflicts which, if serious enough, result in neurosis.

Repression and Dreams

Freud discovered that during free association patients fail to remember, or hesitate to express, certain painful or embarrassing items. Explaining this resistance, Freud formulated his famous theory of repression: the Ego relegates unpleasant desires, memories, and ideas to the unconscious and resists the analyst's efforts to bring them to the surface. (However, in the course of time patients develop a strong attachment or "transference" to the analyst, which aids in breaking down this resistance.) The repressed items, generally sexual in nature, constantly seek outward expression. They may be identified, Freud found, by interpreting the patient's dreams.

During sleep, according to Freud, the Ego is relaxed; hence repressed desires and ideas may slip into consciousness as dreams. However, they are disguised. The true meaning is portrayed symbolically. Freud set about interpreting dream symbolism. Take an example, somewhat clearer than most of his interpretations:

A man and a woman who were in love had spent a night together; he described her nature as maternal, she was one of those women whose desire to have a child comes out irresistibly during caresses. The conditions of their meeting, however, made it necessary to take precautions to prevent the semen from entering the womb. On waking the next morning, the woman related the following dream:

An officer with a red cap was pursuing her in the street. She fled from him and ran up the staircase, with him after her. Breathless, she reached her rooms and slammed and locked the door behind her. The man remained outside and, peeping through the keyhole in the door, she saw him sitting on a bench outside, weeping.

In the pursuit by the officer with the red cap and the breathless climbing of the stairs you will recognize the representation of the sexual act. That the dreamer shuts her pursuer out may serve as an example of the device of inversion so frequently employed in dreams, for in reality it was the man who withdrew before the completion of the sexual act. In the same way she has projected her own feeling of grief on to her partner, for it is he who weeps in the dream, his tears at the same time alluding to the seminal fluid.

Freud does not give all dreams a sexual meaning. Essentially, he says, they fulfill wishes. Some gratify thirst, hunger, or a desire for liberty. But disguised and distorted dreams are mainly sexual. He lists the most common sexual symbols.

A house represents the human body. Male genital organs are symbolized by sticks, poles, trees, pencils, tools, weapons, balloons, and airplanes. Female genitalia are indicated by pots, caves, bottles, boxes, doors, rooms, and gates. Apples, peaches, or other fruit mean the female breast. Pubic hair of both sexes is symbolized in dreams by woods and thickets. Sexual intercourse is represented by dancing, climbing, and experiencing violence like being run over. Emerging from water signifies the act of birth.

Freud defends his interpretations by pointing out similar symbolism in fairy tales, folklore, songs, jokes, and epithets. For instance, the New Testament refers to woman as "the weaker vessel." Symbols are invariable, Freud says, though he admits the importance of knowing a patient's personality and life conditions in order to extract the real meaning from his dreams. Many psychoanalysts disagree with Freud, insisting that the meaning of all symbols depends upon the dreamer's experience. But all agree that interpreting dreams helps the analyst understand a patient's conflicts and the content of his unconscious.

FREUDIAN DYNAMISMS

Everyone adopts a device or "dynamism," according to Freudian theory, in order to resolve the inconsistency between his primitive, animal-like Id and the demands of reality. Repression is a common dynamism; it leashes unacceptable ideas and prevents their entering consciousness. Another device is "sublimation," by which the libido is channeled toward socially acceptable ends. Vocational interests, hobbies, civic activities, and even religion are considered examples of sublimation. "Rationalization" protects the Ego, or self, against awareness of unsocial motives by substituting socially approved reasons for behavior. "Projection" means assigning to other persons desires and urges that one's own Ego repudiates. "Regression" is a return to childish behavior and infantile types of gratification. "Conversion" signifies converting a conflict into physical symptoms; it is the mechanism underlying hysteria. Unconsciously adopted, these dynamisms are the Ego's attempt to resolve conflicts. They show up most clearly in neurotic persons, where the conflicts are greatest.

OTHER MAJOR CONTRIBUTORS TO PSYCHOANALYSIS

In the early years of the twentieth century a number of European psychiatrists became interested in psychoanalytic theories and methods of treatment, and a small, active group gathered about Freud and began to hold scientific meetings. In 1910 the International Psychoanalytic Association was formed. Soon differences of opinion appeared, and some of the disciples began to break away, proclaiming their own doctrines and setting up new schools. The two most important of those who separated from Freud were Alfred Adler and Carl G. Jung.

Alfred Adler's school came to be called "individual psychology." Adler disagreed with Freud's emphasis on sex and his distinction between the conscious and unconscious. For Adler the basic urge is a striving for superiority. When this is thwarted, as frequently happens, the person feels inferior and an "inferiority complex" results. He then attempts to compensate for this inferiority by asserting himself in other ways. If this compensation activity gains recognition, the inferiority feeling may be removed. If the compensation is ill-advised and anti-social, it constitutes neurosis. Not sex repressions, but thwarted self-assertion, says Adler, causes neurotic disorders.

Carl G. Jung, the first Swiss psychoanalyst, set up in Zürich the school of "analytical psychology." Jung believed that the libido is not primarily sexual; it may take many forms. In the child it appears as hunger, while later it becomes self-assertion or sex desire. For Jung the unconscious is not, as Freud believed, entirely unmoral or animal. It also includes moral and even religious principles. It is partly personal, and partly "collective"; the collective part consists of inherited primitive or racial ways of thinking and feeling. Neuroses occur, said Jung, partly because complexes built up in childhood persist and partly because some present difficulty overtaxes the person's capacity to adapt.

Other psychoanalysts also differed from Freud, particularly as to therapeutic technique. Among these are Rank, Horney, Fromm, and Sullivan.

Otto Rank proposed a "birth trauma" theory; the shock of leaving the womb and entering an unfriendly world is a more important cause of emotional troubles than the Oedipus complex. He also stressed the significance of social relationships in producing mental illness, which made him a precursor of the "neo-psychoanalysts," Horney, Fromm, and Sullivan.

Karen Horney was trained in Germany and moved to New York shortly after 1930. She reinterpreted Freud to emphasize cultural influences: conflicts and neuroses do not arise from instinctual sources but are produced by the contradictions in our culture. For example, we are taught brotherly love and unselfishness, but competition for success is strongly stressed on every side. Out of such conflict come basic anxiety, hostility, and other neurotic symptoms. The child's need for security is frustrated. Neurotic needs develop which give rise to inner conflicts. Horney felt that neurotic persons in a given society are essentially alike because their conflicts are products of their common culture.

Erich Fromm, also a leading European-trained analyst, came to America about the same time as Horney. Fromm's background was in sociological and psychological study as well as psychoanalytical. As mentioned earlier, Fromm believes personality is shaped by society's way of life, as mediated by the family, which reflects personal and subcultural influences as well as the broader cultural pattern. As man becomes more civilized he also becomes more lonely and isolated; he needs to belong and to find meaning in life, so he constantly searches for relatedness and significance. Some men may "escape from freedom" by submitting to dictatorship. Others are drawn into the "exploitative," "hoarding," or "marketing" orientation, which basically lead to frustration. Others may choose (possibly through psychotherapy) the "productive" orientation and find self-fulfillment.

Harry Stack Sullivan viewed mental illness in more social terms than either Horney or Fromm. He went so far as to say that psychiatry is the study of interpersonal relations, which could include a person's imaginary figures. Anxiety, explained Sullivan, always grows out of interpersonal relations. Persons having a disturbed childhood develop severe early anxiety, which leads to dissociations and distorted images of themselves and their relations to others. If these are not corrected or "validated" through comparing oneself with others, and communicating with others, mental illness—neurosis or even schizophrenia—may occur. Not only psychotherapy, but life itself may be corrective of one's distortions if one has close friends and sound interpersonal relations with his peer group.

Let us turn now to therapy—to mental hygiene, drugs, and psychotherapy.

Chapter XV

MENTAL HYGIENE, DRUGS, AND PSYCHOTHERAPY

PINEL   DIX   BEERS   KRAFFT-EBING
SAKEL   CERLETTI
FREUD   ADLER   JUNG   FERENCZI   STEKEL
ROGERS   KORZYBSKI   MAY

When did modern methods of treating mental disease begin? Why did psychosurgery and shock therapy give way to treatment by drugs? What is the essence of psychoanalytic therapy? What alternative types of psychotherapy have developed?

As we have seen, mental disease was little understood until very recent times. Afflicted persons were often mistreated as witches, or accused of being possessed by demons; at best, they were ridiculed or shunned. But here and there a ray of light broke through.

PINEL'S HUMANE ATTITUDE

During the French Revolution, Philippe Pinel, a doctor interested in mental diseases, broke daringly with tradition. He insisted on treating mental patients humanely. Appointed director of the Bicêtre, a grim and filthy Paris hospital where the insane were chained like animals, he first of all removed the chains. He treated the patients with kindness and consideration. He studied each individually and drew up individual case histories. He classified mental disorders.

Though his simple classification soon was replaced by better ones, it marked the beginning of scientific psychiatry.

Insane persons have sick brains, Pinel argued. They should be treated with kindliness, like anyone with a physical ailment. Against bitter opposition he put into practice his theory of humane treatment. And he was rewarded by seeing many patients recover.

OTHER PIONEERS IN HUMANE TREATMENT

While Pinel was reforming the Bicêtre, an English Quaker named William Tuke became aware of the horrible condition of English lunatic asylums. He established "York Retreat," a pleasant country house where mental patients lived, worked, and rested in a kindly, religious atmosphere.

Tuke's experiment attracted considerable attention. In America a similar venture called the "Hartford Retreat" was founded by Dr. Eli Todd in 1824; it became a model for American mental institutions.

Treatment of the insane improved rather slowly until about 1840. Then Dorothea Lynde Dix, a Massachusetts school teacher, became aroused by shocking conditions which she encountered in prisons and asylums. With determination and energy, Miss Dix investigated further and presented her findings to the public. In time she influenced the legislatures of 20 states to establish or improve 30 mental institutions. Addressing a "memorial" to Congress, she described the appalling conditions: she had seen "more than 9000 idiots, epileptics and insane in the United States, destitute of appropriate care and protection . . . bound with galling chains, bowed beneath fetters and heavy iron balls attached to dragchains, lacerated with ropes, scourged with rods and terrified beneath storms of execration and cruel blows; now subject to jibes and scorn and torturing tricks; now abandoned to the most outrageous violations."

Indefatigable Miss Dix carried her crusade to Europe. She succeeded in establishing numerous mental institutions, notably in Scotland. Her influence became worldwide. It extended to prison reform and work with mental defectives, besides the mentally diseased. Seldom has one person put across so vast a social reform as Dorothea Dix.

CLIFFORD BEERS AND MENTAL HYGIENE

Early in the present century Clifford W. Beers, a patient in a mental hospital, noted in his lucid moments the shocking stupidity, inefficiency, and ill-advised treatment of patients which still characterized our institutions. Later he recovered and left the hospital. In a book called A *Mind That Found Itself* he describes his experiences. Beers was able to interest a number of famous people, such as William James and Theodore Roosevelt, in his plan to reform conditions in mental hospitals.

Out of his work grew the "mental hygiene movement," dedicated to improving the personnel and procedures in our hospitals for the insane. The National Committee for Mental Hygiene, later expanded into the National Association for Mental Health, with active state and local affiliates, has carried on the compaign for humane treatment and education in the prevention of mental disease. Child guidance clinics, adult psychiatric centers, pastoral counseling services, and other agencies for dealing with personality and behavior problems have been established under its auspices. In 1946 the government established the National Institute for Mental Health as one of the Institutes of Health of the U. S. Public Health Service. This agency carries on large-scale research programs of both practical and theoretical importance. It has authority to expend federal funds for research, training, and community services in the mental health field. American mental health groups cooperate also with the World Federation for Mental Health, and the World Health Organization in their global efforts to prevent and eradicate mental illness.

CHEMICAL TREATMENT OF MENTAL DISEASE

A few mental maladies seem incurable. So far it has not been possible to repair the damaged structures underlying senile psychoses or to arrest the deteriorating processes. On the other hand, medical and psychological treatment may aid a patient even if it does not cure him completely. Alcoholic psychosis, for example, is alleviated when the patient stops drinking, builds himself up physically, and begins to tackle his unsolved problems. After drug treatment, an epileptic prone to severe seizures may leave the hospital, though he will have to continue with drugs and live under a planned regime.

Since the late nineteenth century notable progress has been made in discovering the chemical and bacteriological causes of certain mental disorders, and in treating them. Following leads given by several researchers, Richard von Krafft-Ebing, Viennese psychiatrist, showed that general paresis results from syphilis. He inoculated paretic patients with syphilitic germs and found that they failed to show outward signs of the disease, which suggested strongly that they already had it in less obvious form. Later, Hideyo Noguchi, Japanese bacteriologist at the Rockefeller Institute in New York, proved the case by discovering syphilitic spirochetes in the brain and nervous system of paretic cases. A few years later, Julius Wagner-Jauregg, another Viennese psychiatrist, found that high fever kills syphilitic germs and cures paretic patients. After experimenting with various fevers he selected malaria, since it could be readily stopped with quinine after it had done its work. For many years infection with malaria was the outstanding treatment for paresis, and in 1927 Wagner-Jauregg was awarded a Nobel Prize for his work. In 1943, J. F. Mahoney and his co-workers reported that penicillin proved an even better way to destroy the syphilitic spirochetes. One of the researchers in this area, W. L. Bruetsch, found that malaria therapy produced full recovery in 35% of the cases; moderate dosage of penicillin raised the figure to 50%; and heavy doses raised the recovery rate to 80% or better, though unfortunate side effects sometimes developed.

Bleuler believed that schizophrenia can be cured. For many years no specific cure was found; drugs, oxygen, hormone treatments, fever therapy, and prolonged sleep brought little or no success. About 1932 a Viennese doctor, Manfred Sakel, discovered by accident that giving insulin until it produced shock improved the mental state of schizophrenics. Why this type of coma, induced by decreasing the sugar in the blood, should help cure schizophrenia is not clear. Unfortunately the spectacular successes reported at first were not borne out by later studies. However, insulin shock is still an accepted method of treatment, though many psychiatrists find that one or another tranquilizing drug produces results as good as, or better than, insulin shock.

In 1935 Ladislas J. Meduna of Budapest reported that a similar convulsion, induced by the camphor compound metrazol, could cure schizophrenia. It had certain disadvantages, however, and has been superseded chiefly by electroshock treatment. Two Italian researchers, Ugo Cerletti and L. Bini, were primarily responsible for electroshock therapy (EST) or electroconvulsive therapy (ECT). The shock is induced by a mild current applied through electrodes placed upon the temples. Actually, EST has proved far more useful in treating depression, either in manic-depressive psychosis or in involutional melancholia, than it has in cases of schizophrenia.

The most striking development in chemical treatment of mental disease, of course, is the tranquilizing drug. Since 1952 a large number of preparations have been produced, such as meprobamate (Miltown, Equanil), chlorpromazine (Thorazine), promazine (Sparine), and many others, all of which have the effect of quieting agitation and tension. In a recent summary article, Dr. Paul Hoch, Commissioner of Mental Hygiene for the State of New York, noted that tranquilizers are not indicated for treating depression, but are used effectively in quieting manic conditions and agitation and in treating schizophrenia. Many such patients, however, also need supportive psychiatric treatment. It has been said that the tranquilizer calms the patient and makes him amenable to psychotherapy. Tranquilizers, more than any other single factor, are responsible for changing the whole atmosphere of our mental hospitals and making straitjackets, sedative baths, needleshowers, and even violent wards a thing of the past. It should be added that tranquilizers are also widely used for reducing anxiety and tension in neurotic patients and out-patient psychotics, often in conjunction with psychotherapy.

The complete story of drug therapy is long and complex.

Many phases we have not touched upon, such as the development of new types of medication by Lennox and others, for the treatment of epilepsy, of which the best known is dilantin. We referred earlier to benzedrine; other stimulants such as dexedrine have been synthesized for treating apathy, depression, and other abnormal conditions.

PSYCHOSURGERY

"Psychosurgery" is defined as a surgical operation upon the intact brain for the relief of mental symptoms. It was originated by a Portuguese psychiatrist, Egaz Moniz, who reported of his first twenty patients in 1936 that one-third recovered, one-third improved, and one-third remained unimproved. Moniz' technique was to sever connections between the frontal lobes and the rest of the brain, thus altering personality by destroying "the more or less fixed arrangements of cellular connections that exist in the brain." Richard Brickner had already reported on the effects of removing a patient's frontal lobes on both sides because of tumors. The operation did not affect intelligence or sensorimotor functions, but seemed to impair the patient's ability to combine or synthesize and his restraint of egotistical and unsocial impulses.

Two American neurologists, Walter Freeman and J. L. Watts, carried forward the work of Moniz. They found that after surgery patients became less anxious, less concerned about inner experiences, more responsive to the environment. They discovered also that the operation, "pre-frontal lobotomy" (or "lobectomy"), could relieve unbearable pain. However, the resulting changes in behavior are often unfortunate, including loss of attention and initiative, along with increasing tactlessness and social offensiveness. Because the operation is irreversible, psychosurgery has given way to shock treatments, which are less radical, and to tranquilizers, except for patients who can be helped in no other way.

Is the future likely to bring discovery of physical or chemical cures for most forms of mental illness? Some leaders in medicine believe so. In 1956, Dr. Percival Bailey, Director of the Illinois State Psychopathic Institute, addressed the

American Psychiatric Association, noting that psychosurgery, shock therapy, and psychoanalysis had all raised high hopes at first, but had failed to fulfill their initial promise. He concluded by stating his conviction, much as his predecessors Pierre Janet and even Freud himself had done, that the problem of schizophrenia, and perhaps even of the neuroses, will ultimately be solved by the biochemist. Only time will tell.

PSYCHOTHERAPY

We noted in the last chapter that the understanding of neuroses grew out of mesmerism and hypnotism, which led to the work of Liébeault, Bernheim, and, most important of all, Charcot, the famous neurologist with whom Freud studied in the 1880's. After Freud left Paris and returned to his native Vienna, he experienced only partial success from treating his patients with hypnosis. He went back to France for further inspiration, this time visiting Liébeault and Bernheim at Nancy, where he learned more about their hypnotic methods. Even after this he found hypnosis of doubtful value, because some patients could not be hypnotized, and others who could failed to recover.

FREUDIAN PSYCHOANALYTIC THERAPY

Freud began to work with a former colleague, Josef Breuer, who had developed a "talking out" treatment. Breuer discovered that a patient was helped if encouraged, under hypnosis, to "talk out" his emotional troubles. Breuer and Freud called this technique "catharsis" because it seemed to purge the patient of pent-up or repressed emotions. Shortly after they published a book in 1895 called *Studies in Hysteria*, Breuer withdrew from the partnership and Freud carried on alone.

Freud soon gave up hypnosis and concentrated on the talking-out method of free association. He told patients to relax, think about their troubles, and say everything that came to mind. He found this technique superior to hypnosis because the patient remained in an active, cooperative state, while coping with his difficulty.

Freudian psychoanalysis is based upon two major assumptions or theories:

First, every mental happening has a cause, presumably the psychic events which preceded it. Thoughts and feelings do not occur "for no reason at all," as people often say. This principle of psychic determinism underlies Freud's investigations of dreams, forgetting, slips of the tongue, and other areas previously dismissed as being of no significance.

Second, most of mental life is unconscious rather than conscious, contrary to popular belief. Actually, the primary causes of behavior, according to psychoanalysis, are commonly found in the urges and impulses of the Id.

Freud pointed out that all persons have childhood sexual complexes, with minor conflicts and repressions. But these are handled reasonably well by normal individuals. Neuroses result when the libido fixates on childhood love objects, such as oneself or one's parents, or when the delicate relationship between Ego, Superego, and Id gets out of balance, resulting in serious conflict. The frustration is facilitated when the demands of reality become excessively severe.

Psychoanalytic treatment aims to free the libido from its unfortunate fixations and to build up the Ego until the patient can cope with his problems. By free association and dream interpretation the analyst comes to understand his patient's conflicts. When the patient is brought to the point in his treatment where he can accept the analyst's interpretation of his difficulties, he is on the way to recovery.

ADLERIAN AND JUNGIAN PSYCHOTHERAPY

We referred earlier to Alfred Adler and Carl Jung, disciples of Freud who broke away from the master. Adler insisted that to treat neurosis according to "individual psychology," one must discover the "style of life" or role which the patient adopted early in childhood, chiefly as a result of his position in the family. All this is duly explained to the patient, so that he understands his inferiority complex and the failure of his compensatory efforts. He then is guided toward goals more socially acceptable and more within his capacity for achievement.

Jung, on the other hand, started by studying the present problem and the patient's way of meeting it. He believed that emotional upset develops from disharmony between the "persona" (a person's social mask), the ego, and the collective unconscious. Conflict can also arise from a person's becoming too extroverted or too introverted. Like Freud, Jung used free association and dream analysis, but Jung tailored his interpretations to the personality-type of the patient. Jungian analysis deals with both past and present, and seeks to integrate conscious and unconscious trends of personality.

OTHER PSYCHOANALYSTS

Several associates of Freud came to differ with one or another aspect of psychoanalysis. For example, Wilhelm Reich suggested focusing on the patient's character, and found that this had to be analyzed before psychoanalysis could proceed. The "character armor" of many patients, said Reich, is a kind of defense and makes up the major resistance to analysis of the unconscious processes. Self-dramatizing, intellectualizing, ingratiation, and overaggressiveness are examples of such resistance. These have to be brought into the open and analyzed before free association can proceed productively, according to Reich.

Two other early Freudians, Sandor Ferenczi and Wilhelm Stekel, objected to the length of time consumed by the orthodox "passive" technique of therapy. They favored the analyst taking a more active part in directing a patient's free associations. By one or another form of this method both Ferenczi and Stekel claimed that good results could be obtained in a few months, instead of the year or more usually involved in a Freudian analysis.

In the United States, Franz Alexander and T. M. French have differed even more from orthodox Freudian techniques. They have modified the frequency of treatment sessions and have interrupted therapeutic contacts; they have sometimes given up use of the couch and of free association in terms of the particular needs and problems of individual patients. Alexander and French have not only evaluated their procedures critically but have made significant efforts to assess the success and failure of their psychotherapy.

While the "neo-analysts," whose work we discussed in the preceding chapter, have generally followed psychoanalytic therapeutic techniques, a few variations are worthy of comment. Horney, for example, believed the therapist has to interpret actively to the patient his neurotic needs and the conflict between reality and his idealized self-image. Sullivan saw psychotherapy as a particular type of interpersonal relationship in which the therapist emphasizes and observes, then interrogates and communicates, constantly searching for the cause of the patient's difficulty. Free association may be used to aid the process of communication, which the therapist makes every effort to keep active until he feels that termination is in order. He then summarizes and interprets for the patient. Sullivan was especially interested in schizophrenics and in discovering the traumatic conditions of childhood which caused their overwhelming dissociations; these had then to be attacked directly by the patient and therapist working together.

CLIENT-CENTERED THERAPY

A relatively new, and essentially American, development is "non-directive counseling" or "client-centered" psychotherapy, which is the contribution of psychologist Carl R. Rogers and his associates. Following the lead of Otto Rank, Rogers stressed a permissive attitude toward the patient or client, on the assumption that the client knows himself and his needs best, and that he has within him the possibilities for growth and development. The therapist's role is to understand the client's thought and feeling, and to accept it completely. He does not interpret, but often reflects or summarizes expressed feelings. The therapist's aim is to encourage the patient to be more fully himself, to reorganize himself so as to achieve self-realization. Client-centered therapy is the least directive, least interpretive, least manipulative type of psychotherapy.

Rogers and his colleagues support their claims with a great deal of research and with many complete recordings of therapeutic sessions. Generally speaking, their approach is accepted as a valuable type of therapy for intelligent and mildly disturbed clients, but not for seriously disturbed or psychotic patients. Frederick Thorne, a psychologist and psychiatrist who supports "directive" psychotherapy, doubts that a completely non-directive therapy is possible because of the nature of the therapist-client relationships. The client expects help and direction from a person of superior experience and training; and the sicker the patient, the more true this is. He concludes that the need for direction is inversely correlated with the person's potentialities for effective self-regulation.

PSYCHOTHERAPY AND LEARNING

Rogers' non-directive therapy represents one reaction against traditional psychotherapy. Another is found in the efforts of several psychologists to place psychotherapy on the firm scientific base of learning theory. (See Chapter VI for a discussion of major learning theories.) Robert Sears, for example, interpreted repression, fixation, regression, displacement, and other basic psychoanalytic concepts according to the findings from experimental learning studies. John Dollard and Neal Miller depicted both personality and psychotherapy in terms of Hull's reinforcement theory. Hobart Mowrer has analyzed neurosis and psychotherapy according to his somewhat more complex "twofold learning" theory.

Practicing psychotherapists, too, have been applying theories of conditioning and learning in their work. One of the best known of these, Joseph Wolpe, developed "psychotherapy by reciprocal inhibition." Basically his method consists of evoking positive or pleasurable responses (assertive, sexual, relaxation, and so forth) in the presence of anxiety- or fear-producing stimuli so that responses to these stimuli are weakened. Wolpe claims more striking and longer-lasting results with his reciprocal inhibition technique than have been obtained by psychoanalytic or other methods.

OTHER PSYCHOTHERAPEUTIC APPROACHES

The years since World War II have given rise to many types of psychotherapy. One of these has centered about "semantics" and verbal communication. Count Alfred Korzybski wrote a book called *Science and Sanity* in which he maintained that neurosis results largely from faulty understanding of words and their meanings. When a person's use of words lacks clarity, he tends to be confused or misled about his problems and ways of solving them. One of Korzybski's successors, Wendell Johnson, makes an even stronger case for semantic therapy. The way a person sees himself, formulates his problems, and interprets his environment all depend upon words and concepts. Through language symbols a person can talk and think himself into frustrations and conflicts. (Consider, for example, the world of difference, therapeutically speaking, between "I have failed again" and "I am a failure.") The aim of semantic therapy is to teach a person to conceptualize his problems more clearly and realistically, and through improved communication to develop more effective interpersonal relations.

"Existential analysis" is an outgrowth of the existential philosophy which was derived from the views of Sören Kierkegaard by Martin Heidegger and Jean-Paul Sartre. It seems to have a special appropriateness for the newer generation in that it seeks to overcome personal apathy in the patient by emphasis on the value of greater commitment to worthwhile and creative activities. It centers about understanding man's existence, his values, his personal world, his essential nature. A knowledge of a person's drives and mechanisms is useful, says Rollo May, the leading American existential analyst, and so is information about his gestures, his social conditioning, and his interpersonal relationships. But all these fall on to quite a different level, he continues, when we confront the overarching, most real fact of all—namely, the immediate, living person himself. The existential therapist seeks, somewhat like the client-centered therapist, to empathize with his patient in order to understand his way of feeling and of living. He has no unique therapeutic procedures, but tries

to relate warmly to the patient and to encourage in him
healthy efforts toward self-realization.

MENTAL HEALTH AND THE FUTURE

The treatment of mental illness has been revolutionized
within the past century, and has changed considerably in the
period since World War II. Humane treatment of the mentally ill made great strides with the work of Dorothea Dix
and Clifford Beers. But as Albert Deutsch has said, the task
of assuring enlightened treatment for the mentally ill is a
continuing one which must be shouldered by each generation. The progress made by the report of the Joint Commission on Mental Illness and Health will be described in our
last chapter.

Chapter XVI

MAN AS A SOCIAL BEING

WUNDT   SPENCER   TARDE   LE BON   ROSS
MC DOUGALL   BEKHTEREV   ALLPORT   MORENO   LEWIN
SHERIF   BOGARDUS   KATZ   CANTRIL   MURPHY   NEWCOMB
KLINEBERG   RIESMAN   HOVLAND   OSGOOD

How does social psychology differ from individual psychology? Why has the study of groups become so important? Does leadership depend upon the person or the group? How do our attitudes arise? How can they be changed? Can prejudice be reduced? What is meant by "the communication process"? Do social class differences exist in the United States?

Until now our attention has focused on how we behave as individuals. Another aspect of our behavior is social. We are affected tremendously by the persons we see and talk to daily. They in turn are affected by us. Social psychology deals with the ways persons influence each other.

Philosophical Background

Many great thinkers, ancient and modern, have speculated on men's relations to each other and to society in general. Plato's *Republic* proposes an ideal state in which each man finds a niche according to his abilities, and in which a rational social organization protects the individual against aggressions by others. For Aristotle man is a "political animal," inherently

possessing possibilities for social organization and social reactions.

Thomas Hobbes writes that man's life in the natural state
—without organized society—would be "solitary, poore, nasty,
brutish and short." Man's hunger, thirst, sex urge, fear, desire
for honor, pleasure-seeking, and pain-avoiding are the basis
of social organization. Men formed societies to gratify their
needs and avoid attack. Society grew out of man's fear and
self-interest.

Several nineteenth-century thinkers anticipated social psychology. In England, Jeremy Bentham originated "utilitari-
anism." According to this doctrine man's self-interest—his
tendency to seek pleasure and avoid pain—causes much social
inequality and injustice. Guided by enlightened social leadership, however, it can lead to the greatest good of the greatest
number. Bentham's theories, developed by James Mill and
John Stuart Mill, encouraged psychological analysis of social
and economic behavior.

In 1860 a group of German anthropologists (then called
"folk psychologists") founded a journal devoted to the folklore, customs, and languages of primitive peoples. They were
particularly interested in the contrasting "group minds" of
various races. Inspired by the folk psychologists, Wilhelm
Wundt began to study primitive languages, which he believed
best expressed the mind of each social group. He published
a five-volume work in 1900, called *Folk Psychology*. Anthropologists later criticized his conclusions on the ground that
language undergoes so much borrowing and diffusion that
it cannot be considered an index of the mind of any group.
Nevertheless, Wundt's studies made linguistics a major concern of anthropology and social psychology.

An important step toward establishing social psychology
was taken by Herbert Spencer, an evolutionist even before
Darwin published *The Origin of Species*. Spencer applied
evolutionary interpretations to social behavior and social institutions. Complex modern society can be understood only
in terms of preceding social development, he says. He used
the term "superorganic environment" to describe the build-
ings, tools, language, customs, religion, and other man-made
products, in contrast to natural environment. This man-made

environment, later called "culture" or the "social heritage," became a primary concern of all social scientists, including social psychologists.

BEGINNINGS OF SOCIAL PSYCHOLOGY

Social psychology became a separate field of study in the 1890's when laws and principles regulating man's behavior toward other men were formulated.

A Frenchman, Gabriel Tarde, published *The Laws of Imitation*. We react to each other mainly by conscious and unconscious imitation, Tarde says. Social changes, customs, fashions, inventions, religious hysteria, and other kinds of social behavior come about by imitation. Actually, much of what Tarde included under "imitation" now is called "suggestion." He was influenced by the work of Liébeault and Bernheim on hypnosis and suggestibility.

Gustave Le Bon, also impressed by psychiatric studies of suggestion, wrote *The Crowd*. In it he explained crowd behavior, mobs, and mass movements on the basis of group suggestibility. The crowd is less rational, intelligent, and moral than are its component individuals. It also is more emotional, suggestible, and likely to follow leaders uncritically, just as a hysterical patient accepts a hypnotist's suggestions.

Le Bon's theory of a "group mind," existing independently of the minds of individuals composing the group, became a bone of contention in social psychology. Current theories hold that no group mind exists. They explain crowd behavior by the increased emotionality and suggestibility occurring *in each individual* because he is part of a mob or crowd situation.

In 1908 the first two books actually called *Social Psychology* appeared. One, written by Edward A. Ross, clarified the terms "suggestion" and "imitation" and showed how they brought about contemporary social, political, and economic events. The other, by William McDougall, interpreted social behavior on the basis of instincts. (McDougall's list of innate urges is described in Chapter IX.) Social life, according to him, is native to each of us in the instincts of repulsion, pugnacity, gregariousness, and others. Social psychology can be understood through individual psychology. McDougall's views were approved and widely quoted until a reaction against instinct developed in the 1920's.

BEGINNINGS OF EXPERIMENTATION

While the battle raged over instincts and over the group mind, social psychologists began to experiment instead of theorize. Before 1900 Norman Triplett, experimental psychologist, tested how children are stimulated by competition. He had them compete at winding reels that moved little flags toward a goal. Half his forty subjects worked faster when competing with others than when working alone. Ten children did worse in competition, and ten equally well in either situation. Triplett also experimented on suggestion. He did sleight-of-hand tricks for a large group of children 10 or 12 years old. When he made the motions of throwing a ball into the air, about half the children reported seeing the ball go up and disappear.

Psychologists began to realize that experiment is possible even in the complex field of social behavior. Just after World War I a wave of experimentation resulted in several significant discoveries.

An experiment by Walther Moede tested how well individuals work when other persons are present. One test measured strength of hand grip; Moede found it increased when the subject competed with a rival. In another test boys bore a great deal more pain when pitched against rivals to test endurance. Letters or figures on a printed page were canceled more rapidly but less accurately under competitive than under noncompetitive conditions. Lee E. Travis compared students' accuracy in following a movable target when alone and when in the presence of spectators. Most subjects did better with an audience. Georgina S. Gates, however, in a number of tests found insignificant differences between lone performance and performance before either small or large groups of spectators. John F. Dashiell found in a similar experiment that persons tend to work faster but less accurately when spectators are present. This conclusion is confirmed in many other studies on the subject.

SOCIAL INTERACTION

When co-workers instead of spectators are present, much the same thing results, according to Floyd H. Allport. Having co-workers generally steps up performance. Slow persons speed up more than fast ones, though many individual differences occur. Julius B. Maller tested the relative effectiveness of different kinds of competition. He studied school children in several competitive situations. Working for oneself acted as a strong incentive, but sometimes it was surpassed by working against members of the opposite sex, or working with members of a congenial group against everyone else. When asked under what conditions they would like to compete, three-fourths of the children picked self-competition. Competing as a member of a whole class or as one of an arbitrary group furnished the smallest incentive for accomplishment.

Cooperation in the form of group thinking was studied by the famous Russian psychologist, Vladimir Bekhterev. Group members discussed the probable length of a time interval, what details they saw in a picture, ethical judgments, and creative thinking. Group discussion in general seemed more advantageous than individual work in terms of correctness and quality of decisions.

Cooperative thinking of the jury deliberation variety was studied by Dashiell, among others. He required witnesses of certain events to testify before a jury group, which then discussed the evidence. From their reports Dashiell concluded that jurors, after hearing witnesses, can tell nearly as complete a story and a slightly more accurate one than the average witness can. The whole jury, after discussion, gives a more complete and accurate account of details than any one jury member. Dashiell admitted that his results are only trends. Different events or different types of witnesses and jurors might change the results considerably.

Early students of social psychology also experimented upon suggestion and imitation. Alfred Binet, for example, told

hoolboys to estimate the lengths of lines shown one at a
me. The length of the first five increased progressively; after
at, to thirty-six, they were equal. A constant gradual in-
ease was suggested by the first five, hence the rest were
verestimated. Some of the children were taken in much more
an others; according to Binet they had greater "suggesti-
lity." Older children showed less suggestibility than younger
es. "Prestige suggestion" also was noted by Binet. Here
e person's authority or reputation helped induce unreason-
g responses from others.

Henry T. Moore tested two kinds of prestige suggestion.
e asked a hundred students to make numerous linguistic,
hical, and musical judgments. Later they were told what
dgments most of their group had made, and were given a
ance to change their minds. Still later they were told what
dgments had been made by an expert in each field and
gain were permitted to alter their own reactions. Both the
ajority and expert judgments induced much change of opin-
n, except in regard to musical preferences.

Using several tests, Warner Brown studied the difference
etween men and women in suggestibility. Women proved
enerally more suggestible than men, though not in all cases.
rown also discovered that the most suggestible persons in
onnection with one test were not necessarily so in connection
ith others. He concluded there is no one personality trait
at can be called "suggestibility."

Two British psychologists, Francis Aveling and H. L. Har-
reaves, tried out a battery of suggestion tests. Some resem-
led hypnosis: a child was told that his hand muscles were
iffening, then was asked to open his hand in order to test
hether the suggestion worked. Other items resembled Bi-
et's or included leading questions, as in court procedure. In-
restingly enough, some children reacted negatively to
restige; they did just the opposite of what the experimenter
ggested. Some correlation between the tests was found, how-
ver. Aveling and Hargreaves concluded that suggestibility is
fairly general personality trait. Other psychologists disagree.
t present the matter remains unsettled.

A new attack on the problem of suggestibility was made by
Muzafer Sherif in his study of the autokinetic effect (see

Chapter VII). In a completely dark room subjects were shown a moving point of light. Their estimates of the distance it moved varied considerably because they had no standard by which to judge. As Sherif put it, they lacked a "frame of reference." Under these conditions the judgments of someone having prestige—the instructor, for example—influenced greatly the reactions of others. Sherif found in addition that the socially determined standards set up by suggestion persisted later in a re-test.

Suggestion also provided a criterion, Sherif found, in an experiment on literary preferences. He determined subjects' degree of like or dislike for several authors such as Dickens, Poe, Scott, Conrad, and Stevenson. Later he chose several passages, all from Stevenson's writings, which he attributed to different authors. When asked to rate the passages for literary merit, the subjects judged them, in general, according to their attitudes toward the supposed authors. Similarly Paul R. Farnsworth and a colleague found that college students liked Mark Twain, Will Rogers, and Thomas A. Edison, and tended to agree with their views. When the same views were assigned to Aimee Semple McPherson or William Randolph Hearst, whom the students did not like, greater disapproval of their views was registered. Thus suggestion was found to influence "logical" and "rational" behavior.

Another type of social interaction, imitation, was a very popular concept in the early days of social psychology. As already mentioned, Gabriel Tarde explained most social behavior via operation of the process or force of imitation. Other social psychologists soon criticized such all-inclusive interpretations, noting that behavior similarities may occur for several reasons, including pure chance. Even when imitation does take place, as Ellis Freeman pointed out, it does not occur blindly. We imitate only acts which have meaning for us and harmonize with our desires. A girl gets a hairdo like the reigning movie actress's, said Junius F. Brown, not because of a force called imitation, but because she believes the new coiffure will make her more like the actress or the heroine she portrays.

In 1941 Neal Miller and John Dollard, in their book *Social Learning and Imitation*, portrayed imitation as a type of learning. Similarities in behavior are often not strictly imitative (e.g., motorists stopping at a red light); persons simply have been conditioned in the same way. Conscious copying of another's behavior may properly be called "imitation," but this too is a learned response, not found in animals or very young children. Much of what has been called "imitation" is simply "matched-dependent behavior," according to Miller and Dollard. This is a kind of generalized modeling on the behavior of superior persons which the child learns because he is rewarded for doing so.

Social Groups

By the time of the Second World War interest in social interaction had led social psychologists to the study of social groups. Previously this had been the province of sociology which, indeed, had been defined by some as the "science of social groups." Social psychologists trained in sociology were familiar with the theories of the German, Georg Simmel, distinguishing between in-groups and out-groups. Even earlier, Charles H. Cooley had contrasted primary and secondary groups—the intimate face-to-face relationships found in the family or play group, as compared with the more impersonal, indirect, far-removed groups such as a professional society or political party. Psychologists in the 1930's learned of the industrial studies of Fritz Roethlisberger and W. J. Dickson, in which it was demonstrated that the influence of his work group upon the individual was far more important than illumination, temperature, or rest periods—and even than hours of work or wage rates!

In 1934 J. L. Moreno, a psychiatrist, introduced "sociometry," a method for studying interpersonal relations within a group. By asking each member to indicate which of the other members he would like to live with, work with, or play with, Moreno could construct a "sociogram," which showed the pattern of attractions and repulsions within the group. The sociogram also revealed the leaders and isolates; it is thus a generally useful tool for arranging congenial grouping and improving morale within the group and larger institution.

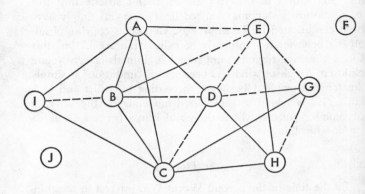

A Typical Sociogram
Solid lines indicate acceptance; broken lines rejection.
Thus A likes everybody and is liked by all but E. ED
and IB are mutual rejections. J and F are isolates.

An even more important contribution to the psychology of
social groups is found in the work of Kurt Lewin, a Gestalt
psychologist who came to the United States from Germany in
1932. Lewin stimulated many important studies, such as the
research into authoritarian and democratic group atmospheres
which will be described later. During World War II Lewin
and his associates demonstrated, for example, that group discussion and "group decision" were much more effective methods of changing people's food habits than either the lecture
method or individual instruction. Alex Bavelas showed that
group decision on the part of a group of factory sewing
machine operators raised their level of production from an index of 75 to one of 87, and maintained it at the latter figure
for more than nine months. Lewin concluded that "it is usually easier to change individuals formed into a group than to
change any one of them separately."

In 1944 Lewin established the Research Center for Group
Dynamics at Massachusetts Institute of Technology, and
with his young associates launched a vigorous program of
social research. Progress was severely handicapped by Lewin's
sudden death in 1947. Shortly after this the Center moved to

the University of Michigan where it has continued under the leadership of Dorwin Cartwright, Ronald Lippitt, Alvin Zander, John R. P. French, Jr. and others.

CHARACTERISTICS OF SOCIAL GROUPS

Cooley's distinction between primary and secondary groups has already been mentioned. Herbert Hyman later suggested a distinction between "membership groups" and "reference groups." Membership groups are those to which we actually belong, such as family, neighborhood, gang, school, or fraternal order. Reference groups are those to which a person aspires or "refers" himself, often to gain in status, such as being considered a professional or being in "society." Muzafer Sherif and Hadley Cantril noted that a child desires to belong and to be accepted by his peers, so he takes over the norms and standards of his membership and reference groups. This process has much to do with determining his ego-structure and his whole personality, including his relationships with other persons and groups.

But what, after all, is a social group? Ernest W. Burgess, the sociologist, defined it as a "unity of interacting personalities." Theodore M. Newcomb was more specific in suggesting that "a group consists of two or more persons who share norms about certain things with one another and whose social roles are closely interlocking." The concepts of "norm" and "role" have become very important to social psychologists, since they are significant aspects of all social groups. Sherif showed that social norms serve as frames of reference which guide the feelings, opinions, and actions of group members, whether or not the latter are aware of them. The group norms—rules, customs, and standards—regulate what is approved and what is "not done" by the members of the group.

"Role" or "social role" is a term taken over from anthropology and sociology, where it referred primarily to the behavior prescribed as appropriate for persons of specified age and sex. Ralph Linton identified seven such roles in all societies: infant, boy, girl, adult man, adult woman, old man, old woman. Social philosopher George H. Mead found that the child learns very early to take or assume roles, and this is essential to his socialization. Sociologist Willard Waller likewise saw the role as a means of social growth, with the child first learning the roles of others in the family, then reaching further afield. Social psychologists give the concept a slightly different twist. Theodore Sarbin, for example, sees a role as a pattern of learned actions performed in a social situation; its nature and function depend upon the person's perception of the situation and the expectations of the others in the group. For psychologists a social role represents the pattern of a person's behavior in social groups; it becomes an essential link or bridge between the individual and society.

Some have asked: what is the optimum size of a social group? The question, of course, is impossible to answer apart from a knowledge of the group's function, that is, whether it is a work group, play group, study group, or therapy group. Paul Hare has given an answer for problem-solving groups: on the whole a group of about five persons seemed to function best and to give most satisfaction to its members.

Another question relates to the cohesiveness of a group (or to what Raymond B. Cattell calls its "syntality"). To some extent cohesiveness depends upon size. Stanley E. Seashore found that factory work groups of between 4 and 22 persons stuck together better than larger groups. Cohesiveness may also hinge upon physical factors, as was shown in a housing project studied by Leon Festinger, Stanley Schachter, and Kurt Back. The occupants formed friendships with those living nearest them, with preference for those living opposite rather than alongside.

CONFORMITY

One of the most interesting and important aspects of group behavior is conformity. To what extent do members adhere to the group norms? Actually most of us conform to some degree, partly to save time and effort and to avoid disapproval.

Just how much we conform, even in the small ways of common situations, was studied by Floyd Allport and his students. He observed 1000 pedestrians at a traffic light guarded by a policeman. Almost 90% obediently waited at the curb until the green light appeared. About 8% waited just off the curb.

Two percent ventured to the middle of the intersection, then waited, while a negligible .3% struck across, defying the light altogether. Other studies dealt with employees' punctuality in arriving at work, Catholics taking part in the Holy Water ceremony, and workers' promptness in registering for employment. In each situation an overwhelming majority conformed to the usual behavior. A few departed slightly, but practically no one proved completely nonconformist.

More recently Solomon Asch demonstrated that under certain conditions a person may display extreme conformity. For example, when all but one individual in a group have been coached to call two unequal lines "equal," the naïve subject may conform, even when the lines are obviously different in length. Richard Crutchfield devised an experimental technique involving five booths and a system of signals by which the experimenter presumably tells each subject how the others have reacted. Like Asch, Crutchfield found that under strong pressure many persons "yielded" on fact and logic items, as well as in the area of opinions and attitudes. To give one example: 19% of a sample of college students, questioned privately, agreed with the somewhat undemocratic statement, "Free speech being a privilege rather than a right, it is proper for a society to suspend free speech whenever it feels itself threatened." In the experimental situation, however, when each individual was led to believe all the rest of the group endorsed the statement, no less than 58% expressed agreement!

Of course, conformity is affected by many factors such as the difficulty level of the problem, the individual's certainty about his judgment, and personality differences in tendency to yield or conform. Conformity also depends upon the individual's relationship to the group, as Newcomb showed in a study made in a college community. Those students who identified with the college and participated in its activities increased most in liberalism of socioeconomic attitudes; that is, they conformed most with the predominant faculty attitudes. Those students whose attitudes changed little (i.e., who did not conform) were negative or indifferent toward the college community and identified themselves with outside groups, notably their families.

THE FUNCTIONING OF GROUPS

Moreno's sociogram, described above, is a method for depicting the interpersonal relations within a group. Others have described these processes in more detail. R. F. Bales, for example, worked out a schema of 12 categories for "interaction process analysis," which has been used for a wide variety of groups. Individual members are rated on their behavior—e.g., on agreeing or disagreeing, on giving or asking for suggestions and information, on laughing or otherwise releasing tension, on helping others, on withdrawing, being cooperative, or antagonistic. Launor Carter and his associates developed a much longer list of categories, covering personal feelings, ways of proposing and initiating action, and of arguing and disagreeing, along with a number of "leader," "follower," and "nonproductive" roles. It has been difficult to obtain a reasonably short list of categories applicable to all kinds of social situations.

John Thibaut and Harold H. Kelley have presented a theory of group functioning based upon learning. Each individual in a group explores and samples the various possibilities of social behavior; his social acts which are reinforced, or rewarded by success, will be repeated. Thus various patterns of interaction may be found among different groups, depending upon the types of responses which were tried out and rewarded.

Other social psychologists have turned to the function of perception and problem-solving in social behavior. Fritz Heider stresses the importance of "balance" or consistency in our thinking; when imbalance occurs we do something about it. For example, if X and Y are judged by a person to be beneficial to him, and if X and Y are antagonistic to one another, a "cognitive imbalance" exists. It might be removed by changing the person's judgment of X or of Y, or of the relation between them, or perhaps in some other way. In any event, the person is distressed until he resolves this inconsistency. Similarly Leon Festinger has elaborated a "theory of cognitive dissonance": awareness of a discrepancy in his knowledge or beliefs motivates one to reduce this dissonance. If a person is unsuccessful in rationalizing or in changing his beliefs or actions, he may seek social support to help bolster the beliefs, which would do away with the dissonance.

On the more practical side, many psychologists have sought to increase the efficiency of group functioning. Following the lead of Kurt Lewin, John R. P. French and his associates studied industrial productivity with reference to communication between employer and employee. When supervisors held a group discussion, with employees participating, to explain a change in assignment or procedure, the group production rate went up noticeably. Robert Tannenbaum and Fred Massarik find many advantages result when decision-making is shared with employees. Not only does production increase, but there is a reduction in turnover, absenteeism, and tardiness, and in general there are fewer grievances and more cooperative relations.

The functioning of groups should deal with relations between groups as well as with interpersonal relations within a group. In a notable series of real-life experiments involving boy campers, Muzafer Sherif and his associates were able to produce stable in-groups which competed with each other almost to the point of overt conflict. Then, by introducing superordinate goals—tasks requiring the cooperation of the antagonistic groups—Sherif showed that intergroup tensions could be eliminated. Similarly, Robert R. Blake and Jane S. Mouton studied the pathology of labor-management conflict. They discovered that a major cause of difficulty lies in the "win-or-lose" attitude, which does motivate each group and increase its cohesion, but leads to belittling of the adversary and distorting of his position. Hence areas of agreement are overlooked and a deadlock is likely to result. Blake and Mouton found, however, that through catharsis-inducing conferences it was possible to shift toward collaborative, problem-solving approaches based upon mutual respect and trust.

LEADERSHIP

Early studies of leadership emphasized the characteristics of leaders. Leaders are dominant persons, yet leadership and domination are not the same thing. As P. J. W. Pigors said, leadership means guiding human beings in pursuit of a common cause. Domination means assuming superiority and using it to regulate others' activities for one's own ends.

Lewis Terman studied the characteristics of leaders among children, as rated by their companions. Leaders tended to be either very good or very bad in appearance, health, social status, school work, boldness, and fluency of speech. They stood out from others in having atypical characteristics.

Elton D. Partridge studied Boy Scout leaders selected by vote of the scouts and endorsed by the scoutmaster. These leaders were taller, heavier, better looking, more athletic, more intelligent, and more independent than the other boys. Partridge found that boys chosen as leaders one year remained leaders a year later.

Floyd H. Allport and Luther L. Bernard, among others, list qualities possessed by leaders. Included are good appearance and physique, high intelligence, energy, initiative, persistence, and ability to deal with people. Socioeconomic factors are also important, as shown by Catharine Cox Miles in her studies of eminent men and women. She found that 52% came from noble or professional families, and another 29% from business and the "gentry." Only 5% came from families representing semiskilled or unskilled labor. S. S. Visher found much the same thing when he examined the background of some 800 prominent American scientists. Forty-six percent of their parents were in the professions, 23% in business, 22% in farming, and only 9% in labor.

Psychoanalytic interpretations of leadership have also been made. Harold D. Lasswell, a political scientist, studied the personalities of many political leaders and traced their dynamics to father or brother hatred, sex repression, feelings of guilt or inferiority, and the like. Later Lasswell emphasized a power-seeking theme, based upon compensation for feelings of weakness and a poor self-image. In his book *Escape from Freedom*, Erich Fromm depicted Hitler as a product of the German authoritarian character structure. Hitler and the hierarchical Nazi state satisfied the combined sadistic and masochistic drives resulting from years of frustration.

But leadership does not derive solely from personal qualities; it depends also upon time and place, particularly the social situation. A successful leader, says J. F. Brown, cannot be an outsider; he must be regarded as one who has the attitudes and reactions common to the group. At the same time his characteristics must set him above and somewhat apart from the others.

One of the best-known studies of leadership was done by Kurt Lewin and two associates, Ronald Lippitt and Ralph K. White. Equated groups of 10-year-old boys were placed under three types of adult leadership: authoritarian, democratic, and *laissez-faire*. In the authoritarian group the leader dictated all policies and activities. Under democratic leadership the boys decided their own program, aided and encouraged by the leader. The *laissez-faire* leader remained completely aloof from his boys unless asked questions directly.

In general, boys under autocratic leadership were either more hostile or more apathetic than those in the other groups. Often hostility took the form of aggression against a "scapegoat" in the group—obviously an outlet for the frustration experienced under the autocratic leader. Lewin also found that boys accustomed to authoritarianism could not change easily to a freer setting or atmosphere. Democratic leadership was preferred by the great majority of the boys; as might be expected it produced the fewest examples of unfavorable social behavior.

Social Attitudes

An attitude is more than a state of mind. It is a tendency to act. A person's attitudes have a great deal to do with how he will behave. Some social psychologists go so far as to define social psychology as the scientific study of attitudes.

Usually attitudes are divided into the favorable and unfavorable, or positive and negative. But we may also classify attitudes as specific and general, temporary or permanent, public or private, common or individual.

Gordon W. Allport, who defined attitude as a "neuropsychic state of readiness for mental and physical activity," noted that attitudes are built up in several ways. They may arise as a kind of residuum from many similar experiences. They may originate in a single dramatic instance, such as a great emotional shock. Or they may be taken over ready-made from parents, teachers, companions, and others.

Various techniques are used for measuring attitudes. One is the "public opinion poll," which will be described shortly. Probably the most widely used method for research purposes is the questionnaire, or attitude scale, on topics such as radicalism, conservatism, militarism, pacifism, and the like. Louis L. Thurstone improved the technique of measurement so that a few dozen items of known value would give a good index of a person's attitudes in a particular area. Rensis Likert proposed a simpler method for determining the value of each item; many psychologists believe his method is just as satisfactory as the Thurstone technique. Both types have been widely used as models for the development of attitude tests. Let us look at a few of the results obtained by attitude investigators.

Manly H. Harper, educational psychologist, developed a test to show our degree of liberalism or conservatism. Giving it to school superintendents all over the country, Harper found southerners more conservative than average, westerners and midwesterners more liberal. Others using Harper's test showed that professional people were more liberal than others, and that students became increasingly liberal as they continued in college, especially if they took social science courses. Conservative or radical teachers were found to influence students in line with their own attitudes. Both George B. Vetter and Ross Stagner found that radicalism and conservatism were fairly consistent patterns of response, with some degree of generality. Theodore F. Lentz defined this factor as "degree of opposition or favor toward social change."

About 1930 Daniel Katz and Floyd Allport tested many attitudes of more than 4000 students at Syracuse University. Their attitudes toward religion were clearest. Women inclined more to religion than men, and lowerclassmen believed more strongly in a personal God and in prayer than upperclassmen. But most kept the same religious belief through college that they held on entering. Orthodox students tended to change their attitude more than atheists or those with liberal religious views.

Later research, such as that reported in Nevitt Sanford's

American College, generally confirms the findings of Katz and Allport on religious attitudes, and indicates also that students become more liberal during their college years. However, as Newcomb showed in his analysis of Bennington College, attitude change is related both to the student's interests and to the prevalent values or atmosphere of the college community.

Actually, a person's attitudes are related to a number of other variables. Thomas H. Howells, for example, compared fifty students who were extremely radical in their religious beliefs with fifty who were extremely conservative. He found the radicals could endure more pain, were less suggestible, more intelligent, and more persistent than the conservatives. Studies by Peter H. Odegard and by Goodwin B. Watson showed that radicals and liberals tended to have more information and knowledge than conservatives.

The relation between attitudes and a person's beliefs and predictions was explored by Hadley Cantril. This social psychologist, in 1937, asked a varied group of persons to forecast economic, social, and military events, such as who would win the Spanish war and whether a depression would occur in the U.S. within a few years. The respondents were also given a short attitude test. Cantril found that most of the subjects, including businessmen, lawyers, and communists, made predictions in line with their prevailing attitudes. If they favored Franco, they forecast his victory in Spain. Social scientists in the group, however, were able to predict independently of their wishes.

An intensive analysis of attitudes in relation to personality was made by Brewster Smith, Jerome S. Bruner, and Robert W. White, who studied ten men having varying attitudes toward the Soviet Union. Detailed clinical research revealed that the individual's attitude provided a key to his personal and social adjustment; it was closely involved with his needs, wants, and relationships with other people. Often the attitude seemed to represent a way of coping with problems, personal as well as international.

One feature of attitudes is very significant—their tendency to become generalized, disregarding exceptions and individual variations. In 1922 Walter Lippmann noted that our attitudes

and opinions often become "stereotypes"—that is, rigid an
standardized pictures in our heads. We notice a trait, conside
it a type, give it a name, and then we fill in the rest of the
picture. "Agitator," "intellectual," "plutocrat," "foreigner,
"Harvard man," "Greenwich Villager," and "internationa
banker" were some stereotypes of the '20's, and some of them
have lasted to the present. Such stereotypes persist, Lipp
mann found, because they provide a consistent picture o
the world in which we come to feel at home. Also, they be
come emotionally charged, so any disturbance or threat t
them becomes an attack upon our universe, which we resis
strongly. The sociologist Stuart Rice presented to a numbe
of people newspaper photos of a bootlegger, a prime minister
a Bolshevik, a labor leader, an editor, and so on, and asked
that they be identified from the picture alone. Responses
proved the existence of stereotypes, though some of them
were quite erroneous.

PREJUDICE AND ITS BACKGROUND

Social scientists have done numerous studies of prejudice,
which is basically a stereotyped negative attitude. In 1925 Em
ory S. Bogardus, a sociologist, published his "social distance
test." A large number of subjects were asked to which of the
following categories they would admit members of several
groups (Armenians, Canadians, Chinese, English, Germans,
Italians, Jews, Negroes, Spaniards, Turks, etc.):

1. To close kinship by marriage
2. To my club, as personal friends
3. To my street as neighbors
4. To employment in my occupation in my country
5. To citizenship in my country
6. As visitors only to my country
7. Would exclude from my country

Interesting though hardly unexpected results emerged. Canadians, English, and north Europeans were favored. Antip-
athy appeared toward Hindus, Japanese, Negroes, and Turks.
Prejudice or "social distance" was smallest where subjects considered themselves closely related to the groups in question.
Curiously enough, a subject's experience with individuals of

the various races affected his attitude only slightly. Bogardus found most prejudice at that time toward Turks, yet few subjects had known or even seen a Turk. Again this shows how we take over our attitudes ready-made; this prejudice could be explained by atrocity stories that appeared during and after World War I.

Bogardus found few changes in the rankings of different ethnic groups as much as twenty years later. Eugene L. Hartley found little variation in the rankings given by several disparate college groups. Except for placing their own group high, the ratings made by Negro students were similar to those of other groups. About 1930 Daniel Katz and Kenneth W. Braly found Princeton students consistent in their stereotypes of Negroes, Jews, Germans, and other ethnic groups, though definiteness of the stereotype was not related to the amount of prejudice. Twenty years later G. M. Gilbert studied Princeton students again and found their attitudes much the same, except for greater dislike of Germans and Japanese, attributable to the war. However, Gilbert found that the stereotypes were not as definite in 1950 as they had been earlier; the postwar college students seemed more hesitant to make racial and national generalizations.

How is prejudice perpetuated in our society? Several psychologists have studied the ways in which it is learned by children. Kenneth B. and Mamie P. Clark studied children's choices between white and colored dolls, and found that even at three years of age children could select the doll that "looked like the white or colored child." In their studies Eugene L. and Ruth E. Hartley called the next stage "identification," in which the child responds to the request "show me the one that looks like you." Later, in the "evaluation" stage, the child becomes aware of superiority and inferiority. By the time he has completed elementary school the youngster has pretty well absorbed the prejudices of his parents, relatives, and family friends.

Personality dynamics also enter the picture. When people are frustrated and insecure, according to Gordon W. Allport, they are likely to engage in "scapegoating" behavior—that is, displacement of hostility and aggression upon minority groups. A California team of investigators (T. W. Adorno,

Else Frenkel-Brunswik, Daniel J. Levinson, and R. Nevitt Sanford) found the roots of much prejudice and ethnocentrism in the "authoritarian" personality structure. This refers to a pattern of conformity, rigidity, herd-mindedness, and overcontrol of impulses and feelings, which was found in some of the persons studied. (Compare Erich Fromm's *Escape from Freedom* mentioned above.)

Social scientists, of course, have investigated alleged ethnic differences in intelligence and personality, to see whether significant variations actually exist. The question is complicated by a misunderstanding of terms. "Race" frequently is confused with "nation," "language," and "culture." It is incorrect to speak of the "French race," "Aryan race," or "American race." To avoid ambiguity social scientists prefer the term "ethnic differences," to refer to variations among groups differing in race, religion, language, culture, or some combination of these. Except for actual physical differences, these ethnic variations are cultural (environmentally produced) phenomena.

Turning to race, we find that anthropologists do not agree on the exact number of human races. They do agree that a race is a sizable portion of mankind having similar physical characteristics known to be transmitted by heredity. The Caucasian, Mongolian, and Negro races form the simplest division; many subdivisions of each have been suggested on the basis of skin color, hair, shape of head, and many other anatomical characteristics.

Two questions arise: Do psychological differences between races exist? If so, do they result from innate or from cultural factors?

The civilization and contribution of almost every race and nation has been called superior by some writer—generally one belonging to the group in question. Nordic or "Aryan" superiority has been claimed vigorously by Count de Gobineau, Houston S. Chamberlain, and many officials of the Nazi party. According to Otto Klineberg, a specialist in race psychology, it is very hard to prove the superiority of any one race. Civilizations rise and fall, and borrow from each other. Criteria of true superiority are doubtful; is our advanced culture, so given to warfare, better than that of the primitive but peaceful Es-

kimo? Within each race is great variability; contrast the cultivated Chinese with the simple nomadic tribes of Siberia. In
Europe the Nordic, Alpine, and Mediterranean racial groups
are distributed among a dozen nations and cultures.

Many experiments have tested the intelligence of different
races. The I.Q.'s of whites generally average higher than those
of Negroes or Indians; early psychologists took this as proof of
white superiority. Soon questions were raised by Klineberg,
Stanley D. Porteus, Thomas R. Garth, and others. Intelligence tests, they pointed out, contain materials based on the
culture and experience of whites; the questions are not fair to
test other races. Motivation also is important; if one does not
exert maximum effort and speed his score suffers. Most Indians and many Negroes are unaccustomed to competition
and speed. They are also handicapped by poor schooling and
lack of facility with language, both of which affect intelligence
test results.

Klineberg proved that so-called race differences in intelligence decrease greatly as environments of each race become
more similar. He compared I.Q.'s of New York white children
and southern Negroes who had migrated to New York. The
Negro children's average I.Q.'s rose in proportion to the
length of time they had been living in the northern environment. Average Negro intelligence never rose as high as
white, but the Negro socioeconomic and educational background has always been poorer than that of whites.

Myrtle McGraw tried to measure racial differences before
social and cultural factors had a chance to operate. She administered Charlotte Bühler's "baby tests" to several dozen
Southern white and Negro infants between two and eleven
months of age, and found the white babies were superior
mentally. However, as critics of the study noted, the white
babies were also superior in height and weight, suggesting a
more favorable environment which could also have influenced
the mental performance. Later, a research psychiatrist, Benjamin Pasamanick, studied the development of Negro and white
New Haven babies during World War II when rationing
made nutrition fairly constant for the two groups. He found
that development of the two groups was practically identical
up to one year of age but that after that their unfavorable

environmental conditions began to affect the Negro infants adversely. We may conclude that only when many individuals from two or more racial groups have similar environments over a period of years starting with birth can we discover whether innate psychological differences between races exist.

Clearly, social psychologists have learned a great deal about prejudice. Whole books about it have been written by Gordon W. Allport, Gerhart Saenger, and Alfred J. Marrow. A two-volume work on research methods in social relations, centering around prejudice, was prepared by Marie Jahoda, Morton Deutsch, and Stuart W. Cook. Much is known about the origin and development of prejudice, its extent, and the reasons for its persistence. But what about that most practical matter of all: can prejudice be reduced or eliminated? This is a phase of the larger question of attitude modification and change. Fortunately a good deal of research has been done on the subject.

The Changing of Attitudes

First of all, knowledge or information does not necessarily change attitudes. Donald Young gave nearly 500 students a test on racial and national attitudes before and after they took a course in race problems. He found little or no change in their attitudes about the inborn ability of various races. On the other hand, Arthur Kornhauser noted an increase in liberalism after a year's survey course in economics. Hermann H. Remmers, of Purdue University, and an associate found the same true after a semester course in sociology.

In general, attitudes change more through real life experiences than through classroom lectures and discussions. Milton Hall compared the attitudes of employed and unemployed engineers during the early depression years. Those unemployed for a considerable time showed a loss of religious faith and marked cynicism about the value of hard work and of traditional American ideals. Their political views became less orthodox, though not necessarily communist or socialist. About a fourth agreed that a revolution might be good for the country, but nearly as many felt the same about a dictator!

Tredwell Smith, at Teachers College, Columbia University, showed how racial attitudes can change through firsthand experience. About fifty graduate students spent two weekends in Harlem, New York's Negro section. There they met prominent Negro editors, doctors, social workers, and artists. They had tea with Negro college alumni and visited a hospital, churches, and cooperative apartments. Four attitude tests, given before and after, indicated that the experience brought significantly more favorable attitudes toward Negroes. The change lasted at least a year, a re-test showed.

Similarly, a War Department study at the close of World War II showed that prejudice of white against Negro soldiers diminished markedly when they had served in the same units, especially if they had been under fire together. Morton Deutsch and Mary E. Collins found less prejudice in integrated than in segregated housing projects, due to the frequent contacts between Negro and white families as well as to the social norms favoring friendly relations.

Intercultural education may produce change in attitude, especially when it deals directly with problems of prejudice. Henry E. Kagan, a rabbi and psychologist, found that indirect methods of dealing with anti-Semitism were ineffective compared with frank discussion of the anti-Jewish attitudes and experiences of the students. However, some researchers believe that additional measures are necessary. Bruno Bettelheim and Morris Janowitz, for example, found that prejudiced persons are frustrated socially and economically, which suggests the need for the combined approaches of psychotherapy and social reconstruction.

The legislative and judicial approach to improving ethnic relations is directed primarily at eliminating discrimination (i.e., behavior), though presumably it will also reduce prejudice (i.e., attitude). Social psychologists played a prominent role in bringing about the major governmental action in this area. Led by Kenneth B. Clark and Isidor Chein, the Society for Psychological Study of Social Issues sponsored a brief signed by 32 leading social scientists on the harmful effects of segregation upon the personality of the Negro child. Presented to the Supreme Court, this document was instrumental in bringing about the unanimous decision of May 17

1954 which decreed that segregated public education is unconstitutional.

The Supreme Court decision has materially reduced and sometimes eliminated discrimination in the schools of many cities and states of our nation. Fair Employment Practice acts and similar legislation have prohibited ethnic discrimination in much of our business and industry. In all probability the resulting increase of interpersonal contacts between ethnic groups will reduce prejudice substantially, though this has not yet been conclusively demonstrated.

PROPAGANDA AND PERSUASIBILITY

The changing of attitudes in a desired direction is the chief function of propaganda. Leonard W. Doob described propaganda as a systematic attempt to control people's attitudes (and hence their actions) by suggestion. Propaganda was neatly distinguished from education by Everett Dean Martin, who noted that an educator tries to produce an open mind, while a propagandist strives for a closed mind—closed, that is, to everything but his message.

Many studies have been done on the propaganda effects of movies and other mass media. L. L. Thurstone gave attitude tests to high school youngsters a few days before and immediately after seeing a film, with a follow-up test after several months. *All Quiet on the Western Front* increased pacifistic attitudes; *The Birth of a Nation* altered attitudes toward Negroes in an unfavorable direction. Many of the effects were found to be lasting. More recently the effects of orientation films upon our Armed Forces were reported by Carl I. Hovland, A. A. Lumsdaine, and F. D. Sheffield. Attitude change was found to be affected by already existing attitudes as well as by social and educational background. For example, films on Negro themes when shown in the South produced no basic change in perception of the Negro and his problems. Also, presenting both sides of an argument or issue was more effective in influencing the better-educated men, while a one-sided argument carried more weight with the men having less education.

Other experiments on propaganda have been performed. Albert D. Annis and Norman C. Meier, for instance, contrived to insert into their university daily several editorials about an Australian prime minister, previously unknown to the students. Half the editorials were laudatory, half derogatory. After students had read a series of "pro" or of "con" editorials, their attitudes toward the Australian changed significantly—a change that lasted through several months. Apparently propaganda can influence opinion noticeably in a short time if the matter discussed is new. If persons already have strong feelings about a question it is harder for the propagandist to change them.

George W. Hartmann conducted a unique experiment comparing the relative strength of rational and emotional propaganda appeals. Running as a Socialist candidate for state office, Hartmann presented persuasive arguments to the voters in certain wards of a city, asking them to vote Socialist if they believed in the principles outlined. In several other wards his campaign material consisted of highly emotional appeals playing up the sadness of depression days, the imminence of war, duty to one's children, and the like. Using as a control other wards of the city where no Socialist appeals were presented, Hartmann found the following:

WARDS RECEIVING:	INCREASED IN SOCIALIST VOTE:
Emotional appeals	50%
Rational appeals	35%
No appeals (control group)	24%

Thus emotional appeals were shown to be considerably more effective than rational appeals as a propaganda device. The finding is not exactly surprising, but Hartmann obtained quantitative results in a real situation, which no one had succeeded in doing before.

One of the early experimenters on propaganda, William W. Biddle, found that high school students and college freshmen became less susceptible to propaganda the more they understood its devices and methods.

In 1937 Clyde R. Miller of Columbia University, with several associates, founded the Institute for Propaganda

Analysis. The aim of this organization was to train people to analyze, understand, and evaluate the many kinds of propaganda, and thus protect themselves against dangerous and undemocratic appeals. The Institute published reports on many current campaigns—those of radical groups, reactionary and fascist groups, business organizations, foreign governments, labor unions, and many more.

The "Seven Devices of the Propagandist," as described by the Institute, became widely known. They are:

1. *Name-calling*—applying emotion-arousing terms to one's opponents. Examples: "Communist," "Fascist," "un-American," "Traitor."

2. *Glittering generalities*—using high-sounding words for favored persons or causes. Examples: "100% American," "Patriotism," "Liberty."

3. *Transfer*—associating persons or causes with items already liked or disliked. Example: a cartoon of one's political candidate swathed in the American flag.

4. *Testimonial*—as in advertising, using prominent names as endorsers.

5. *Plain folks*—being a man of the people, like a politician in galluses who is photographed with his feet on the porch rail.

6. *Card-stacking*—presenting distorted facts or figures; falsifying or omitting essential parts of the story.

7. *Bandwagon*—getting everybody to join the procession; "everybody's doing it."

The Institute also described other typical propagandist appeals. Among them are reinforcement of ideas by repetition; playing up to people's fears, worries, and frustrations; and displacement, or blaming one's troubles on a convenient scapegoat.

The Institute ceased to function just after Pearl Harbor, but its work was carried on for some time after the war by two sociologists, Alfred McClung Lee and Elizabeth Briant Lee.

Several new contributions to understanding attitude change and propaganda have appeared. For example, Irving Janis, Carl Hovland, and their colleagues found evidence for a personality factor of general persuasibility, a readiness to accept social influence regardless of person and content, although a number of more specialized factors were also discovered. They were able to compare the personalities of "attitude changers" (need for social approval, passive feelings of inferiority) and "non-changers" (high on self-expression, creative strivings, feelings of adequacy) among high school students. They even identified a third group, the "negative changers," who went off in a direction opposite to the communicated material; these were the rebels who rejected authority, were cynical, and, no doubt, were the ones who are labeled by the middle-aged "typical adolescents"!

Another postwar trend is called "communications analysis" or "content analysis," developed by Harold D. Lasswell, Paul F. Lazarsfeld, Robert K. Merton, Bernard Berelson, and others. In their studies, positive and negative symbols appearing in mass media may be counted and tabulated; also, the ethnic characteristics of short story or TV heroes and villains may be compared. Such techniques, of course, are essential to the understanding not only of propaganda but of advertising, entertainment, education, and any other kind of symbolic social interaction.

COMMUNICATION

Social psychologists have become increasingly interested in language and other forms of communication as a most significant aspect of interpersonal relations. Many are partial to the theory originated by Edward Sapir and elaborated by Benjamin Whorf that our perception and thinking are shaped by our language. Scientific thinking according to this view could hardly develop among the Hopi, since their concepts of mathematics and time are so different from those found in Western culture.

Along with the advantages of language communication, however, lurk various dangers as noted by Count Alfred Korzybski, the founder of "semantics," and his followers.

S. I. Hayakawa has shown how all of us are affected every waking moment by the words we hear and see, and by our unconscious assumptions about them. Wendell Johnson goes further, to insist that semantic difficulties produce much personal and social maladjustment. A person may see himself as a "failure" unless he has unquestionably succeeded; his semantic error consists in classifying everything into blacks and whites, forgetting the many intervening shades of gray.

Semanticists have clarified the distinction between "denotative" and "connotative" meanings. The former signifies the object, person, or event to which the word actually refers. Connotation, on the other hand, means that which is suggested or associated by the term. When the connotations of a term diverge considerably from the denotation, confusion is likely to result, as Stuart Chase demonstrated in his well-known book *The Tyranny of Words*. The emotionally toned words used by political orators are a case in point. The power of terms like "home," "mother," "our flag," "cooperation," "appeasement," and the like lies in their emotional connotations.

As mentioned earlier, Charles E. Osgood and associates have succeeded in measuring connotative meanings through what he calls the "semantic differential" technique. Three general factors of meaning emerge: the evaluative factor (good-bad, beautiful-ugly); the potency factor (strong-weak, large-small); and the activity factor (active-passive, fast-slow). By asking a person to rate a term on a seven-point scale, for example, from fair to unfair, strong to weak, etc., it is possible to learn the meaning of the term for the person. Meanings obtained in this way correlate very highly with attitudes as determined on other scales.

Some believe that symbolic speech derives from gestures. Both Floyd Allport and Charlotte Bühler noted the great significance of gestures in the infant's life. George H. Mead considered the gesture the primary element in communication, and thought of vocal responses as gestures occurring in social interaction. B. F. Skinner, the behavioristic psychologist, focuses upon language as "verbal behavior"; he emphasizes the functions of verbal responses and the conditions determining them rather than subjective meanings.

Others have sought to analyze the communication process.

Franklin Fearing says that, first of all, any item of communication (traffic signal, editorial, photograph, conversation, gesture, prayer, etc.) is produced by a person with the purpose of shaping or steering behavior in a particular direction. Second, the item is responded to in terms of what it stands for. Third, the item establishes a relationship between the producer of the stimulus and the respondent in terms of shared meaning. Last, the response to a given stimulus is quite variable, depending on the cultural and personality factors each respondent brings to the situation. Thus, concludes Fearing, communication is a dynamic, two-way human relationship, and by no means a simple mechanical transmission of ideas or information, as some have erroneously thought.

Public Opinion

Everyone thinks he knows what is meant by public opinion, but finds it hard to define. Leonard W. Doob stated that public opinion refers to people's attitudes on an issue when they are members of the same social group. Kimball Young described four stages in the evolution of public opinion. First, an issue or problem arises; it is then explored and discussed; solutions are suggested; and sides are taken. Finally, consensus evolves, or at least majority opinion is derived. Floyd H. Allport has insisted that public opinion inheres in individuals and has no existence or meaning apart from the members of the group. Such views gave support to the public opinion polls which were developed in the 1930's by George Gallup, Elmo Roper, and others.

Polling procedures, including interviewing and scientific sampling, are quite widely understood, especially the pre-election polls. Many social scientists—among them Paul F. Lazarsfeld, Hadley Cantril, Herbert Hyman, Angus Campbell, and Arthur W. Kornhauser—have been active in studying errors in polling techniques, new procedures in interviewing, the treatment and analysis of results, and the limitations and misuses of polls. In 1962 Stuart Chase published *American Credos*, drawing upon polls and surveys to depict American attitudes on foreign policy, politics, education, religion, and various personal problems.

NATIONAL CHARACTER AND SOCIAL CLASS

In Chapter XI we described anthropological studies of cultural influences upon the developing child. Social psychologists, with other social scientists, have depicted the "national character" of several peoples, notably the Japanese, Russians, Germans, British, and Americans. Of course, the experts do not always agree, which is hardly surprising in view of the breadth of the undertaking.

Consider, for example, the "American character." Geoffrey Gorer, a British anthropologist, notes particularly our rejection of authority, our female and child dominance, our need for love and attention, and our interest in material things. Robin M. Williams, a sociologist, highlights our active and moral orientation, our restlessness and discontent with the status quo, and our belief in equality and independence paralleled by our simultaneous sensitivity to group pressure which results in conformity.

David Riesman, in his widely read *The Lonely Crowd*, finds that few Americans are as bound by tradition as are people in primitive societies. Most Americans are "inner-directed," meaning that they operate according to goals and ideals implanted by their parents and teachers, which function as a kind of internalized gyroscope. More recently, says Riesman, a new mode which he calls "other-direction" has developed, especially in the upper middle class of our larger cities. The other-directed man depends upon other persons for approval and guidance; he orients toward his peers and associates to insure success. Instead of a gyroscope, he has evolved something like a sensitive radar set to keep him in touch with his world.

American society has also been analyzed in regard to social class. W. Lloyd Warner, an anthropologist-sociologist, studied a New England city in terms of wealth, occupations, social affiliations, residential areas, and the like. He came up with six social classes: an upper, middle, and lower, each divided into an upper and lower segment. Some other investigators, like Allison Davis and B. B. and M. R. Gardner, found the same sixfold division in "Old City" in the South. But August

B. Hollingshead reported five classes in the midwestern city he surveyed. James West could identify only two classes in a midwestern village, and Granville Hicks reports the same division in his upstate New York "Small Town."

More important than wealth, job, or residential area is the subjective side of social class, according to Richard Centers; with which class does a person identify himself? Using a number of national samples, Centers found that very few people consider themselves "upper class" or "lower class." Almost half of our people think of themselves as "middle class" and about the same number as "working class."

As mentioned in an earlier chapter, many researchers report that social class has considerable effect upon personality. Robert and Helen Lynd found that the fact of being in the business or the working class largely determines what one does and how one thinks. Arthur Kornhauser noted great differences between upper and lower economic groups with respect to politics, labor, government controls, distribution of wealth, and also in personal satisfaction. Likewise Herbert Hyman discovered class differences in such areas as the value of a college education or the importance of liking one's job. But the differences were small. Two-thirds of the professional and business people valued a college education highly, but so do half the manual workers—although their reasons may be different.

Social class has many other implications in American society. To mention but one, a sociologist, August Hollingshead, and a psychiatrist, Frederick C. Redlich, have explored the relation between social class and mental illness. Neurosis was found to be prevalent in the higher, and psychosis in the lower classes, according to the diagnoses made. Individual psychotherapy was much more likely to be given to higher class patients, and shock or drug therapy to those from the lower classes.

Thus the psychologist has come a long way in the study of man's social behavior. Since World War II the major emphasis has been upon social groups—their dynamics, characteristics, and functioning. Some of the older themes have continued—e.g., attitudes, prejudice, public opinion, and national character. Others have changed somewhat, such as propaganda and attitude modification tending to fall under the heading of the newer category "communication." But the social psychologist continues as before to be interested both in theory and in application of his findings to help solve human problems.

Chapter XVII

THE APPLICATIONS OF PSYCHOLOGY
TO DAILY LIVING

TAYLOR   GILBRETH   MÜNSTERBERG   POFFENBERGER
VITELES   RYANS   PRESSEY   SKINNER   BINGHAM
STARCH   WITMER   BURTT   JACOBSON   JOHNSON   WIENER

*How has psychology helped to improve working con-
ditions? What psychological applications are found
in the world of business? What is the function of a
clinical psychologist? What is meant by "Action for
Mental Health"? How does a teaching machine
work? What is psychology doing to meet the challenge of the computer and the space age?*

In countless ways the findings of the great psychologists affect our daily living. Some psychological discoveries result
directly from a practical need. Lewis Terman, for instance,
developed intelligence tests because schools and the business
world were in need of some method for the measuring of
ability. Sigmund Freud was concerned mainly with curing
neurotic patients; psychoanalysis, which affects all clinical
work profoundly, grew out of his day-to-day experience.

We are also influenced by abstract psychological principles, discovered by men of science whose chief concern is to
unearth new knowledge about human behavior regardless of
applications. Francis Galton, inquirer into heredity and
individual differences, originated statistical methods that facilitate all kinds of quantitative studies, like those in educational, personnel, and vocational psychology. Hermann von
Helmholtz, intent on discovering how the eye and ear really

function, paved the way for studies of illumination effects in industry and for various tests of sensory capacities used today in many civilian and military enterprises. Hermann Ebbinghaus working on memory, and Ivan Pavlov and Edward L. Thorndike on learning, were forerunners of educational psychology. B. F. Skinner's learning studies led to the development of teaching machines and "programed" learning.

Walter Cannon, the physiologist who studied visceral effects of human emotions, contributed much to understanding physical symptoms in nervous disorders and to later work on lie detection. Shepherd Franz and Karl Lashley, studying how parts of the brain function in monkeys and rats, made possible the retraining of patients with brain injuries.

Research has been stepped up in all areas of psychology, and efforts are being made continually to apply the findings. These have helped to increase efficiency in business and industry, to fit the right persons into the right jobs, and to improve human relations generally. The fruits of research have aided in relieving people's maladjustments and in opening up new fields such as helping the handicapped and preparing for retirement and old age. Teaching methods have been improved and new devices for learning, notably teaching machines, have been introduced. Research efforts have been extended to electronic and space age developments as well as to many problem areas of complex social relations.

INDUSTRIAL PSYCHOLOGY

The keynote of industrial psychology is the increasing of efficiency. It began with the studies of Frederick W. Taylor, a pioneer in "scientific management." Taylor found that more efficient work methods step up production vastly. The average amount of pig iron a man could load on a car was 12½ tons a day. When Taylor dictated how to bend, how to pick up the iron, when to move, when to rest, some men increased their quota to 47½ tons a day, and all increased their output considerably.

Frank and Lillian Gilbreth analyzed many jobs into their

elemental operations. Motions made and time taken for each movement were checked to see where the efficiency could be improved. Hundreds of such "time and motion" studies have been made, and several new principles discovered. For example: both arms should move simultaneously and in opposite symmetrical directions; continuous curved motions are better than jerky movements; foot pedals should relieve hands wherever possible; tools should be conveniently placed. Application of these principles increases production a great deal.

Hugo Münsterberg, one of the first applied psychologists, regarded the study of fatigue as very important in industrial psychology. His successors studied daily and weekly work curves in many factories. A typical daily production chart shows that output increases slightly until mid-morning, then falls off as lunch hour approaches. After lunch productivity rises again, though not as high as in the morning; near the end of the day it falls off sharply. Weekly output shows a similar rise and fall. Production on Monday is fair; Tuesday and Wednesday show the best record; then a gradual decline occurs until Saturday.

Fatigue studies show when rest periods should be introduced. Employers were slow to adopt rest periods, but, as Albert T. Poffenberger noted, practically all rest periods, even when introduced in hit-or-miss fashion, increase production. Length of rest periods varies with the kind of work done. Usually a 10- or 15-minute period in the morning and afternoon is satisfactory. Surveying several British industries, Horace M. Vernon reported an average production rise of 5% to 10% where rest periods were part of the routine. Others found almost phenomenal efficiency increases—100% or more. A rest period should be a complete change, physical and mental, from the work. Modern methods introduce rest periods when output is at its maximum, to *prevent* fatigue rather than *cure* it. They help workers' morale as well as productivity.

Closely related is the problem of optimum work day and work week. Formerly men worked 10 or 12 hours a day, 6 and sometimes 7 days a week. Employers frowned on any reduction as they did in the case of rest pauses. When convinced that shorter hours could increase total output, they yielded. A striking example was furnished during World War I and again after Dunkerque in World War II, when British workers began, patriotically, to work 60 and 70 hours a week. Fatigue and nervousness increased so much that production actually declined. Vernon found that a reduction in hours from 66 to about 50 per week increased hourly output enormously and weekly output by 15%. Since 1945, and particularly since the advent of automation, the work week has been reduced to 40 hours or less. Labor's demand to set the work week at 36 or even 32 hours involves, of course, many other issues along with productivity.

Employees' motives and grievances are important to production. Whiting Williams, who worked as a laborer to observe industrial conditions, reported that a worker's desire for self-respect, for accomplishment, and for job security counts far more than his weekly wage. A study by Rexford Hersey notes four major motives in workers: freedom in work methods, opportunity to use experience, permanence of the job, and a chance for promotion. Outstanding grievances concern monotony and standardization of work, worry about possible unemployment, and fear of being exploited. Minor grievances and some major ones often are handled successfully by conferences between grievance committees of unions and the plant personnel manager.

Industrial accidents have been reduced greatly as a result of psychological studies. Morris Viteles and others found some persons "accident-prone"; that is, they tend to have more than their expected share of accidents. Clinical study of accident-prone persons reveals fatigue, sickness, inexperience, worry, and emotional disturbances as the most likely causes. Hersey noted recurring emotional cycles, or ups and downs of mood, in workers. Most accidents occur during their "low" periods. Clinical treatment helps these persons. Teaching workers not to be careless, installing accident-proof equipment, and requiring frequent inspection of factories also reduces industrial mishaps.

All aspects of a working environment are examined for possible psychological improvement. Clarence E. Ferree and Gertrude Rand developed standards for optimal lighting in different kinds of work. In general, uniform indirect lighting of the "daylight lamp" variety is best. Experimenting with different-colored lights, they found least eye fatigue from unsaturated yellow light, more from orange-yellow and greenish-yellow, and most from bluish-green.

Painting rooms and machinery in colors often brings excellent results. Pastel greens and blues relieve eye strain. Putting color on certain dangerous or movable parts of machines reduces accidents. "Color engineers" are learning which hues seem coolest, induce cheerfulness, and make for greater safety.

Studies of distraction show that loud intermittent noises cause fatigue and inefficiency. But one kind of sound—music—may reduce fatigue and increase production, particularly if intensive concentration or creative work is not involved.

The bad effects of poor ventilation result primarily from increased temperature and humidity, with lack of air circulation. Ellsworth Huntington found that the greatest physical activity occurred when temperature averaged 60 to 65 degrees, and the maximum mental activity when outside temperatures averaged 38 degrees—i.e., during frost season. In studies of high-altitude effects, Ross A. McFarland discovered that when barometric pressure is about half that found at sea level (i.e., at 16,000 feet or more), reaction time, coordination, and association are impaired considerably.

Along with the importance of work curves, rest periods, hours, wages, etc., industrial psychologists have become aware of social influences. The Western Electric studies, mentioned in Chapter IX, revealed the significance of morale, of group organization, and of human relations generally upon industrial productivity. Several such examples of group influences operating in industry were given in the last chapter.

Out of the study of industrial efficiency came another form of applied psychology—"Engineering Psychology" or "Human Engineering"—which is concerned primarily with adjusting machines to man. Impetus given to this field by the military demands of World War II, and today's complex machinery, ranging from computers to missiles, assures continuing development. Engineering psychologists, to mention but one phase of their work, have rearranged and simplified instrument dials and signal systems in the cockpit of a plane, and have discovered through experimentation the proper types of dials to use for optimum control. Some of the leaders in engineering psychology are Alphonse Chapanis, Paul M. Fitts, Walter F. Grether, and Ernest J. McCormick.

PERSONNEL PSYCHOLOGY

Personnel work involves hiring employees, placing them in the right positions, training them, supervising, recommending promotion, transfer, or dismissal, planning welfare programs, adjusting grievances, and conducting research.

Psychologists have studied the value of traditional employment devices: application blanks, letters of recommendation, photographs, and interviews. Much information called for on application blanks proves of little help. Morris Viteles found 18 of 25 questions on one blank useless in judging fitness for the job. Letters of recommendation are inadequate unless the employer requests answers to specific questions. The complimentary generalizations usually written by an applicant's friends cannot be relied on. Harry L. Hollingworth proved the futility of trying to judge character from photographs, though photographs help give an impression of the applicant's appearance.

Although Hollingworth and Walter Dill Scott found that interviewers judge applicants very differently, practically all firms regard the interview as the most important hiring device. Walter V. Bingham and Bruce V. Moore, among others, analyzed interviewing. An interview may be standardized or it may be informal and flexible. The latter is superior if the interviewer is skilled. The best interview is conducted privately, without rush, by a trained interviewer who lets applicants do most of the talking, who is free from bias, and who records his data immediately, before forgetting any items. On the other hand, Robert N. McMurry found that a well-standardized interview covered the significant items systematically, and correlated well with success on the job and with stability of employment.

Personnel workers size up their applicants with the aid of tests and scales, including intelligence and aptitude tests such as were described in Chapter II. Trade tests of skill and achievement may also be used, particularly in selecting workers of manual skill and dexterity, such as compositors, typesetters, carpenters, and machinists.

Another psychological tool often used in business and industry is the rating scale. It is a brief personality estimate made by those who know the individual best, such as a teacher, foreman, or former employer. Bingham and Hollingworth, among others, analyzed the advantages and disadvantages of rating scales. To be valuable a scale must deal with specific traits, they found. (It is hard to rate John Jones accurately on "loyalty" or "personality." He can be rated better on "punctuality," "appearance," or "originality," where more specific examples can be given.) "Halo effect," or the tendency for a rater's favorable or unfavorable general impression to affect all his specific judgments, must be avoided. Raters should not be asked to judge a person either "good" or "bad," but should be given several choices, such as "excellent," "good," "fair," "poor," and "very poor." Several persons should rate each individual; if their judgments agree they probably are valid. With these precautions a personality sketch can be obtained that helps in hiring, assigning to certain jobs, transferring, promoting, or dismissing, though at best it is not very thorough.

ADVERTISING AND SELLING

Psychology is used daily in business, notably in advertising, selling, and market research. Appeals and attention-getting devices were tested by Starch, Hollingworth, Poffenberger, and others. They found that headlines should be short and legible, and should arouse interest and curiosity. Strong black-and-white contrasts are effective; color is even better, though no one color proves generally superior to others. At present consumers prefer aesthetic color effects—even reproductions of old masters—and photographs of the article itself or of persons in action. The upper right-hand portion of a page gets most attention. Front- and back-page magazine advertisements, double-page spreads, and page one of the advertising section are favorable locations.

Richard W. Husband has shown that advertising appeals are most frequently keyed to quality, price, health, appearance, testimonials, time and energy saving, comfort, durability, or dependability. Others have shown that the appeals vary with the product and with age, sex, income, and geographical location of groups appealed to.

The Psychological Corporation, an organization of psychologists mostly engaged in business research work, finds that the choice and use of trade names often lack effect because certain rules are not followed. Herbert Moore lists some of the rules. A short, attractive, and distinctive name associated with a want of the product or with the act of purchasing should be chosen. Salesmen should use the name whenever possible. The trade mark or trade name should be reproduced in the advertisements just as it appears on the product itself.

Henry C. Link, of the Psychological Corporation, noted that the most important qualities of successful salesmen are loyalty to company, knowledge of products, good moral habits, ability to judge people, sense of humor, social aggressiveness, good judgment, and common sense. Both Richard W. Husband and V. V. Anderson, studying successful salesmen, found their personalities dominant and extroverted.

Many psychologists have helped advertisers and manufacturers survey consumer preferences. George Gallup and Daniel Starch, among others, initiated cross-sectional surveys of the buying public to study their preferences and buying habits. Shortly after World War II Ernest Dichter and others developed "motivation research," the object of which was to discover the consumer's deeper dynamics, and to gear advertising appeals to them. The strategy of motivation research, or "M. R.," was publicized by Vance Packard in *The Hidden Persuaders*, which became a best-seller in the late 1950's. We shall cite but one example, Dichter's study of "mistress vs. wife." The strong male interest in convertibles represents a symbolic desire for a mistress, according to Dichter's analysis. The four-door sedan on the other hand symbolizes the practical side, the plain girl he married, the girl who would make a fine wife and mother. How could the union of these trends be achieved? Through the hardtop, reasoned Dichter, which represents a combination of the marital, family motives with the romance and adventure desired in a mistress. The hardtop became an outstandingly successful new auto style!

In the 1930's "consumer research" suggested scientific evaluation of advertised products for the purpose of helping the consumer buy more intelligently and economically. After World War II, however, consumer research came to mean analysis of consumer habits and attitudes primarily in the interest of advertising and business. A few psychologists, notably George Katona, have taken a more scientific direction and are seeking a psychological interpretation of economic man and thus developing the new field of economic psychology or "psychoeconomics."

CLINICAL PSYCHOLOGY

Broadly speaking, clinical psychologists are members of the mental health treatment team along with psychiatrists, psychiatric social workers and nurses, occupational therapists, and others. (The origins of the mental hygiene movement were described in Chapter XV.)

The first psychological clinic was founded by Lightner Witmer in 1896 at the University of Pennsylvania. A few years later the first public clinic for behavior problem children, the Institute for Juvenile Research, was established in Chicago under the direction of psychiatrist William Healy. Other pioneer clinical psychologists were H. H. Goddard of the Vineland Training School, who first introduced the Binet test to America, and J. E. Wallace Wallin, who set up in 1910 a psychological laboratory at the New Jersey Village for Epileptics.

Following World War I the mental health movement, founded by Clifford W. Beers, stimulated the growth of child guidance clinics. By 1940 more than 100 such clinics were operating, usually involving psychiatrists, psychologists, and social workers. By 1954 the number had grown to about 600, and by 1964 to a thousand or more. By the latter date several thousand clinical psychologists were practicing. In

1962 the Division of Clinical Psychology of the American Psychological Association reported a membership of about 3000 and estimated there were another 3000 clinical psychologists who were not members of the division. Most of these 6000 psychologists are engaged primarily in clinical practice.

Clinical psychologists work in universities, hospitals, public and private clinics, industries, schools, prisons, and in private practice. What may we say is the common unifying thread in their work? Laurance F. Shaffer states that clinical psychologists use the hypotheses of their science and the techniques of their profession to gain understandings which will help people to help themselves. Whether their activities are called "diagnosis," "therapy," or something else, the major concerns of clinical psychologists are to understand people and to help them.

The clinical psychologist's work with children is typically done in a child guidance clinic. Children's behavior problems, according to Luton Ackerson, may be either conduct or personality problems. Conduct problems include fighting, stealing, truancy, sex offenses, and other types of delinquent behavior. Personality problems involve feelings of inferiority, jealousy, fears, anxiety, depression, excessive daydreaming, and the like. Child guidance clinics may also deal with youngsters failing in school, those with special deficiencies, or children to be adopted or put into foster care. They may evaluate and diagnose mentally defective children and refer them for training in special classes, schools, or institutions.

Treatment in a child guidance clinic may involve extensive psychotherapy of the child, and sometimes of one or both parents, since the problem often includes the whole family. Recently, the psychologist John E. Bell, and the psychiatrist Nathan W. Ackerman, working independently, have initiated "family group therapy," and report greater success through having the whole family present as a single therapeutic unit.

Environmental therapy (also called "situational" or "milieu" therapy) may be employed as well as, or instead of, psychotherapy. For example, a shy, unsocial child may be placed in a scout troop with proper supervision, or sent to a camp where he will have boxing lessons and other kinds of exercise to build up his self-confidence as well as his physique. A delinquent or a difficult problem child may be sent to a selected foster home or referred to an institution. Obviously child guidance cases must be followed over a long period of time, often with continued therapeutic interviews. Only when the problem has abated markedly is the case finally dropped.

Eli Rubenstein and Maurice Lorr have surveyed clinical practice in psychology. In addition to child guidance clinics, they find that clinical psychologists also work in public school systems, in juvenile courts and training schools, and in certain specialized settings such as reading, hearing, and speech clinics. Actually, more clinical psychologists work with adults than with children. Many are employed by government agencies, especially the Veterans Administration, the Army, the Navy, the Air Force, and the Public Health Service. Some are in clinics and counseling centers conducted by colleges and universities. Others work in state or federal hospitals for the mentally ill, in prisons, or in centers for alcoholics, for the aged, or for those needing vocational rehabilitation. In 1960 a division on "psychological aspects of disability" was added to the American Psychological Association; it consists largely of clinical and counseling psychologists interested in problems of the handicapped.

In 1955 a Joint Commission on Mental Illness and Health was set up by Congress to analyze and evaluate the needs and resources of the mentally ill in America and make recommendations for the national mental health program. This was done in a series of studies culminating in a report entitled "Action for Mental Health." This frank and outspoken document noted that a great deal more should be done for the mentally ill than is being done by individuals and by government—local, state, and national. With proper treatment, for example, the schizophrenic patient has 3 or 4 chances in 5 of improving enough to lead a useful life in the community. Unfortunately, society fears and rejects the mentally ill because they seem different and irresponsible. While perhaps only 1% of our population is severely disturbed, a survey showed that about 15% have sought some kind of psychological help (from clergymen, physicians, psychiatrists and psychologists, social agencies, and marriage clinics). Even so, current needs are not being met, says the report, and our nation faces a real shortage in mental health manpower. Furthermore, an increased long-term and large-scale research attack must be undertaken.

The recommendations of the Joint Commission found embodiment in the President's Mental Health message to Congress early in 1964. He cited our neglect of the mentally ill and called for new treatment methods and great increases in research. He proposed a program of expanded federal aid to the states to stimulate establishment of community mental health centers, improvement of mental hospital care, and increased research and training. He also proposed additional grants to the states to help set up long-range master plans. The American Medical Association supported the President and launched a new mental health program of its own. By 1964, the prospects for dealing effectively with the problem of mental illness were brighter than ever before.

EDUCATIONAL PSYCHOLOGY

Much of the work of educational psychologists has already been discussed in earlier chapters, principally in connection with intelligence and aptitude testing, motivation, learning, memory, and personality.

Scientific Study of Educational Methods. The most powerful influence shaping educational methodology in recent times has been John Dewey, whose followers and interpreters have sometimes overgeneralized their procedures, based on studies of permissiveness versus authoritarianism, or project method versus subject-matter method. Since the 1950's, however, educational psychologists have made greater efforts to investigate their methods scientifically. Teacher characteristics have been studied, notably by David G. Ryans, in the hope of shedding light on teacher selection and training, and the relationship between teacher characteristics and pupil performance. Ryans' research disclosed three major patterns of teacher beavior: 1. warm, understanding, and friendly vs. aloof, egocentric, and restricted; 2. responsible, businesslike, and systematic vs. unplanned, slipshod, and evading; 3. stimulating, imaginative, and surgent vs. dull and routine. These factors in teacher performance have been found to be related, in part, to aspects of pupil behavior. Educational psychologists like Lee J. Cronbach have also emphasized the desirability of deriving teaching practices from scientifically established principles of learning.

Instructional Devices. Instructional media have gained the attention of educational psychologists since 1950. Formerly films, film strips, tape recorders, television sets, and other so-called audio-visual aids were used merely as incidental supplements in classroom instruction. Through the work of A. A. Lumsdaine, Robert Glaser, and others, the effects of instructional media are being scientifically studied, and a sound basis for the use of instruments is being formed. Instructional devices are being used increasingly to supplement or supplant lectures and demonstrations and thus take over one function of the teacher—presentation of material to the student.

According to B. F. Skinner, however, these devices, good as they are, do not contribute to another most important function: the interaction between student and teacher as in a tutorial situation. There is danger that the student will become a passive recipient of instruction if only the usual audio-visual aids are employed. A means of providing for student-tutor interchange is desirable. A modern teaching machine can do this, concluded Skinner, whose learning theory has contributed greatly to the development of such machines.

Teaching Machines. Actually the first teaching machines were developed in the 1920's by a pioneering educational psychologist, Sidney L. Pressey. The early machines were primarily for testing, but they could also be used for instruction. Pressey envisioned an "industrial revolution in education" through the use of teaching machines, but the times were not yet ready for it. The educational world had to wait until the pressures of student population, technological advances, and maturity of learning theory developed to the point where significant methodological changes in teaching could be achieved and could be proved to be of value.

Basic to the development of teaching machines is presentation of material to the student in small, orderly, "programed" steps, to each of which a response is required. Every correct response is reinforced or rewarded, generally by informing the student as to the proper answer. Notable advantages of automated instruction are: 1. material is presented systematically, each level based upon previously mastered levels; 2. students are motivated partly because of the interesting presentation, but even more because they are rewarded frequently and their failures are infrequent; 3. individual differences are recognized, since students can proceed at their own rates; 4. teachers have additional time to devote to more complex and creative tasks.

Programed sequences may be presented by machines of varying complexity or simply in booklet form. Two major approaches to the programing of material have developed. In Skinner's *linear* method, small, orderly steps or "frames" are given in such a way as to make failure virtually impossible, thus assuring continuous reinforcement. The pupil completes an item by providing responses for omissions in a statement, as shown in the example on page 335. The frames constituting a series are arranged in the machine or on different pages of a book so that no two frames of the series can be seen at the same time. At the side of the next frame the answer to the preceding frame appears, thus providing the reinforcement.

In the *branching* method of Norman Crowder, the material is organized into a series of multiple-choice items; the particular choice determines the next step to be made. With a branching program the capable student will proceed more rapidly, since he will not be routed through as many intermediate steps as the less capable one.

Educational Guidance and Counseling. Psychological applications to methodology, instructional media, and programing are matched by equally important applications to educational, vocational, and personal guidance of school children. Psychologists Donald E. Super, Robert L. Thorndike, and Irving Lorge have contributed mightily to the field of educational measurement, which is fundamental to the counseling and guidance of large numbers. Carroll L. Shartle pioneered in classifying occupations and in providing job analyses and

SAMPLE FRAMES FROM A LINEAR PROGRAM

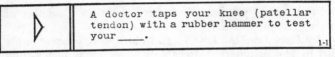

Set 1	PART 1 Reflex Behavior Simple Reflexes Estimated time: 23 minutes Begin ▶

STATEMENT TO BE COMPLETED

▷	A doctor taps your knee (patellar tendon) with a rubber hammer to test your ____. 1-1

ANSWER TO PRE-
CEDING STATEMENT   NEXT STATEMENT

reflexes (reflex) 1-1	If your reflexes are normal, your leg ____ to the tap on the knee with a slight kick (the so-called knee jerk). 1-2

ANSWER   NEXT STATEMENT

responds (reacts) 1-2	In the knee jerk or patellar-tendon reflex, the kick of the leg is the ____ to the tap on the knee. 1-3

ANSWER   NEXT STATEMENT

response (reaction) 1-3	The stimulating <u>object</u> used by the doctor to elicit a knee jerk is a(n) ____. 1-4

ETC.

(The above example is from the programed text, *The Analysis of Behavior* by Holland and Skinner. Copyright 1961, McGraw-Hill Company. Used by permission.)

descriptions. With increasing population pressure, and the concomitant necessity for proper vocational placement, the need for school psychologists and counselors is mounting. This has been recognized not only by educational psychologists, but also by analysts of American education such as James B. Conant, and by the United States Government—notably through passage of the National Defense Education Act in 1960.

Other Applications

Psychological principles have been useful in a number of other practical situations.

Psychology and the Law. Hugo Münsterberg was one of the first to demonstrate the unreliability of testimony such as that given by witnesses in court. In a typical experiment a dramatic event is planned: a masked bandit appears before an audience, fires three shots, shouts a few words, and runs from the room. The audience is asked to testify as to the man's height, clothing, the number of shots fired, his words, and the length of time he remained in the room. Generally, the testimony of most people is unreliable.

Why testimony is unreliable Harold Burtt explained in his book, *Legal Psychology*. Some persons have defective senses; their seeing or hearing may be impaired or limited, so they do not observe events correctly. Possibly their attention is not directed to important details which, as a result, escape their notice; witnesses, for instance, usually fail to note the license number of a hit-run car. A detective, trained to observe carefully, gets these details. Because memory is unreliable after a few hours, testimony should be taken immediately after the event if possible. The element of emotional shock can affect memory greatly. A witness is apt to be less accurate in recalling than in recognizing, but most witnesses are asked to recall and describe events. Suggestion plays an important role in court. Leading questions can trip almost any witness, though children and mentally defective persons are most susceptible to them.

Psychiatrists are called into court to testify on sanity. Perhaps psychologists should be called to check the general reliability of a witness giving testimony; such a report could suggest how much credit a witness's testimony should receive.

Other applications in what has been called "legal psychology" have to do with guilt detection, which was described in Chapter X, and with juvenile delinquency, whose causes we dealt with briefly in Chapter XI. Since World War II the problem has been increasing. Vernon Jones has found that delinquent associates make up the strongest influence determining whether a youth will commit a crime and what type of crime it will be. On the other hand, according to William W. Wattenberg and J. J. Balistrieri, not all delinquents operate in gangs. They found many non-gang delinquents who came from average neighborhoods—although usually from unhappy home situations.

No single solution for delinquency exists. In a famous study of 1000 juvenile delinquents, Sheldon and Eleanor Glueck found that, despite treatment, 88% became repeaters, of whom 70% were later convicted for more serious offenses. Sociologist Clifford Shaw's "area project" in Chicago showed that supervised recreational activities help reduce the delinquency rate, especially if community leaders participate. More recent community projects in the Harlem section of New York and in Cambridge, Massachusetts, have demonstrated that intensive work with neighborhood gangs can turn the youth from delinquent to more constructive activities. Both social conditions and personality problems have to be dealt with.

Psychology and Physical Well-Being. Some personal uses of psychological principles are very helpful.

Important to all of us is knowing how to relax. Geared to high-pressure living, we drain our energies without realizing it, by keeping certain muscles tense. Edmund Jacobson has found that tension which causes muscular contraction, even though no motion is apparent, results in general fatigue. It may cause insomnia, nervousness, indigestion, and even colitis. He recommends recognizing which muscles are tense and learning how to relax them. In time he believes we can learn to use only those muscles involved in necessary movement and to keep other muscles relaxed. This will relieve our bodies—and minds—of much unnecessary strain. The work of Hans Selye on "stress" was described in Chapter X.

Interesting facts about how we sleep and what kind of sleep is best are shown by H. M. Johnson. We commonly assume that sleeping "like a log" is efficient sleep and that restless tossing and turning indicates sleep of poor quality. Johnson built a special bed, balanced on pivots, which vibrated whenever its occupant moved. The vibrations were charted on a recording drum. A camera, focused on the bed, snapped photos whenever the sleeper moved. Normal sleeping positions were shown to change every 5 to 20 minutes. College men stayed motionless longest, averaging 13 minutes. Middle-aged men stayed still 9 minutes, and their wives 10.5 minutes. Children 2½ to 4 years old shifted every 7.4 minutes. The earlier hours of sleep showed less movement than later ones. A striking difference between adults and children appeared in the time required to fall asleep. Adults normally drop off in 15 minutes; kindergarten children require 36 minutes. Johnson's subjects slept in all kinds of positions, including grotesque ones. He concludes that there is no one proper posture for sleeping; the body relieves strains in its various parts by shifting from one position to another.

Nathaniel Kleitman, a physiologist, has studied patterns or cycles of sleeping. In the adult a rhythm of sleep and wakefulness becomes established, with accompanying fluctuations in temperature, as a result of the organism's needs and sleeping arrangements. However, Kleitman showed, in a study conducted in the depths of Mammoth Cave, that after a week or two a person could change his usual rhythm to that of a 28-hour day.

In the battle against traffic accidents, psychology plays an important part. To improve driving, Harry R. De Silva, after long laboratory research, conducted a nationwide series of drivers' clinics, teaching drivers how to avoid accidents. One of the commonest tests measures reaction time. How quickly can one apply a brake after seeing a danger signal? An average person's time lies between one-half and three-quarters of a second. Other tests measure a driver's ability to steer, his sensitivity to color and to glare, and the general quality of his hearing and vision.

An interesting finding of reaction time tests is that women perform as well as men. Alvah Lauer and Albert P. Weiss, studying uniformity or consistency of driving, found that men do considerably better than women, probably because they are more experienced. Men handle apparatus better, but women are more careful in making stops. The investigators concluded that women are more conscientious but less skillful drivers.

Some drivers, like industrial workers, are "accident-prone," De Silva found. About 20% of 1800 taxi drivers caused more than 50% of the total accidents; another 20% had no accidents. Rexford Hersey studied 400 cases of industrial accidents and found that more than half occurred when the worker was worried, apprehensive, or otherwise in a low emotional state. J. W. Parker, Jr. investigated over 100 truck drivers to see what factors were associated with low accident rate. He discovered that good visual acuity and depth perception were important, which is hardly surprising. But he also found that drivers who were married, who had high mechanical interest, and who scored high on a test of emotional stability had relatively low accident rates. Thus it is possible to identify accident-prone persons and to treat them by clinical methods or to shift them into less dangerous types of work.

CURRENT AND FUTURE TRENDS

Psychology is still a young science, and applied psychology is younger still. But, as we have seen, both are mature enough to have affected in many ways the lives of all of us.

What of the future? The world has entered an age of electronic computers, of high-speed transportation and communication—in fact, we are now in the "space age." How is psychology helping to meet this challenge?

The advent of electronic computers and servomechanisms (self-correcting devices) has brought about the emergence of a new science. It was ushered into the world by Norbert Wiener, a mathematician from the Massachusetts Institute of Technology, who named it "cybernetics," after the Greek word meaning "steersman" or "helmsman." It refers to control and communication in both animal and machine.

The new electronic machines frequently simulate human behavior very closely. For example, machines have been "programed" to write music, to translate from one language to another, and to play elaborate games. Servomechanisms are goal-seeking, self-correcting devices which make possible the control of missiles, planes, ships, and complicated machinery. The obvious parallel here is the goal-seeking organism whose responses toward the goal are controlled by "feedback," meaning that the responses which are made then operate as new stimuli to the organism. The following diagram illustrates these operations in man, computer, and servomechanism, and involves the concepts "input," "throughput," "output," and "feedback":

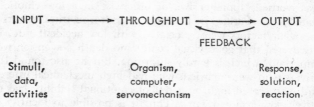

When an organism is hungry, internal stimuli act upon it and result in a class of responses which are likely to lead to food rather than being random, undirected responses. This is true because responses in the direction of food meet with "success," "hope," "positive reinforcement," or "positive feedback." If responses are made which lead away from food, they meet with "failure," "fear," "lack of positive reinforcement," or "negative feedback." The same is true for the computer, the output of which is continuously controlled by the degree of harmony between the feedback and the "program" or instructions, until finally a solution is reached. When a servomechanism is activated, feedback from the reactions controls further output, just as when an old-fashioned steam engine operates too fast, the spinning governor attached to the flywheel automatically shuts down the heat source, thus maintaining a constant speed.

What are the implications of the age of electronics and of automation? Pessimists see growing unemployment, while optimists foresee a reduction in the work week and an age of leisure and affluence. Both are potentially correct, it would seem; it will require combined efforts of science and politics to solve the new problems.

Russia's Sputnik late in 1957 ushered in the space age, and the world has already seen remarkable achievements by both American and Russian astronauts. Engineering psychologists have been called on in our country, along with other scientific specialists, to aid the National Aeronautics and Space Administration. One psychologist, Robert B. Voas, played a key role in Project Mercury. Psychological contributions included testing in the selection of astronauts, design of training equipment and planning of training methods, and analysis of factors relating to the astronaut's observation and manual control of his capsule, including its position or "attitude." Many physicians and physiologists as well as psychologists are studying psychophysiological aspects of space flight. But other factors are also receiving attention. For example, Saul B. Sells, a psychologist who has edited a book on human factors in jet and space travel, has applied to aerospace flight some of the findings from the psychology of small groups.

The world has become more complex in terms of human and social relationships as well as in technical advances. One attempt to cope with difficult problems is generally called "decision theory." In the 1940's mathematician John von Neumann expressed in sophisticated, quantitative form the theory of games, which may become one of the most important developments of our times. It sets forth principles of strategy in decision-making—how to make the best of a bad situation or how to avoid the worst of a good situation. It was the basis for a large contract supported by the Office of Naval Research to study competitive American-type economics. When there is no clear-cut way of winning, game theory can indicate the strategy which will maximize the chances of winning. Game theory has been used by both sides in the cold war, and some have suggested it may partly account for the avoidance of another world war.

Economists have used game theory in making mundane predictions such as when to launch new publications or musical recordings, or when to introduce innovations in automobiles. Recently psychologists, notably Ward Edwards, have sought to apply decision theory to the behavior of individuals. A major proposal is that people make choices or decisions according to "subjectively expected utility," a concept which resembles classical economics and also the "valences" hypothesized by Kurt Lewin in the 1930's. Part of the difficulty of application is that in predicting the behavior of one person statistics are less helpful than in forecasting the behavior of a group, where the criterion is simply the *percent* of persons responding in a particular way, and it makes no difference which persons do the responding.

We have presented here several examples of scientific psychology applied to the solution of current human problems. Some readers may be wondering if all the efforts of psychologists are in the direction of aiding the technicians. Actually psychology is growing fast and is developing in all directions! At the same time that some psychologists were devising improved teaching machines or giving technical aid to Project Mercury, others were forming a new Division of Philosophical Psychology and an American Association for Humanistic Psychology. James F. T. Bugenthal, a leader among the humanistic psychologists, believes that two great traditions—science and the humanities—are at last converging, and that psychology now has matured to the point where its major concern will be not part functions, but the functioning and experience of the whole human being. An increasing number of psychologists are coming to feel the same way.

BIOGRAPHICAL NOTES

ADLER, ALFRED (1870–1937). Viennese psychiatrist and one-time associate of Sigmund Freud. Broke away to found school of "individual psychology." Originated the concept of the "inferiority complex." Lectured and practiced in the United States during the latter years of his life. Among his books are: *The Neurotic Constitution, Problems of Neurosis, Understanding Human Nature.*

ALLPORT, FLOYD HENRY (1890–   ). Pioneer social psychologist, noted for his work on personality traits, attitudes, and conformity behavior. Taught at Syracuse University; wrote *Social Psychology, Institutional Behavior,* and *Theories of Perception and the Concept of Structure.*

ALLPORT, GORDON WILLARD (1897–   ). Authority in personality and social psychology, especially prejudice. Professor of Psychology at Harvard for many years. Author of *Personality, Pattern and Growth in Personality,* and *The Nature of Prejudice.*

ANGELL, JAMES ROWLAND (1869–1949). One of the founders of functional psychology, with John Dewey, at the University of Chicago early in the century. Dr. Angell was President of Yale University (1921–37) and, later, educational director of the National Broadcasting Company.

ARISTOTLE (384–322 B.C.). The great Greek philosopher, who is also considered one of the first scientists because of his empirical viewpoint (basing knowledge on observation and experience). His interpretations of knowledge, sensation, and memory foreshadowed the association psychology of the seventeenth, eighteenth, and nineteenth centuries. Two of his most important works are *Concerning the Soul* and *Concerning Memory.*

BAIN, ALEXANDER (1818–1903). Probably the first writer and teacher to devote his full efforts to psychology. A close friend of John Stuart Mill, he divided his time between free-lance writing in London and teaching in Scotland. His books, *The Senses and the Intellect* and *The Emotions and the Will,* became standard British psychological texts for two generations.

BALDWIN, JAMES MARK (1861–1934). American philosopher and psychologist, who founded the psychological laboratories at Toronto and Princeton Universities. His great interest was mental development; his writings were very popular and were translated into many languages. His most lasting work was the *Dictionary of Philosophy and Psychology*.

BARD, PHILIP (1898–   ). American physiologist. Taught at Harvard, Princeton, and Johns Hopkins; known chiefly for his investigations of the nervous system.

BEERS, CLIFFORD WHITTINGHAM (1876–1943). An American, internationally famous as the founder of the mental hygiene movement. He wrote *A Mind That Found Itself*, describing his unfortunate experiences while a mental patient.

BEKHTEREV, VLADIMIR MIKHAILOVITCH (1857–1927). Famous Russian experimental and social psychologist. He advocated an objective type of psychology, much like behaviorism, shortly before Watson founded his school.

BELL, SIR CHARLES (1774–1842). British physiologist and neurologist. Proved that "specific energies" or separate functions exist for the sensory and motor nerves.

BENEDICT, RUTH FULTON (1887–1948). Distinguished anthropologist and teacher at Columbia University. Author of *Patterns of Culture* and *Race: Science or Politics?*

BENUSSI, VITTORIS (1878–1927). Outstanding Italian psychologist, whose studies of respiratory changes during emotion paved the way for scientific methods of lie detection.

BERKELEY, GEORGE (1685–1753). Distinguished Irish philosopher, psychologist, and bishop, who contributed in his *New Theory of Vision* to the psychology of depth perception and of meaning.

BERNARD, LUTHER LEE (1881–1951). American sociologist and social psychologist, noted for his book *Instinct*, which exposed the absurdities of instinct theories. Taught at Washington University in St. Louis.

BERNHEIM, HIPPOLYTE MARIE (1840–1919). French physician, associated with Liébeault in investigating hypnosis. He proved that some degree of hypnosis can be induced in almost anyone.

BETTELHEIM, BRUNO (1903–   ). He was professor of educational psychology at Chicago. His main work was in child psychoanalysis and child development; works include *Love Is Not Enough*, *Symbolic Wounds*, and *Truants from Life*.

BINET, ALFRED (1857–1911). Probably the most noted French psychologist. Originated intelligence tests; also contributed to the psychology of memory, thinking, suggestibility, and individual development. Founded the first psychological laboratory and first psychological journal in France. Author of *The Development of Intelligence in Children* and *The Psychology of Reasoning*.

BINGHAM, WALTER VAN DYKE (1880–1952). An outstanding authority on personnel work and aptitude testing. Formerly director of the Personnel Research Federation; then chief psychologist of the U. S. Adjutant General's Office. Author of *Aptitudes and Aptitude Testing*, and of *How to Interview* (with B. V. Moore).

BLATZ, WILLIAM E. (1895–1964). Canadian child psychologist and director of the Institute of Child Study at the University of Toronto. Author of *The Management of Young Children* (with H. Bott) and *The Five Sisters*.

BLEULER, EUGEN (1857–1939). Swiss psychiatrist, best known for his introduction of the term "schizophrenia" in place of "dementia praecox." Author of *A Textbook of Psychiatry*.

BOGARDUS, EMORY STEPHEN (1882–   ). Prominent sociologist and social psychologist, noted for his studies of attitude toward various races and nationalities. Taught at the University of Southern California.

BORING, EDWIN GARRIGUES (1886–   ). One of the outstanding American experimental psychologists; for many years director of the psychological laboratory at Harvard University. His *History of Experimental Psychology* is a standard reference work in the field.

BRIDGES, KATHERINE M. BANHAM (1897–   ). British-born psychologist, who has taught and practiced in Toronto and Montreal and at Duke University. Did pioneer studies on the development of the child's emotions.

BROCA, PAUL (1824–80). French physiologist, who in 1861 discovered the "speech center" of the brain.

BROWN, THOMAS (1778–1820). Scottish philosopher-psychologist, who contributed to the understanding of learning and memory by elaborating several laws of mental association. Author of *Lectures on the Philosophy of the Human Mind*.

BRUNER, JEROME S. (1915–   ). Student of cognition and social behavior. Professor at Harvard University. Author of *A Study of Thinking* (with J. J. Goodnow and G. A. Austin).

BÜHLER, CHARLOTTE (1893–   ). Viennese child and clinical psychologist, noted for her studies of the child's social development. Has taught and practiced in the United States since 1940.

BÜHLER, KARL LUDWIG (1879–1963). Experimental psychologist, famous for his studies of thought processes. Taught at Würzburg, Munich, and Vienna; moved to the United States in 1940.

BURKS, BARBARA STODDARD (1902–43). California research psychologist, an associate of Lewis Terman, who did famous studies of gifted children and of hereditary and environmental determinants of intelligence.

BURT, CYRIL LUDOWIC (1887–   ). Outstanding British specialist in child and educational psychology and in juvenile delinquency. Taught at the University of London. His best-known book is *The Young Delinquent*.

BURTT, HAROLD ERNEST (1890–   ). Applied psychologist, long at Ohio State University. Author of *Legal Psychology* and *Principles of Employment Psychology*.

CANNON, WALTER BRADFORD (1871–1945). One of the outstanding American physiologists, noted for research on physiological factors in emotion. Taught at Harvard Medical School. His most important books are: *Bodily Changes in Pain, Hunger, Fear and Rage* and *The Wisdom of the Body*.

CANTRIL, HADLEY (1906–   ). Social psychologist, associated with Princeton University and head of the Institute for International Social Research. Author of the *Psychology of Social Movements, Invasion From Mars*, co-author with M. Sherif of *Psychology of Ego-Involvements*.

CARMICHAEL, LEONARD (1898–   ). Leading physiological and experimental psychologist. Taught at Brown University, became president of Tufts College, and later was appointed director of the Smithsonian Institution.

CATTELL, JAMES MCKEEN (1860–1944). A student of Wilhelm Wundt at Leipzig in the 1880's. Taught at University of Pennsylvania and Columbia University. Did famous studies of reaction time, mental testing, and backgrounds of American men of science. For many years edited *Science, Scientific Monthly, School and Society*. Founder and first president of the Psychological Corporation.

CATTELL, RAYMOND BERNARD (1905–   ). British-born researcher into intelligence, personality, abnormal and social behavior. Research professor at University of Illinois. Author of *Description and Measurement of Personality, Factor Analysis, Personality and Motivation.*

CERLETTI, UGO (1877–   ). Italian neuropsychiatrist who, with the collaboration of L. Bini, developed the technique of electric shock therapy.

CHARCOT, JEAN MARTIN (1825–93). Brilliant French neurologist, famed for his studies of hysteria and hypnosis.

CLAPARÈDE, EDOUARD (1873–1940). Distinguished Swiss educational and experimental psychologist, on the faculty of the University of Geneva. Author of significant studies of intelligence and thinking.

COOLEY, CHARLES HORTON (1864–1929). Eminent sociologist, interested in the effects of society upon the developing personality. Author of *Human Nature and the Social Order.*

DARWIN, CHARLES (1809–82). World-famous British scientist, author of the theory of evolution, which soon revolutionized biology, psychology, and the social sciences. His views on instinct and expression of emotions were of direct importance in psychology. In addition to *Origin of Species* and *Descent of Man,* Darwin wrote *Expression of the Emotions in Man and Animals.*

DASHIELL, JOHN FREDERICK (1888–   ). Prominent experimental and social psychologist, associated with the University of North Carolina.

DA VINCI, LEONARDO (1452–1519). Renowned Italian artist, inventor, and scientific investigator. His observations and experiments on perception of depth and distance preceded by many centuries the work of experimental psychologists.

DESCARTES, RENÉ (1596–1650). Most famous as a philosopher, Descartes was interested also in mathematics, physics, physiology, and psychology. He proposed a dualism between mind and body, with interaction occurring via the pineal gland at the base of the brain. The body he considered a machine; he noted many automatic acts later called reflexes. Man also has rational powers and suffers from "passions" or emotions. His most important psychological book is *The Passions of the Soul.*

DEWEY, JOHN (1859–1952). Distinguished American philosopher. One of the founders of "functional psychology" early in the twentieth century. Best known in psychology for his work on thinking, learning, and educational theory. Among his many books are: *How We Think, Democracy and Education, Human Nature and Conduct, Experience and Nature.*

DIX, DOROTHEA LYNDE (1802–87). New England schoolteacher, whose crusades for humane treatment of the insane, feebleminded, and criminal brought about improvement in institutions all over the world.

DOLL, EDGAR ARNOLD (1889–   ). Noted for studies of mental defectives. For many years director of research at the Vineland Training School. Originator of the Vineland Social Maturity Scale.

DOLLARD, JOHN (1900–   ). Psychiatrically oriented sociologist, long associated with the Institute for Human Relations, Yale University. Author of *Criteria for the Life History, Caste and Class in a Southern Town,* and co-author with N. E. Miller of *Personality and Psychotherapy.*

DONDERS, F. C. (1818–89). Dutch physiologist and oculist, one of the first scientists to study reaction time.

DOOB, LEONARD WILLIAM (1909–   ). Social psychologist at Yale University. Author of *Public Opinion and Propaganda.*

DUNLAP, KNIGHT (1875–1949). Noted experimental psychologist and contributor to many branches of psychology. Helped overthrow instinct doctrines, studied emotional expression, devised a new technique for breaking bad habits. Taught many years at Johns Hopkins University, then at University of California at Los Angeles. Among his best-known books are *Civilized Life* and *Habits; Their Making and Unmaking.*

EBBINGHAUS, HERMANN (1850–1909). One of the most famous German experimental psychologists. His studies of memory set the stage for most of the later work in that field. Also pioneered in the measurement of intelligence. His most significant book bears the simple title *Memory.*

EHRENFELS, CHRISTIAN VON (1859–1932). Austrian philosopher. He introduced the expression "Gestalt" into psychology; pioneered in treating the concept of value psychologically, as a function of desire.

ELLIS, HAVELOCK (1859–1939). British philosopher and psychologist, famous for his studies of genius and of sex. Two of his most important books are A Study of British Genius and the many-volumed Studies in the Psychology of Sex.

ERIKSON, ERIK (1902–   ). American psychoanalyst associated with Harvard Medical School. Noted for studies on the human life cycle, institutions, and personality.

EYSENCK, HANS JURGEN (1916–   ). A University of London experimental-clinical psychologist famous for his analytic studies of the structure of personality and his emphasis on learning principles as the basis of behavior. Author of Dimensions of Personality.

FECHNER, GUSTAV THEODOR (1801–87). German physicist and philosopher, who became interested in E. H. Weber's work on psychophysics—a study of the relation between stimuli and sensations. Fechner extended and improved upon Weber's work. His best-known book is Elements of Psychophysics.

FERENCZI, SANDOR (1873–1933). Hungarian psychoanalyst, whose theories differ somewhat from those of the orthodox followers of Freud.

FLOURENS, PIERRE (1794–1867). Early French neurologist, and the first to show that the brain and nervous system act as a unit.

FRANK, LAWRENCE KELSO (1890–   ). Student of child development, projective techniques, and of cultural effects on personality. Director of the Carolyn Zachry Institute for Human Development and more recently associated with Massachusetts Institute of Technology.

FRANZ, SHEPHERD IVORY (1874–1933). American physiological psychologist, noted for his work on localization of brain functions and re-education of patients with cerebral injuries. Taught at the University of California at Los Angeles.

FREEMAN, FRANK NUGENT (1880–   ). Educational psychologist, author of significant studies of mental testing and of effects of environment on intelligence. Taught at the University of Chicago; later dean of the school of education at the University of California. Among his books are Mental Tests and Twins—a Study of Heredity and Environment (with H. H. Newman and K. J. Holzinger).

FREUD, SIGMUND (1856–1939). World-famous Austrian psychiatrist, who founded psychoanalysis at the turn of the present century. He practiced and taught in Vienna until the Nazi conquest of 1938 drove him to England, where he died the following year. His many books include: *A General Introduction to Psychoanalysis, The Psychopathology of Everyday Life, The Interpretation of Dreams, Wit in Relation to the Unconscious, Beyond the Pleasure Principle, Totem and Taboo, The Future of an Illusion, Civilization and Its Discontents.*

FROMM, ERICH (1900–   ). German-born clinical and social psychologist, with psychoanalytic training. Has taught and practiced in New York City and the University of Mexico. Author of *Escape from Freedom, Man for Himself,* and *The Sane Society.*

GALTON, FRANCIS (1822–1911). Starting life as a child prodigy, Galton dabbled in a number of scientific pursuits, including medicine, anthropology, and meteorology. Later he turned to biology and psychology, studying inheritance of physical traits and of talent, and devising new statistical methods for measuring individual differences. He also founded eugenics. Other researches include mental imagery, and the senses of hearing and of smell. His books are *Hereditary Genius* and *Inquiries into Human Faculty.*

GARRETT, HENRY EDWARD (1894–   ). Prominent experimental and differential psychologist, who taught at Columbia University and later at the University of Virginia. Author of *Great Experiments in Psychology, Psychological Tests, Methods and Results* (with M. R. Schneck), and *Statistics in Psychology and Education.*

GATES, ARTHUR IRVING (1890–   ). An outstanding educational psychologist and specialist in the psychology of reading. Long associated with Teachers College, Columbia University.

GESELL, ARNOLD LUCIUS (1880–1961). One of the foremost American child psychologists, best known for his experimentally determined norms of child development. Director of the Yale Clinic of Child Development. He wrote: *Infancy and Human Growth, The First Five Years of Life* (with associates), *Infant and Child in the Culture of Today* (with F. L. Ilg).

GIBSON, JAMES J. (1904–   ). Experimental psychologist, and author of *The Perception of the Visual World.* Professor at Cornell University.

GILBRETH, FRANK B. (1868–1924) and GILBRETH, LILLIAN M. (1878–   ). Early industrial psychologists, noted for their "time and motion" studies. Joint authors of *Fatigue Study* and *Applied Motion Study.*

GODDARD, HENRY HERBERT (1866–1957). One of the first American psychologists to make systematic studies of mental deficiency. He translated and introduced the Binet test into this country. He coined the term "moron" for the highest grade of the feebleminded. Goddard was director of psychological research for many years at the Vineland (N. J.) Training School; later he taught at Ohio State University. His writings include *The Kallikak Family* and *Feeblemindedness—Its Causes and Its Consequences*.

GOLDSTEIN, KURT (1879–1963). German-born neurologist and psychiatrist, founder of organismic psychology. Author of *The Organism* and *Human Nature in the Light of Psychopathology*.

GOODENOUGH, FLORENCE LAURA (1886–1959). Well-known contributor to child and genetic psychology and to mental testing. Taught at the University of Minnesota Institute of Child Welfare. Author of *Developmental Psychology* and *The Measurement of Intelligence by Drawing*.

GUILFORD, JOY PAUL (1897–   ). Experimental and differential psychologist and statistician. He has taught at the University of Nebraska, and at the University of Southern California. Author of *Psychometric Methods*, and *Fundamental Statistics in Psychology and Education*.

GUTHRIE, EDWIN RAY (1886–1959). University of Washington psychologist, best known for his book *The Psychology of Human Conflict*.

HALL, G. STANLEY (1846–1924). Having studied under Wundt at Leipzig, Hall returned to found the first psychological laboratory in America at Johns Hopkins University in 1882. A few years later he became president of Clark University. His research centered in child and adolescent psychology and in education. He founded the first American psychological journal, and became the first president of the American Psychological Association. His best-known books are: *Adolescence, Senescence, Morale*.

HAMILTON, SIR WILLIAM (1788–1856). Brilliant Scottish philosopher and psychologist, who originated the theory of "redintegration."

HARLOW, HARRY FREDERICK (1905–   ). Student of comparative psychology, especially primates. Professor at the University of Wisconsin.

HARTLEY, DAVID (1705–57). British neurologist and pioneer in physiological psychology. He insisted upon a bodily basis—vibrations in the nerves and brain—for ideas, images, and associations. His theories were published in a book called *Observations on Man*.

HARTMANN, GEORGE WILFRIED (1904–55). Social and educational psychologist, of Teachers College, Columbia University and of Roosevelt University. Author of *Gestalt Psychology*.

HARTSHORNE, HUGH (1885–   ). Yale University psychologist, best known for his studies of character and personality. Wrote *Studies in Deceit* (with M. A. May).

HAVIGHURST, ROBERT J. (1900–   ). Professor of Education at Chicago and chairman of the Committee on Human Development. Studied the social and intellectual development of children in various societies. He wrote *Human Development and Education*.

HEALY, WILLIAM (1869–   ). Distinguished Boston psychiatrist and authority on juvenile delinquency. Author of *The Individual Delinquent* and *Reconstructing Behavior in Youth* (with associates).

HEBB, DONALD OLDING (1904–   ). Outstanding contributor to the study of brain function. Professor at McGill University. Author of *The Organization of Behavior*.

HEIDBREDER, EDNA (1890–   ). Experimental psychologist at the University of Minnesota, and later at Wellesley College. Author of *Seven Psychologies*.

HELMHOLTZ, HERMANN VON (1821–94). Probably the most brilliant of the nineteenth-century German physiologists. Of his many original contributions those on vision, hearing, and reaction time are the most significant for psychology. His theories of color vision and of hearing are still considered seriously. His major publications are *Physiological Optics* and *On the Sensations of Tone*.

HERBART, JOHANN FRIEDRICH (1776–1841). German philosopher, educator, and psychologist, famous for his theory of the dynamic nature of mental processes. He sought to apply psychological principles in education, and introduced a theory of the unconscious. He wrote a *Textbook of Psychology* and *Psychology as Science*, the first important books to use the word "psychology" in the title.

HERING, EWALD (1834–1918). One of the most famous German physiologists; noted particularly for his theories of color vision and of temperature sensation.

HESS, WALTER R. (1881–   ). Swiss physiologist and Nobel Prize winner. His main work concerns ophthalmics and cerebral localization.

HIPPOCRATES (460–356? B.C.). Famous Greek physician, often called the father of medicine. His diagnoses of mental disease and his fourfold classification of personality types were influential until the seventeenth or eighteenth centuries.

HOBHOUSE, LEONARD TRELAWNEY (1864–1929). British philosopher and psychologist, famed for his early experiments on animal learning and thinking. Wrote *Mind in Evolution*.

HÖFFDING, HARALD (1843–1931). Outstanding Danish philosopher and psychologist. One of the first to react against Wundt's structural psychology; also to propose a theory of the subconscious. Except for his early *Outlines of Psychology* his writings are philosophical.

HOLLINGWORTH, HARRY LEVI (1880–1956). Pioneer in applied psychology and contributor to almost every psychological field. Noted for his studies in personnel, physiological, and abnormal psychology and for his systematic viewpoint emphasizing "redintegration." Taught at Barnard College, Columbia University. His books include: *Vocational Psychology, Psychology of the Functional Neuroses, Mental Growth and Decline, Abnormal Psychology*.

HOLLINGWORTH, LETA STETTER (1886–1939). Best known for her work with gifted children; also contributed to intelligence testing and understanding the subnormal child. Wife of Harry L. Hollingworth, she was Professor of Education at Teachers College, Columbia University. Among her books are: *The Psychology of Subnormal Children, Special Talents and Defects, Gifted Children*.

HOLZINGER, KARL JOHN (1892–1953). Statistician and author of research studies in mental measurement, especially of effects of heredity and environment on intelligence. Co-author of *Twins—A Study of Heredity and Environment*.

HORNEY, KAREN (1885–1952). German-born psychoanalyst who practiced in New York and emphasized cultural factors in the production of neurosis. Author of *The Neurotic Personality of Our Time* and *New Ways in Psychoanalysis*.

HOVLAND, CARL IVER (1912–62). Professor of Psychology at Yale who was an authority on learning and communication. Author of *Communication and Persuasion*.

HULL, CLARK LEONARD (1884–1952). One of the foremost American authorities on learning. Also did important experimental studies of hypnosis, suggestibility, and effects of tobacco. Taught at Yale University. His books include: *Aptitude Testing, Hypnosis and Suggestibility*, and *Principles of Behavior*.

HUME, DAVID (1711–76). Famous Scottish philosopher, historian, and psychologist, who stressed the distinction between sense impressions and images. He also wrote on the laws of association. Author of *A Treatise on Human Nature* and *Inquiry Into Human Understanding*.

HUNTER, WALTER SAMUEL (1889–1954). Experimental psychologist who taught at Clark and Brown Universities. One of the early behaviorists, he performed significant experiments on animal learning and reasoning.

ITARD, JEAN MARC GASPARD (1775–1838). Associate of the great French psychiatrist Philippe Pinel, Itard won enduring fame by his patient efforts to educate the "Wild Boy of Aveyron."

JACOBSON, EDMUND (1888–   ). Chicago physiologist and physiological psychologist, noted for his studies of muscular activity. Author of *Progressive Relaxation*.

JAENSCH, ERICH RUDOLF (1883–1943). German psychologist, of the University of Marburg, famous for his work on eidetic imagery.

JAMES, WILLIAM (1842–1910). Greatest figure in early American psychology. Educated in Europe as well as in the United States, James was trained first in anatomy and physiology before he turned to psychology and philosophy. His *Principles of Psychology* (1890) became the standard psychological text for a generation. His most original contributions concern the theory of emotions, instinct, transfer of training, "the stream of consciousness," and the unconscious. James was connected with Harvard as student and teacher for most of his life.

JANET, PIERRE (1859–1947). Distinguished French psychiatrist, noted for his studies of hysteria and other neuroses. Author of *Major Symptoms of Hysteria* and *Psychological Healing*.

JASTROW, JOSEPH (1863–1944). One of G. Stanley Hall's first students at Johns Hopkins University, Jastrow went to the University of Wisconsin and founded a psychological laboratory there. He was one of the first to devise and administer mental tests, and made many contributions to experimental psychology. His many books include *Fact and Fable in Psychology*, *Temperament and Character*, and *Effective Thinking*.

JOHNSON, HARRY MILES (1885–1953). Experimental and applied psychologist; taught at Tulane University. Best known for his studies of sleep.

JONES, HAROLD ELLIS (1894–1960). Educational and child psychologist, noted for studies of intellectual development. For many years director of the Institute of Child Welfare at the University of California.

JONES, MARY COVER (1896–). Child psychologist at the University of California, famed for her studies on the conditioning of children's emotions. Wife of Harold E. Jones.

JUNG, CARL GUSTAV (1875–1961). Distinguished Swiss founder of the school of analytical psychology, a variety of psychoanalysis. His work included important research on emotions. He originated the concepts of introvert and extrovert personality types. Author of *Analytical Psychology* and *Psychological Types*.

KARDINER, ABRAM (1891–). American psychiatrist. Taught at Cornell, Columbia, and Emory. He wrote *The Individual and His Society* and *Sex and Morality*.

KATZ, DANIEL (1903–). Social psychologist, specializing in attitudes and public opinion. Teacher at Princeton and the University of Michigan.

KITSON, HARRY DEXTER (1886–1959). One of the best-known specialists in vocational psychology; was professor at Teachers College, Columbia University. Author of *The Mind of the Buyer* and *Psychology of Vocational Adjustment*.

KLINEBERG, OTTO (1899–). Social psychologist, noted for studies of ethnic differences and the psychology of international relations. After retiring from Columbia University he went to teach at the Sorbonne in Paris. Author of *Race Differences*, *Tensions Affecting International Understanding*.

KOFFKA, KURT (1886–1941). One of the founders of Gestalt psychology. Born and educated in Berlin; taught at Smith College from 1927 until his death. His most noted book is *The Growth of the Mind*.

KÖHLER, WOLFGANG (1887–   ). A founder and leader of Gestalt psychology. Did his famous experiments on apes in the Canary Islands where, as a German, he was interned during World War I. Taught in Germany until the 1930's, when he came to Swarthmore College. His best-known books are *The Mentality of Apes* and *Gestalt Psychology*.

KORZYBSKI, ALFRED (1879–1950). Polish-American scientist. Developed general semantics and wrote *Manhood of Humanity: The Science and Art of Human Engineering*, and *Science and Sanity: An Introduction to Non-Aristotelian Systems and General Semantics*.

KRAEPELIN, EMIL (1856–1926). Achieved fame for his experiments on drugs and fatigue before he turned to psychiatry. Outstanding among German psychiatrists, Kraepelin classified mental diseases so well that his list became the basis for present-day classifications.

KRAFFT-EBING, RICHARD VON (1840–1912). Viennese psychiatrist, best known for his studies of abnormal sex behavior. Author of *Textbook of Psychiatry* and *Psychopathia Sexualis*.

KRETSCHMER, ERNST (1888–1964). German psychiatrist, best known for his studies and theories of constitutional type in relation to personality. Wrote *Physique and Character*.

KUDER, GEORGE FREDERIC (1903–   ). Professor of Psychology at Duke University. He developed techniques for measuring aptitudes and vocational preferences. He wrote *The Construction of Occupational Scales*.

KÜLPE, OSWALD (1862–1915). German experimental psychologist, director of the Würzburg laboratory, where important experiments on thinking took place. Author of an influential early book called *Outlines of Psychology*.

LADD-FRANKLIN, CHRISTINE (1847–1930). Originator of one of the three most widely accepted theories of color vision. Taught at Columbia University.

LANDIS, CARNEY (1897–1962). Psychologist at Psychiatric Institute, Columbia University. Best known for his experimental studies of emotions.

LANGE, KARL GEORG (1834–1900). Danish physiologist, whose theory of emotions was amplified by William James and came to be known as the "James-Lange Theory."

LANGFELD, HERBERT SIDNEY (1879–1958). American experimental psychologist, trained in Germany. Has contributed to aesthetics and the study of emotions. Taught at Princeton University.

LASHLEY, KARL SPENCER (1890–1958). Physiological psychologist, famed for his experiments on localization of brain functions. Taught at Minnesota, Chicago, and Harvard Universities. His research is described in *Brain Mechanisms and Intelligence*.

LE BON, GUSTAVE (1841–1931). French writer, author of *The Crowd*, a book influential in establishing social psychology as a separate field of study.

LEWIN, KURT (1890–1947). First identified with the Gestalt School in Germany, Lewin came to the United States and taught at the University of Iowa. Later he founded the Research Center for Group Dynamics at the Massachusetts Institute of Technology. His three best-known books are *Dynamic Theory of Personality*, *Principles of Topological Psychology*, and *Field Theory in Social Science* (edited by D. Cartwright).

LIÉBEAULT, AMBROISE AUGUSTE (1823–1904). French physician and psychiatrist, who pioneered in using hypnosis to cure hysterical patients.

LIKERT, RENSIS (1903–   ). A specialist in psychological and sociological research and scaling methods. Director of the Institute of Social Research of the University of Michigan.

LINDSLEY, DONALD BENJAMIN (1907–   ). Authority on psychophysiology of visual perception, brain organization, and neurophysiology of emotion. Professor at University of California in Los Angeles.

LINTON, RALPH (1893–1953). American anthropologist. He taught at Wisconsin, Columbia, and Yale; he undertook studies of complex cultural-psychiatric relationships of varying groups. He wrote *The Science of Man in the World Crisis*, *Most of the World*, and *The Tree of Culture*.

LOCKE, JOHN (1632–1704). Renowned British philosopher, who insisted that all knowledge is obtained through sensory experience, and that learning and memory depend upon "association of ideas." His most important work is the *Essay concerning Human Understanding*.

LYND, ROBERT S. (1892–   ). American sociologist. He made, with his wife, Helen Merrill Lynd, the famous sociological study of

Muncie, Indiana. The results of this study were published as *Middletown: A Study in Contemporary American Culture* and *Middletown in Transition*.

McCLELLAND, DAVID CLARENCE (1917–   ). A leading American psychologist in the fields of human motivation and socialization. Author of *The Achievement Motive*.

McDOUGALL, WILLIAM (1871–1938). Internationally famous figure in psychology. Born in England, he taught at Oxford before coming to Harvard and Duke Universities. He contributed to every branch of psychology from physiological to social. He stoutly opposed mechanism and behaviorism and espoused the purposive nature of behavior. His many books were influential; they include *Introduction to Social Psychology, The Group Mind, Modern Materialism and Emergent Evolution*.

MacKINNON, DONALD WALLACE (1903–   ). Student of motivation and of personality, and co-director of psychological studies in the Office of Strategic Services. Became director of the Institute of Personality Assessment and Research at the University of California.

McNEMAR, QUINN (1900–   ). An outstanding psychologist in the fields of statistics, experimental design, and test theory. Professor at Stanford University. Author of *The Revision of the Stanford-Binet Scale*.

MAIER, NORMAN RAYMOND FREDERICK (1900–   ). Professor at the University of Michigan, noted for his studies of reasoning, of neurosis in animals, and of industrial psychology. Author of *Frustration, Psychology in Industry*.

MASLOW, ABRAHAM HAROLD (1908–   ). Student of motivation, personality, and abnormal psychology; pioneer in humanistic psychology. Professor at Brandeis University. Author of *Motivation and Personality* and *Toward a Psychology of Being*.

MAY, MARK A. (1891–   ). Director of the Institute of Human Relations at Yale University; noted for his studies of personality and character. Author of *Studies in Deceit* (with H. Hartshorne).

MAY, ROLLO (1909–   ). Noted American existential psychoanalyst. A fellow and faculty member of the William Alanson White Institute and professor of clinical psychology at New York University. Author of *Man's Search for Himself* and *Existential Psychology*.

MEAD, GEORGE HERBERT (1863–1931). Distinguished philosopher, of the University of Chicago, who emphasized the part played by society in developing a child's selfhood or personality. Wrote *Mind, Self and Society.*

MEAD, MARGARET (1901–   ). American anthropologist and social psychologist, noted for her studies of primitive peoples in the South Seas. Author of *Coming of Age in Samoa, Growing Up in New Guinea, Sex and Temperament in Three Primitive Societies.*

MEIER, NORMAN CHARLES (1893–   ). Co-author of the Meier-Seashore Art Judgment Test. Professor for many years at the University of Iowa.

MENDEL, GREGOR (1822–84). Austrian monk, whose experiments on plant breeding proved that laws exist by which inheritance of characteristics can be predicted.

MESMER, FRANZ ANTON (1733–1815). Viennese doctor, who discovered "animal magnetism," later called "mesmerism." Though scientists considered Mesmer a charlatan, his work stimulated research which led to later understanding of suggestion and hypnosis.

MEYER, ADOLF (1866–1950). Internationally famous psychiatrist and neurologist. Born in Switzerland; practiced and taught in the United States for over fifty years, mainly at Johns Hopkins University.

MILES, CATHARINE COX (1890–   ). Best known for her work with Terman on studies of genius and of sex differences. Wife of Walter R. Miles, she has taught at Yale University and engaged in private practice.

MILES, WALTER RICHARD (1885–   ). Experimental psychologist, noted for his studies of alcohol, of visual functions, and development of mental ability. Professor at Yale University and later director of the U. S. Naval Medical Research Laboratory in New London.

MILL, JAMES (1773–1836). British historian, economist, and psychologist, noted for his simplification of the laws of association. Author of *Analysis of the Phenomena of the Human Mind.*

MILLER, NEAL ELGAR (1909–   ). Contributor to learning and motivation theory; professor at Yale University. Co-author with J. Dollard of *Social Learning and Imitation* and *Personality and Psychotherapy.*

MINKOWSKI, MIECZYSLAW (1884–   ). Swiss neurologist and embryologist (born in Warsaw, Poland), whose studies of fetuses showed that mass action precedes specific responses in fetal development.

MORENO, J. L. (1892–   ). He has been professor of sociology at New York University, the New School, and Columbia University. He developed the concepts of psychodrama and of the sociogram. He is the author of *Sociometry, Experimental Methods and the Science of Society*, and *Who Shall Survive?*

MORGAN, C. LLOYD (1852–1936). Versatile British scientist, noted as a geologist, zoologist, and psychologist. He is considered the founder of scientific comparative psychology through his pioneer experiments on animal learning and thinking. Author of *Animal Life and Intelligence, Emergent Evolution*, and *Animal Mind*.

MORGAN, JOHN JACOB BROOKE (1888–1945). Child and clinical psychologist for many years at Northwestern University; also known for his experimental studies of distraction. Author of *Psychology of the Unadjusted School Child* and *The Psychology of Abnormal People*.

MOSSO, ANGELO (1846–1910). One of the most famous Italian psychologists, known particularly for his work on fatigue.

MOWRER, ORVAL HOBART (1907–   ). Learning theorist, with interest in motivation, language, personality and psychotherapy. Has taught at Yale, Harvard, and University of Illinois. Author of *Learning Theory and Personality Dynamics* and *Psychotherapy, Theory and Research*.

MÜLLER, GEORG ELIAS (1850–1934). Distinguished German experimental psychologist, noted for his work in memory and psychophysics. He taught at the University of Göttingen and built up there a famous laboratory.

MÜLLER, JOHANNES (1801–58). One of the greatest German physiologists. Made original contributions on the function of the nervous system; wrote internationally famous textbook, *The Elements of Physiology*.

MÜNSTERBERG, HUGO (1863–1916). Born in Germany, Dr. Münsterberg, pioneer experimental psychologist, spent his last twenty years at Harvard, where he promoted legal, industrial, and other applications of psychology. Author of *Psychotechnics, Psychology and Industrial Efficiency*, and *On the Witness Stand*.

MURPHY, GARDNER (1895–   ). Social and personality psychologist who taught for many years at Columbia University and College of the City of New York, then became Director of Research for the Menninger Foundation. Author of *Historical Introduction to Modern Psychology*, *Experimental Social Psychology* (with L. B. Murphy and T. M. Newcomb), and *Personality—A Biosocial Approach*.

MURPHY, LOIS BARCLAY (1902–   ). Teacher at Sarah Lawrence College and student of social behavior in young children; more recently a research psychologist at the Menninger Foundation. She is co-author of *Experimental Social Psychology*, and wrote *Personality in Young Children* and *The Widening World of Childhood*.

MURRAY, HENRY ALEXANDER (1893–   ). Psychologist and M.D. noted for his studies of personality; long associated with Harvard University. Principal author of *Explorations in Personality* and *Assessment of Men*.

NEWCOMB, THEODORE MEAD (1903–   ). Social psychologist for many years at Bennington College and later at the University of Michigan. Co-author of *Experimental Social Psychology* (with G. and L. B. Murphy); author of *Personality and Social Change* and *The Acquaintance Process*.

NEWMAN, HORATIO HACKETT (1875–1957). University of Chicago biologist and geneticist; specialist on twins. Collaborated with F. N. Freeman and K. J. Holzinger on *Twins—A Study of Heredity and Environment*. He also wrote *Multiple Human Births*.

NIETZSCHE, FRIEDRICH WILHELM (1844–1900). Famous German philosopher, who proposed in his *Birth of Tragedy* two contrasting philosophies of life, or personality types, the Apollonian and the Dionysian.

OSGOOD, CHARLES EGERTON (1916–   ). Research specialist in cognition and communication and professor at the University of Illinois. Devised the semantic differential technique. Co-author of *The Measurement of Meaning* (with G. J. Suci and P. H. Tannenbaum) and author of *An Alternative to War or Surrender*.

PATERSON, DONALD GILDERSLEEVE (1892–1961). Educational and clinical psychologist who taught at the University of Minnesota. Best known for his scale of performance tests (with R. Pintner) and the Minnesota mechanical ability tests (with associates). He wrote *Physique and Intellect*.

PAVLOV, IVAN PETROVICH (1849–1936). Russian physiologist, internationally famous for discovering the "conditioned reflex." His years of subsequent research established conditioning as one of the most fundamental types of learning. Pavlov contributed also to abnormal psychology by producing "experimental neurosis" in dogs. His chief scientific findings are included in *Lectures on Conditioned Reflexes*.

PEARSON, KARL (1857–1936). British mathematician and scientist, a disciple of Francis Galton. He originated new statistical techniques, notably correlation. In his *Grammar of Science* he insisted that science is defined by the methods it uses rather than by the nature of its subject matter.

PENROSE, LIONEL SHARPLES (1898–   ). British physician and psychologist, specializing in the study of mental deficiency. His book *Mental Defect* is a standard reference work in the field.

PIAGET, JEAN (1896–   ). Famous Swiss child psychologist, teaching at the University of Geneva. Author of *The Child's Conception of the World*, *The Language and Thought of the Child*, and *Construction of Reality in the Child*.

PILLSBURY, WALTER BOWERS (1872–1960). Prominent psychologist, associated with the University of Michigan for nearly 50 years. Author of *Attention* and *The History of Psychology*.

PINEL, PHILIPPE (1745–1826). French psychiatrist, famed for introducing humanitarian treatment of the mentally diseased.

PINTNER, RUDOLF (1884–1942). Authority on the measurement of intelligence. Co-author of the Pintner-Paterson Performance Tests; student of the psychology of deaf, physically handicapped, and mentally deficient persons. Taught at Ohio State University and Teachers College, Columbia University. His books include *Intelligence Testing*, *Educational Psychology*, *The Psychology of the Physically Handicapped* (with associates).

PLATO (427–347 B.C.). The famous Greek philosopher, pupil of Socrates and teacher of Aristotle. Plato's *Dialogues*, dealing with the whole range of philosophical ideas, contain also the earliest theories of sensation, memory, and association of ideas.

POFFENBERGER, ALBERT THEODORE (1885–   ). Distinguished experimental and applied psychologist, professor for many years at Columbia University. Author of *The Psychology of Advertising* and *Applied Psychology*.

PORTEUS, STANLEY DAVID (1883–   ). Differential and social psychologist, who taught at the University of Hawaii. He devised the Porteus Maze Test.

PRESSEY, SIDNEY LEAVITT (1888–   ). Educational psychologist, long at Ohio State University. He constructed an early teaching machine. Author of *Psychology and the New Education*.

PREYER, WILHELM (1842–97). German physiologist, famous for his book, *The Mind of the Child*, the first systematic account of child development.

RANK, OTTO (1884–1939). Austrian psychoanalyst, best known for his proposal of the "birth trauma" theory of neurosis. Dr. Rank came to the United States a few years before his death. Among his books are: *The Trauma of Birth, Art and Artist, Modern Education*.

REICH, WILHELM (1897–1957). He was chief associate at Freud's Psychoanalytic Polyclinic in Vienna. In this country, he taught at the New School and founded the controversial Orgone Institute.

REID, THOMAS (1710–96). Scottish philosopher, he is identified with the theory of natural realism, a common-sense view of perception.

RIBOT, THÉODULE ARMAND (1839–1916). One of the foremost French psychologists, Ribot worked in both the experimental and abnormal fields. His books include *Diseases of Memory, Psychology of the Emotions*, and *Essay on Creative Imagination*.

RIESMAN, DAVID (1909–   ). Professor of Social Sciences at Chicago, Yale, and Harvard. Wrote, with collaborators, *The Lonely Crowd: A Study of the Changing American Character* and *Individualism Reconsidered*.

ROGERS, CARL RANSOM (1902–   ). Outstanding clinical psychologist and founder of "non-directive therapy." Taught at Ohio State University, and Universities of Chicago and Wisconsin. Author of *Counseling and Psychotherapy, Client-Centered Therapy*, and *On Becoming a Person*.

RORSCHACH, HERMANN (1884–1922). Swiss psychiatrist, who originated the widely used inkblot test of personality which bears his name.

ROSS, EDWARD ALSWORTH (1866–1951). Prominent sociologist, long associated with the University of Wisconsin. Wrote the first book called *Social Psychology*.

RYANS, DAVID G. (1909–   ). He was director of National Teacher Examinations for the American Council of Education, and is known for his theory of personality measurement. He wrote *Teacher Personality and Its Evaluation*.

SAKEL, MANFRED (1900–   ). He is director of the Manfred Sakel Foundation for Emotional and Mental Disorders. He was a pioneer in the development of shock treatments and the use of the therapeutic, neurotropic value of insulin.

SEARS, ROBERT RICHARDSON (1908–   ). Child and social psychologist; has taught at Yale, Iowa, Harvard and Stanford Universities. Author of *Patterns of Child Rearing* (with E. E. Maccoby and H. Levin).

SEASHORE, CARL EMIL (1866–1949). Devised the widely used Seashore test of musical talent. Co-author of the Meier-Seashore Art Judgment Test. He was Professor of Psychology and Dean of the Graduate College, University of Iowa. His best-known book is *The Psychology of Musical Talent*.

SEGUIN, ÉDOUARD (1812–80). Frenchman and pupil of the famous Dr. Jean Itard, Seguin devised new methods of educating and treating mental defectives. His form-board is still used as part of the Pintner-Paterson Performance Tests.

SELYE, HANS (1907–   ). Medical researcher and educator, he wrote *Encyclopedia of Endocrinology*, *Stress*, and *The Story of the Adaptation Syndrome*.

SHAFFER, LAURANCE FREDERIC (1903–   ). Prominent clinical psychologist; has taught at Carnegie Institute of Technology and Teachers College, Columbia University. Author of *The Psychology of Adjustment* (revised with E. J. Shoben).

SHAW, CLIFFORD R. (1896–1957). Chicago sociologist, noted for his studies of community factors in juvenile delinquency. His books include *Delinquency Areas* (with associates), *The Jack-Roller*, and *Brothers in Crime*.

SHELDON, WILLIAM H. (1899–   ). M.D. and psychologist who elaborated morphological types of physique and proposed a theory of constitutional psychology. He wrote *Varieties of Human Physique* and *Varieties of Temperament*.

SHERIF, MUZAFER (1905–   ). Turkish-born social psychologist, for many years professor at the University of Oklahoma and director of its Institute of Group Relations. He is author of *The Psychology of Social Norms, Psychology of Ego-Involvements* (with H. Cantril), *Groups in Harmony and Tension* (with C. W. Sherif), and *Social Judgment* (with C. I. Hovland).

SHERRINGTON, SIR CHARLES SCOTT (1857–1952). Distinguished British neurologist and physiological psychologist, famed for his experiments on the physiological basis of emotions. His *Integrative Action of the Nervous System* is a classic in both neurology and psychology.

SHIRLEY, MARY MARGARET (1899–   ). Child psychologist and student of infant development who taught at Smith and Wellesley Colleges. Wrote *The First Two Years*.

SIMON, THÉOPHILE (1873–1961). French psychologist, famous as the collaborator of Alfred Binet in devising the first intelligence tests.

SKINNER, BURRHUS FREDERIC (1904–   ). Major developer of the reinforcement concept of learning, which stresses "operant conditioning." Has taught at Minnesota, Indiana, and Harvard Universities. Author of *Behavior of Organisms, Verbal Behavior*, and *Science and Human Behavior*.

SPEARMAN, CHARLES EDWARD (1863–1945). One of the most distinguished British psychologists. Known for his theory of a "general factor" in intelligence and for several contributions to statistical method. Taught at the University of London. Author of *The Nature of Intelligence* and *The Abilities of Man*.

SPENCE, KENNETH WARTENBE (1907–   ). Learning theorist following in the tradition of Clark Hull. Professor at the University of Iowa. Author of *Behavior Theory and Conditioning*.

SPENCER, HERBERT (1820–1903). British philosopher, psychologist, and sociologist, who introduced evolutionary principles into psychology. He is regarded as one of the forerunners of social psychology. His books include *Principles of Psychology, Synthetic Philosophy*, and *Essays on Education*.

SPRANGER, EDOUARD (1882–   ). German psychologist, noted for his classification of six personality types, based on differences in fundamental interests and attitudes. Author of *Types of Men*.

STAGNER, ROSS (1909–   ). Personality and social psychologist who has taught at Dartmouth and at Illinois and Wayne State Universities. Author of *Psychology of Personality* and *Psychology of Industrial Conflict*.

STARCH, DANIEL (1883–   ). Applied psychologist, founder of a New York firm specializing in business and personnel psychology and in studies of consumer attitudes.

STEKEL, WILHELM (1868–1940). Viennese psychoanalyst, whose technique of therapy differs from that of the Freudians.

STERN, WILLIAM (1871–1938). German psychologist, professor of psychology at the University of Hamburg. Famous as the founder of differential psychology and originator of the intelligence quotient. He wrote *Differential Psychology* and *General Psychology from the Personalistic Standpoint*.

STODDARD, GEORGE DINSMORE (1897–   ). Educational psychologist; has been professor at the University of Iowa, Commissioner of Education for New York State, President of the University of Illinois, and Dean of the School of Education at New York University. Author of *The Meaning of Intelligence*.

STRONG, EDWARD K. (1884–1963). Applied psychologist noted for his studies of interests. Originated the Strong Vocational Interest Blank. Author of *Vocational Interests of Men and Women*.

SULLIVAN, HARRY STACK (1892–1949). Psychiatrist and "neo-psychoanalyst" famous for his emphasis on interpersonal factors in mental illness. He was president of the William Alanson White Foundation and director of the Washington School of Psychiatry. Author of *Interpersonal Theory of Psychiatry* and *Conceptions of Modern Psychiatry*.

SUPER, DONALD EDWIN (1910–   ). Authority on vocational counseling, testing, and personnel selection. Author of *Appraising Vocational Fitness*.

SYMONDS, PERCIVAL MALLON (1893–1960). Educational and clinical psychologist at Teachers College, Columbia University. Author of *Diagnosing Personality and Conduct, The Psychology of Parent-Child Relationships*, and *Dynamic Psychology*.

TARDE, GABRIEL (1843–1904). French sociologist, considered one of the founders of social psychology because of his book, *The Laws of Imitation*.

TAYLOR, FREDERICK WINSLOW (1856–1915). Because of his pioneer studies of efficiency in industry, Taylor is known as the father of scientific management. He was a member of the American Academy of Mechanical Engineers. He wrote *Principles of Scientific Management*.

TERMAN, LEWIS MADISON (1877–1956). World-famous as the author of the Stanford-Binet intelligence test, first published in 1916. Other contributions include studies of gifted children, of factors in marital happiness, and of sex differences. He wrote: *The Measurement of Intelligence*, *Genetic Studies of Genius* (with associates), *Psychological Factors in Marital Happiness* (with associates), *Sex and Personality* (with C. C. Miles).

THEOPHRASTUS (372–287 B.C.). Famous Greek philosopher and naturalist, a pupil of Aristotle. Credited with originating the early form of personality study called "character writing."

THORNDIKE, EDWARD LEE (1874–1949). Often called the founder of animal psychology because of his original studies of learning in cats, dogs, chicks, fish, and monkeys. Later he became famous for his contributions to educational psychology, especially intelligence testing, transfer of training, adult learning, and motivation. He was professor of education at Teachers College, Columbia University. Among his most important books are *Animal Intelligence*, *Educational Psychology*, and *Adult Learning*.

THURSTONE, LOUIS LEON (1887–1955). One of the outstanding authorities on mental measurement. He pioneered in measuring attitudes and in developing new statistical techniques, especially factor analysis. Taught at University of Chicago. Wrote *The Nature of Intelligence* and *Multiple Factor Analysis*.

TITCHENER, EDWARD BRADFORD (1867–1927). An Englishman, trained in Germany, who brought Wundtian structural psychology to America. At Cornell University, where he taught until his death, Titchener expounded his rigidly defined psychology in a series of manuals and texts. He also wrote *The Psychology of Feeling and Attention* and *The Psychology of the Thought Processes*.

TOLMAN, EDWARD CHACE (1886–1959). Experimental and comparative psychologist, noted for his researches on motivation and learning. Taught at the University of California. His most important book is *Purposive Behavior in Animals and Men*.

TREDGOLD, ALFRED FRANK (1870–1952). Outstanding British authority on mental defect. His book *Mental Deficiency* has become a classic in the field.

VERNON, PHILIP EWART (1905–   ). British educational psychologist and student of personality. Has taught at the University of Glasgow and the University of London. Author of A *Study of Values* (with G. W. Allport).

VITELES, MORRIS SIMON (1898–   ). Prominent industrial psychologist, associated with the University of Pennsylvania. Author of *Industrial Psychology* and *The Science of Work*.

WARDEN, CARL JOHN (1890–1961). One of the foremost American comparative psychologists, famous for his study of the relative strength of animal drives and for his 3-volume *Comparative Psychology* (with T. N. Jenkins and L. H. Warner).

WATSON, GOODWIN BARBER (1899–   ). Educational and social psychologist, for many years at Teachers College, Columbia University. Author of *Action for Unity*.

WATSON, JOHN BROADUS (1878–1958). Founder of Behaviorism. An early animal psychologist and student of learning, Watson also did original investigations of newborn babies. Taught at the University of Chicago and Johns Hopkins, then engaged in advertising. He wrote *Behaviorism*, and other books expounding behaviorist views; also *Psychological Care of the Infant and Child*.

WEBER, ERNST HEINRICH (1795–1878). German anatomist and physiologist, famed as the founder of psychophysics. His chief discovery—that we perceive relative, not absolute, changes in the intensity of stimuli—has become known as "Weber's Law." Weber also did original research on the sense of touch.

WECHSLER, DAVID (1896–   ). Originator of the well-known tests of intelligence which bear his name. Chief psychologist at Bellevue Psychiatric Hospital in New York for many years. Author of *The Measurement of Adult Intelligence*.

WELLS, FREDERIC LYMAN (1884–1964). Experimental and clinical psychologist at Harvard University and Boston Psychopathic Hospital. Author of *Mental Tests in Clinical Practice*.

WERTHEIMER, MAX (1880–1943). Discoverer of the "phi phenomenon," or illusion of motion, and one of the founders of Gestalt psychology. Taught for many years at the Universities of Frankfurt and Berlin; and then at the New School for Social Research in New York.

WHORF, B. L. (1897–1941). He formulated, with some ideas of Edward Sapir, what was known as the Sapir-Whorf Hypothesis: that every language is a systematic presentation or analysis of reality as seen by its speakers. A selection of his writings was published posthumously as *Language, Thought and Reality*.

WIENER, NORBERT (1894–1964). American mathematician and educator; he taught at Massachusetts Institute of Technology and was best known for his theory of cybernetics. He wrote *The Human Use of Human Beings*.

WITMER, LIGHTNER (1867–1956). Clinical and educational psychologist for many years at the University of Pennsylvania. Famed as the founder of the first psychological clinic.

WOLFF, HAROLD G. (1898–   ). American neurologist, he taught at Cornell University, and is best known for his study of conditioned reflexes and psychosomatic problems.

WOODWORTH, ROBERT SESSIONS (1869–1962). One of the most eminent American psychologists. Trained in the United States, and in England under C. S. Sherrington. Author of notable studies in learning, thinking, motivation, and personality. Taught at Columbia University. Wrote *Dynamic Psychology*, *Contemporary Schools of Psychology*, and *Experimental Psychology*.

WUNDT, WILHELM (1832–1920). German physiologist and psychologist, called the father of experimental psychology because he established at Leipzig in 1879 the first psychological laboratory in the world. In addition to doing much valuable research himself, he taught many men who later became leaders in psychology; among them were Cattell, Titchener, Hall, Kraepelin, Münsterberg, Külpe, Witmer, and Judd. He also founded the first journal for experimental psychology. His best-known book is *Physiological Psychology*.

YERKES, ROBERT MEARNS (1876–1956). Noted as a comparative psychologist. Also served in a high official capacity during World War I, helping administer the Army testing program. Taught at Yale University. His best-known books are *The Dancing Mouse, Army Mental Tests* (with C. S. Yoakum), and *The Great Apes* (with A. W. Yerkes).

INDEX